New Frontiers in Entrepreneurial Finance Research

New Frontiers in Entrepreneurial Finance Research

Anita Quas *University of Milan, Italy*
Yan Alperovych *em**lyon business school**, France*
Cristiano Bellavitis *Auckland Business School, New Zealand*
Ine Paeleman *University of Antwerp, Belgium*
Dzidziso Samuel Kamuriwo *Cass Business School, UK*

World Scientific

NEW JERSEY • LONDON • SINGAPORE • BEIJING • SHANGHAI • HONG KONG • TAIPEI • CHENNAI • TOKYO

Published by

World Scientific Publishing Co. Pte. Ltd.

5 Toh Tuck Link, Singapore 596224

USA office: 27 Warren Street, Suite 401-402, Hackensack, NJ 07601

UK office: 57 Shelton Street, Covent Garden, London WC2H 9HE

Library of Congress Cataloging-in-Publication Data

Names: Quas, Anita, editor. | Alperovych, Yan, editor. | Bellavitis, Cristiano, editor.

Title: New frontiers in entrepreneurial finance research / edited by: Anita Quas (EMLyon Business School, France), Yan Alperovych (EMLyon Business School, France), Cristiano Bellavitis (University of Auckland, New Zealand), Ine Paeleman (Ghent University, Belgium) and Dzidziso Samuel Kamuriwo (Cass Business School, UK).

Description: New Jersey : World Scientific, 2019. | Summary: "This book provides an updated view of new trends in entrepreneurial finance, with the aim of guiding academics and non-academics alike that want to gain a deeper understanding of this field. It collects recent contributions from scholars from all over the world. Each chapter provides new empirical or theoretical evidence on fundamental issues related to entrepreneurial finance, including business angels, crowdfunding, Initial Coin Offerings, Mini bonds, public support and more. Besides reviewing the recent trends in the field, the book also highlights new avenues for research, and implications for practitioners"-- Provided by publisher.

Identifiers: LCCN 2019013764 | ISBN 9789811202759 (hardcover)

Subjects: LCSH: Business enterprises--Finance. | Angels (Investors) | Crowd funding. | Venture capital.

Classification: LCC HG4026 .A437 2019 | DDC 658.15/224--dc23

LC record available at https://lccn.loc.gov/2019013764

British Library Cataloguing-in-Publication Data

A catalogue record for this book is available from the British Library.

For any available supplementary material, please visit
https://www.worldscientific.com/worldscibooks/10.1142/11344#t=suppl

Desk Editors: Anthony Alexander/Sandhya Venkatesh

Typeset by Stallion Press
Email: enquiries@stallionpress.com

Foreword

The subject of funding of entrepreneurial ventures has been discussed by many authors and on many occasions. However, the pace of funding mechanisms has substantially accelerated and we have witnessed their unprecedented development in recent times. Looking in the past, it is possible to identify parallels between these mechanisms and modern times. However, what exactly is an entrepreneurial venture today? Why do entrepreneurs need long-term capital? What sources of funding are available for entrepreneurial ventures? And what are these new funding models available to modern entrepreneurs?

An entrepreneurial venture is born from the interaction of three fundamental characteristics that have traditionally remained stable. The first ingredient relates to the emergence of a project or idea that is global in scale and has the potential to revolutionize current practices or ways of thinking. It can bring long-term competitive advantages to whoever dominates the issue. It must be a worthwhile cause, one that justifies the risk. The ambitiousness of the project is obviously the first determining factor in terms of funding. The greater the ambition, the greater the sums of capital available to invest, in line with the potential return on investment. But even such an ambitious proposition, put forward as a carefully structured project, is not in itself sufficient to attract funding.

The second ingredient required to set an entrepreneurial project in motion relates to the concept of innovation. A new idea often comes about by chance when an everyday reality meets a different way of seeing it. The innovation might be technical or technological, but it is not always so, it can also be connected to company projects that relate to the traditional economy, industry or services. While we most often think of cutting-edge technology with the power to disrupt — which is often the case for projects that produce the kind of radical changes leading to improvements in quality of life for humanity — innovation can nonetheless take very different forms. It might simply be an innovative use that represents a bonus in terms of what already exists but does not revolutionize current practice. It might also take the form of a new way of doing ordinary things, a procedural improvement, a new way of doing business or an original market positioning. Wherever it comes from, this innovative dimension is essential in that it offers the person who masters it, or is the first to harness it, a long-term competitive advantage that will establish a new practice and standard.

However, entrepreneurial ventures do not emerge solely on the basis of an innovation with a universal character. If such were the case, the success of an innovative project would depend only on the strength of its inventiveness, a result of observation and intelligence — essentially, the product of in-depth academic research. But for the process of funding to be put in place, a third essential ingredient must be added to the recipe: a person (or team) able to assume the risks inherent in carrying out the project. In this respect, the human dimension is the determining and essential element of the entrepreneurial venture. The entrepreneur must be able to demonstrate a sound view of the nature of the project's risks and potential benefits. But he or she also needs charisma and audacity: these are the qualities that inspire respect and confidence in his or her ability to build, manage and lead a team beyond the difficulties they will surely encounter on that journey full of unexpected situations, surprises and pitfalls.

Once these three fundamental elements have been brought together, one final element is required for an entrepreneurial venture to emerge — a spark, the fuel, that allows the action to be carried out. The birth of an idea capable of revolutionizing the existing system, supported by an individual and a bold team, inevitably raises the question of how to fund its implementation. Not just any old funding will do — such a project requires patient funding that does not expect rapid returns. It is risky funding with the possibility of total loss of funds committed, a kind of funding which represents a magnitude of potential loss equal only to the level of return expected if the project succeeds. This expected return is not just financial. It must be able to provide the contributor with a positional advantage or additional clout in the global competitive game.

When in the 15th century Admiral Christopher Columbus conceived the idea to discover a sea route to the East Indies, with Cipango (Japan) as his original objective, he set the framework for an ambitious project. Contrary to popular belief, he was neither the first human to set foot in America (human beings migrated there from Asia more than 10,000 years ago) nor the first human to cross the Atlantic (according to historians, Vikings or Normans did so before him). His company was first and foremost a commercial business, based on the hope of discovering faster trade routes for spices, gold and rare pearls. A seasoned navigator, considered one of the best of all time, he used the "breakthrough technologies" of his time, such as the compass, the Etambot rudder and the caravel, a ship that was relatively affordable to equip and had a shallow draught that allowed him to approach the coast without the risk of running aground.

Aiming to bring to fruition a project of global ambition that promised unimaginable reward at the time, Christopher Columbus is considered a true entrepreneur who knew how to surround himself with an experienced crew boasting all the characteristics of a team ready to succeed. Many of the scientific experts at the time considered that his plan to reach the Levant by going west was plausible and technically feasible, although it was in fact based on a calculation error leading him to underestimate the size of the seas separating the Canary Islands from the eastern tip of the Asian continent. He then met John II, King of Portugal, from whom he solicited the necessary funds to prepare his venture. Despite the great rewards expected in the event of success, a group of experts mandated by John II recommended against engaging in such a dangerous project. The risk of failure was considered too high and the probability of success too low. Continuing his quest with tenacity and perseverance, he later met Queen Isabella of Castile. Following a first refusal, his request was on the brink of acceptance, but he demanded to be appointed Viceroy of all the discovered lands and given assurance of a share of the spoils as well as a noble title. He was thus refused a second time. He finally obtained the financial support of Queen Isabella of Castile through the treasurer of her kingdom, to whom he promised huge potential economic benefits, since, after a modest initial investment, the discovery of a new route to the Indies would free him from reliance on eastern intermediaries. When he signed the Capitulations of Santa Fe with the Catholic Monarchs in 1492, it took him more than 8 years to mobilize the resources and obtain the required titles and benefits.

This story is often told by teachers of entrepreneurial finance as it illustrates the combination of all the ingredients mentioned above: an ambitious project likely to "change the world", prior validation of the innovative technical dimension by scientific experts, thereby giving credibility to the project's feasibility, the use of the most recent technologies to carry it out, and a renowned and demanding leader able to show tenacity and perseverance despite multiple refusals. He was therefore able to access a timely and patient source of funding that was only authorized once the expected benefits were understood and once the entrepreneur had finally succeeded in gaining acceptance for his terms on how the dividends would be shared.

For a very long time, the state has played a decisive role in providing financial resources to bold entrepreneurs for political or economic purposes. States pursue a development strategy based on a long-term period and on abundant and renewable resources. They have been and still are one of the most powerful drivers of entrepreneurial funding. Lenders similar to today's banks also existed in the past. These large money lenders already knew how to lend capital against interest, but in return required a concrete guarantee to secure their loans. However, these funds were not fully adapted to the financing of entrepreneurial ventures, since the entrepreneur was not in a position to ensure a rapid and certain return of the sums borrowed and could not offer sufficient guarantees to secure such loans. It is not in the nature of banks to take more risk than entrepreneurs themselves. This is why banks require the latter to raise equity capital (their own or from others) — long-term capital at high risk, which they may supplement.

In more recent times, when new technologies that surpassed the power that could be generated by animals (such as the steam engine in the 18th century or electricity in the 19th century) appeared, these great inventions heralded an era of industrial development that really soared in the 20th century. In a way, the industrial entrepreneurs of the last century shaped modern capitalism and led states to gradually realize that the entrepreneurial dimension could play an essential role in societal structuring and organization. Despite the attractiveness of the entrepreneurial phenomenon, many projects were hampered by the financial world's reluctance to face the risk of failure. In order to encourage and strengthen the involvement of banks in the funding of entrepreneurial ventures, guarantee mechanisms were devised by governments so that private financiers could be protected via a risk compensation mechanism provided by the public authorities. These mechanisms, still in place in many countries today, have greatly encouraged banks to take risks and fostered the development of an entrepreneurial spirit.

It was not until the middle of the 20th century that a new method of funding companies, known as "venture capital", appeared, under the impetus of an obstinate Frenchman. Georges F. Doriot came from a family of automotive manufacturers, settled in the United States and studied at MIT. In the 1940s, he created the American Research & Development Corporation (ARD) with private capital and assistance from MIT, having refused the Pentagon's offer of a position managing a department to fund companies whose research or production could have military applications. Founding INSEAD in 1957, he invested that same year $70,000 in a start-up called Digital Equipment Corporation (DEC), which would become an industrial conglomerate and give ARD a return on investment of 7,800 times the initial investment! He is recognized as the father of venture capital. This new and innovative method of funding is different from banks in that the capital is invested at risk (i.e., without guarantee in the event of failure) and expects neither interest nor immediate returns. This new approach to funding would be copied by American industrialists in the San Francisco region, who, by investing in entrepreneurs in the electronics and IT sectors, would go on to create the Silicon Valley.

The emergence of venture capital represented a real breakthrough in the financing mechanisms of entrepreneurial ventures. Brought to Europe in the 1970s, this original funding model was first launched confidentially, supported by a small number of pioneers, before intensifying at the end of the 1990s with the emergence of the Internet, underpinned by the development of high-speed optical telecommunications infrastructures. The emergence of a "new economy" driven by new kinds of entrepreneurs creating "start-ups" disrupted the traditional economy and changed its codes.

The Internet represented a new Eldorado offering the most daring entrepreneurs huge scope for commercial conquest with opportunities for rapid enrichment. The codes of these start-ups were radically different from those of the old economy, and the strategic positions of the leaders were fundamentally at odds with the times. Even the speech peppered with Anglicisms and the format of the presentation materials become characteristic of a radical change in the way business was presented and one of the keys to raising capital from the "VCs". Even when the telecoms bubble burst in 2000 it would not slow the enthusiasm of entrepreneurs or investors for this new economy. In less than 20 years, new world champions, whose capital now exceeds that which the largest industrial conglomerates took more than a century to build, have emerged in many fields.

Under the impetus of this new economy, the acceleration continued, yet some entrepreneurs noticed that VCs were no longer fully playing their role of funding and providing seed capital because they refused to invest in projects considered immature or unproven. These entrepreneurs, having made their fortunes through selling their companies as quickly as possible, started to support the creation of new businesses by providing young start-ups with the financial resources and sound advice required, with a view to repeating their success and further increasing their wealth. The emergence of "business angels" as a new driving force for funding entrepreneurial ventures first experienced rapid development in the United States before going international. However, not many of these business angels had huge fortunes ready to invest in many projects, and not all early investments were successful either. The illiquidity of some investments and the failures of others slowed the pace of this new financial manna. In this situation, states decided to intervene by creating different tax benefit mechanisms to encourage the wealthiest people to invest their savings in young companies. These tax advantages were first directed toward an indirect financing method to strengthen the capacities of professional investment funds supporting start-ups. In order to amplify this phenomenon, the advantages were quickly extended to all taxpayers, allowing them to make their own investment choices. But in order for these private investors to have access to investment opportunities, they had to form clubs and began to pool their investments at the seed stage. Even so, these clubs often only had access to opportunities that were geographically close to their members, potentially missing a new spark igniting at the same time in another part of the world.

Seeing these limits naturally gave rise to the idea of putting entrepreneurs in contact with a mass of individual investors who wanted to choose what to do with their savings and use them for something meaningful. Thus, about 10 years ago, the first crowdfunding platforms appeared on the Internet. Initially, this new funding method allowed individuals to give funds to support a project or cause, or to finance the development of a product in return for the privilege of being among the first customers to receive it as soon as the product was released. The 2008 financial crisis, which shook the global banking system, gave rise to a variant of this funding method at a time when banks had reduced their support for businesses. Crowdlending thus appeared as a new way of opening up access to business funding from individuals.

Since the postwar period that saw the emergence of venture capital, and even more so since the 2000s, history has shown an effervescence and dazzling proliferation of ideas for how to overcome the obstacles or limits of existing mechanisms in order to provide funding to bold entrepreneurs. Entrepreneurship is more alive than ever and is interfering in the creation of these new funding mechanisms. In a world disrupted by an unstable global context, the foundations of the capitalist system that has been in place for more than 50 years are being shaken. The public or private authorities that govern the capitalist economy by controlling money, whatever its currency (dollar, euro, yen, etc.), are being called into question by the development of cryptocurrencies, in particular Bitcoin and Ethereum. Based on technology for storing and transmitting information without a control body, these electronic currencies offer a new field of exploration for both investors and entrepreneurs, who see them as a new way to finance the real economy. Blockchain-based mechanisms now make it possible to create smart contracts that are automatically unlocked on condition that future events occur. Based on the Initial Public Offering (IPO) mechanism, the first Initial Coin Offering (ICO) appeared. This innovation makes it possible to offer a new investment solution to electronic currency holders.

The increase in the pace of innovation in the world of entrepreneurial venture funding is unprecedented. It is developing under the impetus of new technologies and seeks to overcome the obstacles that hinder entrepreneurs' desire to find funding to carry their projects forward. New entrepreneurs are even specializing in this discipline by creating fintech companies at the crossroads of the worlds of finance and technology. This book offers an open and up-to-date view of these new funding dimensions, tracing the development of a phenomenon that is experiencing constant change.

Sébastien Touvron, author of this foreword, serves as the President of KREAXI since November 2016. Previously, since 2012, he served as the President of Rhône-Alpes Création, a group of investment funds focusing on investing in innovative start-ups based in Auvergne Rhône-Alpes area. In 25 years, KREAXI has become a key player in the financing landscape for early stage start-ups in France.

About the Editors

Anita Quas is a Senior Researcher in Corporate Finance at Università degli Studi di Milano (Milan, Italy) since April 2019. She previously worked as an Associate Professor of Corporate Finance at em**lyon** **business school**. Anita obtained her PhD at Politecnico di Milano in 2012. She had visiting research experiences at Harvard Business School (Fall 2011) and the SPRU Department of University of Sussex (Spring 2012). She also worked as an Innovation and Policy Consultant at Technopolis group, in the UK, in 2013. Her research is focused in entrepreneurial finance. Specifically, she studies venture capital and public initiatives to support entrepreneurial ventures. She published her research in international peer-reviewed journals including *Research Policy*, *Entrepreneurship: Theory and Practice*, *Journal of Business Venturing* and *Small Business Economics*. She won several awards for her research, including the Coller Institute of Venture Best Paper Award in 2017 and Runner-up Prize in 2016.

Yan Alperovych is an Associate Professor of Corporate Finance at em**lyon business school**, which he joined in 2011. Yan obtained his PhD degree at the University of Liège (Belgium) in 2011. He also was a Centre for Management Buyout Research Fellow. His research interests lie in the area of entrepreneurial finance, venture capital and private equity. He is also interested in the assessment of the impact of public sector initiatives to promote regional entrepreneurship. He published his works in international peer-reviewed journals such as *Economics Bulletin* (2018), *Venture Capital* (2018), *Journal of Business Venturing* (2015), *Small Business Economics* (2013), *European Journal of Operational Research* (2013), and *Research in International Business and Finance* (2011). He also won several best paper awards such as the FMA Applied Finance Conference Best Paper Award (2017), the Coller Institute of Venture (Runner-up Prize, 2016), the Best Paper in Corporate and Entrepreneurial Finance award (AFFI, 2016).

Cristiano Bellavitis is the Lecturer (Assistant Professor) of Innovation and Entrepreneurship at the Faculty of Management and International Business of Auckland Business School, and is a member of the editorial board of *Venture Capital: An International Journal of Entrepreneurial Finance.* His research interests include network theory, strategic partnering and interfirm networking in entrepreneurial finance settings, and two-sided platforms. His research has been published in leading international journals such as *Organization Science, Strategic Entrepreneurship Journal, British Journal of Management*, and *Journal of Small Business Management.*

Ine Paeleman is an Assistant Professor at the University of Antwerp (Belgium). She received her PhD in Business Administration from Ghent University in 2015. She was twice a visiting scholar at the Carlson School of Management (University of Minnesota) and did an internship at the National Bank of Belgium. Prior to joining the University of Antwerp in October 2018, she was a Postdoctoral Research Fellow of the Flemish Fund for Scientific Research (FWO) at Ghent University. Ine's research interests cross the traditional boundaries between entrepreneurship, management and finance disciplines. Her research focuses on entrepreneurial finance, slack resources and international entrepreneurship. She has published in academic journals including *Journal of Management Studies* (2013, 2015), *Journal of World Business* (2017), *Small Business Economics* (2013), the *Academy of Management Best Paper Proceedings* (2012), and *Frontiers of Entrepreneurship Research* (2010, 2012).

Dzidziso Samuel Kamuriwo is an Associate Professor in Strategy at Cass Business School and before joining Cass in 2008, he had extensive executive-level industry experience in Africa. Sam's research is on organizational and funding innovations in technology in new firms, and the diffusion, adoption and application of innovation through projects. His research work has been published in leading innovation journals such as *Research Policy* and *Journal of Product Innovation Management* and management journals such as *Leadership Quarterly*, *Entrepreneurship Theory and Practice*, *British Journal of Management*, and *Journal of Business Research*.

Contents

Foreword v

About the Editors xiii

Chapter 1 Introduction: Entrepreneurial Finance — From the 18th Century to Modern Times 1
Yan Alperovych, Cristiano Bellavitis, Dzidziso Samuel Kamuriwo, Ine Paeleman and Anita Quas

Part 1 Beyond Traditional Venture Capital 11

Chapter 2 The Role of Angel Syndicates on the Demand and Supply of Informal Venture Capital 13
Stefano Bonini, Vincenzo Capizzi and Paola Zocchi

Chapter 3 To the Rescue: Government Intervention in Venture Capital Markets 51
Thomas Standaert

Chapter 4 Guarantee Instrument Obsolete or Future-Oriented? 93
Rudy Aernoudt

Part 2 Fintech Revolution and Entrepreneurial Finance **119**

Chapter 5 New Frontiers in Green Project Financing: Leveraging on the Crowd 121
Saman Adhami, Giancarlo Giudici and Huy Pham Nguyen Anh

Chapter 6 Linguistic Style and Crowdfunding: Moving the Current Debate Forward 149
Riccardo Maiolini, Francesco Cappa and Francesco Fasano

Chapter 7 An Introduction to Blockchain, Cryptocurrency and Initial Coin Offerings 181
Pierluigi Martino, Kevin Jue Wang, Cristiano Bellavitis and Carlos M. DaSilva

Chapter 8 Mini-Bonds: An Emerging Link in the Intermediation Chain in Europe 207
Luisa Anderoni and Maria Debora Braga

Part 3 Soft Characteristics and Entrepreneurial Finance **241**

Chapter 9 Construed Shared Expectations: Facilitating Access to Early-Stage Equity Financing in Developing Countries 243
Carlos Martínez

Chapter 10 Financial Literacy and Entrepreneurship 271
Riccardo Calcagno, Yan Alperovych and Anita Quas

Chapter 11 Social Entrepreneurship Competitions: Hoping for Funding and Gaining Valuable Experience in the Process — An Exploratory Study 299
Moriah Meyskens, Rachel Christensen and Patricia Márquez

Index 331

Chapter 1

Introduction: Entrepreneurial Finance — From the 18th Century to Modern Times

Yan Alperovych*
em**lyon business school**
alperovych@em-lyon.com

Cristiano Bellavitis†
Auckland Business School, Auckland University
c.bellavitis@auckland.ac.nz

Dzidziso Samuel Kamuriwo‡
Cass Business School, City University of London
d.s.kamuriwo@city.ac.uk

Ine Paeleman§
University of Antwerp
ine.paeleman@uantwerpen.be

Anita Quas¶
University of Milan and em**lyon business school**
anita.quas@unimi.it

---

* 23, Avenue Guy de Collongue, Ecully, 69134, France.
† 12, Grafton Road, Auckland, 1010, New Zealand.
‡ 106, Bunhill Row, London, EC1Y 8TZ, UK.
§ 13, Prinsstraat, Antwerpen, 2000, Belgium.
¶ 7, Via Conservatorio, Milan, 20122, Italy; 23, Avenue Guy de Collongue, Ecully, 69134, France.

Entrepreneurial firms are the backbone of economies and drivers of both economic development and employment. Young and innovative entrepreneurial firms are germane to the creation, development, and growth of new technologies, industries, markets and create the most jobs (Bellavitis *et al.*, 2017; Megginson, 2004). Without start-ups, it will be much more difficult to generate net job growth in the economy. It is estimated that, for example in the US, new ventures create three million jobs a year (Kane, 2010).

Although the cost of starting a business has declined over the years, raising finance is one of the crucial milestones of any new venture. New technologies, open-source software (e.g., GitHub), co-working spaces (e.g., WeWork), APIs (e.g., WordPress), virtual services (e.g., virtual personal assistant), low cost telecommunication (e.g., Skype), cloud computing and storage (e.g., Amazon Web Services), have reduced the fixed and overall costs to start a new technology venture. Some new ventures can even be created during the course of a weekend (e.g., Start-up Weekend). These factors, coupled with a cultural shift pushed by an entrepreneurial wave and pulled by open-minded customers, have led to an unprecedented Cambrian moment — an explosion of life — for tech start-ups (*The Economist*).[1] However, according to research from CB Insights,[2] running out of cash is the second most predominant reason for start-up failure, attracting 29% of responses. Therefore, securing enough capital to start and grow a business is still crucial.

Luckily, entrepreneurs have rarely experienced such an abundance of capital and funding sources. In fact, although entrepreneurial finance has always been available to new ventures, in one form or another, today's entrepreneurs have a much broader set of instruments at their disposal.

For centuries, the world has experienced a thriving connection between finance and innovation. Venture-style investing can be seen in

---

[1] *The Economist* (2014), last accessed 10 December 2018: https://www.economist.com/sites/default/files/20140118_tech_startups.pdf.

[2] Last accessed 10 December 2018: https://www.cbinsights.com/research/startup-failure-reasons-top/.

the way that the Columbus adventures were structured in the 15th century, or the early whaling industry in the 18th century — with its emphasis on capital pooling, partnerships, principal–agent relationships, and long-tail investments (Nicholas and Akins, 2012; Nicholas, 2016). The US industrial revolution in New England textiles was promoted by the Boston Associates, a group of investors who were willing to finance risky technological development (Dalzell, 1987). The rise of Midwestern cities like Cleveland as entrepreneurial hotspots in the 19th century depended on financiers such as Andrew Mellon (Lamoreaux *et al.*, 2006).

However, it is not until 1946 that a formal venture capital (VC) industry emerged with the establishment of the American Research & Development (ARD) Corporation. ARD was formed by Georges Doriot (Dean of Harvard Business School) with the support of Ralph Flanders (Senator for Vermont), and Karl Compton (President of MIT). ARD had a number of important characteristics. First, unlike modern VC firms, which are mostly organized as limited liability partnerships (LLPs) with multiple closed-end funds under management and a finite lifetime of approximately 10 years (extendable) each, ARD was formed as a single closed-end fund (Hsu and Kenney, 2005). This structure was aligned with the objective to select investments and govern them effectively over the long run (Nicholas, 2016). Second, due to regulatory constraints, no institutional investor could own more than 9.9% of the fund (Ante, 2008). Finally, ARD had an internal structure to facilitate deal flow and investment due diligence. ARD prized a robust technical advisory board that encompassed a mix of financial, technological and legal expertise. ARD maintained high standards for selecting investments, focusing on commercially viable ventures with patent protection and high profit potential (Etzkowitz, 2002; Nicholas, 2016). Although sound investment criteria led to some early successes such as an investment in Flexible Tubing, the bulk of returns came from one venture, Digital Equipment Corporation (DEC), a company that developed circuit board modules and efficient computers. DEC valuation jumped from approximately $100,000 when it received its first investment from ARD in 1957 to $355 million in 1971, granting an outstanding return to the original investors (Liles, 1977, p. 83). The early successes of ARD drew attention to the VC industry and, coupled with regulatory changes implemented in the US at the end of the 1978–1979,[3] literally kick started the modern VC industry.

Over the last few years, a whole set of relatively "new" sources of financing has emerged (e.g., Bruton *et al.*, 2015). Entrepreneurs can now raise financing from numerous sources such as incubators and accelerators, crowdfunding platforms, proof-of-concept centers, university-based seed funds, and IP-backed financial instruments and, more recently, initial coin offerings (ICOs). Strikingly, although VC is a significant portion of entrepreneurial finance, other sources are becoming more prevalent. In 2017, US VC investments totaled $76 billion.[4] However, only $14 billion were invested in seed and early stage ventures, with the rest going to expansion and late stage ventures. In comparison, entrepreneurial projects raised $17 billion from crowdfunding platforms.[5] Although the first ICO was launched in 2013 only (Bellavitis *et al.*, 2018), recent statistics indicate that ICOs contributed $1.7 billion to US-based ventures in 2017 (globally ICOs raised $7 billion in 2017, and $13.7 billion in the first 5 months of 2018).[6]

Considering the importance of new ventures for economic growth and wealth creation, and the changing landscape of the entrepreneurial finance ecosystem, there is a need for research to understand how "old" and "new" sources of finance impact start-ups (Bellavitis *et al.*, 2017). Extant research has only skimmed the surface in terms of exploring these new sources of entrepreneurial finance. It is with this broad objective that

---

[3]The 1978 Revenue Act reduced the capital gains rate from 49.5% to 28%. The flow of monies into venture capital funds jumped from $68 million to nearly $1 billion. Then in 1979, Congress passed the ERISA "Prudent Man" Rule that allowed pension funds to invest in venture capital. Again, venture capital benefited. By 1983, new commitments exceeded $5 billion (Bellavitis *et al.*, 2019).

[4]PWC Money Tree report: https://www.pwc.com/us/en/industries/technology/moneytree.html.

[5]Last accessed 10 December 2018: https://www.statista.com/statistics/946659/global-crowdfunding-volume-worldwide-by-region/.

[6]PWC and CryptoValley, last accessed 10 December 2018: https://cryptovalley.swiss/wp-content/uploads/20180628_PwC-S-CVA-ICO-Report_EN.pdf.

this book collects contributions that aim at tackling this gap, and that identify exciting new directions for research in this field.

Part 1: Beyond Traditional Venture Capital

The first part of the book focuses on some of the relatively most established providers of entrepreneurial funding: angel investors and government interventions. Such investors are key sources of capital specifically targeted to innovation and firm development (Drover *et al.*, 2017). Because of the substantial importance of business angels in the entrepreneurial ecosystem, these investors attracted substantial academic interest in recent years (e.g., Huang and Pearce, 2015). However, recently the focus has shifted from single business angels, to business angels networks. Accordingly, in Chapter 2, Bonini, Capizzi and Zocchi discuss first the relation between the membership in a business angel network (BAN) and the investment decisions of the BAN members which is measured as the share of personal wealth each angel invests in a given deal or the angel's share of equity stakes in the portfolio companies. Next, they also provide insights on the valuation of the contributions provided by business angels to the survival and growth of the angel-backed companies. The authors propose a performance index as an original proxy for survival and growth.

Further, the role of the government in entrepreneurial finance also spurred considerable academic and public debate, especially aimed at identifying the most promising form of governmental intervention. Chapters 3 and 4 discuss alternative policy approaches.

In Chapter 3, Standaert is devoted to an in-depth literature review on the efforts made by governments to support VC markets directly by injecting them with public funds. The author discusses rationales as well as concerns related to direct government intervention in VC markets. Next, he also highlights how distinct types of direct government intervention ((1) GVCs following a go-it-alone strategy; (2) GVCs syndicating with private VCs; and (3) governments investing in private VC funds) determine whether and how the objectives of the government intervention are achieved.

In Chapter 4, Aernoudt focuses on guarantees which are often wrongly considered as obsolete bureaucratic instruments leading to moral hazard at lenders' level. The author explains that a guarantee instrument is not only a valid policy instrument to cope with the financing gap but also to give a positive impetus to the use of VC as the American SBIC system shows. This chapter provides an overview of policy recommendations and criteria that have to be fulfilled to realize a well-conceived public guarantee system.

Part 2: Fintech Revolution and Entrepreneurial Finance

The second part of this book focuses on alternative entrepreneurial financing options offered through technology-based innovations, spurring from the so-called "fintech revolution". The most prominent example of such innovation is probably crowdfunding. Crowdfunding is a growing trend in peer to peer business and consumer lending, whose overall magnitude now dominates conventional financing instruments (Chapter 8). The four chapters in this part provide an update on funding innovations related to the crowdfunding phenomenon.

Chapter 5 by Adhami, Giudici and Nguyen Anh examine the success factors related to crowdfunding for "green" projects such as renewable energies. Their study employed a large sample of renewable projects on 27 specialized European crowdfunding platforms and highlights success factors related to the motivations of investors as well as specific contextual factors that include institutional quality and the degree of the problem the projects are meant to resolve. The study key contribution is how innovative fund raising is possible for projects that may likely suffer from market failure because of their public goods characteristics.

Chapter 6 is an interesting contribution by Maiolini, Cappa and Fasano, who unpick a different success factor for crowdfunding related to the problem of information asymmetry between fund raisers and investors. The authors propose communication enhancement measures that involve linguistic style approaches to gain empathetic attention from investors. The study examines the use of recurrent words and linguist models representing narrative styles and provides evidence of the necessity of using communication to leverage emotions and achieve engagement by ventures that are raising funds from "the crowd".

Chapter 7 by Martino, Wang, Bellavitis and DaSilva is a comprehensive summary of blockchain technology to date. It also provides insight into blockchain-enabled initial coin offerings (ICOs), which are shaping the future of entrepreneurial finance by providing a relatively low cost and speedy fund-raising process through a global pool of participants. The chapter provides a brief summary of blockchain technology and how its initial and best-known application in cryptocurrencies is now being leveraged to provide a new way to raise entrepreneurial finance through ICOs. ICOs issue newly-created cryptocurrencies (such as bitcoins) or tokens (cryptographically-secured digital assets) that are sold to the public in exchange for capital by start-ups. The main takeaway is the surprising exponential expected growth of this mode of funding from insignificant in 2014 to an expected $12 billion (OECD estimate) by end of 2018. However, ICOs seem to be open to blockchain-related companies only at present and is not risk-free.

Chapter 8, by Anderloni and Braga, discusses a very interesting recent development in major European markets — the development of the mini-bond market for SMEs. An underdeveloped area, the chapter discusses institutional changes made in the countries under study — such as lighter regulation and setting up of relevant market platforms and legislation, to provide an enabling environment for institutional investors and potential entrepreneurial ventures wishing to trade. Although there is variability in the evolution of these markets in different countries, of interest is that crowdfunding to retail investors is possible for mini-bonds in several European countries.

Part 3: Soft Characteristics and Entrepreneurial Finance

The last part of the book consists of three chapters that discusses how the qualities of entrepreneurs, relate to success in fund raising. The three chapters focus on three key soft characteristics, namely (1) the lack of social capital for isolated entrepreneurs in developing countries, (2) the financial literacy and (3) self-efficacy development.

In Chapter 9, Martínez analyzes the difficulties for socially-isolated entrepreneurs in non-developed countries to access early-stage financing. By employing a grounded study of potential brokers — individuals who have made it their mission and goal to connect entrepreneurial venture teams to potential angel investors in central American contexts, the study unveils barriers to engagement between ventures and investors, and provides a set of solutions to how these barriers can be mitigated — thus, allowing hitherto isolated ventures to access early stage funding.

In Chapter 10, Calcagno, Alperovych and Quas focus on entrepreneurs' financial literacy. They begin by discussing how limited is our understanding of this topic, which naturally calls for substantially greater academic attention. While prior scholars mainly focused on financial literacy as the ability of households to manage their personal finance in a healthy way, the financial literacy of entrepreneurs affects their ability to make good financial decisions when managing their business activity daily. Therefore, financial literacy could determine entrepreneurial outcomes such as start-up creation, growth and survival. The recent policy interest for this topic highlights the potential important policy implications of academic studies in the field.

Lastly, Chapter 11 by Meyskens and Márquez illustrates the pedagogical value of social entrepreneurship competitions at the individual level. They empirically show that although funding promises might initially entice students to join a competition, the learning gained through participation in the competition has far greater value than the funding alone. Through experiential learning, they experience how difficult it is to actually start a venture. The authors conclude with avenues for future research and practitioner recommendations.

References

Ante S. E. (2008) *Creative Capital: Georges Doriot and the Birth of Venture Capital.* Harvard Business Press, Boston.

Bellavitis C., Cumming D., and Vanacker T. (2018) The cross-country diffusion of initial coin offerings: An institutional theory perspective. Working paper.

Bellavitis, C., Rietveld, J., and Filatotchev, I. (2019). The effects of prior co-investments on the performance of VC syndicates: A relational agency perspective. *Strategic Entrepreneurship Journal*, forthcoming.

Bellavitis C., Filatotchev I., Kamuriwo D. S., and Vanacker T. (2017) Entrepreneurial finance: New frontiers of research and practice: Editorial for the special issue *Embracing Entrepreneurial Funding Innovations*. Venture Capital.

Bruton G., Khavul D. S., and Wright M. (2015) New financial alternatives in seeding entrepreneurship: Microfinance, crowdfunding, and peer-to-peer innovations, *Entrepreneurship Theory and Practice*, 39, 9–26.

Dalzell R. F. (1987) *Enterprising Elite: The Boston Associates and the World They Made*. Harvard University Press, Cambridge, MA.

Drover W., Busenitz L., Matusik S., Townsend D., Anglin A., and Dushnitsky G. (2017) A review and road map of entrepreneurial equity financing research: Venture capital, corporate venture capital, angel investment, crowdfunding, and accelerators, *Journal of Management*, 43(6), 1820–1853.

Etzkowitz H. (2002) *MIT and the Rise of Entrepreneurial Science*. Routledge, London.

Hsu D. H. and Kenney M. (2005) Organizing venture capital: The rise and demise of American Research & Development Corporation, 1946–1973. *Industrial and Corporate Change*, 14(4), 579–616.

Huang L. and Pearce J. L. (2015) Managing the unknowable: The effectiveness of early-stage investor gut feel in entrepreneurial investment decisions, *Administrative Science Quarterly*, 60, 634–670.

Kane T. J. (2010) The importance of startups in job creation and job destruction. Available at SSRN: https://ssrn.com/abstract=1646934.

Lamoreaux N. R., Levenstein M. C., and Sokoloff K. L. (2006) Mobilizing venture capital during the second industrial revolution: Cleveland, Ohio, 1870–1920, *Capitalism and Society*, 1.

Liles P. R. (1977) *Sustaining the Venture Capital Firm*. Management Analysis Center, Boston.

Megginson W. L. (2004) Towards a global model of venture capital, *Journal of Applied Corporate Finance*, 16, 89–107.

Nicholas T. (2016) The origins of high-tech venture investing in America, *Research Foundation Publications*, 2016(3), 227–241.

Nicholas T. and Akins J. P. (2012) *Whaling Ventures*. Harvard Business School Case 813–086 (October).

Part 1

Beyond Traditional Venture Capital

Chapter 2

The Role of Angel Syndicates on the Demand and Supply of Informal Venture Capital

Stefano Bonini*

School of Business, Stevens Institute of Technology

sbonini@stevens.edu

Vincenzo Capizzi†

Department of Economics and Business Studies, University of Piemonte Orientale

vincenzo.capizzi@uniupo.it

Paola Zocchi†

Department of Economics and Business Studies, University of Piemonte Orientale

paola.zocchi@uniupo.it

*1 Castle Point Terrace, Hoboken, NJ 07030, USA.

†18, Via E. Perrone, Novara, 28100, Italy; SDA Bocconi School of Management, Milan, Italy.

Abstract

The recent explosion of the informal venture capital is stimulating finance scholars to deeply investigate the major determinants, characteristics and possible implications of this phenomenon within the start-up ecosystems. The rising literature on business angels (BAs) still misses to adequately cover many investigation areas, such as the operations and the role played by the different typologies of BA networks (BANs) and the valuation of the contributions provided by BAs to the performance of the angel-backed companies. The contributions of Bonini *et al.* (2018, 2019) are part of the ongoing debate on these two research areas that have not yet been exhaustively explored. The two papers show that the affiliation to an angel community affects BAs' investment decisions, though it doesn't seem to have a significant impact on the survival and profitability of the funded ventures. On the contrary, by co-investing in an angel syndicate, BAs may enjoy risk- and information-sharing benefits that structurally affect both their investment practices and the performance of the funded ventures. Also, the BAs' willingness to play an active role does have a positive impact on angel-backed companies' survival and growth. Finally, the intensity of BAs' soft monitoring seems negatively related to the performance of the funded ventures because of the impact on the trust-based entrepreneur–angel relationship. However, angel communities might be able to decrease and distribute within the network the need for individual monitoring while increasing members' confidence in the angel investments.

1. Introduction

The growing relevance of the role played by business angels (BAs) within the entrepreneurial finance eco-system emerges unambiguously by looking at market data at both the US and the European level (US ACA, 2016; Kraemer-Eis *et al.*, 2016; OECD, 2016; EBAN, 2017; Invest Europe, 2017).

BAs are: *high net worth individuals who invest their own money in small unlisted companies, with no family connections, typically assuming a minority equity stake as well as active involvement in portfolio companies* (Mason, 2008). Thanks to their growth as well as increasing professionalization angel investors have filled the so-called "funding gap" existing between the demand and supply of early-stage equity capital, thus becoming crucial drivers of entrepreneurship and economic growth (Mason and Harrison, 2000; Johnson and Sohl, 2012; Mason *et al.*, 2013; Capizzi, 2015; Bonini and Capizzi, 2017). As a matter of fact, from the one hand, BAs meet a demand for an equity ticket size (on average between 100k and 300k euros) usually neglected by venture capitalists because of the relatively high costs required for due diligence, contracting and monitoring (Gompers, 1995; Jeng and Wells, 2000; Kaplan and Strömberg, 2001; Carpenter and Peterson, 2002; Mason, 2009; Cumming and Johan, 2013; Bernstein *et al.*, 2016). From the other hand, BAs, alongside with monetary resources, provide non-monetary resources, such as industrial knowledge, management experience, mentoring and personal relationship networks (Harrison and Mason, 1992; Landström, 1993; Politis, 2008).

The growing relevance of this informal segment of the equity capital markets gave rise to the development on a worldwide basis of a vast literature focused on business angels, adopting various theoretical perspectives, research scopes and methodologies (Landstrom and Mason, 2016; Edelman *et al.*, 2017; Tenca *et al.*, 2018). Relying on a well-accepted classification approach based on research themes, we can identify at least five focused streams of contributions, summarized in the following.

The first research theme examines the main features of both BAs and their investment decision-making process (Mason and Harrison, 2000; Van Osnabrugge, 2000; Shane, 2000; Paul *et al.*, 2007; Sudek *et al.*, 2008; Wiltbank *et al.*, 2009; Macht, 2011; Bammens and Collewaert, 2014; Harrison and Mason, 2017; Bonini *et al.*, 2018).

The second group comprises studies focusing on the comparison between the operations and the investment practices of angel investors and venture capitalists (VCs), trying also to investigate the nature of the relationship between BAs and VCs (Van Osnabrugge, 1998; Harrison and Mason, 2000; Madill *et al.*, 2005; Sohl, 2006; Ibrahim, 2008; Wong *et al.*, 2009; Johnson and Sohl, 2012; Vanacker *et al.*, 2013; Chemmanur and Chen, 2014; Hsu *et al.*, 2014; Kerr *et al.*, 2014; Hellmann *et al.*, 2017).

The third stream of contributions addresses the issue of the transformation of the angel market taking place after the rising of angel investment organizations (business angel networks (BANs), angel clubs or syndicates), identifying the major monetary and non-monetary contributions provided to either the entrepreneurs of the BA joining a given group of angels (Mason and Harrison, 1997; Mason, 2008; Paul and Whittam, 2010; Collewaert *et al.*, 2010; Brush *et al.*, 2012; Mason *et al.*, 2013; Carpentier and Suret, 2015; Lahti and Keinonen, 2016; Croce *et al.*, 2017; Gregson *et al.*, 2017; Bonini *et al.*, 2019).

The fourth research topic deals with the identification and the measurement of the determinants of the profitability of BAs' investments (Lumme, 1996; Harrison and Mason, 1999; Mason and Harrison, 2002; Wiltbank, 2005; Wiltbank and Boeker, 2007; Werth and Boeert, 2013; De Gennaro and Dwyer, 2014; Capizzi, 2015; Politis, 2016).

The final group of studies, leveraging on the literature on venture capital and private equity (Gompers and Lerner, 2001; Davila *et al.*, 2003; Dimov and Shepherd, 2005; Hsu, 2006; Søresen, 2007; Colombo and Grilli, 2010; Chemmanur *et al.*, 2011; Croce *et al.*, 2013; Grilli and Murtinu, 2014) focuses on the analysis of the performance of the angel-backed companies, disentangling also the impact of the different typologies of value-added contribution on the success of the funded ventures (Manigart *et al.*, 2002; Harrison and Mason, 2008; Pommet, 2012; Alemany and Villanueva, 2015; Lerner *et al.*, 2016; Levratto *et al.*, 2017; Cumming and Zhang, 2018; Bonini *et al.*, 2019).

Despite the notable flourishment of research on angel financing, however, what we do know about the behavior, operations and performance of BAs and angel investment organizations is still limited and hard to generalize, mostly because of the intrinsic limitations of either the anecdotal-based evidence or the survey-based empirical analysis so far performed to shed light over so opaque an asset class.

In this chapter, we aim at pointing out the major findings dealing with some BA-specific investment practices, as emerging from two recent related studies providing some original and incremental contributions to existing literature.

The two papers focus, respectively, on the supply (Bonini *et al.*, 2018) and the demand (Bonini *et al.*, 2019) for angel financing in the early stage segment of the Italian capital market sharing as a starting point for the build-up of the datasets a common information base: the annual survey of the Italian Business Angel Network (IBAN) delivered since 2007 to its associates and other unaffiliated BAs, which provides valuable qualitative and quantitative information on the companies invested, the characteristics of the deals and the investment practices of the surveyed angels.

The first paper moves, among the others, from the previous contributions of Shane (2000), Sohl (2007), Paul and Whittam (2010), Mason *et al.* (2013), Mason and Botelho (2016) and Croce *et al.* (2017). These studies reveal the importance of the role played by angel groups, from the one hand, in collecting, processing, filtering, and disclosing information among members about possible investment opportunities and, from the other hand, in sharing within the group angels' previous experience as well as competences and relational networks. In the first paper, the authors aim at investigating the existing relationship between the membership in a BAN and the investment decisions of the BAN members, as measured by the share of angel personal wealth invested in a given deal or the amount of equity stakes in the portfolio companies.

The second paper focuses on the angel-backed companies, showing the impact on the performance and the probability of survival of the funded ventures played by some angel-specific factors, among which the presence of angel syndicates. One critical methodological issue underlying such a research goal is the selection of an accurate measure for the performance of the invested companies, given it's hard to adopt the same metrics developed in the literature investigating the impact of private equity and VC investors on the performance of portfolio companies (Bran and Gompers, 1997; Black and Gilson, 1998; Hellmann and Puri, 2000; Kortum and Lerner, 2001; Engel, 2002; Manigart *et al.*, 2002; Davila *et al.*, 2003; Bertoni *et al.*, 2011; Chemmanur *et al.*, 2011; Croce *et al.*, 2013; Cumming and Johan, 2013; Grilli and Murtinu, 2014).

Different from venture-backed companies, angel-backed firms are mostly pre-revenues, not yet able to produce a constant stream of future cash flows. In many cases, they are not fully active and running their business, up to the point that for most of them it's concrete the case they shut down without having generated any sale or having capitalized significant assets. Therefore, in the earliest stages of their life-cycle, accounting measures of performance (turnover or its growth, ebitda, market share, return on equity and capital assets) are likely to have a low informative power about a company's future survival and growth. Similarly, other commonly-used metrics in the literature on venture capital such as innovation, patent licensing, employment growth, productivity or successful exits through IPOs or acquisitions can hardly be applied in the context of angel financing, where the funded ventures quite often operate in traditional low tech industries, do not show accelerated growth paths in limited time frames nor are ready to be listed in officially regulated capital markets. Therefore, in order to address the limitations of the above-mentioned metrics, Bonini *et al.* (2019) propose an original proxy (the *Performance Index, P.I.*) for the survival and growth of the angel-backed companies that, as explained in the following section, is an ordinal variable that can assume five different values, based on different combinations of revenues, assets and income reported for the sample companies.

The major finding empirically confirmed from both contributions points out the crucial role played by angel syndicates in both sides of the investigated informal venture capital market: from the supply side, angel investors affiliating to an angel investment organization show a higher propensity to invest in a given deal when compared to unaffiliated angels; from the demand side, angel syndicates are a major determinant of the performance and the probability of survival of angel-backed companies.

2. Unit of Analysis, Sample Data and Dependent Variables

The IBAN administered 3,000 questionnaires to 929 affiliates and 2071 non-affiliates from 2009 (2008 investment data) through 2015 (2014 investment data), with an overall response rate of 41.7% (47.2% for the sub-sample of affiliated angels and 39.2% for the non-affiliated angels). Each survey — resembling the typical structure of the questionnaires delivered on an annual basis by the national federations of BAs and BANs all over the world — enquired about investments in the previous year.

The first paper by Bonini *et al.* (2018) assumes as unit of analysis the investments made by Italian angel investors in the 2008–2014 time period, as shown in Table 1, Panel A.

After discarding incomplete or inconsistent filled IBAN questionnaires, the authors were able to build a final dataset based on 439 responses reporting an aggregate of 810 deals, for 619 unique companies, by 330 unique investors. Such sample was used to investigate the impact of a

Table 1: Sampling procedure.

PANEL A — Paper#l: The determinants of BAs investment decisions			
	Surveys sent (2008–2014)	**Final filled surveys selected**	**No. of deals reported**
Full Sample	3,000	439 (14.6%)	810
BAN Members	929	246 (26.5%)	438
Non-BAN Members	2,071	193 (9.3%)	372

PANEL B — Paper#2: The performance of angel-backed companies			
No. of deals reported (2008–2012) (1)	**No. of fully identified deals (2)**	**Panel firms (3)**	**(3)/(2)**
695	302	111	37%

preselected set of factors related to BAs' investment practices on the angels' propensity to invest part of their wealth in a given deal. Two variables have been used as a measure of the BAs' investment decisions: the amount of capital invested as a share of the individual BA's personal wealth (Y_1 = *Wealth*%) and the amount of capital invested by an individual BA expressed as a share of the equity capital of the funded venture (Y_2 = *Participation*%).

Table 3, Panels A and B, provides descriptive statistics related to the two dependent variables: the average BA allocate about the 15.5% (median 14%) of his wealth in a given deal, which results in the acquisition of a minority equity-stake of about the 14.7% (median 8%) of the common equity of the investee company. Interesting to note, the number of observations for variable *Wealth*% (669) is considerably lower than for the variable *Participation*% (808); this is due to the lower number of surveyed angels who have answered the specific question asking for a disclosure about an angel's personal wealth, confirming one relevant and intrinsic selection bias affecting all the empirical analyses dealing with survey-based questionnaires.

The second paper by Bonini *et al.* (2019) bases its analysis on a sample of 111 companies invested by the surveyed angels in the period 2008–2012. During those years, 695 deals were reported by IBAN respondents, but full information on the names of the target companies was only reported for 302 deals. The 111 companies were the target of those deals Table 1, panel B. The companies were monitored along a time horizon of four years (for a total of 444 observations), where *t*0 is the time of the BA investment. Table 2 provides descriptive statistics of the temporal and industry distribution of the sample deals and companies investigated in both papers. The number of firms investigated in this work is significantly lower than that of both the deals and the angel-backed firm considered in the first paper for several reasons. Firstly, the explicit unit of analysis of the first paper is constituted by the individual investments made by each BA, implying that the same company can be present in the investigated sample as many times as the BAs that have invested in it at the same time or in different years. Secondly, for a remarkable number of deals the responding angel did not indicate the name of the investee company or wrote in the questionnaire a name that could not be traced back to any real company, preventing the subsequent data collection required by the empirical analysis to be run by Bonini *et al.* (2019). Finally, the need to observe angel-backed companies in a post-investment time horizon of at least three years did not allow the authors to use for the second paper the 2013 and 2014 IBAN questionnaires, as at the time when the data collection process was carried out, the last official annual financial statement was that of 2015.

The performance of the funded ventures has been measured through the creation of an original indicator, the P.I. is an ordinal variable based on pre-selected combinations of accounting variables relating to revenues, net income and net asset value. The P.I. can assume five different ordinal scores:

(1) Revenues, net asset value and net income are positive → P.I. = 2
(2) Revenues and net asset value are positive, but net income is negative → P.I. = 1
(3) Revenues are positive, but net asset value and net income are negative → P.I. = 0

(4) Revenues are zero, net income is negative, but net asset value is positive → P.I. = –1
(5) Revenues are zero, net income and net asset value are negative → P.I. = –2

Table 2: Sample descriptive statistics.

PANEL A — Temporal distribution

	Paper#1: The determinants of BAs investment decisions No. of deals	**Paper#2: The performance of angel-backed companies No. of firms**
2008	95	2
2009	142	12
2010	137	27
2011	159	23
2012	162	47
2013	58	
2014	57	
Total	810	111

PANEL B — Industry distribution

	Paper#1: The determinants of BAs investment decisions	**Paper#2: The performance of angel-backed companies**
Biotech	17.06%	17.12%
Cleantech	13.08%	13.51%
Commerce and distribution	10.09 %	9.01%
Electronics	9.34%	15.32%
Information and Communications Technology (ICT)	20.80%	18.02%
Media & Entertainment	9.96%	9.01%
Other sectors	19.68%	18.02%
Total	100.00%	100.00%

Table 3: Dependent variables: descriptive statistics.

PANEL A — Dependent variable = *Wealth*%	
Mean	15.48
Median	14
Maximum	60
Minimum	5
Standard deviation	11.8
No. of observation	669
PANEL B — Dependent variable = *Participation*%	
Mean	14.74
Median	8
Maximum	100
Minimum	1
Standard deviation	19.54
No. of observation	808
PANEL C — Dependent variable = *Performance Index*	
Ordinal Value	**Total by value**
2	91
1	179
0	40
−1	54
−2	16
No. of firms without financial statement in $t0$	64
Total	444

In the 404 sample of company-years observations used in Bonini *et al.* (2019), 4.21% were in the lowest category of P.I., with negative income and net assets, and no revenues. 14.21% had only positive net assets, 10.53% only had positive revenues, 47.11% had both positive revenues and positive net assets and 23.95% also had positive net income.

Although many alternative combinations of outcomes are technically possible from a mere computational standpoint, the authors argue their five selected outcomes are consistent with the five performance scenarios commonly outlined in financial accounting literature (Anthony and Ramesh, 1992; Black, 1998; Fame and French, 2000; Nissim and Penman, 2001; Omrani and Karami, 2010; Dickinson, 2011) and practice (Damodaran, 2015; Fabozzi *et al.*, 2015).

The basic rationale underlying the P.I. is that it takes time for a small company receiving an equity injection to (i) fully deploy the projected operating investments disclosed in the fundraising process, (ii) adjust the business model and company operations, and (iii) start experiencing cash inflows, earnings and increase in the equity capital base. As a consequence, a common growth path to many angel-backed start-ups implies some years of zero or low revenues, negative profits and equity capital erosion, followed by either the increase of sales, earnings and cash flows, or the death of the company.

It's therefore a crucial issue understanding the major contributions provided by BAs and leading some companies after a few years since their foundation to be able to be alive and grow their business, differently from some others experiencing low performance and undergoing liquidation or bankruptcy procedures within the same time frame.

3. Main Research Hypotheses

The main research hypotheses set by the authors of both papers aim at investigating whether BAs' investment decisions and the performance of angel-backed companies are affected by two main typologies of factors: the interaction across angel investors and the interaction between BAs and the funded venture.

As for the first factor, Bonini *et al.* (2018) measure the interaction across BAs through an original pair of variables related to the investment practices of the surveyed angels: the membership to a BAN and the number of BA co-investing in a given deal.

Also the second factor, i.e., the interaction between BAs and the angel-backed company, is measured by two distinct variables, both based on the answers provided by the surveyed angels to specific questions about their investment decision-making process. The first measure discriminates between passive angel investors and actively involved ones, the formers being BAs investing just for financial purposes, the latters also providing relevant non-monetary contributions, such as mentoring, management advisory, networking, sharing industry or product market knowledge related to their previous experience. The second measure is the intensity of the post-investment monitoring effort, that in the case of BAs, different from VCs, takes place basically through company visits and meeting with the funded entrepreneurs.

The main research hypotheses developed in the two works are presented in the following section.

3.1. *Affiliation to an angel community*

A significant transformation driver affecting the angel market in the last two decades is the emergence of angel investment organizations (Shane, 2000; Josè *et al.*, 2005; Aernoudt *et al.*, 2007; Ibrahim, 2008; Paul and Whittam, 2010; Brush *et al.*, 2012; Gregson *et al.*, 2013; Lahti and Keinonen, 2016; Mason *et al.*, 2016). It's now well clear that by joining an angel syndicate BAs can enjoy multiple benefits, mostly due to the information and knowledge sharing taking place inside the community. In particular, less experienced angels by getting in touch with more experienced angels may have the opportunity to increase their human capital, developing a better understanding about how to implement effective value-creating investment decisions.

Therefore, Bonini *et al.* (2018) argue the affiliation to an angel syndicate does have a double impact on BAs' investment decision. Firstly, due to the information sharing and screening contribution provided by angel investment organizations, which decreases the opaqueness as well as the perceived risk profile of BAs' typical investment opportunities, affiliate members should invest in companies belonging to this peculiar asset class more of their personal wealth than unaffiliated angels.

Secondly, BAs joining a BAN benefit from the deal flow disclosed inside the angel community and, therefore, are provided with both a higher number of and better quality investment opportunities compared to non-BAN members. However, given that the impact of angel syndicates on BA investments should not necessarily result in structural changes in either angels' risk aversion or angels' historical asset allocation strategies, affiliated angels offset the increase in the number and the unit size of deals with a decrease in the equity stake acquired in the investee companies.

Table 4: Business angels' investment intensity.

No. of deals in business angles' portfolios	Whole sample (%)	BAN members (%)	Non-BAN members (%)
>10	17.9	18.16	9.13
6–10	26.05	28.32	9.14
2–5	33.46	35.16	51.34
1	22.59	18.26	20.38
χ^2 (portfolio > 5)		32.02***	

In support of such hypothesis, Table 4 shows that the Italian angels joining an angel syndicate have in their asset portfolio a number of angel deals higher than that of the unaffiliated angels: Only 18% of BAs who are not members of any given BAN own a portfolio with more than five investments, against about 47% of those angel investors affiliated with a BAN.

Finally, assuming the standpoint of the angel-backed companies, Bonini *et al.* (2019) observe many BANs arrange on a regular basis courses and training programs targeted to both their own affiliates or potential entrepreneurs, in order to increase the quality of the entrepreneur–investor relationship and maximize the post investment value contribution provided by BAs.

Additionally, BAN membership gives affiliated angels the opportunity to enjoy some common services, such as due diligence and contract designing, as well as to optimize BAs' decision-making styles according to their investment behavior in a trust-based environment, ultimately increasing the probability of the funded venture to run follow-on investment rounds (Wiltbank, 2009; Fili *et al.*, 2013; Bonnet *et al.*, 2013; Bammens and Collewaert, 2014). It is therefore possible that the contribution of angel syndicates is not limited to the generation and screening of investment opportunities, rather positively impacting the growth path and the value creation potential of the angel-backed companies.

The causal relationships above argued have been tested through the use of the dummy variable *BAN-membership*, that assumes the value of one if at least one BA joining a given deal shows a BAN affiliation.

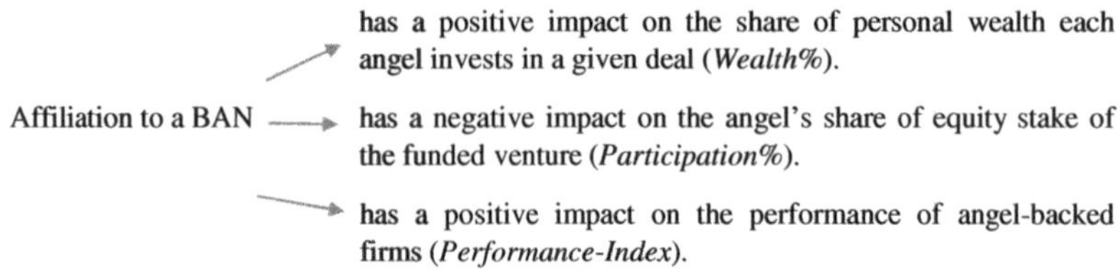

Figure 1: Hypothesized effects of the affiliation to an angel community.

The expected relationships between the dummy *BAN-membership* and the dependent variables investigated in the two papers are depicted in Figure 1.

3.2. *The co-investment across BAs*

Alongside with angel investment organizations, another rising phenomenon affecting the informal venture capital market is the emergence of the practice of co-investment, that can be pursued according to more or less structured modes, involving a plurality of investments or just a single deal raising the interests of multiple BAs forming an investment syndicate (or "club deal") on a spot basis.

From the IBAN data on the Italian market, a rather heterogeneous scenario emerges, where the number of co-investors varies from a maximum of 15 to a minimum of 0, assumes an average value of 4 and a median value of 2, confirming co-investment as a structural investment practice within the angel market.

The co-investment yields some valuable advantages to BAs. First, it allows them to reduce their individual equity stake in the investee companies, without sacrificing the opportunity to play an active role and eventually provide value-added contributions, due to the cumulative equity position held by all the BAs co-investing in a given deal, that is higher than "solo" angels' equity stake (Paul and Whittam, 2010). Second, consistent with modern portfolio theory (Elton and Gruber, 2005), the co-investment option is a pure rational diversification strategy aimed at reducing the risk from a given investment opportunity and, therefore, at relying on more diversified investment portfolios (Harrison and Mason, 2002; Mason *et al.*, 2013). Third, similar to an analogous argument developed about angel syndicates, BAs, by co-investing in a given deal, can get access to risk-reducing information coming from the reciprocal knowledge, background and previous experience (Aernoudt, 2005; Sohl, 2012).

As a consequence of the above said, Bonini *et al.* (2018) assume rational BAs deciding to co-invest are likely to adopt a risk-sharing perspective also when deciding the amount of their personal wealth to allocate to a given deal, therefore individually investing a smaller amount of capital than "solo" angels.

When assuming the perspective of the investee ventures, Bonini *et al.* (2019) argue a company being funded by a syndicate of angels might enjoy a wider set of both monetary and non-monetary contributions than that possibly provided by a solo angel, thus increasing its growth potential as well as its future probability of survival. As for the monetary contributions, it's clear a high number of co-investing angels implies the opportunity to immediately start the business with a higher size scale, market potential and an increased probability to run follow-on investment rounds over time. A further monetary contribution for the angel-backed companies comes from the possibility to benefit from the sharing taking place across co-investing angels of the costs of due diligence, contracting and monitoring. As for the non-monetary contributions, the angel-backed companies can enjoy multiple sources of coaching and mentoring and can benefit from each BA's industrial knowledge, previous investment experience and relationship network.

The magnitude of the co-investment, as measured by the number of co-investors in a given deal, therefore implies a higher quality selection process and a more effective post-investment involvement than those of the "solo" angels, because of the possibility to benefit from wider experience, knowledge and social capital.

Such research hypothesis has been tested through the variable *Co-investors*, which corresponds to the number of BAs joining a given deal. The expected relationships between the variable *Co-investors* and the dependent variables selected in the two papers are described in Figure 2.

3.3. *Active or passive investors?*

As anticipated in the previous section, the contribution BAs can provide in a given deal is often not limited to just the subscription of equity capital,

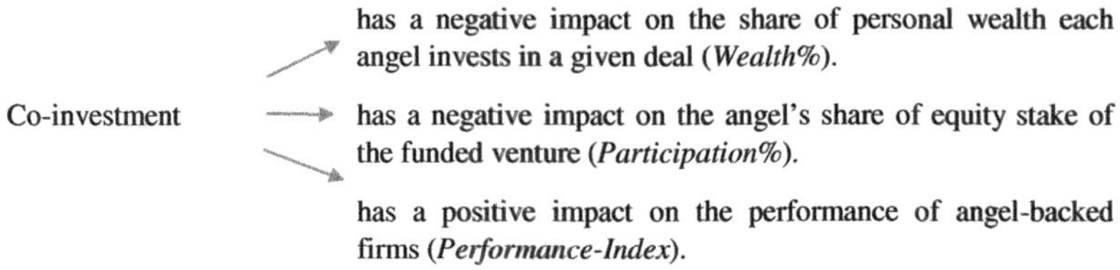

Figure 2: Hypothesized effects of the co-investment in a given deal.

but, as pointed out by the literature, it might be aimed at seeking active involvement with their portfolio companies, supporting them in the value creation process through a hands-on approach. The willingness to share with the entrepreneur own industry skills, to offer mentoring and advisory services, to participate in the strategic design process, to optimize corporate governance, to provide previous experience, to make the funded venture benefit from their own network of industry and financial relationships are all examples of non-monetary contributions possibly available to angel-backed companies (Mason and Harrison, 2000; Mason, 2006; Politis, 2008; Landström and Mason, 2016; Croce *et al.*, 2018).

On the contrary, it is not uncommon to observe BAs not willing and/or able to play such an active role in the funded ventures: rather, they behave according to a hands-off approach typical of purely financial investors, being attracted by potential capital gains and by the portfolio diversification benefits associated to angel investments.

Hence, Bonini *et al.* (2018) assume that "active" and "passive" investors exhibit a structurally different investment pattern. More in detail, the exclusive orientation to financial yields and diversification benefits is likely to have a negative impact on both the share of BAs' personal resources to be invested and the size of their equity stakes in the funded ventures.

Such hypothesis has been tested through the dummy variable *Passive investor*, that takes a value of one if the responding angel states that the investment decision was driven exclusively by capital gain motivation and not by other reasons suggesting his willingness to play an active role in the angel-backed company.

The expected relationships between the dummy *Passive investor* and the variables *Wealth%* and (*Participation%*) are represented in Figure 3.

Passive investment → has a negative impact on the share of personal wealth each angel invests in a given deal (*Wealth%*).

Passive investment → has a negative impact on the angel's share of equity stake of the funded venture (*Participation%*).

Figure 3: Hypothesized effects of the BAs' "passive" investment behavior.

Active involvement → has a positive impact on the performance of angel-backed firms (*Performance-Index*).

Figure 4: Hypothesized effects of the BAs' "active" involvement.

Differently from controversial findings from the venture capital industry, the impact of BAs' active involvement on portfolio companies is generally found to be positive as for the possibility of angel-backed companies to both raise follow-on funds and create value for their stockholders (Madill *et al.*, 2005; Chua and Wu, 2012; Landström and Mason, 2016). In line with these evidences, Bonini *et al.* (2019) hypothesize a positive relationship between the *Performance Index* of the funded ventures and BAs' active involvement in company operations (Figure 4).

3.4. *The intensity of monitoring*

Finance literature has deeply addressed the role of the monitoring as a way to reduce the problems related to information asymmetry and moral hazard stemming from any type of securities investments (Jensen and Mecking, 1976; Diamond, 1984; Aghion and Bolton, 1992).

As far as VC and private equity investments are concerned, a wide stream of studies has extensively investigated how institutional investors monitor target companies and the major contingent contracts, clauses and mechanisms used to manage such problems and realign incentives between investors and company owner-managers (Sahlman, 1990; Triantis, 2001; Kaplan and Strömberg, 2003; Gompers and Lerner, 2004; Chemmanur *et al.*, 2011; Cumming, 2008; Wong *et al.*, 2009; Metrick and Yasuda, 2010; Cumming and Johan, 2013; Bernstein *et al.*, 2016; Erenburg *et al.*, 2016).

In the case of angel financing, however, several contributions point out that BAs hardly adopt the typical monitoring mechanisms used by venture capitalist, preferring instead to implement "non-aggressive" and informal control mechanisms which Bonini *et al.* (2018, 2019) define as "soft monitoring" ones, such as geographical proximity to the angel-backed company, BAs' knowledge of the industry, experience gained from previous investments and, most importantly, interactions with entrepreneurs through periodic meeting or company visits (Van Osnabrugge, 2000; Kelly and Hay, 2003; Wiltbank and Boecker, 2007; Ibrahim, 2008; Chemmanur and Chen, 2014; Goldfarb *et al.*, 2014; Bonini and Capizzi, 2017).

It is then reasonable to assume the more intense the soft monitoring effort put by BAs, the lower the investment risk perception by BAs in their investment decision-making process, hence positively impacting on both the amount invested and the size of their equity stakes in the funded ventures.

However, when considering the perspective of the angel-backed companies, one has to remind the tight fiduciary relationship existing between the BA and the entrepreneur, mutually nurtured by reciprocal trust (Chua and Wu, 2012; Bammens and Collewaert, 2014). Therefore, it might be the case that tightening the degree of soft monitoring could harm the trust-based relationship between the entrepreneur and the angel investor, negatively impacting on the mutual perception on each other's contribution, possibly worsening the future company performance.

The above-developed research hypothesis has been investigated using the variable *Soft-monitoring*, that may take a value from 1 to 5, depending on the frequency of the visits a BA makes to its portfolio companies. The expected relationships between the variable *Soft-monitoring* and the dependent variables being studied in the two papers are shown in Figure 5.

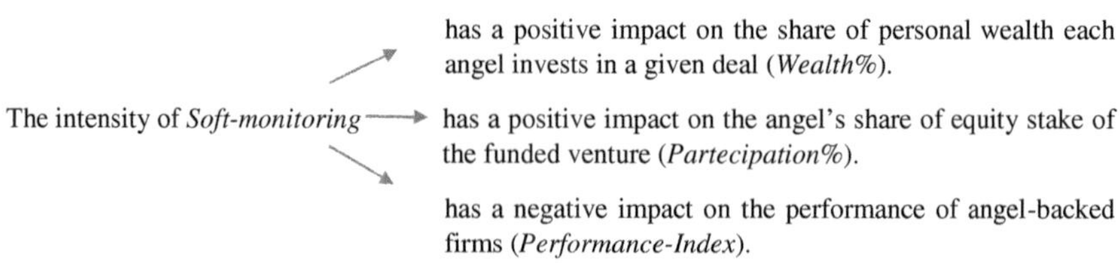

Figure 5: The intensity of the *Soft-monitoring*.

4. Methodology and Main Results

In the first paper, the authors investigate the determinants of BAs' investment decisions by running an ordinary least squares (OLS) regression model between the two selected dependent variables (*Wealth*% and *Participation*%) and a set of independent variables related to the research hypotheses developed in the previous sections: *BAN membership*, *Co-investors*, *Passive investor* and *Soft-monitoring*.

In addition to the four independent variables defined above, the model also introduces control variables related to the characteristics of the BAs (age, education, wealth, previous investment experience, professional background), the characteristics of the funded ventures (company size, age and stage in the life cycle, geographical location) and to the characteristics of the reference industry (industry price-to-book value ratio and industry capital intensity). Finally, the authors add to some model specifications time and industry-fixed effects to account for possible heterogeneity in BAs' behavior.

The analysis is then replied for the sub-samples of affiliated and unaffiliated BAs separately, in order to be able to identify structural differences in BAs' investment practices likely driven by the different degree of networking, information and knowledge sharing across the two groups.

In the second paper, being the dependent variable the five-stage ordinal variable *Performance Index*, the authors run a set of ordinal logistic (Ologit) regression analysis.

The explanatory variables are related to the main research hypotheses: *BAN_membership, Co-investors, Active-Involvement, Soft-Monitoring.* Moreover, the authors included firm-specific controls (company age, size, location and stage in the life cycle) and angel-specific controls (BA's age, experience and equity stake in the funded venture), together with fixed temporal and industry effects.

The results, reported in Table 5, show that being a member of an angel community increases the share of wealth invested in a deal by approximately 16% (column 2) and reduces the size of the equity stake in the investee venture by approximately 14% (column 5), thus confirming the authors' hypotheses about the role of angel syndicates on BAs' investment decisions.

Table 5: Huber–White heteroskedasticity-consistent standard errors are reported in parentheses under each coefficient.

	Y = Wealth%			Y = Participation%			Y = Performance-Index
	Whole sample	BAN Member	Non-BAN Member	Whole sample	BAN Member	Non-BAN Member	Whole sample
Independent variables	**(2)**	**(3)**	**(4)**	**(5)**	**(6)**	**(7)**	**(8)**
BAN_membership	0.155***			–0.139*			0.225
	(0.05)			(0.07)			(0.37)
Co-investors	–0.017***	–0.035***	–0.007	–0.067***	–0.075***	–0.069***	0.063**
	(0.01)	(0.01)	(0.01)	(0.01)	(0.01)	(0.01)	(0.03)
Passive Investor	–0.064	–0.023	–0.163**	–0.186**	–0.262**	–0.264***	
	(1.08)	(0.25)	(2.08)	(0.08)	(0.13)	(0.09)	
Active Involvement							0,479
							(0.31)
Soft-Monitoring	0.054*	–0.053	0.154***	0.214***	0.116**	0.287***	–0.316***
	(1.92)	(1.62)	(4.60)	(0.04)	(0.05)	(0.06)	(0.12)
ANGEL F.E.	YES	YES	YES	YES	YES	YES	YES
FIRM F.E.	YES	YES	YES	YES	YES	YES	YES
INDUSTRY F.E.	YES	YES	YES	YES	YES	YES	YES
YEAR F.E.	YES	YES	YES	YES	YES	YES	YES
cut 1							–7.129***
cut 2							–5.354***
cut 3							–4.874***
cut 4							–2.235*
R^2	0.27	0.35	0.37	0.56	0.51	0.67	0.10
Observations	569	292	277	569	292	277	303

Notes: *, **, *** indicate statistical significance at the 10%.

However, the affiliation to an angel network does not seem to have a statistically significant impact on the performance of angel-backed companies (column 8), maybe due to the intrinsic features of the authors' survey-based dataset, which does not allow the possibility to account for the qualitative differences in the various forms of potentially existing angel investment organizations.

Ceteris paribus, a one-unit increase in the number of co-investors reduces the percentage of BA's personal wealth invested in a single *deal* by 2% (column 2) and decreases the individual participation in the investee company by an economically significant 7%; therefore, co-investing appears to be an effective way to pursue risk-minimizing investment decisions while enjoying the upside of portfolio diversification.

Moreover, by comparing affiliated angels to unaffiliated angels, Bonini *et al.* (2018) observe the BAs' wealth allocation is affected by the presence of co-investors only for the sub-sample of the BAs affiliated to an angel community, implying that there could be a positive effect played by the trust established within a given angel community. On the opposite, the absence of an effect for unaffiliated angels might be interpreted as the result of a lack of knowledge of other investors' profiles and characteristics, eventually preventing BAs from co-investing because of potential free-riding and/or opportunistic behavior (columns 3 and 4).

As for the variable *Participation*%, results confirm the expected negative relationship between the number of co-investors and the equity stake in the investee company for both sub-samples (columns 6 and 7), though showing higher significance for affiliated angels. The phenomenon of co-investment also positively affects the performance of angel-backed companies, as expected (column 8).

When considering BAs' motivations to invest, it is confirmed the existence of a negative relationship between a "passive" investment aptitude and BAs' investment decisions, though limited to just unaffiliated angels. Bonini *et al.* (2018) argue that within an angel community the possibility of benefitting from co-investing with other affiliated angels, the possibility of enjoying other angels' experience and knowledge may provide incentives that ultimately positively affect the percentage wealth invested by passive BAs, similarly to actively involved BAs' investment decisions.

Finally, the variable *soft-monitoring*, is significant and has a positive impact on both the dependent variables *Wealth%*, (column 2) and *Participation%* (column 5), confirming the authors' hypothesis. By looking at the results of the analysis run separately for affiliated and unaffiliated BAs, it turns out that the impact of BAs' monitoring is statistically significant only for investors not joining an angel community, thus confirming the quality of the contribution in terms of deal flow and screening provided by angel groups to their members. In fact, it is likely that affiliated angels put a higher effort in monitoring only on ventures perceived as riskier and, thus, more opaque. When considering the impact of soft monitoring on the performance of angel-backed companies, the results of the empirical analysis show a statistically significant negative relationship, supporting the argument that tightening the control on the funded venture might damage the underlying trust-based fiduciary relationship and eventually worsen the future probability of survival and growth.

In Bonini *et al.* (2018), the authors provided further support to their results by performing multiple robustness checks (including a set of two-stage instrumental variable regressions and propensity score matching regressions) to face possible sample bias or endogeneity issues dealing with the decision to join a given angel investment organization. Results, not reported in this chapter, are qualitatively unchanged.

In Bonini *et al.* (2019), on top of the various robustness checks performed, the authors tested the predictive power of their P.I. by creating a dummy variable (*Survival*) assuming the value one for those ventures that have survived four years after the initial investment, or zero otherwise. They then run a set of logistic regressions on such variable against the P.I. as explanatory variable on both the sample of angel-backed companies and a homogeneous sample of control companies not funded by BAs. Table 6 shows the results of this regression analysis, which confirms the predictive power on the survival of angel-backed firms of the P.I. for both samples, differently from other traditional accounting measures (total assets and revenues).

Table 6: Predictive power of different performance measures.

	(1)		(2)		(3)	
	Angel-backed firms	**Control sample**	**Angel-backed firms**	**Control sample**	**Angel-backed firms**	**Control sample**
Performance-Index	0.623**	0.359*				
	(0.29)	(0.191)				
Total Assets			–0.163	0.038		
			(0.18)	0.141		
Revenues					0.081	0.032
					(0.06)	0.043
Industry-FE	YES	YES	YES	YES	YES	YES
Intercept	0.759	0.682**	3.497	0.557	0.49	0.728
	(0.53)	(0.341)	(2.48)	(1.764)	(0.76)	(0.495)
Pseudo R^2	0.159	0.06	0.131	0.03	0.119	0.04
N	80	114	80	114	80	114

Notes: In this table are presented results for a set of logistic regressions estimating the survival of firms through the Performance Index and two other traditional measures of performance. The dependent variable is a dummy ("Survival") assuming value one for those firms that have survived four-years after the initial investment, or zero otherwise. Huber–White heteroskedasticity-consistent standard errors are reported in parentheses under each coefficient. *, **, *** indicate statistical significance at the 10%, 5% and 1% levels, respectively.

5. Conclusions

The recent explosion of the informal venture capital market all over the world is stimulating finance scholars to deeply investigate the major determinants, characteristics and possible implications of this phenomenon within the start-up ecosystems. Though now rather developed and well differentiated by major research themes, literature on BAs still misses to adequately cover many actual investigation areas where, up to date, the knowledge is still limited. Examples of relatively low explored topics deal with the operations and the role played by the different typologies of BA networks or, also, the valuation of the contributions provided by BAs to the survival and growth of the angel-backed companies.

The contributions of Bonini *et al.* (2018, 2019) are part of the ongoing debate on these two research areas that have not yet been exhaustively explored. The two papers show that the affiliation to an angel community does affect BAs' investment decisions, though it doesn't seem to have a significant impact on the survival and profitability of the funded ventures, except for the weakest performing ones. On the contrary, by co-investing on a deal-specific basis in a given angel syndicate, BAs may enjoy risk-sharing and information-sharing benefits that structurally affect both their investment practices and the performance of the funded ventures.

Also the BAs' willingness to play an active role by providing value-added contributions in terms of industry skill, experience, mentoring and networking opportunities plays a major role in driving the angel-backed companies to survival and growth.

On the contrary, the intensity of BAs' soft monitoring seems negatively related to the performance of the funded ventures because of the impact on the trust-based entrepreneur–angel relationship. However, angel communities might be able to decrease and distribute within the network the need for individual monitoring while increasing members' confidence in the angel investments.

Future research will have to shed more light on the pivotal role played by angel syndicates — both inside and outside angel communities — within the entrepreneurial finance ecosystem, given their intrinsic potential as mechanisms for sharing across BAs information, experience and knowledge. Another promising area of future research stems from the extension of the analysis at an international level through worldwide-based BA samples, in order to find out best practices inside angel investment organizations as well as focused public policies aimed at creating favorable environments for angel investors.

One concrete example of one possible policy measure could be the design of dedicated financing facility schemes leveraging on the value-adding potential of BAs, such as the creation of public–private angel co-investment funds.

Finally, the analyzed contributions suggest a number of possible action schemes also for BAs, on the one hand, and entrepreneurs, on the other hand. As a matter of fact, the business model of "solo angels" looks like less effective and value-adding than that of BAs deciding to co-invest and, therefore, to enjoy the many benefits associated to an angel syndicate, ultimately positively impacting the investment risk and the performance of the funded venture. From the entrepreneurs' side, it is crucial to consider the major contribution provided by angel investors is not just a pure monetary one: therefore, involving as equity investors a pool of co-investors is a unique opportunity to exploit multiple background experiences, know how, industry and product market knowledge, networks of personal relationships as well as the standing and reputation of all the angels co-investing in a given deal.

References

Aernoudt R. (2005) Business angels: the smartest money for starters? PLEA for a renewed policy focus on business angels. *International Journal of Business*, 19(5), 271–284.

Aghion P. and Bolton P. (1992) An incomplete contracts approach to financial contracting. *Review of Economic Studies*, 59(3), 473–494.

Alemany L. and Villanueva J. (2015) Early stage investors' criteria and new venture financial performance: are they related? Working paper, available at: https://www.researchgate.net/publication/279275482.

Alexy O. T., Block J. H., Sandner P., and Ter Wal Ann L. J. (2012) Social capital of venture capitalists and start-up funding. *Small Business Economics*, 39(4), 835–851.

Anthony J. H. and Ramesh K. (1992) Association between accounting performance measures and stock prices: A test of the life cycle hypothesis. *Journal of Accounting and Economics*, 15(2–3), 203–227.

Ardichvili A., Cardozo R. N., Tune K., and Reinach J. (2002) The role angel investors in the assembly of non-financial resources of new ventures: conceptual framework and empirical evidence. *Journal of Enterprising Culture*, 10(1), 39–65.

Audretsch and Lehmann (2004) Financing high-tech growth: the role of banks and venture capitalists. *Schmalenbach Business Review*, 56(4), 340–357.

Baldock R. and Mason C. (2015) Establishing a new UK finance escalator for innovative SMEs: The roles of the enterprise capital funds and angel co-investment fund. *Venture Capital: An International Journal of Entrepreneurial Finance*, 17(1–2), 59–86.

Bammens Y. and Collewaert V. (2014) Trust between entrepreneurs and angel investors: exploring positive and negative implications for venture performance assessments. *Journal of Management*, 40(7), 1980–2008.

Benjamin G. A. and Margulis J. (2000) Angel Financing, Weley & Sons, Hoboken, NJ.

Bergemann D. and Hege U. (1998) Venture capital financing, moral hazard and learning. *Journal of Banking and Finance*, 22, 703–735.

Bertoni F., Colombo M. G., and Grilli L. (2011) Venture capital financing and the growth of high-tech start-ups: disentangling treatment from selection effects. *Research Policy*, 40(7), 1028–1043.

Black B. S. and Gilson R. J. (1998) Venture capital and the structure of capital markets: banks versus stock markets. *Journal of Financial Economics*, 47(3), 243–277.

Black E. L. (1998) Life-cycle impacts on the incremental value-relevance of earnings and cash flow measures. *Journal of Financial Statement Analysis*, 4(1), 40–56.

Bonini S. and Capizzi V. (2017) The effects of private equity investors on the governance of companies. In Gabrielsson J. (ed.), *Handbook of Research on Entrepreneurship and Corporate Governance*, Edward Elgar Publishing, Camberley, UK.

Bonini S., Capizzi V., Valletta M., and Zocchi P. (2018) Angel network affiliation and business angels' investment practices. *Journal of Corporate Finance*, 50(6), 592–608.

Bonini S., Capizzi V., and Zocchi P. (2019) The performance of angel-backed companies. *Journal of Banking & Finance*, 100(3), 328–345.

Bonnet C. and Wirtz P. (2012) Raising capital for rapid growth in young technology ventures: when business angels and venture capitalists coinvest. *Venture Capital: An International Journal of Entrepreneurial Finance*, 14(2–3), 91–110.

Brander J. A., Amit R., and Antweiler W. (2002) Venture-capital syndication: improved venture selection vs. the value-added hypothesis. *Journal of Economics & Management Strategy*, 11(3), 423–452.

Brav A. and Gompers P. A. (1997) Myth or reality: the long-run underperformance of initial public offerings: evidence from venture and nonventure capital-backed companies. *Journal of Finance*, 52(5), 1791–1821.

Brush C. G., Edelman L. F., and Manolova T. S. (2012) Ready for funding? Entrepreneurial ventures and the pursuit of angel financing. *Venture Capital: An International Journal of Entrepreneurial Finance*, 14(2–3), 111–129.

Burt R. S. (2005) *Brokerage and Closure: An Introduction to Social Capital*. Oxford University Press, New York, NY.

Capizzi V. (2015) The returns of business angel investments and their major determinants. *Venture Capital: An International Journal of Entrepreneurial Finance*, 17(4), 271–298.

Carpenter R. E. and Petersen B. C. (2002) Capital market imperfection, high-tech investment and new equity financing. *The Economic Journal*, 112(477), F54–F72.

Carpentier C. and Suret J.-M. (2015) Angel group members' decision process and rejection criteria: A longitudinal analysis. *Journal of Business Venturing*, 30(6), 808.

Chemmanur T. J., Krishnan, K., and Nandy D. K. (2011) How does venture capital financing improve efficiency in private firms? a look beneath the surface. *Review of Financial Studies*, 24(12), 4037–4090.

Chemmanur T. J. and Chen Z. (2014) Venture capitalists versus angels: The dynamics of private firm financing contracts. *Review of Corporate Finance Studies*, 3(1–2), 39–86.

Christensen J. L. (2011) Should government support business angel networks? The tale of Danish business angels network, *Venture Capital: An International Journal of Entrepreneurial Finance*, 13(4), 337–356.

Chua J. and Wu Z. (2012) Value Added by Angel Investors through Post-investment Involvement: Exploratory Evidence and Ownership Implications. In Cumming D. (ed.), *The Oxford Handbook of Venture Capital*, Oxford University Press, New York, NY, pp. 721–750.

Coleman J. S. (1988) Social capital in the creation of human capital. *American Journal of Sociology*, 94, s95–s120.

Collewaert V. and Manigart S. (2016) Valuation of angel-backed companies: the role of investor human capital. *Journal of Small Business Management*, 54(1), 356–372.

Colombo M. G. and Grilli L. (2010) On growth drivers of hightech start-ups. The role of founders' human capital and venture capital. *Journal of Business Venturing*, 25(6), 610–626.

Croce A. and Martí J. (2016) Productivity growth in private-equity-backed family firms. *Entrepreneurship Theory and Practice*, 40(3), 657–683.

Croce A., Martí J., and Murtinu S. (2013) The impact of venture capital on the productivity growth of European entrepreneurial firms: "Screening" or "value added" effect? *Journal of Business Venturing*, 28(4), 489–510.

Croce A., Tenca F., and Ughetto E. (2017) How business angel groups work: rejection criteria in investment evaluation. *International Small Business Journal*, 35(4), 405–426.

Cumming D. (2008) Contracts and exits in venture capital finance. *The Review of Financial Studies*, 21(5), 1947–1982.

Cumming D. and Dai N. (2010) Local bias in venture capital investments. *The Journal of Empirical Finance*, 17(3), 362–380.

Cumming D. and Johan S. (2013) *Venture Capital and Private Equity Contracting: An International Perspective*, 2nd Edition. Elsevier Science Academic Press, Amsterdam, The Netherlands.

Cumming D. and Walz U. (2010) Private equity returns and disclosure around the world, *Journal of International Business Studies*, 41(4), 727–754.

Cumming D. and Zhang M. (2018) Angel Investors Around the World. *Journal of International Business Studies*, First Online September 2018, doi: https://doi.org/10.1057/s41267-018-0178-0.

Damodaran A. (2015) *Applied Corporate Finance*, 4th Edition. Wiley & Sons, Hoboken, NJ.

Davila A., Foster G., and Gupta M. (2003) Venture capital financing and the growth of startup firms. *Journal of Business Venturing*, 18(6), 689–708.

De Clercq D., Fried V. H., Lehtonen H., and Sapienza H. J. (1996) An entrepreneur's guide to the venture capital galaxy. *Academy of Management Perspectives*, 20(3), 90–112.

De Clercq D. and Sapienza H. J. (2006) Effects of relational capital and commitment on venture capitalists' perception of portfolio company performance. *Journal of Business Venturing*, 21(3), 326–347.

De Gennaro R. P. and Dwyer G. P. (2014) Expected returns to stock investments by angel investors in group. *European Financial Management*, 20(4), 739–755.

De Leeuw E. D. (2005) To mix or not to mix data collection modes in surveys. *Journal of Official Statistics*, 21, 233–255.

Diamond D. W. (1984) Financial intermediation and delegated monitoring. *The Review of Economic Studies*, 51(3), 393–414.

Dickinson V. (2011) Cash flow patterns as a proxy for firm life cycle. *The Accounting Review*, 86(6), 1969–1994.

Dillman D. A., Smyth J. D. and Christian L. M. (2009) *Internet, Mail, and Mixed-Mode Surveys: The Tailored Design Method.* Wiley & Sons, Hoboken, NJ.

Dimov D. P. and Shepherd D. A. (2005) Human capital theory and venture capital firms: Exploring "home runs" and "strike outs". *Journal of Business Venturing*, 20(10), 1–21.

Dimov D., Shepherd D. A., and Sutcliffe K. M. (2007) Requisite expertise, firm reputation, and status in venture capital investment allocation decisions. *Journal of Business Venturing*, 22(4), 481–502.

EBAN (2015) *Activity Report 2015*. Available at: www.eban.org.

EBAN (2017) European Early Stage Market Statistics. *2016 EBAN Statistics Compendium*. Available at: www.eban.org.

Elton E. J. and Gruber M. J. (2005) *Modern Portfolio Theory and Investment Analysis,* 5th Edition. Wiley & Sons, Hoboken, NJ.

Engel D. (2002) The impact of venture capital on firm growth: an empirical investigation. ZEW Discussion Paper (January 2, 2002). doi: http://dx.doi.org/10.2139/ssrn.319322.

Engel D. and Keilbach M. (2007) Firm-level implications of early stage venture capital investment — an empirical investigation. *Journal of Empirical Finance,* 14(2), 150–167.

Erenburg G., Smith, J. K., and Smith R. (2016) Which institutional investors matter for firm survival and performance? *The North American Journal of Economics and Finance,* 17, 348–373.

EVCA (2014) *EVCA Report 2014,* Available at: www.evca.eu.

Fabozzi F. J., Peterson Drake P., and Polimeni R. S. (2015) *The Complete CFO Handbook: From Accounting to Accountability*. Wiley & Sons, Hoboken, NJ.

Fama E. F. and French K. R. (2000) Forecasting profitability and earnings. *Journal of Business,* 73(2), 161–175.

Fili A., Berggren B., and Silver L. (2013) The impact of financial capital, human capital and social capital on the evolution of business angel networks. *International Journal of Corporate Governance,* 4(3), 209–228.

Forsfält T. (1999) The effects of risk aversion and age on investments in new firms. Research Papers in Economics, Stockholm University, Department of Economics No 1999:18.

Freear J., Sohl J. E., and Wetzel W. E. (1992) The investment attitudes, behavior and characteristics of high net worth individuals. In Churchill N. C, Birley S., Bygrave W. D., Muzyka D. E., Wahlbin C., and Wetzel W. E., Jr. (eds.), *Frontiers of Entrepreneurship Research 1992*. Babson College, Babson Park, MA, pp. 374–387.

Goldfarb B., Hoberg G., Kisch D., and Triantis A. (2014) Are Angels Different? An Analysis of Early Venture Financing. Robert H. Smith School Research Paper (RHS 06-072, October 2014).

Gompers P. A. (1995) Optimal investing, monitoring and the staging of venture capital. *Journal of Finance,* 50, 1461–1489.

Gompers P. and Lerner J. (2004) *The Venture Capital Cycle*. The MIT Press, Cambridge, MA.

Gompers P. and Lerner J. (2001) The Venture Capital Revolution. *Journal of Economics Perspectives,* 15(2), 145–168.

Granovetter M. (1992) Problems of explanation in economic sociology. In Nohria N. and Eccles R. G. (eds.), *Networks and Organizations: Structure, Form, and Action*, Harvard Business School Press, Boston, MA, pp. 25–56.

Gregson G., Mann S., and Harrison R. (2013) Business angel syndication and the evolution of risk capital in a small market economy: Evidence from Scotland. *Managerial and Decision Economics*, 34(2), 95–107.

Grilli L. and Murtinu S. (2014) Government, venture capital and the growth of European high-tech entrepreneurial firms. *Research Policy*, 43(9), 1523–1543.

Harrison R. T. and Mason C. M. (1992) International perspectives on the supply of informal venture capital. *Journal of Business Venturing*, 7(6), 459–475.

Harrison R. T. and Mason C. M. (eds.) (1996) *Informal Venture Capital: Evaluating the Impact of Business Introduction Services.* Prentice Hall, Hertfordshire, UK.

Harrison R. T. and Mason C. M. (2002) Is it worth it? The rates of return from informal venture capital investments. *Journal of Business Venturing*, 17, 211–236.

Harrison R. T. and Mason C. M. (2008) Sampling and data collection in business angels research. *Venture Capital: An International Journal of Entrepreneurial Finance*, 10(4), 305–308.

Harrison R. T., Mason C. M., and Robson P. J. A. (2010) Determinants of long-distance investing by business angels in the UK. Entrepreneurship and Regional Development, 22(2), 113–137.

Harrison R. T. and Mason C. M. (2017) Backing the horse or the jockey? Due diligence, agency costs, information and the evaluation of risk by business angel investors. *Venture International Review of Entrepreneurship*, 15(3), 269–290.

Harrison R. T. (2017) The internationalisation of business angel investment activity: a review and research agenda. *Venture Capital: An International Journal of Entrepreneurial Finance*, 19(1–2), 119–127.

Hellman T., Schure P., and Vo D. (2013) Angel and venture capitalists: Complements or substitutes? NBER Working Paper. Available at: http://strategy.sauder.ubc.ca/hellmann.

Hellmann T. and Thiele V. (2015) Friends or foes? The interrelationship between angel and venture capital markets. *Journal of Financial Economics*, 115(3), 639–653.

Hellmann T. and Puri M. (2000) The interaction between product market and financing strategy: the role of venture capital. *Review of Financial Studies*, 13(4), 959–984.

Hellmann T. and Puri M. (2002) Venture capital and the professionalization of start-up firms: Empirical evidence, *Journal of Finance*, 57, 169–197.

Hochberg Y. V., Ljungqvist A., and Lu Y. (2007) Whom you know matters: venture capital networks and investment performance. *Journal of Finance*, 62(1), 251–301.

Hopp C. (2010) When do venture capitalists collaborate? Evidence on the driving forces of venture capital syndication. *Small Business Economics*, 35(4), 417–431.

Hsu D. H. (2004) What do entrepreneurs pay for venture capital affiliation? *Journal of Finance*, 59(4), 1805–1844.

Hsu D. H. (2006) Venture capitalists and cooperative start-up commercialization strategy. *Management Science*, 52(2), 204–219.

Hsu D. K., Haynie J. M., Simmons S. A., and McKelvie A. (2014) What matters, matters differently: A conjoint analysis of the decision policies of angel and venture capital investors. *Venture Capital: An International Journal of Entrepreneurial Finance*, 16(1), 1–25.

IBAN, *Annual Survey* (2007–2014). Available at: www.iban.it.

Ibrahim D. M. (2008) The (not so) puzzling behavior of angel investors. *Vanderbilt Law Review*, 61(5), 1405–1452.

Inova+ (2017) *Understanding the nature and impact of the business angels in funding research and innovation*. European Union Commission Study, November, 2017. Available at: http://www.eban.org/eu-commission-study-understanding-nature-impact-business-angels-funding-research-innovation.

Invest Europe (2017) 2016 European Private Equity Activity. *Annual Activity Statistics*. Available at: www.investeurope.eu.

Jeng L. A. and Wells P. C. (2000) The determinants of venture capital funding: evidence across countries. *Journal of Corporate Finance*, 6(3), 241–289.

Jensen M. C. and Meckling W. H. (1976), Theory of the firm: Managerial behavior, agency costs and ownership structure. *Journal of Financial Economics* 3(4), 305–360.

Johan S. and Zhang M. (2016) Private equity exits in emerging markets. *Emerging Markets Review*, 29(4), 133–153.

Johnson W. C. and Sohl J. (2012) Angels and venture capitalists in the initial public offering market. *Venture Capital: An International Journal of Entrepreneurial Finance*, 14(1), 27–42.

José S. A., Roure J., and Aernoudt R. (2005) Business angel academies: unleashing the potential for business angel investment. *Venture Capital: An International Journal of Entrepreneurial Finance*, 7(2), 149–165.

Kaplan S. and Stromberg P. (2003) Financial contracting theory meets the real world: Evidence from venture capital contracts. *Review of Economic Studies*, 7(2), 281–315.

Kaplan S. and Schoar A. (2005) Private equity performance: returns, persistence, and capital flows. *Journal of Finance*, 60(4), 1791–1823.

Kerr William R., Josh Lerner, and Antoinette Schoar (2014) The consequences of entrepreneurial finance: a regression discontinuity analysis. *Review of Financial Studies*, 27, 20–55.

Kraemer-Eis H., Botsari A., Gvetadze S., Lang F., and Torfs W. (2017) European small business finance outlook: December 2017. EIF Research & Market Analysis, working paper (2017/46).

Kraemer-Eis H., Lang F., Torfs W., and Gvetadze S. (2015) European small business finance outlook. EIF Research & Market Analysis, working paper (2015/32).

Kraemer-Eis H., Signore S., and Prencipe D. (2016) The European venture capital landscape: an EIF prespective. EIF Research & Market Analysis, working paper (2016/34).

Lahti T. and Keinonen H. (2016) Business angel networks: a review and assessment of their value to entrepreneurship. In Landström H. and Mason (eds.), *Handbook of Research on Business Angels*. Edward Elgar Publishing, Cheltenham, UK, pp. 354–380.

Lahti T. (2011) Angel investing: an examination of the evolution of the Finnish market. *Venture Capital: An International Journal of Entrepreneurial Finance*, 13(2), 147–173.

Landström H. (1993) Informal risk capital in Sweden and some international comparisons. *Journal of Business Venturing*, 8(6), 525–540.

Landström H. and Mason C. (2016) Business angels as a research field. In Landström H. and Mason (eds.), *Handbook of Research on Business Angels*. Edward Elgar Publishing, Cheltenham, UK, pp. 1–24.

Landström H. and Mason C. (eds.) (2016) *Handbook of Research on Business Angels*. Edward Elgar Publishing, Cheltenham, UK, pp. 1–432.

Lerner J. (1994) The syndication of venture capital investments. *Financial Management*, 23(3), 16–27.

Lerner J. (1998) "Angel" financing and public policy: An overview. *Journal of Banking & Finance*, 22(6–8), 773–783.

Lerner J., Schoar A., Sokolinski S., and Wilson K. (2016) The globalization of angel investments: evidence across countries, HBS Working Paper (16-072).

Levratto N., Tessier L., and Fonrouge C. (2017) Business performance and angels presence: a fresh look from France 2008–2011. *Small Business Economics*, First Online: January, 2017. doi:10.1007/s11187-016-9827-5.

Li Y., Jiang S., Long D., Tang H., and Wu J. (2014) An exploratory study of business angels in China: a research note. *Venture Capital: An International Journal of Entrepreneurial Finance*, 16(1), 69–83.

Macht S. A. (2011) Inexpert business angels: How even investors with 'nothing to add' can add value. *Strategic Change*, 20(7–8), 269–278.

Macht S. A. and Robinson J. (2009) Do business angels benefit their investee companies? *International Journal of Entrepreneurial Behaviour and Research*, 15(2), 187–208.

Madill J. J., Haines Jr., G. H., and Riding A. L. (2005) The role of angels in technology SMEs: a link to venture capital. *Venture Capital: An International Journal of Entrepreneurial Finance*, 7(2), 107–129.

Manigart S., Baeyens K., and Van Hyfte W. (2002) The survival of venture capital backed companies. *Venture Capital: An International Journal of Entrepreneurial Finance*, 4(2), 103–124.

Mason C. (2016), Researching business angels: definitional and data challenges. In Landström H. and Mason (eds.), *Handbook of Research on Business Angels*. Edward Elgar Publishing, Cheltenham, UK, pp. 25–52.

Mason C. and Botelho T. (2016) The role of the exit in the initial screening of investment opportunities: The case of business angel syndicate gatekeepers. *International Small Business Journal*, 34(2), 157–175.

Mason C. M. (2006) Informal sources of venture finance. In Parker S. C. (ed.), *The Life Cycle of Entrepreneurial Ventures*. Springer, New York, NY, pp. 259–299.

Mason C. M. (2008) The real venture capitalists: a review of research on business angels. Working Paper WP08-06, Hunter Center for Entrepreneurship, University of Strathclyde, September 2008, pp. 1–55.

Mason C. M. (2009) Public policy support for the informal venture capital market in Europe: A critical review. *International Small Business Journal*, 27(5), 536–556.

Mason C. M. (2016) Researching business angels: definitional and data challenges. In Landström H. and Mason (eds.), *Handbook of Research on Business Angels*. Edward Elgar Publishing, Cheltenham, UK, pp. 25–52.

Mason C. M. and Harrison R. T. (2000) The size of the informal venture capital market in the United Kingdom. *Small Business Economics*, 15, 137–148.

Mason C. M. and Harrison R. T. (2002) Is it worth it? the rates of return from informal venture capital investments. *Journal of Business Venturing*, 17(3), 211–236.

Mason C. M., Botelho T., and Harrison R. T. (2016) The transformation of the business angel market: empirical evidence and research implications. *Venture Capital: An International Journal of Entrepreneurial Finance*, 19(4), 321–344.

Maula M., Autio E., and Arenius P. (2005) What drives micro-angel investments? *Small Business Economics*, 25(5), 459–475.

May J. (2002) Structured angel groups in the USA: The dinner club experience. *Venture Capital: An International Journal of Entrepreneurial Finance*, 4(4), 337–342.

Morrisette S. G. (2007) A profile of angel investors. *The Journal of Private Equity*, 10(3), 52–66.

Mueller D. (1972) A life cycle theory of the firm. *Journal of Industrial Economics*, 20(3), 199–219.

Nissim D. and Penman S. (2001), Ratio analysis and equity valuation: From research to practice. *Review of Accounting Studies*, 6(1), 109–154.

OECD (2012) *Financing High-Growth Firms: The Role of Angel Investors*. OECD Publishing. doi: http://dx.doi.org/10.1787/9789264118782-en.

OECD (2016) *Business and Finance Outlook*. OECD Publishing. Available at http://www.oecd.org.

Omrani H. and Karami G. (2010), The effect of firm's life cycle and conservatorism on firm value. *Journal of financial accounting*, 3(5), 49–64.

Paul S. and Whittam G. (2010) Business angel syndicates: An exploratory study of gatekeepers. *Venture Capital: An International Journal of Entrepreneurial Finance*, 12(3), 241–256.

Paul S., Whittam G., and Wyper J. (2007) Towards a model of the business angel investment process. *Venture Capital: An International Journal of Entrepreneurial Finance*, 9(2), 107–125.

Payne W. H. and Mccarty M. J. (2002) The Anatomy Of An Angel Investing Network: Tech Coast Angels. *Venture Capital: An International Journal of Entrepreneurial Finance*, 4(3), 336.

Penrose E. G. (1959) *The Theory of the Growth of the Firm*. Blackwell, Oxford.

Politis D. (2008) Business angels and value added: What do we know and where do we go? *Venture Capital: An International Journal of Entrepreneurial Finance*, 10(2), 127–147.

Pommet S. (2012) The survival of the venture backed companies: an analysis of the French case. GREDEG Working Paper Series, WP No. 2012–14.

Proksch D., Stranz W., Röhr, N., Ernst C., Pinkwart A., and Schefczyk M. (2017) Value adding activities of venture capital companies: a content analysis of investor's original documents in Germany. *Venture Capital: An International Journal of Entrepreneurial Finance*, 19(3), 129–146.

Puri M. and Zarutskie R. (2012) On the lifecycle dynamics of venture capital and non-venture-capital-financed firms. *Journal of Finance*, 67, 2243–2297.

Rosenbaum P. R. and Rubin D. B. (1983) The central role of the propensity score in observational studies for causal effects. *Biometrika*, 70(1), 41–55.

Sahlman W. A. (1990) The structure and governance of venture capital organizations. *Journal of Financial Economics*, 27, 473–524.

Samuelson P. A. (1997) How best to flip-flop if you must: integer dynamic stochastic programming for either-or. *Journal of Risk and Uncertainty*, 15(3), 183–190.

Schuessler K. F. (1979) *Sociological Methodology*, Vol. 10. Blackwell Publishers, Cambridge, MA, pp. 276–302.

Shane S. (2000) Prior knowledge and the discovery of entrepreneurial opportunities. *Organization Science*, 11, 448–469.

Snijkers G., Haraldsen G., Jones J., and Willimack D. (2013) *Designing and Conducting Business Surveys.* John Wiley and Sons, Hoboken, NY, USA.

Sohl J. E. (2007) The organisation of the informal venture capital market. In Landström H. (ed.), *Handbook of Research on Venture Capital.* Edward Elgar, Cheltenham, UK, pp. 347–368.

Sohl J. E. (2012) The changing nature of the angel market. In Landström H. and Mason C. (eds.), *Handbook of Research on Venture Capital: Volume 2,* Chapter 2. Edward Elgar, Cheltenham, UK, pp. 17–41.

Sørensen M. (2007) How smart is smart money? a two-sided matching model of venture capital. *Journal of Finance*, 62(6), 2725–2762.

Sørheim R. (2003) The pre-investment behaviour of business angels: a social capital approach. *Venture Capital: An International Journal of Entrepreneurial Finance*, 5(4), 337–364.

Sørheim R. and Botelho T. (2016) Categorizations of business angels: an overview. In Landström H. and Mason (eds.), *Handbook of Research on Business Angels.* Edward Elgar Publishing, Cheltenham, UK, pp. 76–91.

Strätling R. S., Wijbenga F. H., and Dietz G. (2012) *The impact of contracts on trust in entrepreneur–venture capitalist relationships, International Small Business Journal*, 30(8), 811–831.

Sudek R. (2006) Angel investment criteria. *Journal of Small Business Strategy*, 17, 89–103.

Sudek R., Mitteness C., and Baucus M. (2008) Betting on the horse or the jockey: The impact of expertise on angel investing. *Venture Capital: An International Journal of Entrepreneurial Finance*, 14(4), 241–267.

Tian X. (2011) The causes and consequences of venture capital stage financing. *Journal of Financial Economics*, 101(1), 132–159.

Tian X. (2012) The role of venture capital syndication in value creation for entrepreneurial firms. *Review of Finance,* 16, 245–283.

Triantis G. G. (2001) Financial contract design in the world of venture capital. *University of Chicago Law Review*, 68, 305–312.

US Angel Capital Association (2015) Introducing Angel Investing as an asset class for all investors. *The Go Beyond Investor Report*. Available at: http://www.angelcapitalassociation.org.

Van Osnabrugge M. (2000) A comparison of business angel and venture capitalist investment procedures: An agency theory-based analysis. *Venture Capital: An International Journal of Entrepreneurial Finance*, 2(2), 91–109.

Vanacker T., Collewaert V., and Paeleman I. (2013) The relationship between slack resources and the performance of entrepreneurial firms: the role of venture capital and angel investors. *Journal of Management Studies*, 50(6), 1070–1096.

Werth J. C. and Boeert P. (2013) Co-investment networks of business angels and the performance of their start-up investments. *International Journal of Entrepreneurial Venturing*, 5(3), 240–256.

Wetzel W. E. (1986) *Entrepreneurs, Angels and Economic Renaissance*. Lexington Books, Lexington, MA.

White B. A. and Dumay J. (2017) Business angels: a research review and a new agenda. *Venture Capital: An International Journal of Entrepreneurial Finance*, Published online: February 7, 2017. doi: http://dx.doi.org/10.1080/13691066.2017.1290889.

Wiltbank R. (2005) Investment practices and outcomes of informal venture investors. *Venture Capital: An International Journal of Entrepreneurial Finance*, 7(4), 343–357.

Wiltbank R. and Boeker W. (2007) Returns to angel investors in groups. Report, Ewing Marion Kauffman Foundation and Angel Capital Education Foundation, November.

Wiltbank R., Dew N., Read S., and Sarasvathy S. D. (2006) What to do next? The case for non-predictive strategy. *Strategic Management Journal*, 27(10), 981–998.

Wiltbank R., Read S., Dew N., and Sarasvathy S. D. (2009) Prediction and control under uncertainty: Outcomes in angel investing. *Journal of Business Venturing*, 24(2), 116–133.

Windmeijer F. A. G. and Santos Silva J. M. C. (1997) Endogeneity in count data models: An application to demand for health care. *Journal of Applied Econometrics*, 12(3), 281–294.

Wong A., Bhatia M., and Freeman Z. (2009) Angel finance: The other venture capital. *Strategic Change*, 18(7–8), 221–230.

Wooldbrige J. M. (2002) *Econometric Analysis of Cross Section and Panel Data.* The MIT Press, Cambridge, MA.

Wright M., Westhead P., and Sohl J. (1998) Editors' introduction: Habitual entrepreneurs and angel investors. *Entrepreneurship Theory and Practice*, 22(4), 5–21.

Zacharakis A., Erikson T., and George B. (2010) Conflict between the VC and entrepreneur: the entrepreneur's perspective. *Venture Capital: An International Journal of Entrepreneurial Finance*, 12(2), 109–126.

Chapter 3

To the Rescue: Government Intervention in Venture Capital Markets

Thomas Standaert*

Department of Accounting, Corporate Finance and Taxation, Ghent University

thomasb.standaert@ugent.be

Abstract

Research on direct government intervention in venture capital (VC) markets has expanded rapidly over the last decade. This chapter reviews the extant literature on direct government intervention in VC markets, providing a classification of existing studies according to the three identified types of direct government intervention under analysis. As such, this chapter provides an assessment of the degree to which the government's objectives of alleviating the equity gap and generating social returns have been achieved by these three types of direct intervention. Furthermore, this chapter highlights how future research on the interrelationships between governments, private VC investors, portfolio companies, and the external environment, offers the potential to increase the effectiveness of direct government intervention in VC markets.

---

*7, Sint-Pietersplein, Ghent, 9000, Belgium; Université de Lille, Lille, France.

1. Introduction

Many successful firms such as Apple, Skype, Spotify and Tesla raised VC financing to fund their growth in the early stages of their life cycle. Interestingly, each of the aforementioned firms received part of this financing from governments (European Investment Fund, 2016; Small Business Administration, 2017). This is not surprising since governments in developed and developing countries have become an important player in the area of entrepreneurial finance by supporting VC markets through direct intervention (Block *et al.*, 2018). Although governments can also support VC markets *indirectly* by making changes to a country's legal framework,[1] this chapter will solely focus on the efforts made by governments to support VC markets *directly* by injecting them with public funds.

Research on direct government intervention in VC markets has expanded rapidly over the last decades. While Colombo *et al.* (2016a) provide an excellent academic overview of the existing literature on direct government intervention in VC markets, this chapter aims to discuss this debate in a non-academic manner. To policymakers, the chapter provides an answer to the question whether direct government intervention leads to the achievement of desired outcomes, based on the extant state of knowledge in the area. More specifically, the chapter demonstrates that the effectiveness of direct government intervention is determined by the *modus operandi* of the intervention as well as the features of the external environment. To scholars, the chapter proposes an analytical framework for direct government intervention in VC markets and intends to help establish a research agenda by identifying interesting avenues for future research.

The chapter continues as follows. In Section 2, we explain the rationales for as well as concerns related to direct government intervention in VC markets. Section 3 highlights the importance of acknowledging the heterogeneity in types of direct government intervention when interpreting existing findings. Section 4 uses the proposed typology to review the empirical literature.

---

[1] The legal framework refers to laws related to the level of investor protection (Groh *et al.*, 2010), bankruptcy laws (Armour and Cumming, 2006), labor market regulation (Jeng and Wells, 2000), regulation of pension funds and other institutional investors (Jeng and Wells, 2000), and taxation of investors (Armour and Cumming, 2006).

More specifically, we provide an overview of the real effects of each type of direct government intervention. Section 5 concludes by discussing existing findings and identifying interesting avenues for future research.

2. Direct Government Intervention in VC Markets: Rationales and Concerns

2.1. *Rationales*

The reason of existence of any government intervention should always be clearly motivated. Therefore, we start by focusing on two rationales for government intervention in VC markets highlighted in the literature.

The first rationale for direct government intervention in VC markets is the existence of a market failure in the provision of financing for new technology-based firms (NTBFs). NTBFs are considered an important source of innovation and employment growth (Audretsch, 1995), and have therefore received a lot of attention from policymakers. Due to their technological nature, NTBFs are characterized by a lack of collateral and high information asymmetries, which makes them unlikely to secure debt financing (Carpenter and Petersen, 2002). Through the use of rigorous screening methods before investment and powerful monitoring mechanisms after investment, VCs[2] are able to resolve the aforementioned problems (Amit *et al.*, 1998). Therefore, VC financing has proved to be an effective tool for alleviating the financial constraints (Bertoni *et al.*, 2010) and improving the growth perspectives of NTBFs (Puri and Zarutskie, 2012). The supply of VC financing, however, is limited and highly concentrated in specific regions (De Prijcker *et al.*, 2017; Mueller *et al.*, 2012) and industries (Bertoni *et al.*, 2015; Kovner and Lerner, 2015), leading to the emergence of an equity gap, in which promising firms are not able to raise VC financing (Murray and Lott, 1995; Wilson *et al.*, 2018). Governments can therefore alleviate the equity gap by increasing the supply of VC.

The second rationale is based on the assertion that direct government intervention in VC markets will generate social returns (Lerner, 2002). Since independent VCs are solely focused on generating financial returns,

[2] In the remainder of the text, we refer to VC investors as "VCs".

they may decide to not select or drop firms from their portfolio that are not expected to deliver a financial return higher than a minimum threshold, destroying the firm's potential of generating social returns (Abrardi *et al.*, 2018). Governments can therefore take up the role of investing in those firms that are able to generate social returns. By social returns, governments typically refer to job creation and knowledge spillovers from innovative activities (Bertoni and Tykvová, 2015; Colombo *et al.*, 2016a). However, governments can also establish other objectives with social payoffs for their direct intervention in VC markets, such as the development of the innovation ecosystem (Pierrakis and Saridakis, 2017).

2.2. *Concerns*

Even when the objectives of the government intervention are agreed upon, flaws in the design or implementation of government VC programs can undermine its effectiveness. The following paragraphs explain how badly designed government VC programs can damage rather than support VC industries and how distortions in the allocation process can lead to suboptimal outcomes.

It is feared that the availability of VC financing coming from public sources might not lead to an increase in the aggregate supply of VC. In this case, government intervention will effectively lead to the "crowding-out" rather than the "crowding-in" of private investors. Table 1 provides a summary of papers that have studied the existence of a crowding-out effect at the market-level. The empirical literature has either found support for (Armour and Cumming, 2006; Cumming and MacIntosh, 2006; Da Rin *et al.*, 2006) or rebuttal to (Brander *et al.*, 2015; Cumming, 2014; Leleux and Surlemont, 2003) the existence of a crowding-out effect in Canada and Europe. However, it is plausible that findings are driven by the inclusion or exclusion of specific government programs. For example, the existence of a crowding-out effect in Canada seems to be caused by one specific government program, the Labor Sponsored Venture Capital Corporation (LSVCC) (Cumming *et al.*, 2017b). This program provided generous tax benefits to retail investors in mutual funds, called LSVCCs, that invested in private entrepreneurial firms. The immediate returns to investors from tax credits and deductions lowered the LSVCCs' required rate of return,

Table 1: Selected papers on crowding-out.

Authors	Data sources	Sample	Identification source for government funds	Research question	Key findings
Armour and Cumming (2006)	EVCA, CVCA, Venture Economics	VC investment and fundraising in 15 Western European and North American countries between 1990 and 2003	Europe: EVCA Canada: CVCA US: Venture Economics	Do legislative enactments make a difference to VC finance?	Investment of government funds does not increase the overall amount of VC investment in a particular country: rather, public funds crowd out private funds such that there is no overall change in the total amount invested.
Brander *et al.* (2015)	Thomson One, Asian Venture Capital Journal	20,446 enterprises in 25 countries that received their first VC funding from 5,095 distinct VCs between 2000 and 2008	Thomson One, Capital IQ	Does the activity of GVCs tend to displace or crowd out PVCs?	If GVC investment and PVC investment are both present in an enterprise, that enterprise tends to obtain more total VC funding than if the enterprise receives all of its VC from PVCs, or if it receives all of its funding from GVCs. Markets that receive more GVC funding also receive more funding overall and, strikingly, receive more PVC finance.
Cumming (2014)	EVCA	VC investment activity in 13 European countries between 1989 and 2011	EVCA	Are Da Rin *et al.*'s (2006) findings robust to alternative specifications?	Government VC funds in Europe have not crowded out private VC investment.
Cumming and MacIntosh (2006)	CVCA	VC investment in Canada between 1977 and 2001	LSVCC	Have LSVCCs crowded out, or displaced other forms of VC organizations and have the various government sponsors achieved their goal of expanding the Canadian pool of VC?	LSVCCs have not only crowded out other Canadian funds, but have led to a reduction in the overall size of the VC pool.

(*Continued*)

Table 1: (*Continued*)

Authors	Data sources	Sample	Identification source for government funds	Research question	Key findings
Da Rin *et al.* (2006)	EVCA	VC investment activity in 14 European countries between 1988 and 2001	EVCA	What policies can help create active VC markets?	An increase in the supply of funds has no effect on the innovation ratios.
Leleux and Surlemont (2003)	EVCA	Cumulative funds raised in 15 European countries between 1990 and 1996	EVCA	Do direct public interventions (1) tend to "seed" underdeveloped VC industries; (2) prevent the emergence of active VC markets by "crowding-out" private funds; or (3) facilitate their development by signaling and certifying their social value?	(1) No support for the seeding hypothesis, public VCs appear to come late to the market, more as a response to an already primed industry growth. (2) Public VCs do not crowd-out private VCs from the industry. (3) Public investments in VC may signal or legitimize support for VC investments as a whole, opening the floodgate of private investments in the sector.

Notes: The following abbreviations are used: CVCA (Canadian Venture Capital and Private Equity Association), EVCA (European Private Equity and Venture Capital Association), GVC (government venture capital), LSVCC (Labor Sponsored Venture Capital Corporation), PVC (private venture capital), VC (venture capital).

allowing them to out-bid private VCs, drive up valuations and lower VC returns. As a result, instead of achieving its goal of expanding the aggregate pool of capital, the LSVCC program effectively led to a reduction in the aggregate pool of capital due to a decrease in commitments by institutional investors to private VC funds (Cumming and MacIntosh, 2006). Therefore, when studying the phenomenon of crowding-out, it is of the utmost importance to take into account the type of direct government intervention under analysis, which is the focus of the following section.

For every form of government intervention in private markets, there is a risk that government actions are distorted by the interests of politicians or interest groups, leading to the misallocation of public resources (Lerner, 1999). The literature has provided evidence of this phenomenon in the context of direct government intervention in US and European VC markets. Furthermore, the phenomenon is more apparent in more corrupt regions (Alperovych *et al.*, 2016; Bertoni and Quas, 2016). First, governments have been found to use VC investments to serve their own rather than society's interests. Bertoni and Quas (2016) find that during close elections, governments increase their VC investment activity in an attempt to give a short-term boost to the economy. If voters attribute the boost to the competence of the incumbent government, the strategy has been successful in improving the government's chances of being re-elected. From a societal perspective, the strategy is inefficient since firms selected in those close elections are ultimately more likely to be liquidated and demonstrate lower growth than firms selected during low-stakes elections (Bertoni and Quas, 2016). Second, firms can influence the allocation process of public resources through corporate political connections (Duchin and Sosyura, 2012). Firms that are better connected with government officials through previous public sector experience, shared education networks, lobbying or political contributions have better access to public funds (Alperovych *et al.*, 2016; Denes, 2017; Milosevic, 2018).

3. Types of Direct Government Intervention

Before reviewing the empirical literature on direct government intervention in VC markets, this section presents the typology used to categorize existing findings. This step is crucial since direct government intervention initiatives differ in their definition of responsibilities of government officials. The role performed by government officials in the VC process is expected to be an important determinant of the effectiveness of government initiatives. According to Wilson and Silva (2013), three distinct types of direct government intervention in VC markets can be distinguished.

First, policymakers can decide to have government officials deal with the screening and selection of investment opportunities and the post-investment value-adding and monitoring of portfolio companies, without involving private VCs.[3] In this case, government VCs (GVCs) effectively follow a go-it-alone strategy. Examples of GVCs are the community development venture capital (CDVC) funds in the US and the Business Development Bank of Canada.

Second, GVCs can draw upon the screening, selection, value-adding and monitoring abilities of private VCs through the creation of a mixed syndicate consisting of both GVCs and private VCs. While all GVCs may syndicate with private VCs on an *ad hoc* basis, some programs, such as the New Zealand Seed Co-investment Fund and Scottish Co-investment Fund, require GVCs to syndicate all of their investments.

Third, policymakers can decide to completely outsource the screening, selection, value-adding and monitoring activities to private VCs and limit the government's role to investing in funds raised by private VCs. As such, governments operate as a limited partner (LP), or the so-called government limited partner (GLP), in VC markets (Alperovych *et al.*, 2018). This type of intervention was introduced by the US government in 1958 through the Small Business Investment Company (SBIC) program (Bruno *et al.*, 1985), which continues to exist to date (Lerner, 2009). Examples of similar GLP initiatives are the Israeli Yozma program, the European Investment Fund (EIF) and the British Enterprise Capital Funds (ECF) program. A typical GLP initiative is structured as a 100% public fund-of-funds managed by public fund-of-funds managers, which

[3] Private VCs include independent VCs, which manage funds on behalf of institutional investors and wealthy individuals, and captive VCs, which manage funds on behalf of a parent company such as a bank or corporation (Da Rin *et al.*, 2013).

invests in a portfolio of underlying private VC funds. In order to attract private LPs to the underlying VC funds, GLP initiatives often use profit distribution structures that improve the expected returns for private LPs (Jääskeläinen *et al.*, 2007). For example, both the SBIC and ECF program leverage the returns to private LPs by providing their commitments in the form of an interest-bearing loan (Jääskeläinen *et al.*, 2007). In continental Europe, however, GLPs invest on the same terms as private LPs *(pari passu)* to comply with State aid rules, which limits the potential to attract private LPs (Aernoudt, 2017). The participation of private LPs can be further enhanced by attracting them also to the level of the fund-of-funds. For example, in 2018 the European Commission launched the VentureEU program, through which the EIF invests in six privately-managed funds-of-funds that receive at least half of their financing from private LPs.

With regard to the importance of the types of direct government intervention across regions, GVC investments have been more frequently used in Canada and Europe than in the US (Bertoni *et al.*, 2015; Brander *et al.*, 2010). In the US, direct government intervention has predominantly taken the form of GLPs committing to privately managed VC funds (Abrardi *et al.*, 2018; Brander *et al.*, 2015). In recent years, GLPs in Canada and Europe also have significantly increased their activity (CVCA, 2017; Invest Europe, 2018).

4. Empirical Evidence

This section systematically reviews the empirical literature on the real effects of the three types of direct government intervention: (1) GVCs following a go-it-alone strategy; (2) GVCs syndicating with private VCs; and (3) GLPs committing to private VC funds. For each type of intervention, two major research streams are identified within this literature, which revolve around the following questions: (1) what are the characteristics of the firms that are targeted by the direct government intervention; and (2) what is the impact of the direct government intervention on firm performance? Summaries of papers on the investment patterns and the impact on firm performance of direct government intervention are provided in Tables 2 and 3, respectively.

Table 2: Selected papers on investment patterns.

Authors	Data sources	Sample	Type of intervention	Identification source for government funds	Research question	Key findings
Abrardi *et al.* (2018)	Thomson One	9,610 US VC financing rounds in 7539 ventures between 1998 and 2010	GVC go-it-alone	Thomson One	What are the determinants of switching lead VC when two specific organizational forms of VC are involved: IVCs and GVCs?	Ventures characterized by a low economic return are more likely to be adopted by a new lead GVC that is more reputable than the IVC dropping them. This effect is more significant the lower the reputation of the incumbent IVC is.
Bertoni *et al.* (2015)	VICO, Thomson One	1,663 first VC investments made by 846 VCs in 737 European companies between 1994 and 2004	GVC go-it-alone	VICO	(1) What are the investment patterns of different types of VCs in Europe and (2) how do they compare to those observed in the US?	(1) The investment pattern of GVCs is the reverse of that of IVCs and BVCs. (2) GVC investments are more frequent in Europe than in the US, and IVC is less attracted to risky investments than in the US.
Bertoni *et al.* (2019)	VICO	1,239 first investments by 676 PVCs in 560 European high-tech companies between 1994 and 2004	GVC go-it-alone Syndication	VICO	How does GVC's density in a VC ecosystem influence the characteristics of the companies that are the target of PVC investments?	Syndication is one mechanism that GVC uses to attract PVC in its niche, but not the only one: PVC investors that do not syndicate with GVC are more likely to invest in less-competitive regions and smaller companies when GVC's density is greater.

Buzzacchi *et al.* (2013)	EIF, Thomson One	149 VC funds that received financial support from the EIF and that invested in 1,925 European companies between 1998 and 2007	GLP	EIF	How does the intensity of public ownership affect the investment strategy, reflected both in the (1) *ex ante* selection process for the target companies and in their (2) post-acquisition management, of hybrid VC funds?	(1) The level of public ownership shows a weak negative correlation with the likelihood of observing a write-off. (2) A higher public share is associated with a longer duration for the investment. This effect is more relevant for those investments that generate intermediate financial returns.
Cumming (2007)	AVCAL	280 Australian VC and PE funds and their investments in 845 entrepreneurial firms	GLP	AVCAL	What is the performance of the IIF funds relative to other types of PE and VC funds in Australia?	IIFs are more likely to finance seed and early stage companies as well as riskier companies in high-tech industries than other types of private funds. Managers that operate IIFs are also more likely to finance start-up and early stage firms from their other funds than other types of private funds. IIFs on average are more likely to have one extra staged financing round and one extra syndicated investor, and finance on average 0.3 fewer firms per manager than other types of private funds.

(*Continued*)

Table 2: *(Continued)*

Authors	Data sources	Sample	Type of intervention	Identification source for government funds	Research question	Key findings
Knockaert *et al.* (2010a)	EVCA, regional VC associations, academics	68 early-stage high-tech VCs in 7 European countries	GLP	Questionnaire	To what extent is the selection behavior of different early-stage high-tech VCs associated with differences in their fund characteristics?	Public funding seems to be used for pushing forward new and unique technologies, and the human characteristics of the founding team and financial prospects of the business plan are of less importance at the time of selection.
Knockaert *et al.* (2010b)	EVCA, national VC associations, academics	68 early stage VC investment managers in 7 European countries	GLP	Questionnaire	Which factors explain VC investment managers' attitudes towards academic spin-out investing?	The presence of public sector capital positively affects investment managers' attitudes toward academic spin-out investing.
Kovner and Lerner (2015)	VentureXpert	65,590 VC investments in the US between 1996 and 2009	GVC go-it-alone Syndication	CDVC	What is the impact of CDVC funds?	CDVCs invest in industries that are less likely to receive traditional VC capital and in regions without many traditional VCs. Co-investments share many of the geographic characteristics of the sole CDVC investments. VCs are more likely to invest in regions with less venture activity after co-investment with CDVC.

Mayer *et al.* (2005)	EVCA, national VC associations in Germany, the UK and Israel, survey by Nikkei Kinyu	Sources of finance and investments activities of 187 German, 119 Israeli, 62 Japanese and 140 funds from the UK	GLP	EVCA, national VC associations in Germany, the UK and Israel, survey by Nikkei Kinyu	What is the relation between sources of finance of VC firms and the investment activities in which they are engaged?	Government-backed funds are associated with more early-stage and less late-stage investments. Government funding is closely associated with local and national investment.
Uzuegbunam *et al.* (2017)	Kaufmann Firm Survey	4,925 new US ventures founded in 2004 and tracked over 2004–2008	GVC go-it-alone	Kaufmann Firm Survey	How do new ventures' resources and assets affect GVC funding decisions?	Founders' educational attainment and industry-specific work experience have a positive impact on GVC funding, while the former exerts a stronger effect on GVC funding than the latter. The number of patents owned by the start-up increases GVC funding.

Notes: The following abbreviations are used: AVCAL (Australian Private Equity and Venture Capital Association), BVC (bank-affiliated venture capital), CDVC (community development venture capital), EIF (European Investment Fund), EVCA (European Private Equity and Venture Capital Association), GVC (government venture capital), IIF (Innovation Investment Fund), IVC (independent venture capital), PE (private equity), PVC (private venture capital), UK (United Kingdom), US (United States), VC (venture capital).

Table 3: Selected papers on the impact on firm performance.

Authors	Data sources	Sample	Type of intervention	Identification source for government funds	Research question	Key findings
Alperovych *et al.* (2016)	Thomson One	1,230 firms in 16 European countries that received a first VC round between 1995 and 2011	GVC go-it-alone Syndication	Thomson One, VICO, Internet queries	Under which conditions are GVCs more effective in fulfilling their mission of bridging the equity gap?	GVCs are less successful when they invest in economically lagging regions; when they invest locally, especially in countries with higher perceived corruption; and when they invest solo compared to syndicating with PVC. Solo GVCs that build up industry-specific experience and syndication experience with PVCs are more successful.
Alperovych *et al.* (2015)	Factiva, Venture Economics, Capital IQ, Zephyr	515 Belgian VC-backed firms between 1998 and 2004	GVC go-it-alone	Belgian regional governments	How do differences in types of VCs (GVC/PVC) affect the post-investment efficiency of their portfolio firms?	Within the pool of Belgian VC-backed firms, being financed by PVCs improves the efficiency of portfolio companies significantly. Being financed by a GVC fund implies a significant reduction in productivity.
Bertoni and Tykvovà (2015)	VICO	665 European biotechnology start-ups in 7 European countries that received their first VC investment between 1994 and 2004	GVC go-it-alone Syndication	VICO	Have GVC funds been successful in supporting inventions and innovations in Europe?	GVC has no impact on invention and innovation. IVC-backed companies patent more than GVC-backed companies. The combined effect of IVC and GVC goes beyond the individual effect of the two investors.

Croce *et al.* (2018)	Webcapitalriesgo	384 Spanish early-stage VC-backed companies financed during 2005–2013 (173 GVC-backed and 211 PVC-backed) and a control group of 888 non-VC-backed peers	GVC go-it-alone	Webcapitalriesgo	What is the effect on employment growth of investments carried out by PVCs versus GVCs before and during a period of economic crisis?	PVCs exert a higher impact on employment growth in invested companies than GVCs in investments carried out during a period of crisis whereas the opposite is found in the case of investments completed before the crisis. PVCs enhance their job-creation performance during a period of crisis while GVCs significantly reduce their impact on employment in the investments carried out during the crisis
Cumming *et al.* (2017a)	VICO	8,370 high-tech firms in 7 European countries observed between 1991 and 2010	GVC go-it-alone Syndication	VICO	(1) Are GVCs by their own able to lead to a positive exit in comparison with traditional IVCs?; (2) How do syndicated investments by GVC and IVC funds perform?; (3) Do different structures of mixed IVC–GVC syndicates play a differential effect on the exit performance?	(1) Positive contribution of IVC-backing on the likelihood to reach a positive exit, while the impact of GVC is negligible. (2) Mixed IVC-GVC syndicated investments lead to a higher (but not statistically different) likelihood of a positive exit than that of IVC-backing. (3) The positive impact of IVC-GVC syndicates is not influenced by the composition of the syndicate in terms of size and institutional heterogeneity.

(*Continued*)

Table 3: *(Continued)*

Authors	Data sources	Sample	Type of intervention	Identification source for government funds	Research question	Key findings
Cumming and Johan (2016)	Morningstar, Thomson Reuters SDC, AVCAL, Lexis-Nexis, Hoovers, Bloomberg, Patents IP Australia, Internet searches	All VC- and PE-backed Australian firms and 40% of the population of non-VC/ PE-backed firms followed up until 2012	GLP	AVCAL	How important are VC and PE funds to the Australian economy?	VC- and IIF-backed firms contribute disproportionately to R&D and patents. VC-backed firms have greater market capitalization relative to PE- and non-VC/ PE/IIF-backed firms. IIF investments show the highest proportion of subsequent listings and result in greater market capitalization relative to both VC- and PE-backed firms.
Grilli and Murtinu (2014)	VICO	8,370 high-tech firms in 7 European countries	GVC go-it-alone Syndication	VICO	What is the effect of GVCs in comparison (and conjunction) with IVCs on the growth of European high-tech entrepreneurial firms?	Positive effect by IVCs on firm sales growth, while the impact of GVC alone appears to be negligible. Positive impact of syndicated investments by both GVC and IVC on firms sales growth, but only when led by IVCs. The impact of the syndicates that are led by IVCs on the sales growth is at least partially due to capital injections. No statistically significant impact is exerted by IVCs, GVCs, or their syndicates on the employment growth.
Grilli and Murtinu (2015)	VICO	6,513 European NTBFs in 7 European countries observed between 1992 and 2009	GVC go-it-alone Syndication	VICO	Is the impact of GVCs on NTBF sales growth conditional on the age of the portfolio NTBF?	PVC positively affects the sales growth of NTBFs, especially in very young firms. GVC does not exert any statistically significant impact on the sales growth of NTBFs. There is a positive role of GVC when GVCs target relatively young firms using co-financing with PVCs.

Guerini and Quas (2016)	VICO	8,277 European high-tech companies in 7 European countries	GVC go-it-alone	VICO	Does obtaining GVC financing facilitate a high-tech entrepreneurial company's access to PVC financing because of a certification effect?	GVC funding increases the likelihood that companies receive PVC at least threefold. PVC investments in GVC-backed companies are more likely to reach a second round of PVC than other PVC investments.
Munari and Toschi (2015)	Venture Economics	628 UK companies that received a first VC round between 1998 and 2007	GVC go-it-alone	1998 Competitiveness White Paper	Does the impact of publicly supported VC programs vary (1) with respect to the impact of private VC funds, (2) between regional and governmental public VC funds and (3) among regions according to their level of innovation intensity?	(1-2) Public VC funds, especially those with a specific regional focus, have a lower impact on company performance than private VC funds. (3) These negative consequences tend to be more pronounced in technologically lagging regions. Public intervention, especially with a regional focus, acts as a "certification signal" towards VC investments only in regions already marked by a high level of innovation intensity.
Standaert and Manigart (2018)	Zephyr	108 Flemish portfolio companies that received an investment between 2005 and 2009 from a VC fund accredited by ARKimedes	GLP	PMV	How does the societal impact of the government fund-of-fund differ depending on the sponsor of the VC fund?	Companies backed by hybrid independent VC funds create more jobs compared to both hybrid captive VC funds and government VC funds.

(*Continued*)

Table 3: (*Continued*)

Authors	Data sources	Sample	Type of intervention	Identification source for government funds	Research question	Key findings
Vanacker *et al.* (2014)	VICO	6,813 NTBFs in 6 European countries tracked over 1994–2007	GVC go-it-alone	VICO	How does the type of VC investor affect the use of external financing by private NTBFs?	Firms backed by a government as lead VC are less likely to raise additional equity financing and raise smaller amounts of debt financing compared to firms backed by independent VCs.
Zhang (2018)	PEdata	5,222 Chinese firms that received their first VC round between 1995 and 2011	Syndication	PEdata, VC firm websites, SASAC	What is the impact of mixed GVC-PVC syndication on their investees?	Portfolio companies backed by mixed syndication or by pure PVC syndication show no difference in the likelihood of achieving IPO/M&A. Portfolio companies backed by PVC-led mixed syndication are less likely to survive to the next round than those backed by pure PVC syndication. A similar trend is not found for the portfolio companies of GVC-led mixed syndicates. The underperformance of PVC-led mixed syndication is more pronounced when the lead PVC has a networking position above average.

Notes: The following abbreviations are used: AVCAL (Australian Private Equity and Venture Capital Association), GVC (government venture capital), IIF (Innovation Investment Fund), IPO (initial public offering), IVC (independent venture capital), M&A (mergers and acquisitions), NTBF (new technology-based firm), PE (private equity), PMV (Participatie Maatschappij Vlaanderen), PVC (private venture capital), R&D (research and development), SASAC (State-owned Assets Supervision and Administration Committee), UK (United Kingdom), VC (venture capital).

4.1. *GVCs following a go-it-alone strategy*

4.1.1. *Investment patterns*

Since GVCs and independent VCs have different objectives (Colombo *et al.*, 2016a), the investment patterns of both types of VCs are expected to differ significantly. In particular, portfolio companies of GVCs differ from those of independent VCs with respect to their geographical location, industry, development stage, and resource endowment.

In the US, GVCs invest in firms operating in industries or regions that are less popular with independent VCs (Kovner and Lerner, 2015). More specifically, GVCs are less likely to invest in firms active in industries that are mainstays of independent VCs, including biotech, Internet and computers, and communication and electronics. Further, GVCs are more likely to invest in firms located in non-metropolitan regions and regions with little VC activity. Also, GVCs are more likely to make early-stage investments than their independent counterparts. Examining what human capital and intellectual capital characteristics affect the funding decisions made by GVCs, Uzuegbunam *et al.* (2017) show that GVCs invest in firms that have the potential to generate knowledge spillovers, as measured by the number of patents owned by the firm and the education level of the founders. Further evidence of this investment behavior is provided by Abrardi *et al.* (2018), who show that GVCs invest in firms with expected social returns that fell out of grace with independent VCs because of their unsatisfying financial returns.

In Europe, where independent VCs are less attracted to risky investments than in the US, GVCs take up the role of investing in small, young, early-stage firms that are active in the biotech, R&D and engineering or other high-tech manufacturing industries (Bertoni *et al.*, 2015). At the same time, GVCs neglect large, mature, later stage firms and firms operating in Internet and telecommunication services. GVCs also invest less often across national borders and invest more locally than independent VCs.

4.1.2. *Impact on firm performance*

Even if GVCs are able to select promising firms, their effectiveness still depends on their ability to support their portfolio companies' performance (Bertoni *et al.*, 2011). In this subsection, we provide some possible explanations as to why GVCs do not seem to contribute to their portfolio companies' growth and exit performance. However, we also identify circumstances under which solo GVC investments can become more impactful.

The VC literature has found a positive relationship between VCs' involvement in value-adding activities and a firm's performance or likelihood of a successful exit (Bernstein *et al.*, 2016; Colombo *et al.*, 2017). More specifically, VCs can add value to their portfolio companies by providing access to their networks of customers, suppliers and strategic partners (Hochberg *et al.*, 2007), helping them to raise additional financing (Vanacker *et al.*, 2014), assisting in strategic and operational planning (Sapienza *et al.*, 1996) or helping to recruit additional employees or managers (Hellmann and Puri, 2002). However, GVCs are less involved in value-adding activities compared to independent VCs (Bottazzi *et al.*, 2008; Knockaert *et al.*, 2006; Knockaert and Vanacker, 2013; Luukkonen *et al.*, 2013). A possible explanation for the inferior value-adding by GVCs can be found in the fact that investment managers at GVCs, in contrast to those at independent VCs, typically are not offered a profit-sharing compensation component (Manigart *et al.*, 2002) — called the "carried interest" — and therefore have few incentives to engage in value-adding activities (Sahlman, 1990). Consistent with this argument, Hirsch and Walz (2013) show that GVCs use fewer contract mechanisms that induce active intervention through value-adding activities as compared to independent VCs. Further, the lack of performance-based compensation might make it difficult for GVCs to attract or retain investment managers who possess the necessary skills to make successful VC investments (Leleux and Surlemont, 2003).

Even when GVCs employ skilled investment managers that are willing to provide value-adding services to portfolio companies, their time available to each portfolio company is limited since they have to manage more portfolio companies at a time than their counterparts at independent VCs (Knockaert *et al.*, 2006). Consequently, the suboptimal amount of attention allocated to a portfolio company will result in lower firm performance (Jääskeläinen *et al.*, 2006).

Differences in the objectives of independent VCs and GVCs are also likely to have an effect on the growth and exit performance of portfolio companies. Independent VCs manage closed-end funds with limited lifetimes and therefore must periodically raise follow-on funds well before the termination date of the current fund in order to continue operations (Gompers, 1996). This puts a strong pressure on independent VCs to quickly grow and exit portfolio companies, which positively affects the fund's interim performance and, ultimately, the VCs' ability to raise a follow-on fund (Barber and Yasuda, 2017). In contrast to independent VCs, GVCs are not motivated by financial objectives but rather by social objectives (Manigart *et al.*, 2002). As a result, GVCs aim to influence the strategic decisions of their portfolio companies in such a way that they lead to the generation of social returns. For example, GVCs have a strong positive impact on the establishment of EU-funded R&D partnerships (Colombo *et al.*, 2016b), which can lead to knowledge spillovers. However, these strategic decisions could hamper portfolio companies' ability to grow and realize a successful exit (Bertoni *et al.*, 2013).

Controlling for possible selection effects, the literature has shown that European GVCs following a go-it-alone strategy have overall no or even a negative impact on their portfolio companies' employment growth (Grilli and Murtinu, 2014), sales growth (Grilli and Murtinu, 2014, 2015), operating efficiency (Alperovych *et al.*, 2015), patenting activity (Bertoni and Tykvová, 2015) and likelihood of an IPO or trade-sale (Cumming *et al.*, 2017a). Furthermore, European GVC-backed firms have a smaller likelihood of raising additional equity financing and raise smaller amounts of debt financing compared to their independent VC-backed counterparts (Vanacker *et al.*, 2014).

Overall, GVCs appear to be not as effective in aiding the performance of portfolio companies as private VCs. However, it is credible that GVCs' effectiveness is dependent on the features of the GVC and the external environment. Evidence for this assertion has been brought forward by studies that focused on the experience of GVCs, economic conditions, and the location of portfolio companies when assessing the impact of GVCs. Alperovych *et al.* (2016) find that European GVCs have a more positive impact on their portfolio companies' exit performance if they have built up experience from investing in the same industry as the portfolio company or from syndicating with private VCs. These findings provide evidence of a learning process of GVCs. Using a sample of Spanish VC-backed and comparable non-VC-backed firms, Croce *et al.* (2018) show that GVCs reduced their impact on job creation in portfolio companies after the 2008 financial crisis. In contrast, private VCs enhanced their job creation performance during the same period. According to the authors, the lower employment growth in firms backed by GVCs during crisis times versus normal times can be explained by the pressure exerted by GVCs on portfolio companies to overcome the short-term effects of the crisis on employment levels. This argument is consistent with Colombo *et al.* (2014), who find that portfolio companies of GVCs are less likely to fire employees during sales contractions — which are likely to occur during times of economic crisis — than those of independent VCs. Consequently, in crisis times, portfolio companies of GVCs allocate resources towards the protection of existing employment levels rather than to the improvement of growth prospects. Examining the exit performance of GVC-backed firms in the United Kingdom, Munari and Toschi (2015) find that GVCs have a more positive impact on their portfolio companies' exit performance if they invest in firms located in more innovative regions.

Alternatively, GVCs can be effective if they are able to attract private VCs toward firms that would not have received private VC otherwise. As such, GVCs effectively contribute to the crowding-in of private VC at the firm-level (Brander *et al.*, 2015). On the one hand, through their screening and certification abilities, European GVCs are able to increase their portfolio companies' ability to raise a follow-on round from private VCs (Guerini and Quas, 2016). The effectiveness of this certification effect may however be reduced when the GVC's portfolio company is headquartered in a less innovative or economically developed region (Alperovych *et al.*, 2016; Munari and Toschi, 2015) or when the GVC invests locally, especially in countries with higher perceived corruption (Alperovych *et al.*, 2016). On the other hand, the greater presence of GVCs leads private VCs to alter their investment patterns and invest in firms that are the typical target of GVCs (Bertoni *et al.*, 2019; Kovner *et al.*, 2015).

4.2. *GVCs syndicating with private VCs*

4.2.1. *Investment patterns*

The investment patterns of mixed syndicates are more similar to those of solo GVCs than of private VCs. In the US, mixed syndicate investments share many of the characteristics of solo GVC investments (Kovner and Lerner, 2015), in that they are more likely to be early-stage investments as well as geographically concentrated outside of large metropolitan areas and in areas with less VC activity. Their industry investment focus, however, is more similar to that of private VC investments. In Europe, GVCs have successfully used syndication as a mechanism to attract private VCs to younger and smaller firms, which were typically only served by GVCs (Bertoni *et al.*, 2019). These findings confirm that GVCs use syndication as a mechanism to attract private VCs to their niche.

4.2.2. *Impact on firm performance*

Evaluations of mixed syndicates have been predominantly positive, with firms backed by both investor types demonstrating higher sales growth (Grilli and Murtinu, 2014, 2015), patenting activity (Bertoni and Tykvová, 2015) and likelihood of an IPO or trade-sale (Brander *et al.*, 2015; Cumming *et al.*, 2017a) compared to firms backed by only independent VCs. Deeper examinations of these findings have revealed that the superior performance of firms backed by mixed syndicates can be partially explained by the larger investment amounts raised (Brander *et al.*, 2015; Grilli and Murtinu, 2014).

The only exception to the superior impact of mixed syndicates has been observed in China. Chinese firms backed by a mixed syndicate are less likely to survive to the next financing round or achieve a successful exit directly after the initial round of financing compared to those backed by syndicates of independent VCs (Zhang, 2018). This finding is driven by mixed syndicates led by independent VCs, in which independent VCs use less strict selection criteria as a result of the use of a profit distribution structure that limits the risk for the independent VC (Jääskeläinen *et al.*, 2007). Moreover, the underperformance of mixed syndicates led by independent VCs is more pronounced for syndicates characterized by higher coordination costs. Coordination costs in mixed syndicates increase when the GVC is not able to provide resources that are complementary to those owned by the independent VC (Zhang, 2018).

4.3. *GLPs committing to private VC funds*

The number of studies on the investment patterns or impact on portfolio companies of private VC funds that raised part of their funds from public sources is limited and in most cases restricted to one specific program. This is largely due to the difficulty of obtaining information on the identities of investors in private VC funds (Buzzacchi *et al.*, 2013). For example, Invest Europe, the trade association for the European VC industry and an important source of information on VC fundraising, only provides aggregate statistics on the importance of public sources in fundraising by private VCs (Armour and Cumming, 2006). To the best of our knowledge, Brander *et al.* (2015) and Alperovych *et al.* (2018) are the only studies that collected an international dataset on private VC funds with GLPs.

4.3.1. *Investment patterns*

Examining investment patterns of VC funds in Germany, Israel, Japan and the United Kingdom, Mayer *et al.* (2005) show that the use of public sources of fundraising by VCs is associated with more early-stage, less late-stage, and more local and national investments.

In an evaluation of the Australian Innovation Investment Fund (IIF) program, Cumming (2007) shows that funds participating in the IIF program had a higher propensity to invest in early-stage and high-tech firms compared to other VC funds. This finding demonstrates that GLP commitments to VC funds increase the willingness of private VCs to invest in more risky firms. Interestingly, VCs managing IIF funds exhibited the same willingness to take on risk in their non-IIF funds, which suggests that these VCs developed valuable expertise in financing early-stage firms (Cumming, 2007).

Buzzacchi *et al.* (2013) study the investment patterns of private VC funds that raised part of their funds from the EIF and find that funds with a higher share provided by the EIF select *ex ante* less risky firms, as measured by the lower likelihood of observing a write-off. The authors interpret this finding as evidence of the GLP rendering private VCs to be more concerned about avoiding firms that will not be able to generate social returns due to their higher *ex ante* likelihood of later turning into write-offs. In the same vein, the presence of GLPs in European VC funds positively affects the investment managers' attitudes toward investing in firms with the potential to generate knowledge spillovers, such as firms that develop new and unique technologies (Knockaert *et al.*, 2010a) and academic spin-outs (Knockaert *et al.*, 2010b).

When multiple GLPs are active in a region, there is a risk that the objectives of the GLPs are competing with each other, which reduces their effectiveness. Cumming and Johan (2009) show that the introduction of the Australian Pre-seed Fund (PSF) program diminished the incentives for funds participating in the IIF program to invest in seed stage firms because funds participating in the PSF program were competing with them for deal flow. It would be interesting to examine whether similar phenomena occur in other regions or contexts. A potentially interesting case is Europe, where the EIF as well as national and regional GLPs operate and even act as co-investors in VC funds.

4.3.2. *Impact on firm performance*

According to Cumming and Johan (2016), funds participating in the IIF program have contributed significantly to the R&D and innovation activities of their portfolio companies. Compared to firms backed by other VCs, IIF-backed firms were more likely to be publicly listed, and if they went public, they did so at higher valuations.

Buzzacchi *et al.* (2013) show that funds with a higher public share held onto their portfolio companies for a longer period of time. This phenomenon was more prevalent for portfolio companies that were expected to generate intermediate financial returns. In other words, funds with a higher public share were less interested in quickly exiting portfolio companies that would not become huge successes, but rather pursued a more patient investment strategy. While this investment strategy benefits the achievement of social objectives pursued by the GLP, it comes to the detriment of the pure maximization of financial returns.

Brander *et al.* (2015) show that firms backed by private VC funds with GLPs had a lower likelihood of a successful exit through an IPO or acquisition than those backed by private VC funds without GLPs. Firms backed by both types of private VC funds were most likely to undergo a successful exit.

Comparing the exit values of firms backed by one of the three types of direct government intervention, Cumming *et al.* (2016) find that the only way in which governments are able to positively affect exit value is by investing in private VC funds.

It is important that GLPs commit to funds managed by VCs that have the capabilities to fulfill the government's objectives. For instance, of the four private VC funds participating in the PSF program, one demonstrated markedly superior performance (Cumming and Johan, 2009). Further, GLPs should take into account the heterogeneity among VC investor types. Since bank-affiliated VCs use their VC investments to build lending relationships with portfolio companies (Hellmann *et al.*, 2008), they focus less on firms' growth potential during the screening process (Croce *et al.*, 2015) and are less involved in value-adding activities (Bottazzi *et al.*, 2008; Knockaert *et al.*, 2006) compared to independent VCs. However, in Europe, where bank-affiliated VCs have historically been active investors (Bertoni *et al.*, 2015), GLPs have invested in numerous bank-affiliated VC funds (Knockaert *et al.*, 2006). Standaert and Manigart (2018) show that the bank-affiliated VC funds participating in the Flemish ARKimedes program created fewer jobs in their portfolio companies compared to the participating independent VC funds. The findings above therefore highlight the importance of the selection of fund managers. However, we lack insights into the decision process of GLPs.

5. Lessons for Policymakers and Scholars

5.1. *Lessons for policymakers*

The systematic review of the empirical literature on direct government intervention in VC markets allows to make inferences about the effectiveness of the different types of direct government intervention, which can serve as a guideline for policymakers when establishing or adjusting their programs for direct intervention in VC markets. More specifically, we evaluate to what degree the government's objectives of alleviating the equity gap and generating social returns have been achieved by the three types of intervention.

We find that government intervention is able to bridge the equity gap in a number of ways. First, GVCs are able to screen the market for promising targets and certify them to private VCs (Guerini and Quas,

2016), although the effectiveness of the certification effect is reduced by regional constraints or potential collusion and regulatory capture (Alperovych *et al.*, 2016; Munari and Toschi, 2015). Second, GVCs are able to alter the investment patterns of private VCs and attract them to the GVC's niche, even when GVCs do not syndicate with private VCs (Bertoni *et al.*, 2019; Kovner and Lerner, 2015). Third, there is some evidence that GLP commitments to VC funds have led private VCs to invest more in early-stage and high-tech firms (Cumming, 2007; Mayer *et al.*, 2005). Further, Alperovych *et al.* (2018) show that increases in the importance of GLPs in national VC industries improved the easiness with which European firms can access finance. However, future studies should more deeply examine the mechanisms through which GLP commitments to private VC funds can lead to the desired objective of closing the equity gap.

The picture is more nuanced when the government's ability to generate social returns is evaluated. Firms receiving solo GVC investments generally do not show higher employment growth than non-VC-backed firms (Grilli and Murtinu, 2014), although findings may depend on the features of the GVC and the external environment. Similarly, solo GVC investments do not lead to higher patenting activity by firms (Bertoni and Tykvová, 2015). In order to meet their goal of realizing social returns, governments can follow two strategies. First, during the screening process, GVCs can use models that estimate a firms' growth potential, reducing the required overall screening time and freeing up resources for valuable value-adding activities (Minola *et al.*, 2017). Second, governments can draw upon the superior value-adding abilities of independent VCs by creating mixed syndicates (Bertoni and Tykvová, 2015) or by investing in independent VC funds (Standaert and Manigart, 2018).

Equipped with this knowledge, we are able to formulate policy recommendations for direct government intervention in VC markets. Fundamentally, the ability of governments to involve private VCs seems a precondition for the effectiveness of direct government intervention. If governments are not able to attract private VCs to the firms they aim to support, firms will be constrained in their development (Cumming *et al.*, 2017a; Grilli and Murtinu, 2014, 2015) and face difficulties in attracting follow-up funding (Guerini and Quas, 2016; Munari and Toschi, 2015).

Consequently, the optimal use of the three types of direct government intervention is likely to differ depending on the size of the population of private VCs.

When the number of private VCs that is active in the domestic VC industry is limited, governments should first put efforts into raising this number before implementing GVC initiatives that target the early stages of financing. Governments can achieve this aim by having GLPs take up the role of anchor investor in early-stage funds raised by new fund management teams. Only then can GVCs focus on improving the attractiveness of firms operating in industries that are less popular with private VCs by screening targets and syndicating with private VCs. Importantly, these firms should have the potential to generate significant social returns (Minola *et al.*, 2017). At the same time, GVCs should increase the value of their role as an active early-stage investor by building up industry-specific experience and learning from private VCs (Alperovych *et al.*, 2016).

When the domestic VC industry has reached a critical mass of private VCs, governments should structure their direct intervention initiatives in the following ways. At the early stages of financing, GVCs could play a dual role. First, experienced GVCs could become valuable and long-term syndication partners for private VCs in early-stage investment rounds. Because of their different objectives, GVCs develop non-financial resources that are complementary to those provided by private VCs (Bertoni and Tykvová, 2015). Since early-stage firms are typically constrained in both financial and non-financial resources, the addition of a GVC could positively affect a firms' likelihood of success. Second, GVCs could ensure the availability of early-stage financing when private VCs drift towards later stage deals during times of poorly performing financial markets (Buzzacchi *et al.*, 2015; Cumming *et al.*, 2009). In summary, we argue that, under the conditions explained above, continued government intervention through GVCs is warranted.

While GVCs could contribute to a flourishing early-stage VC industry, they are not suited to provide an answer to the limited supply of VC at later stages of financing (Wilson *et al.*, 2018). Even though private VCs might be willing to invest in later stage rounds, they might not be able to provide the required amounts due to the limited size of their funds (Duruflé *et al.*,

2018). In theory, skilled VCs should be able to attract the interest from outside LPs and consequently raise larger follow-on funds (Kaplan and Schoar, 2005). However, if the targeted fund sizes are too small to be considered by large institutional investors, the increase in size of the follow-on funds could not be sufficient to match the higher demand for later stage financing. Therefore, governments should aim to crowd-in these large institutional investors through GLP initiatives (Aernoudt, 2017).

In conclusion, this section has provided policymakers with some rules of thumb for planning their direct intervention in VC markets. However, it should be acknowledged that the eventual success of these initiatives will be determined by their execution as well as exogenous factors. In order to improve the likelihood of success of government initiatives, we encourage policymakers to collect detailed information on their activities and pursue close collaboration with researchers in order to rigorously evaluate their effectiveness. A good example is the VICO[4] project, which brought forward a number of peer-reviewed studies on the impact of GVC initiatives in seven European countries. Future research projects could further advance our understanding of direct government intervention in VC markets by tackling some of the research questions that are outlined in the following section.

5.2. *Lessons for scholars*

Although there has been a recent wave of research on direct government intervention in VC markets, future research is needed to improve our understanding of the consequences, and therefore the effectiveness, of government initiatives. This section intends to identify questions that have been unexplored up until now. For this purpose, we develop an analytical framework for direct government intervention in VC markets. The analytical framework is depicted in Figure 1. In order to duly examine the

---

[4]VICO is a research project, funded by the 7th Framework Program of the European Commission, aiming to assess the impact of VC investments on the economic performance of entrepreneurial firms in Europe. The project involved nine universities and research centers from seven European countries. For more information on the project, see VICO (2011).

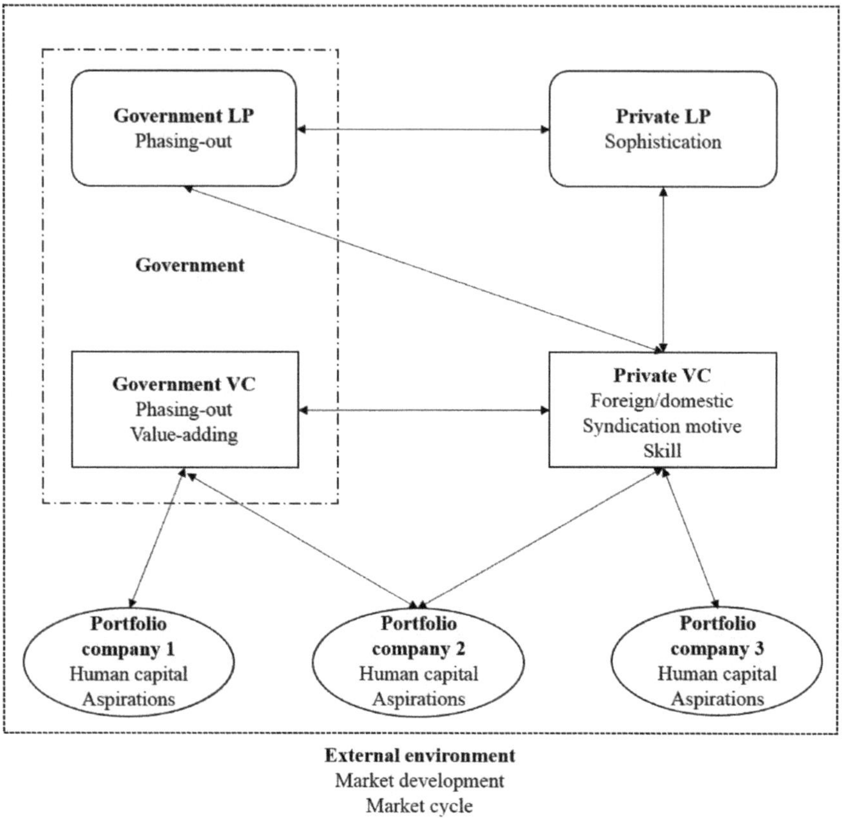

Figure 1: Analytical framework for direct government intervention in VC markets.

effectiveness of direct government intervention, we argue that future research should take into account two important aspects. First, every type of intervention creates interrelationships with private investors and/or portfolio companies. These interrelationships between government and private actors will be affected by the characteristics and interests of both parties. Second, the nature of the interrelationships is expected to be influenced by the external environment. The remainder of this section is structured as follows. In the following subsection, we identify general gaps that are applicable to all types of direct intervention. In the subsequent subsections, we reveal gaps that are specific to each type of intervention.

5.2.1. *General gaps*

Dimensions of government intervention in VC markets that have not received sufficient attention are the characteristics of the external environment, the effects of tapering government intervention and the relationship with foreign VCs.

While evaluations of direct government intervention can be positive, we do not know what factors determine whether government intervention continues to be effective over time. On the one hand, the development of a private VC industry could reduce the need for government intervention and therefore question its continued existence (Lerner, 2009). On the other hand, the cyclical nature of the private VC industry could raise the need for continued government intervention, which can serve the role of smoothening the supply of VC (Gompers *et al.*, 2008).

Previous studies have briefly touched upon the possible consequences of phasing out specific government programs (Avnimelech and Teubal, 2006; Jacob *et al.*, 2016). The disappearance of an hitherto important syndicate partner or GLP could shift investment patterns of VCs or lead to a decrease in the willingness of private LPs to invest in VC funds. Future studies could therefore improve our understanding of the consequences of tapering government intervention for firms and independent VCs by using macro-level data for various countries.

The literature on VC internationalization has focused on the country-level determinants and outcomes of international VC investments (Devigne *et al.*, 2018). While previous studies have highlighted the role of a country's institutional development as an important driver of international VC investments, there is a lack of evidence on the relationship between direct government intervention and the inflow of international VC investments. Since firms backed by syndicates consisting of both domestic and foreign VCs show higher growth and have a higher likelihood of successful exit than other VC-backed firms (Chemmanur *et al.*, 2016; Devigne *et al.*, 2013), governments might be particularly interested in attracting foreign VCs to their national industries. Future studies could therefore examine whether the presence of GVCs attracts foreign VCs, whether foreign VCs syndicate with GVCs, and how syndicates of GVCs and foreign VCs perform relative to syndicates of other investor types.

Similarly, it would be interesting to examine whether GLP commitments to foreign VC funds lead to a sustained increase in the inflow of international investments, and to evaluate how this investment strategy affects the population of domestic VCs.

5.2.2. *Gaps related to the go-it-alone strategy of GVCs*

While the majority of studies aim to account for observable and unobservable heterogeneity of firms when demonstrating the limited impact of solo GVCs on firm growth, there is a possibility that GVCs suffer from the adverse selection of entrepreneurs. In other words, unobservable entrepreneur characteristics, which lead to inferior growth outcomes, might be associated with solo GVC investments. In the entrepreneurship literature, the entrepreneur's human capital and growth aspirations have been advanced as important determinants of firm growth outcomes (Gilbert *et al.*, 2006). On the one hand, independent VCs might invest in firms whose entrepreneurs possess the kind of human capital that is required to realize high growth (Colombo and Grilli, 2010). On the other hand, entrepreneurs with strong growth aspirations might decide to not apply for GVC financing, due to a misalignment of incentives, or only accept investments from independent VCs, who are better able to fulfill the entrepreneurs' growth aspirations due to their higher involvement in value-adding activities (Knockaert *et al.*, 2006). In both cases, GVCs can only invest in a subset of firms owned by entrepreneurs with low human capital or weak growth aspirations, which will lead to low firm growth outcomes. Future research could examine whether this alternative explanation holds.

Future studies could also examine how GVCs can become more successful when following a go-it-alone strategy. A first step in this direction is taken by Alperovych *et al.* (2016), who show that investments by more experienced GVCs demonstrate better performance. Another way in which GVCs could compensate for their limited value-adding role consists of building and drawing upon a network of professionals to provide their portfolio companies with expertise through the board of directors or advisory board.

5.2.3. *Gaps related to syndication of GVCs with private VCs*

With regard to the existence of mixed syndicates, we currently do not have an understanding of the motives for independent VCs' decision to syndicate with GVCs. The literature on syndication by independent VCs has identified different motives for syndication and compared their relative importance across VC firm characteristics (Manigart *et al.*, 2006), but did not consider the heterogeneity of VC investor types. Since the introduction of a GVC in a syndicate could lead to a higher incidence of agency conflicts (Zhang, 2018), future research could examine why and when independent VCs might prefer to syndicate with GVCs rather than with other independent VCs.

Previous studies have found that the superior performance of mixed syndicates can be partially explained by the larger investment amounts raised (Brander *et al.*, 2015; Grilli and Murtinu, 2014). Since governments can also positively affect the average investment amount indirectly by increasing the funds available to independent VCs through GLP commitments, it would be interesting to examine whether the role of GVCs as active investor in mixed syndicates adds more value *vis-à-vis* their role as passive investor in private VC funds.

5.2.4. *Gaps related to GLP commitments to private VC funds*

An interesting question is whether GLP commitments to VC funds have effectively contributed to the existence of a healthy private VC industry. Since the level of public ownership of independent VC funds affects the investment behavior of VCs (Buzzacchi *et al.*, 2013), skilled VCs could decide to avoid sourcing funds from GLPs. This leads to a situation of adverse selection, in which GLPs can only invest in funds of less-skilled VCs. These less-skilled VCs are unlikely to be able to generate the financial returns that are required to attract private LPs. Alternatively, in countries where private LPs are more hesitant to invest in VC funds due to high risk aversion or an inability to evaluate the quality of VCs (Lerner *et al.*, 2007), GLP commitments to VC funds, especially funds for which information asymmetries are high such as first-time funds (Zarutskie, 2010), could serve as a signal to private LPs and consequently facilitate the development of a private VC industry.

Finally, it would be interesting to analyze the fund performance of independent VCs that have access to GLP commitments. On the one hand, the stability provided by a less performance-sensitive incumbent LP could reduce the VCs' time and effort spent on raising follow-on funds, freeing up time for valuable value-adding activities, and consequently boost fund performance. On the other hand, fund performance could be negatively affected due to the restrictions imposed on funds that receive GLP commitments. These restrictions could hinder VCs' ability to pursue the maximization of financial returns (Buzzacchi *et al.*, 2013) by requiring them to invest the available funds within a certain time frame or within certain geographic boundaries, leading them to invest in inferior targets or invest at higher valuations (Heughebaert and Manigart, 2012).

References

Abrardi L., Croce A., and Ughetto E. (2018) The dynamics of switching between governmental and independent venture capitalists: theory and evidence. *Small Business Economics,* 53(1), 165–188.

Aernoudt R. (2017) Executive Forum: the scale-up gap: and how to address it. *Venture Capital: An International Journal of Entrepreneurial Finance*, 19(4), 361–372.

Alperovych Y., Groh A. P., and Quas A. (2016) When can government venture capital funds bridge the equity gap? Available at SSRN: https://papers.ssrn.com/sol3/papers.cfm?abstract_id=2718061.

Alperovych Y., Hübner G., and Lobet F. (2015) How does governmental versus private venture capital backing affect a firm's efficiency? Evidence from Belgium. *Journal of Business Venturing*, 30(4), 508–525.

Alperovych Y., Quas A., and Standaert T. (2018) Direct and indirect government venture capital investments in Europe. *Economics Bulletin*, 38(2), 1219–1230.

Amit R., Brander J., and Zott C. (1998) Why do venture capital firms exist? Theory and Canadian evidence. *Journal of Business Venturing*, 13(6), 441–466.

Armour J. and Cumming D. (2006) The legislative road to Silicon Valley. *Oxford Economic Papers*, 58(4), 596–635.

Audretsch D. B. (1995) *Innovation and Industry Evolution.* MIT Press, Cambridge MA.

Avnimelech G. and Teubal M. (2006) Creating venture capital industries that co-evolve with high tech: insights from an extended industry life cycle perspective of the Israeli experience. *Research Policy*, 35(10), 1477–1498.

Barber B. M. and Yasuda A. (2017) Interim fund performance and fundraising in private equity. *Journal of Financial Economics*, 124(1), 172–194.

Bernstein S., Giroud X., and Townsend R. R. (2016) The impact of venture capital monitoring. *Journal of Finance*, 71(4), 1591–1622.

Bertoni F., Colombo M. G., and Croce A. (2010) The effect of venture capital financing on the sensitivity to cash flow of firm's investments. *European Financial Management*, 16(4), 528–551.

Bertoni F., Colombo M. G., and Grilli L. (2011) Venture capital financing and the growth of high-tech start-ups: Disentangling treatment from selection effects. *Research Policy*, 40(7), 1028–1043.

Bertoni F., Colombo M. G., and Grilli L. (2013) Venture capital investor type and the growth mode of new technology-based firms. *Small Business Economics*, 40(3), 527–552.

Bertoni F., Colombo M. G., and Quas A. (2015) The patterns of venture capital investments in Europe. *Small Business Economics*, 45(3), 543–560.

Bertoni F., Colombo M. G., and Quas A. (2019) The role of governmental venture capital in the venture capital ecosystem: An organizational ecology perspective. *Entrepreneurship Theory and Practice*, 43(3), 611–628.

Bertoni F. and Quas A. (2016) The electoral cycle of government venture capital investments. Available at SSRN: https://papers.ssrn.com/sol3/papers.cfm?abstract_id=2777169.

Bertoni F. and Tykvová T. (2015) Does governmental venture capital spur invention and innovation? Evidence from young European biotech companies. *Research Policy*, 44(4), 925–935.

Block J. H., Colombo M. G., Cumming D. J., and Vismara S. (2018) New players in entrepreneurial finance and why they are there. *Small Business Economics*, 50(2), 239–250.

Bottazzi L., Da Rin M., and Hellmann T. (2008) Who are the active investors? Evidence from venture capital. *Journal of Financial Economics*, 89(3), 488–512.

Brander J. A., Du Q., and Hellmann T. (2015) The effects of government-sponsored venture capital: international evidence. *Review of Finance*, 19(2), 571–618.

Brander J. A., Egan E. J., and Hellmann T. F. (2010) Government sponsored versus private venture capital: Canadian evidence. In J. Lerner, and A. Schoar (Eds.), *International Differences in Entrepreneurship*. University of Chicago Press, Chicago, pp. 275–320.

Bruno A. V., Tyebjee T. T., and Anderson J. C. (1985) Finding a way through the venture capital maze. *Business Horizons*, 28(1), 12–19.

Buzzacchi L., Scellato G., and Ughetto E. (2013) The investment strategies of publicly sponsored venture capital funds. *Journal of Banking and Finance*, 37(3), 707–716.

Buzzacchi L., Scellato G., and Ughetto E. (2015) Investment stage drifts and venture capital managerial incentives. *Journal of Corporate Finance*, 33, 118–128.

Carpenter R. E. and Petersen B. C. (2002) Capital market imperfections, high-tech investment, and new equity financing. *The Economic Journal*, 112(477), F54-F72.

Chemmanur T. J., Hull T. J., and Krishnan K. (2016) Do local and international venture capitalists play well together? The complementarity of local and international venture capitalists. *Journal of Business Venturing*, 31(5), 573–594.

Colombo M. G., Cumming D. J., and Vismara S. (2016a) Governmental venture capital for innovative young firms. *Journal of Technology Transfer*, 41(1), 10–24.

Colombo M. G., D'Adda D., and Pirelli L. H. (2016b) The participation of new technology-based firms in EU-funded R&D partnerships: The role of venture capital. *Research Policy*, 45(2), 361–375.

Colombo M. G., D'Adda D., Malighetti P., Quas A., and Vismara S. (2017) The impact of venture capital monitoring in Europe. Available at SSRN: https://papers.ssrn.com/sol3/papers.cfm?abstract_id=2906236.

Colombo M. G. and Grilli L. (2010) On growth drivers of high-tech start-ups: Exploring the role of founders' human capital and venture capital. *Journal of Business Venturing*, 25(6), 610–626.

Colombo M. G., Piva E., and Rossi-Lamastra C. (2014) The sensitivity of high-tech entrepreneurial ventures' employment to a sales contraction in a negative growth scenario: the moderating role of venture capital financing. *Managerial and Decision Economics*, 35(2), 73–87.

Croce A., D'Adda D., and Ughetto E. (2015) Venture capital financing and the financial distress risk of portfolio firms: How independent and bank-affiliated investors differ. *Small Business Economics*, 44(1), 189–206.

Croce A., Martí J., and Reverte C. (2018) The role of private versus governmental venture capital in fostering job creation during the crisis. *Small Business Economics*, 1–22.

Cumming D. (2007) Government policy towards entrepreneurial finance: Innovation investment funds. *Journal of Business Venturing*, 22(2), 193–235.

Cumming D. (2014) Public economics gone wild: Lessons from venture capital. *International Review of Financial Analysis*, 36, 251–260.

Cumming D., Fleming G., and Schwienbacher A. (2009) Style drift in private equity. *Journal of Business Finance and Accounting*, 36(5-6), 645–678.

Cumming D. J., Grilli L., and Murtinu S. (2017a) Governmental and independent venture capital investments in Europe: A firm-level performance analysis. Journal of Corporate Finance, 42, 439–459.

Cumming D. and Johan S. (2009) Pre-seed government venture capital funds. *Journal of International Entrepreneurship*, 7(1), 26–56.

Cumming D. and Johan S. (2016) Venture's economic impact in Australia. *Journal of Technology Transfer*, 41(1), 25–59.

Cumming D., Johan S., and MacIntosh J. G. (2017b) A drop in an empty pond: Canadian public policy towards venture capital. *Economia e Politica Industriale*, 44(1), 103–117.

Cumming D., Knill A., and Syvrud K. (2016) Government as a source of capital for entrepreneurs: evidence from entrepreneurial exits. Available at SSRN: https://papers.ssrn.com/sol3/papers.cfm?abstract_id=2764927.

Cumming D. and MacIntosh J. G. (2006) Crowding out private equity: Canadian evidence. *Journal of Business Venturing*, 21(5), 569–609.

Da Rin M., Hellmann T., and Puri M. (2013) A survey of venture capital research. In G. Constantinides, M. Harris, and R. Stulz (Eds.), *Handbook of the Economics of Finance*, Volume 2, Part A. Elsevier, Amsterdam, pp. 573–648.

Da Rin M., Nicodano G., and Sembenelli A. (2006) Public policy and the creation of active venture capital markets. *Journal of Public Economics*, 90(8-9), 1699–1723.

Denes M. (2017) When do firms risk shift? Evidence from venture capital. Available at SSRN: https://papers.ssrn.com/sol3/papers.cfm?abstract_id=2875882.

De Prijcker S., Manigart S., and Collewaert V. (2017) Relocation to get venture capital: a resource dependence perspective. *Entrepreneurship Theory and Practice*, doi: https://doi.org/10.1177/1042258717739003.

Devigne D., Manigart S., Vanacker T., and Mulier K. (2018) Venture capital internationalization: synthesis and future research directions. *Journal of Economic Surveys*, 32(5), 1414–1445.

Devigne D., Vanacker T., Manigart S., and Paeleman I. (2013) The role of domestic and cross-border venture capital investors in the growth of portfolio companies. *Small Business Economics*, 40(3), 553–573.

Duchin R. and Sosyura D. (2012) The politics of government investment. *Journal of Financial Economics*, 106(1), 24–48.

Duruflé G., Hellmann T., and Wilson K. (2018) From start-up to scale-up: Examining public policies for the financing of high-growth ventures. In C. Mayer, S. Micossi, M. Onado, M. Pagano, and A. Polo (Eds.), *Finance and Investment: The European Case*. Oxford University Press, Oxford, pp. 179–219.

European Investment Fund (2016) The European venture capital landscape: an EIF perspective, Volume 1: The impact of EIF on the VC ecosystem. EIF Research and Market Analysis. Working Paper 2016/34. Available at: http://www.eif.org/news_centre/-publications/eif_wp_34.pdf.

Gilbert B. A., McDougall P. P., and Audretsch D. B. (2006) New venture growth: a review and extension. *Journal of Management*, 32(6), 926–950.

Gompers P. J. (1996) Grandstanding in the venture capital industry. *Journal of Financial Economics*, 42(1), 133–156.

Gompers P., Kovner A., Lerner J., and Scharfstein D. (2008) Venture capital investment cycles: The impact of public markets. *Journal of Financial Economics*, 87(1), 1–23.

Grilli L. and Murtinu S. (2014) Government, venture capital and the growth of European high-tech entrepreneurial firms. *Research Policy*, 43(9), 1523–1543.

Grilli L. and Murtinu S. (2015) New technology-based firms in Europe: market penetration, public venture capital, and timing of investment. *Industrial and Corporate Change*, 24(5), 1109–1148.

Groh A. P., von Liechtenstein H., and Lieser K. (2010) The European Venture Capital and Private Equity country attractiveness indices. *Journal of Corporate Finance*, 16(2), 205–224.

Guerini M. and Quas A. (2016) Governmental venture capital in Europe: Screening and certification. *Journal of Business Venturing*, 31(2), 175–195.

Hellmann T., Lindsey L., and Puri M. (2008) Building relationships early: banks in venture capital. *Review of Financial Studies*, 21(2), 513–541.

Hellmann T. and Puri M. (2002) Venture capital and the professionalization of start-up firms: empirical evidence. *Journal of Finance*, 57(1), 169–197.

Heughebaert A. and Manigart S. (2012) Firm valuation in venture capital financing rounds: the role of investor bargaining power. *Journal of Business Finance and Accounting*, 39(3–4), 500–530.

Hirsch J. and Walz U. (2013) Why do contracts differ between venture capital types? *Small Business Economics*, 40(3), 511–525.

Hochberg Y. V., Ljungqvist A., and Lu Y. (2007) Whom you know matters: venture capital networks and investment performance. *Journal of Finance*, 62(1), 251–301.

Jääskeläinen M., Maula M., and Murray G. (2007) Profit distribution and compensation structures in publicly and privately funded hybrid venture capital funds. *Research Policy*, 36(7), 913–929.

Jääskeläinen M., Maula M., and Seppä T. (2006) Allocation of attention to portfolio companies and the performance of venture capital firms. *Entrepreneurship Theory and Practice*, 30(2), 185–206.

Jacob M., Johan S., Schweizer D., and Zhan F. (2016) Corporate finance and the governance implications of removing government support programs. *Journal of Banking and Finance*, 63, 35–47.

Jeng L. A. and Wells P. C. (2000) The determinants of venture capital funding: evidence across countries. *Journal of Corporate Finance*, 6(3), 241–289.

Knockaert M., Clarysse B., and Wright M. (2010a) The extent and nature of heterogeneity of venture capital selection behaviour in new technology-based firms. *R&D Management*, 40(4), 357–371.

Knockaert M., Lockett A., Clarysse B., and Wright M. (2006) Do human capital and fund characteristics drive follow-up behaviour of early stage high-tech VCs? *International Journal of Technology Management*, 34(1-2), 7–27.

Knockaert M. and Vanacker T. (2013) The association between venture capitalists' selection and value adding behavior: evidence from early stage high tech venture capitalists. *Small Business Economics*, 40(3), 493–509.

Knockaert M., Wright M., Clarysse B., and Lockett A. (2010b) Agency and similarity effects and the VC's attitude towards academic spin-out investing. *Journal of Technology Transfer*, 35(6), 567–584.

Kovner A. and Lerner J. (2015) Doing well by doing good? Community development venture capital. *Journal of Economics and Management Strategy*, 24(3), 643–663.

Leleux B. and Surlemont B. (2003) Public versus private venture capital : seeding or crowding out ? A pan-European analysis. *Journal of Business Venturing*, 18(1), 81–104.

Lerner J. (1999) The government as venture capitalist: the long-run impact of the SBIR program. *Journal of Business*, 72(3), 285–318.

Lerner J. (2002) When bureaucrats meet entrepreneurs: the design of effective 'public venture capital' programmes. *The Economic Journal*, 112(477), F73–F84.

Lerner J. (2009) *Boulevard of Broken Dreams: Why Public Efforts to Boost Entrepreneurship and Venture Capital Have Failed — and What to Do about It*. Princeton University Press, Princeton NJ.

Lerner, J., Schoar A., and Wongsunwai W. (2007) Smart institutions, foolish choices: the limited partner performance puzzle. *Journal of Finance*, 62(2), 731–764.

Luukkonen T., Deschryvere M., and Bertoni F. (2013) The value added by government venture capital funds compared with independent venture capital funds. *Technovation*, 33(4–5), 154–162.

Manigart S., De Waele K., Wright M., Robbie K., Desbrières P., Sapienza H.J., and Beekman A. (2002) Determinants of required return in venture capital investments: a five-country study. *Journal of Business Venturing*, 17(4), 291–312.

Manigart S., Lockett A., Meuleman M., Wright M., Landström H., Bruining H., Desbrières P., and Hommel U. (2006) Venture capitalists' decision to syndicate. *Entrepreneurship Theory and Practice*, 30(2), 131–153.

Mayer C., Schoors K., and Yafeh Y. (2005) Sources of funds and investment activities of venture capital funds: evidence from Germany, Israel, Japan and the United Kingdom. *Journal of Corporate Finance*, 11, 586–608.

Milosevic M. (2018) Skills or networks? Success and fundraising determinants in a low performing venture capital market. *Research Policy*, 47(1), 49–60.

Minola T., Vismara S., and Hahn D. (2017) Screening model for the support of governmental venture capital. *Journal of Technology Transfer*, 42(1), 59–77.

Mueller C., Westhead P., and Wright M. (2012) Formal venture capital acquisition: can entrepreneurs compensate for the spatial proximity benefits of South East England and 'star' golden-triangle universities? *Environment and Planning A: Economy and Space*, 44(2), 281–296.

Munari F. and Toschi L. (2015) Assessing the impact of public venture capital programmes in the United Kingdom: Do regional characteristics matter? *Journal of Business Venturing*, 30(2), 205–226.

Murray G. C. and Lott J. (1995) Have UK venture capitalists a bias against investment in new technology-based firms? *Research Policy*, 24(2), 283–299.

Pierrakis Y. and Saridakis G. (2017) The role of venture capitalists in the regional innovation ecosystem: a comparison of networking patterns between private and publicly backed venture capital funds. *Journal of Technology Transfer*, 44(3), 850–873.

Puri M. and Zarutskie R. (2012) On the life cycle dynamics of venture-capital- and non-venture-capital-financed firms. *Journal of Finance*, 67(6), 2247–2293.

Sahlman W. A. (1990) The structure and governance of venture capital organizations. *Journal of Financial Economics*, 27(2), 473–521.

Sapienza H. J., Manigart S., and Vermeir W. (1996) Venture capitalist governance and value added in four countries. *Journal of Business Venturing*, 11(6), 439–469.

Small Business Administration (2014) SBIC overview. Available at: https://www.sba.gov/sites/default/files/articles/sbic_program-_overview.pdf.

Standaert T. and Manigart S. (2018) Government as fund-of-fund and VC fund sponsors: effect on employment in portfolio companies. *Small Business Economics*, 50(2), 357–373.

Uzuegbunam I., Liao Y., Pittaway L., and Jolley G.J. (2017) Human capital, intellectual capital, and government venture capital. *Journal of Entrepreneurship and Public Policy*, 6(3), 359–374.

Vanacker T., Heughebaert A., and Manigart S. (2014) Institutional frameworks, venture capital and the financing of European new technology-based firms. *Corporate Governance: An International Review*, 22(3), 199–215.

VICO (2011) Venture capital: Policy Lessons from the VICO project. Available at: https://www.vlerick.com/~/media/Corporate/-Pdf-knowledge/Venture%20Capital_VICO/Venture%20Capital_VICO.pdf.

Wilson K. and Silva F. (2013) Policies for seed and early stage finance: Findings from the 2012 OECD financing questionnaire. OECD science, technology and industry policy papers, NO. 9, OECD Publishing. doi:10.1787/5k3xqsf00j33-en.

Wilson N., Wright M., and Kacer M. (2018) The equity gap and knowledge-based firms. *Journal of Corporate Finance*, 50, 626–649.

Zarutskie R. (2010) The role of top management team human capital in venture capital markets: Evidence from first-time funds. *Journal of Business Venturing*, 25(1), 155–172.

Zhang Y. (2018) Gain or pain? New evidence on mixed syndication between governmental and private venture capital firms in China. *Small Business Economics*, 51(4), 995–1031.

Chapter 4

Guarantee Instrument Obsolete or Future-Oriented?

Rudy Aernoudt*
Department of Accounting, Corporate Finance and Taxation, Ghent University
raernoudt@gmail.com

Abstract

Venture capital, business angels, crowdfunding and mezzanine are among the financing instruments considered as sexy and future-oriented. Therefore, they receive a lot of attention from researchers and policymakers. This is in big contrast to the guarantee instrument often considered as an obsolete bureaucratic instrument leading to moral hazard at lenders' level. Moreover, guarantees are not only linked — as the traditional approach suggests — to credits, but can be a useful instrument, on top of the different co-investment schemes, to boost venture capital. This chapter argues that a guarantee policy should be an integral part of the landscape of financial instruments as it can be very efficient in terms of value for public money and pleads for a renewal of academic research on the matter and ends with concrete research suggestions.

*7, Sint-Pietersplein, Ghent, 9000, Belgium; European Commission, Bruxelles, Belgium.

1. Introduction

This chapter starts by analyzing the rationale of guarantee schemes by referring to the financing gap in general and to the loan and equity gap in particular. Guarantee schemes are discussed coping with the loan gap. But guarantees can be used to cope with the equity gap as well. Both US and the EU models are described, and the chapter ends with policy recommendations and research suggestions.

2. Rationale for Guarantees Schemes

2.1. *The financing gap*

In a perfect world, every viable and sustainable project should find financing. However, many studies show that despite liquid markets and major government efforts the financing gap remains significant. This implies a lot of start-ups not being created and existing enterprises not sufficiently exploiting their growth potential. To illustrate: in a report on the public consultation that preceded the start-up and scale-up initiative, 71% of the respondents identified access to finance as the major barrier for European start-ups to scale up their business (European Commission, 2016). The financing gap indicates that a sizeable share of economically significant enterprises cannot obtain financing from banks, capital markets or other suppliers of finance. In other words, some enterprises and entrepreneurs that have the capability of using funds productively were they available do not have access to those funds (OECD, 2017). Given the liquidity of the capital markets, the financing problem is rather a transmission problem than a lack of financial means problem.

One could argue, referring to the equilibrium rates, that the financing gap is due to price conditions whereby the amount of financing demanded exceeds the amount being supplied. However, peculiarities of finance explain the existence of a financing gap without price distortions because financiers may not supply funds for a variety of reasons. For instance, some issues of primary importance include the complications arising from asymmetric information, such as moral hazard and adverse selection (Stiglitz and Weiss, 1981). Stiglitz and Weiss conclude that there are no competitive forces in action to increase the interest rate in order to bring demand and supply together. A market clearing equilibrated pricing mechanism is hence not an efficient instrument to cope with the financing gap, on the contrary. If a bank for instance, would agree on a higher interest rate, its expected return would decrease due to informational asymmetries. First, an adverse selection effect would be introduced, as a higher interest rate will attract higher risk borrowers while lower risk borrowers drop out. Second, borrowers who receive a loan will prefer higher risk projects to low-risk projects. By driving out lower risk borrowers, high interest rates may lead to a riskier loan portfolio, thus setting in motion a process of adverse credit selection. Third, this would increase the capital requirements imposed by the Basel Regulations and hence the higher interest would not necessarily lead to higher profit margins. For all these reasons, bankers have an incentive to engage in credit rationing and to allocate credits to very creditworthy borrowers. Consequently, bankers do not provide or extend the full amount of credit demanded even when the borrower is willing to pay higher rates. On the demand side, potential borrowers do not apply for a bank loan because they fear their application would be rejected. Studies show that among those discouraged borrowers, only 20% have a high likelihood of being rejected if they applied (Ferrando *et al.*, 2017).

The same reasoning goes for the venture capitalists where the normal market functioning based on risk premium theories fails as the high risk on venture stage doesn't go along with a high return, while the low-risk MBO-type investments are highly rewarded (Aernoudt, 2015).

In the Stieglitz–Weiss formulation, a financing gap is said to occur if among applicants who appear to be identical some receive financing while others do not, or if there are identifiable groups in the population that are unable to obtain financing at any price. Of particular concern is the financing gap for enterprises that have a high potential for future growth and, possibly, for increasing overall productivity and creating new employment (OECD, 2017). These firms often suffer from financing constraints, which limit their growth and threaten their survival (Brown and Earle, 2015; Block *et al.*, 2016). The basic question from a policy perspective is hence how a financial environment can be created allowing financiers to make more financing available as challenges, such as the

Table 1: The loan and equity gap.

Averages in % of GDP	US	FR	D	NL	PL	RO
Loan gap	1.6	4.3	4.9	11.2	9.9	2.6
Equity gap	1.2	2.6	2.6	2.3	8.9	8.9
Financing gap	2.8	6.9	7.3	13.5	18.8	11.5

Note: Own calculations based on Lopez de Silanes *et al.* (2015).

above-mentioned asymmetric information, would be mitigated (IFC, 2017). The financing gap can be divided into the loan gap and the equity gap. The gap varies of course from one country to another, and for some countries we could even wonder if a gap exists *überhaupt* (e.g., Burger and Udell, 1992). Worldwide, the total loan gap — defined as the difference between demand and supply of loans to enterprises — is estimated in the range of US $5.2 trillion (IFC, 2017). The equity gap — defined as the difference without the amount of money that investors will wish to hold in equities and the amount that companies will need to fund growth — is even estimated at US $12 trillion (McKinsey, 2011). These estimates should of course be interpreted with the biggest caution. Focusing on Europe, in most countries the loan gap is more important than the equity gap (Table 1).

2.2. *The loan gap*

Loan finance is the most important source of external financing for most European enterprises. Although we live in a financial environment with a high profile given to capital markets and venture capital, the fact is that 70% of enterprises are still financed through traditional bank loans (Aernoudt, 2017a). Roughly 80–90% of a firm's start-up capital is made up in equal parts of owner equity and bank debt. Therefore, they are very sensitive to changes in bank lending conditions (Robb *et al.*, 2014). The enterprise credit market is characterized by major market failures such as the above-mentioned information asymmetries, high transaction costs for small-scale lending, high concentration in the banking sector as shown by the Herfindahl index, overregulation and high-risk perception. All these elements mean that despite the liquid markets, promising starters and other enterprises cannot always find sufficient credits on the market to finance their projects. The refusal to grant such a loan is, in many cases, a major impediment to the creation of a company and/or the financing of an investment.

The first, necessary but not only, condition to obtain a loan is to prove that you are able to repay. As common sense states it: in order to get a loan, you have to prove you don't need it. Every bank has set up a credit-scoring department in order to estimate, based on complicated models and mainly on historical data, the default ratio (DR) for each (potential) borrower. Depending upon the banks' strategy, if the expected DR goes beyond the bank's target, the loan is refused. Given the low credit margins, banks cannot permit having huge losses on their credit portfolio. Sticking to the "you never know" principle, and arguing that money lent comes from the savings of accountholders, banks are reluctant to grant loans unless sufficient collateral is provided. Therefore, credits on notoriety — this means credits without any request for collateral — are commonly limited to 25% of own funds. As most of the credit requests don't respect that ratio of financial independence, banks want to reduce the loss given default (LGD) by requesting collateral. Even if banks consider that the projects are viable and should, if all goes well, generate sufficient repayment capacity, lack of recognized collateral is often the biggest problem facing enterprises, and in particular start-up companies. No wonder that surveys report that the majority of respondent firms indicate "insufficient collateral" as the main reason for the financial constraints they are experiencing (European commission, SAFE, 2014).

This tendency has even increased due to the Basel regulations. Collateral leads, in Basel jargon, to a haircut. This means the more collateral the bank has on its credit portfolio, the less capital is required. Indeed, the higher the collateral, the lower the LGD and hence the lower the capital requirements. As collateralized loan represents less risk concerning the recovery of the outstanding loan in case of default, less equity has to be reserved by the financial institution. Surveys indeed indicate that the Basel regulations led to a higher request for collateral, in some cases to excessive collateral requirements (Aernoudt, 2017a). We could summarize stating that information asymmetry leads to high collateral requirements and this process has been intensified by the Basel regulations. In answer to this market failure, credit guarantee schemes (CGSs) are the most common form of government intervention. Such a scheme provides third-party credit risk mitigation to lenders with the objective of increasing access to credit for enterprises. Providing through the CGSs a guarantee to the bank might serve as a mechanism mitigating information asymmetries and thus solving the credit-rationing problem. This risk mitigation happens through the absorption of a portion of the lender's losses on the loans made to enterprises in case of default.

2.3. *The equity gap*

Guarantees have always been considered as an instrument that reduces the amount of losses for credit lenders in case of default. "Risk-capitalists" — the continental cultural translation of venture capitalists — are characterized by the fact that they take risks, so it is argued that credit and venture capitalists are two different worlds, with different actions and different tools, fulfilling different needs and appealing for different policies. Therefore, government policy in the field of equity is mainly linked to regulation issues in order to cope with the fragmented capital market such as the capital market union action plan (European Commission, 2017; AFME, 2017). Besides, different investment schemes have been developed such as direct investment schemes, co-investment schemes and fund of fund approaches, with not all types of intervention being as efficient (Alperovych *et al.*, 2015, 2018; Standaert, 2019). These schemes, involving a lot of public money, have proven to be relatively effective in coping with the small equity gap and this gap in Europe narrowed compared to the US (EIF, 2018). In other words, start-ups looking for equity financing may find it easier to get this financing today than a decade ago. However, one of the main problems in Europe linked to equity is the relatively small size of the funds. Often public investment into funds — the so-called fund of fund approach — does not lead to more private funding and there is even a danger of crowding out (Oxford, 2015).

The global equity gap is estimated at 1.25% of GDP in the US against 3% of GDP in the EU (data 2014, in Lopez de Silanes, 2015). But particularly in later stage financing, the US has a clear advantage over Europe, as available equity capital in the US is 21 times that in the EU (AFME, 2017).

The structural weakness of the European venture capital market relates mainly to the small average fund size. Funds in the US have an average size of US $135 million compared to €60 million in Europe. Therefore, the percentage of growth stage deals is significantly higher in the US than in Europe. As funds are smaller and less growth-oriented, it is very hard to find tickets of €15–25 million for later round financing (technically C and D rounds). Therefore, the later stage equity gap is the biggest financial obstacle for start-ups to scale up in Europe (European Commission Survey, 2016) with 90% of the fast-growing companies having problems financing their growth in Europe (Oxford Research, 2015).

Due to this scale-up gap, Europe is not reaping the benefits of the most promising young companies it has nurtured, once they pass the seed, start-up and early expansion stage and embark on an ambitious, global growth path for which they seek higher investment ticket sizes (EIF, 2018). In the process, Europe loses much needed entrepreneurship, technological know-how and jobs. To illustrate, during the period 2003–2015, on average 44% of the venture capital companies backed by European publicly co-financed venture capital funds, were acquired by non-European buyers, in particular from the US. Examples include German robot manufacturer Kuka, Finnish gaming developer Supercell, French digital performance display advertiser Criteo, the Belgian data governance company Collibra and the Estonian global internet giant Skype (EIF, 2018). And how contradictory it might seem at first glance, one of the best ways to cope with this scale-up gap is by using the guarantee instrument in order to stimulate risk-averting investors to into equity funds (Aernoudt, 2017b). As we will see, guarantees can alter the risk-return relationship both for the risk-averting investors as for the risk-taking equity investor. In the next section we will illustrate how guarantees can cope with the loan gap. In a final section, we will analyze how public guarantees can cope with the equity gap.

3. Guarantee Policy and the Loan Gap

3.1. *Collateral as main obstacle*

As shown by the pecking order theory (Myers, 1984), the preferred option entrepreneurs take is to see if they can finance the project through their own resources, generated by earlier savings or cash flow in previous years. They know their business better than anyone else, and they avoid administrative procedures and costs otherwise necessary to convince an external person to lend or to invest money in the company. It is only when self-financing is unavailable that the company turns to external financiers and bankers in the first place. Paradoxically, bankers use the same information asymmetry argument in order to request collateral. Lack of collateral would not be a problem if lenders were able to access accurately borrowers' net present value. However, banks feel that they cannot do so (Cressy, 2000). Therefore, they require collateral and, if possible, personal commitment from the entrepreneur arguing that a banker cannot believe in a project if the entrepreneur does not believe in it him- or herself.

Banks provide liquidity, while the entrepreneur is bearing the risk associated with default through the liens on their personal assets (Robb *et al.*, 2014). Moreover, loans are dumb money. Bankers do not interfere in the business as long as the credit is paid back at the agreed deadline. This implies that they don't have the same insight as, for instance, venture capitalist or business angels who are actively involved or at least have a seat in the board. Both arguments — information asymmetry and lack of involvement — imply that banks want to limit their loss in case of default by obtaining as much in guarantees as possible. Guarantees often far exceed the amount of credits.

Firms are not eager to pledge their collateral because of the risk of losing the collateral in case of default and also because of the costs and the red tape involved. Entrepreneurs — or their family — are often reluctant to offer personal guarantees as, *de facto*, the "limited responsibility" that characterizes many company structures and that often was the main reason to set up a separate legal entity is hollowed out. But even if entrepreneurs do commit their own belongings, often this is not enough to guarantee the amounts of credits in a way that the LGD for the bank is close to zero.

3.2. *Loan guarantee scheme (LGS)*

Loan guarantee mechanisms are intended to address this market failure by reducing the financial loss suffered by the financial institutions in the case of defaults. Therefore, most advanced economies have established publicly

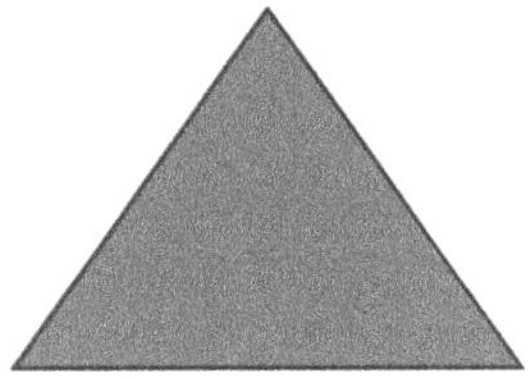

Figure 1: The three parties involved in LGS.

funded guarantee schemes to help enterprises overcome their financing difficulties that are due to imperfect or incomplete financial markets. Relevant players in the guarantee mechanism include the enterprise that demands credit, the financial institution that performs an assessment of the borrower's creditworthiness and the government through the LGS that covers a share of the loan with its guarantee (Figure 1).

In order to avoid confusion, and in contradiction to what some literature suggests (OECD, 2017), a loan guarantee doesn't reduce the risk of default (DR), but impacts the LGD for the beneficiary of the guarantee. So the guarantee instrument is not a risk-reducing instrument but rather a risk-sharing instrument. The loan guarantee implies that, should the lender default, the CGS will reimburse a predefined share of the outstanding loan. One of the major risks linked to the system of LGSs is the moral hazard. Although this cannot be completely avoided, setting the coverage at the optimal level and fine-tuning the risk sharing might reduce its impact.

3.2.1. *The share covered*

A 100% coverage rate would of course lead to great moral hazard, as the beneficiary of the guarantee has nothing to lose, literally. Therefore, in order to reduce the risk of moral hazard, the lender should always bear part of the risk. A public guarantee scheme should hence always be a partial credit guarantee. A too high coverage rate does increase the strategic default option of borrowers and reduces banks' incentives to properly assess and monitor risk. On the other hand, a coverage rate below 50% reduces banks' incentives to participate in the guarantee program, especially because loan administration costs can be quite high (OECD, 2011). In principle, the guarantee coverage ratio should not be lower than 50% (World Bank, 2017). Each system has to find its optimal coverage rate. Case-based analysis suggests that coverage rates should generally be between 60% and 80% (Levitsky, 1997; Honohan, 2010). Rates in this interval are high enough to encourage lender participation and yet low enough to limit moral hazard. From the 76 schemes studied by the World Bank, the median coverage rate was 80% (World Bank, 2015). This is line with earlier research finding (Beck, 2010). This median hides the fact that that the coverage rate varies widely between 14% and goes as high as 100% (AECM, 2018).

3.2.2. *Risk-sharing models*

Different risk-sharing models are possible: the *pari passu* model, where lender and guarantor each absorb a fixed fraction of any loss, and the first-loss, where the guarantor pays out on all the loss up to some fixed fraction of the total loan obligation (Honohan, 2010). Lending should of course never be based on access to collateral only without a decent risk analysis in order to determine the payback capacity. But the risk sharing between the lender and the guarantor should alter the credit analysis at lenders' level enabling viable projects to get financed. In order to reduce adverse selection, the government can cap the amount of losses. In the UK for instance, the Small Firms Loan Guarantee (SFLG), which foresaw a 75% coverage of the outstanding balance of all loans that defaulted, has been replaced by the Enterprise Finance Guarantee (EFG) whereby the government puts a cap of 9.75% of the lending amount on default payments. Once the cap is exceeded, the government bears no risk and any further risk falls entirely onto the lender.

One could argue that the use of collateral at borrowers' level may impose opportunity costs on borrowers, affect business performance and increase the risk of default, to the extent that it ties up assets that might be put to more productive use (Berger *et al.*, 2011). However, completely exempting the entrepreneur from collateral could lead to a kind of agency problem whereby in bad times the entrepreneur has little incentive to do the utmost in order to avoid default. The provision of assets that can be turned to the bank and cashed in if default occurs should prevent the entrepreneur no longer being involved in the risk sharing and become a kind of free-rider only benefitting from good performance. In that case, moral hazard at borrowers' level might occur as the entrepreneur has only a stake in success, not in failure, which could lead to risk-taking behavior. There is indeed some evidence that loan guarantees could be associated with increased default risk of beneficiary firms (OECD, 2017). But the justification of spending or even losing public money, is that, through guarantee schemes, viable projects will be financed by loans, thus creating employment and contributing to economic growth — in other words, assisting in the creation of additional economic wealth. Most studies on the effectiveness of loan guarantees find that these schemes indeed have a positive effect on beneficiaries' growth and performance (Bertoni *et al.*, 2017). Moreover, research shows that in contradiction to common knowledge, government guarantees do not always induce financial institutions to take excessive risk (Allen *et al.*, 2015).

Finally, studies show that the guarantee might affect the cost of borrowing. As a loan guarantee directly reduces the probability of loss for lenders, it reduces the borrowing costs (Soumaré *et al.*, 2016). An analysis of the UK small LGS found that the higher the incidence of publicly guaranteed debt over the total amount of outstanding loans, the lower the spread (Ughetto *et al.*, 2017).

3.3. *Policy recommendations*

In the European Union, most countries and regions have set up guarantee schemes.[1] At European level, the EU can guarantee or counter-guarantee guarantee schemes. An example is the COSME Loan Guarantee Facility, which supports European enterprises' growth and research and innovation. The facility is part of the Programme for the Competitiveness of Enterprises and Small- and Medium-sized Enterprises (SMEs) 2014–2020 (COSME), an initiative launched by the European Commission, managed

[1] It is estimated that there are 3 million outstanding guarantee contracts covering a total credit amount of €125 billion (AECM, 2018). For a comprehensive overview on the use of guarantee schemes for SME, see Chatzouz *et al.* (2017).

by EIF and implemented through a network of financial institutions. Through COSME guarantees and counter-guarantees, including securitization of SME debt finance, portfolios are offered to selected financial intermediaries (e.g., guarantee institutions, banks, leasing companies, etc.) to help them provide more loans.[2] By sharing the risk, COSME aims to facilitate access to debt finance for companies who might otherwise have difficulty in obtaining credits. The guarantee instrument is included in the EU Invest program for the programming period (2021–2027).[3] Besides, within the framework of regional policy, regions use the European structural allocations in order to reinforce their mutual, local and regional guarantee schemes.

Most studies show a positive causal relationship between the public guarantee and the debt leverage of guaranteed firms (Zecchini, 2007). Based on an analysis of 23 countries having a loan guarantee system, the OECD concludes the there is evidence that such schemes are positive for the firms' access to debt finance (OECD, 2017). Therefore, a well-conceived public guarantee system should be part of the financial instruments at national and/or regional level. In order to be efficient and sustainable, certain criteria have to be fulfilled:

1. There should be no involvement of the guarantee fund at the project level. The procedure for request and approval should be automatic at the bankers' level. This means that no separate request should be sent from the intermediate bank to the guarantee system. A framework agreement should clarify the relations between the bank and the guarantee scheme, setting out the modalities to be applied to each individual project. Such a system operates in Europe through the EIF and in countries such as Belgium (Flanders), Germany, the Netherlands and France.

---

[2]COSME is the EU programme for the Competitiveness of Enterprises and SMEs, running from 2014 to 2020, with a budget of €2.3 billion. COSME supports SMEs in the following areas: Facilitating access to finance, supporting internationalization and access to markets, creating an environment favorable to competitiveness and encouraging an entrepreneurial culture.

[3]Proposal for a Regulation of the European Parliament and of the Council, establishing the InvestEU Programme, COM/2018/439 final.

2. Legal certainty should prevail at the level of the financial institution, making involvement of a discretionary external decision authority superfluous. Banks would inform their customers immediately about the credit decision, knowing that they can in turn appeal to the guarantee scheme, provided a number of conditions are fulfilled. In Germany and the Netherlands, for instance, the bank knows that they can draw from the public guarantees in an automatic way as long as the amount of the guarantee request does not exceed 50% of the credit granted to the company. For the remaining 50%, banks can appeal to traditional guarantees, such as mortgages or pledges, or grant the credit without supplementary guarantees.
3. To reduce moral hazard on the parts of both lenders and SMEs, credit risk must be shared appropriately among the three parties involved: government, lenders and enterprises. Sharing credit risk ensures that the right incentives are in place so that default and claim rates are kept as low as possible. The guarantee coverage ratio should be high enough to induce lenders to participate. At the same time, the ratio should allow lenders to assume a meaningful share of credit risk.
4. Securitization must be foreseen and obtaining the public guarantee should have an impact on the reserve obligation of the portfolio at bankers' level (Trujillo, 2011).
5. Special attention should be given to those parts of the market where market failure is the most obvious, such as start-ups, involving a higher coverage rate or even grace periods. In Germany for instance, 60% of public guarantees are oriented toward start-ups. In Brussels, the public guarantee fund can cover up to 80% for start-ups.

4. Guarantees and the Equity Gap

4.1. *Equity guarantee systems*

Putting aside MBO-type funds, most equity funds struggle to raise sufficient capital, especially in Europe (AFME, 2017). In most EU countries, except for UK and the Netherlands, pension funds and insurance companies hardly invest in venture capital funds. Regulation and their risk-averse character imply that only a very small part of their abundant investment capacity finds the way to the venture business. Therefore, many fund managers struggle to attract sufficient investors. This, and the market fragmentation, explains why the average size of European funds is far below their American counterparts. This has different implications. First, return is lower as return is positively correlated with scale. Second, this implies difficulties for the funds to finance follow-on investments. And third, the small size of European funds makes it difficult to find experienced fund managers who are looking for great carried interests. In an attempt to cope with this situation and to break the vicious circle of small funds, low return and less-experienced managers, both at European level and at Member state level, public money has been massively injected into the equity markets mainly into fund-of-fund structures. While 10 years ago 9% of the European venture capital market was public, following estimations, 39% is public today (Aernoudt, 2017b) and government intervenes, on average, in 42.2% of venture capital investments in Europe (Alperovych, 2018). This leads to an increased danger of crowding-out. Therefore, investments schemes should be complemented with new types of intervention based on the guarantee principle.

4.2. *Typology of equity guarantee schemes*

There are two ways to use public guarantees in order to stimulate venture capital. The first is to cover losses that the venture capital fund may realize on its investments. The second is to guarantee the investors investing into the funds. The first way means that fund managers can claim back part of the losses for certain types of investments. This approach has been experimented in different countries (e.g., Denmark, Voekstfonden; Finland, Finnish Guarantee board; France, Banque Publique d'Investissement (BPI) France; Flanders, (Participatiemaatschappij Vlaanderen (PMV)). Most of those schemes foresaw a guaranteeing of 50% of the losses. The adverse selection argument — fund managers used the guarantee for the weakest projects with a big default as result — was so strong that the cost of the schemes largely exceeded the benefits (Avnimelech and Teubal, 2006; Gilson, 2003). Therefore, almost all concerned Member States abolished this way of guaranteeing. This experience led to a hangover in many countries and a profound reluctance to further experiment with the guarantee instrument linked to equity.

Table 2: Asset versus liability based.

Guarantee On	Asset	Liabilities
Beneficiary	(Risk-taking) Investor in projects	(Risk-averse) Investor in venture capital funds
Trigger event	Bankruptcy of investee	Bankruptcy of fund
Guarantee payment	*Pari passu*	Government comes first
Default	Very high due to adverse selection argument	Close to zero due to diversification, liability-based, portfolio based
Used by	Netherlands, Belgium (Flanders), France, Denmark, (in most countries abolished)	US (different attempts to copy remained unsuccessful until now)
Leverage on return	No, on the contrary adverse selection argument	Yes, at risk taking investor level
Value for public money	Costs mostly exceed benefits	Scheme runs at zero cost, high value for public money

These experiments should however not lead to the conclusion that guarantees are incompatible with venture capital. In order to overcome the adverse selection, one should work at the portfolio level only. Such a portfolio approach does not fully avoid the adverse selection argument as guaranteed funds will go to the more risky projects as the partly default coverage reduces the risk-alertness of risk capitalist. So a subtler second way combines a portfolio approach with a guarantee on investors' side into the fund rather than on investors' side in to the investee, so not on an asset-based but on a liability-based approach (Table 2).

We can summarize the two approaches, as given in Table 2.

Given the bad value for public money for the asset-based system, we will focus on the liabilities-based approach and explain how it functions in the US and how it could function in Europe.

4.3. *The US equity guarantee scheme*

A classic misunderstanding is that the venture capital scene in the US is of a purely private nature without public involvement. This is, however, not the case and a large part of the US equity market is publicly driven.

The SBIC program, which stands for Small Business Investment Company, aims to increase the availability of long-term equity and loan financing for enterprises. It is the only program of support for venture capital at the US federal level (though many states have their own programs; mostly investment-type programs). The SBIC program launched in 1958 was substantially reformed in 1992 and 2014.[4]

SBICs, licensed and regulated by the small business administration (SBA), are privately owned and managed investment firms that use their own capital, plus funds obtained at favorable rates with an SBA guarantee. Virtually all SBICs are profit-motivated businesses. They provide equity capital, long-term loans (limited to maximum 10% of the funds raised), debt-equity investments and management assistance to qualifying small businesses. The majority of SBIC investments in SMEs are in the range of $250,000 to $4 million, an investment size usually considered too small by US venture capital companies and giving room for public intervention.

The basic characteristic of the system is leverage. In SBIC jargon, this means that SBICs can raise funding on public capital markets by using a guarantee from the SBA or by selling securities directly to the SBA. The SBA never buys SBIC securities itself — it only guarantees them. To obtain leverage and in order to attract another type of investors to the VC-world — the risk-averters — regular SBICs sell debenture securities guaranteed by the SBA. The effect of the leverage is to reduce the average cost of capital for the SBIC's, in the sense that the equity returns are geared upward if the company's investment portfolio as a whole makes a return above the interest cost (Aernoudt, 2017b). Therefore, a licensed fund can more easily attract money from private investors. In practice, a fund to be created requests a license based on a budgeted commitment of private money. Only thereafter do the fund managers start raising equity using leverage on return as a main incentive for private investors to invest into the new fund. Following SBA rules, a fund manager has to prove within 2 years

[4] The Small Business Investment Company program initially had problematic features, with numerous counterproductive requirements, and then implemented inconsistently, which led to incompetent and even outright crooked funds (Lerner, 2012; for a description of the different reforms, see Aernoudt, 2017a).

after the approval of the conditional license that the equity money has been fully committed.

In the case of SBA-guaranteed debentures — the only type left after the 2014 reform — pools are formed, and SBA-guaranteed participation certificates are sold to investors through a public offering. Under current procedures, the debentures have a term of 5 or 10 years, providing for semi-annual interest payments and a lump sum principal payment at maturity. The interest rate is equal to that of 10-year Treasury Bonds, plus an average of 70 basic points. This is a relatively low cost of capital. An SBIC may leverage up to 300% of its private capital and the maximum leverage is $150 million. Since the cost of capital is far below the risk-adjusted rate of return for the US venture capital market, funds do request the maximum amount of debt available leading to a high debt-to-asset ratio (Kaplan and Schoar, 2005). Concretely, $50 million may lead to a $200 million fund. Based on the sound management rules — a fund should never invest more that 10% in one investee — this permits an average fund to invest $20 million in one venture, exactly the average amount scale-ups are looking for.

4.3.1. *SBIC, Tesla and Apple*

Potential beneficiaries of the SBIC system prepare an 80-page memorandum. The due diligence by the SBA takes 4–7 months, and the SBA has a significant rejection rate for applications. The due diligence includes a clearance based on fingerprints by the FBI. Despite this heavy procedure, around 400 licensed SBICs have made over $25 billion of investments in over 100,000 enterprises, including Tesla, Apple Computer, Federal Express, Intel, Cray Research and America Online. These examples show that the SBICs are mainly financing enterprises with scale-up potential and scale-up ambitions. The SBIC Program is designed to operate on a "zero-subsidy" basis, meaning no tax dollars are used to fund the program. The SBA estimates the cost per job created at $1,000 (it was much higher in the past). For every $1 appropriated, around $200 was invested. The SBA also believes that the net cost to the taxpayer of the SBIC program (taking account of increased tax revenues, etc.) is negative, i.e., the program pays for itself. Therefore, it considers the SBIC as a "zero cost" program. Fees (examination fees, commitment fees, disbursement fees) are adapted if needed to assure that the program remains break-even.

4.3.2. *Equity culture*

The SBIC programme shows that US is still taking the lead in the venture capital world. At the same time, it deconstructs the myth that the venture capital business in the US is a privately driven business. With the SBIC, the government played and still plays a major role in the evolution of the equity culture in the US.[5] Moreover, academic research has shown that equity-holders respond positively to riskier investments when funds are distressed. The agency costs linked to debt financing through the SBIC system have to be neutralized by putting in place mechanisms to constrain managerial investment policy (Denes, 2017). Finally, the SBIC program became a policy tool that can orientate investors toward underserved and rural communities. Venture capital is hence used as a policy tool both for venture and for regional development.

4.4. *The EU equity guarantee scheme*

The European way of combining risk capital and guarantees slightly differs from the American way. Indeed, risk aversion in Europe is higher. Therefore, public investment schemes have been set up at the regional, national and European level in order to increase the availability of risk capital (Standaert, 2019). This approach was effective as it increased the availability of risk capital. But at the same time, there is a risk of crowding-out: as the risk capital sector became too public, private investors became — even more — reluctant to invest into European funds. This way the investment schemes did not succeed in coping with the scale-up gap (Aernoudt, 2017b). Therefore, 60 years after the launch of the SBIC program in the US, an SBIC-inspired program is being launched in the EU, called European Scale-Up Action for Risk Capital (ESCALAR). It is meant to double the investment capacity of venture capital funds active in

[5]To show its importance: between 1958 and 1969, the SBIC program invested 3 billion dollars, or three times the total private venture capital investments these years (Lerner, 2002).

scale-up financing in Europe through quasi-equity financing, financed by private risk-averse investors, such as pension funds, but guaranteed under European Fund for Strategic Investments (EFSI).

The ESCALAR mechanism will activate investments from private, risk-averse investors at European level in order to cope with the later stage equity gap and in this way contribute to the creation of jobs and growth in Europe. The privately owned and managed investment funds (ESCALAR funds) will have to go through a due diligence process, realized by the EIF, and have to raise their own equity (which can be partly public) over a certain amount of time. If they are successful in raising the capital, they receive additional funds (as quasi-equity) borrowed through issuing a bond by the EIB, based on the collective demand of different ESCALAR funds. The bond is guaranteed by the EU (through EFSI) and could be subscribed by risk-averse private investors. Thanks to these features, scale-up financing is being improved without further aggravating the public character of the European VC-landscape.[6] In full conformity with the 3rd pillar of EFSI, ESCALAR will contribute to removing one of the major bottlenecks for scale-up investment in Europe. Once the investments are realized and the fund begins to wind down, the ESCALAR fund will repay its EFSI-guaranteed quasi-equity and share the profits from its investments with the private investors who backed the fund. The mechanism requires that the ESCALAR funds focus on scale-up investments, mainly in Europe (Figure 2).

4.5. *Policy recommendations*

Despite the antagonism at first sight, the guarantee instrument can be a good value for a public money instrument to stimulate the availability of venture capital. The guarantee for the risk-averse investor should allow pension funds and insurance companies to invest in the risk-capital sector. Return is rather low but the investment is risk-less and can offer a nice investment diversification opportunity for the portfolio of the risk-averter.

[6]The pilot phase (2019–2020), financed by the EIB without issuing specific bonds but guaranteed by EFSI, should permit recalibration of the parameters for the programming period (2021–2027).

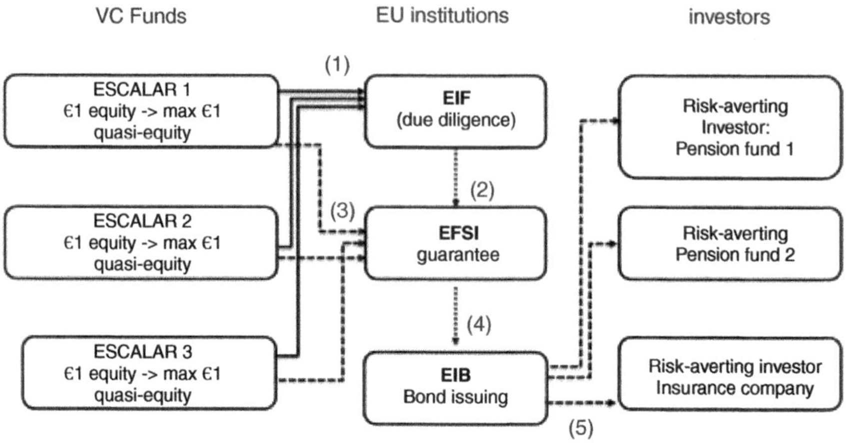

Figure 2: The working of ESCALAR.

Notes: (1) Funds ask agreement for recognition (2) EIF preselects (3) Funds drawn private money (4) EFSI asks EIB to issue a bond; after pilot phase (5) EIB collects money through risk-averting investors.

Given the huge amount they manage, this can bring a bull of oxygen to the risk-capital sector, especially for the later financing rounds looking for big ticket. For the non-guaranteed equity investors, the risk of being subordinated to debt (US case) or quasi-equity (EU case) financing is largely compensated by leverage on return given the relatively cheap cost of the guaranteed financing for the fund. The better risk–return relationship should make it easier to raise equity. For the fund managers, this leverage on return could increase the carried interest. And finally — and that's what this is about — scale-ups would find it easier to obtain scale-up financing.

Guaranteeing venture capital could hence be very good value for public money policy. In order to be efficient, the following criteria have to be fulfilled:

1. The guarantee should never be on project level but always on portfolio level.
2. The guarantee should always be on the money-raising side and not on the asset side as in the latter case the adverse selection argument implies that the taxpayers' cost of the program exceeds the benefits.
3. The scheme should make a clear distinction between the non-guaranteed equity investors and the guaranteed risk-averse investors and a ratio

between both has to be fixed *ex ante*. This ratio could go from 1 (the EU case) up to 3 (the US case) or even to 4 (the US case in distressed areas)

4. As the system is built on leverage on return, focus should be given to well-managed funds only. Therefore, a thorough due diligence process should be part of such a scheme. Moreover, the focus on well-managed funds, the portfolio approach and the less risky scale-up phase should allow a mature guarantee scheme to run at zero cost for the taxpayer.
5. Government involvement should be hands-off with no seats on the board of the funds and no involvement in the investment decisions on project level.

5. By Way of Conclusion

The guarantee instrument, despite its obsolete and bureaucratic image, is still a very valid instrument in order to cope with the financing gap. Guaranteeing as an answer to the information asymmetry problem is however always linked with moral hazard issues and danger of adverse selection. Therefore, the implementation of guarantee schemes, as a tool to facilitate access to long-term financing, should be conceived in an equilibrated way whereby all parties are involved, or better committed. Coverage for lending should be between 50% and 80%. For equity, leverage should be the basis and adverse selection should be avoided by developing market-conform risk-return relationships both for the equity investors as for the risk-averse, guaranteed investors. Finally, guarantee systems can only work when the government is hands-off and decisions are portfolio-based without government interference at the project level.

That said, the guarantee instrument should not be considered as obsolete. Guarantees can be used in the current financial context to cope with the loan gap and even give a positive impetus to the use of venture capital as the American SBIC system shows. Permanent evaluation and monitoring of the system is needed in order to (re)calibrate the parameters. As preliminary research suggests that guarantee schemes can lead to increased default probability, one should wonder if this is a real problem or rather a way of legitimating policy intervention targeting riskier enterprises with a high growth potential.

6. Suggestions for Further Research

Although a lot of research was done in the field of guarantees, there remain many open research questions. The impact of loan guarantees on the banking decision policy, and more generally on the stability of the banking system, remains an open and hugely relevant research issue. As a corollary, more empirical research should be done on the adverse selection argument and the impact of guarantees on DR and on the performance and on the productivity of guaranteed enterprises. Finally, regular evaluation is needed and should include the assessment of net economic benefits of LGS activities, in particular, the identification of economic, as opposed to financial, additionality (OECD, 2017).

On guarantee on equity, almost all research, and especially that in Europe, is focused on asset-based guarantee systems, while the liability-based guarantee approach remains a highly untapped research topic. Research is this field could be focused notably on the impact of the equity revenue kicker on the equity investors' eagerness to invest into funds, the impact of quasi-equity funding at the fund level on the fund managers' investment policy into investees and the willingness of risk-averse investors to invest in funds when their investment is partly or totally guaranteed

References

AECM (2018) Facts and figures, Statistic overview, www.aecm.eu.

AFME (2017) The Shortage of Risk Capital for Europe's High Growth Businesses, www.afme.eu.

Aernoudt R. (2017a) *Financial Management Applied*, Intersentia, Cambridge, Antwerp, New York.

Aernoudt R. (2017b) Scale-Up gap, the scale-up gap: and how to address it, *Venture Capital*, 19(4), 361–372.

Aernoudt R. and Van Rompaey M. (2015) *Entrepreneurship, a Way of Life*, Intersentia, Cambridge, Antwerp, New York.

Allen F., Carletti E., Goldstein I., and Leonello A. (2015) Moral hazard and government guarantees in the banking industry. *Journal of Financial Regulation*, 1(1), 30–50.

Alperovych Y., Quas A., and Standaert T. (2018) Direct and indirect government venture capital investments in Europe. *Economics Bulletin*, 38(2), 1219–1230.

Alperovych Y., Hübner G., and Lobet F. (2015) How does governmental versus private venture capital backing affect a firm's efficiency? Evidence from Belgium. *Journal of Business Venture*, 30, 508–525.

Avnimelech G. and Teubel M. (2006) Creating venture capital industries that co-evolve with high tech: insights from an extended industry life cycle perspective of the israeli experience. *Research Policy*, 35, 1477–1498.

Beck T., Klapper L. F., and Mendoza J. C. (2010) The typology of partial credit guarantee funds around the world. *Journal of Financial Stability*, 6(1), 10–25.

Berger A. and Udell G. (1992) Some evidence on the empirical significance of credit rationing. *Journal of Political Economy*, 100, 1046–2177.

Bertoni F., Martí J., and Reverte C. (2017) The impact of government-supported participative loans on employment growth in entrepreneurial ventures. SSRN.

Block J. H., Colombo M. G., Cumming D. J., and Vismara S. (2016) New players in entrepreneurial finance and why they are here. *Small Business Economics*. doi: 10.1007/s11187-016-9826-6.

Brown J. D. and Earle J. S. (2015) Finance and growth at the firm level: evidenced from SBA loans. IZA Working Paper No. 9267.

Chatzouz M., Gereben Á., Lang F., and Torfs W. (2017) Credit guarantee schemes for SME lending in Western Europe. EIB Working Papers 2017/02, European Investment Bank (EIB).

Cressy R. (2000) Government guarantee schemes in Europe: Who has them? Who pays? Who gains? In B. Green (ed.), *Risk Behaviour and Risk Management in Business Life*, Springer, 247–255.

Denes, M. (2017) When do firms risk shift? Evidence from venture capital. Working Paper. https://papers.ssrn.com/sol3/papers.cfm?abstract_id=2875882.

Doran A. and Levitsky J. (1997) *Credit Guarantee Schemes for Small Business Lending: A Global Perspective*. Graham Bannock and Partners Ltd., London.

European Commission (2017) Communication from the commission on the mid-term review of *the capital markets union action plan*, Brussels, COM (2017), 292 final.

European Commission (2016) Report on the public consultation under the Start-Up Initiative, Brussels.

European Commission (2014) ECB-EC Survey on the Access to Finance of Enterprises (SAFE). *European Commission*, DG Enterprise and Industry, Brussels.

EIF (2018) Equity flagship: Towards a European risk capital platform for starting-up and scaling up Europe's future innovation leaders.

Ferrando A. and Mulier K. (2017) The Real Effects of Credit Constraints: Evidence from Discouraged Borrowers. doi: http://dx.doi.org/10.2139/ssrn.2518980.

Gilson R. J. (2003) Engineering a venture capital market: Lessons from the American experience. *Stanford Law Review*, 55(4), 1067–1103.

Honohan P. (2010) Partial credit guarantees: Principles and practice. *Journal of Financial Stability*, 6(1), 1–9.

IFC (2015) Enterprise finance gap database. *International Finance Corporation*, Washington, DC. http://www.smefinanceforum.org/data-sites/ifc-enterprise-finance-gap.

IFC (2017) MSME finance gap, assessment of the shortfalls and opportunities in financing micro, small and medium enterprises in emerging markets.

Kaplan S. and Schoar A. (2005) Private equity performance: Returns, persistence and capital flows. *The Journal of Finance*, 60, 1791–1823.

Lerner J. (2002) When bureaucrats meet entrepreneurs: the design of effective "public venture capital" programmes. *Economic Journal*, doi: https://doi.org/10.1111/1468-0297.00684.

Lerner J. (2012) Boulevard of broken dreams: Why public efforts to boost entrepreneurship and venture capital have failed — and what to do about it, The Kauffman Foundation Series on *Innovation and Entrepreneurship*.

Lopez de Silanes F., McCahery J., Schoemaeker D., and Stanisic D. (2015) Estimating the financing gap, Duisenberg School of Finance, 1(3).

McKinsey (2011) the emerging equity gap: Growth and stability in the new investor landscape, www.mckinsey.com/industries/private-equity-and-principal-investors/our-insights/emerging-equity-gap.

Myers S. C. and Majluf N. S. (1984) "Corporate financing and investment decisions when firms have information that investors do not have". *Journal of Financial Economics*, 13(2), 187–221. doi: 10.1016/0304-405X(84)90023-0.

OECD (2017) Evaluating Publicly Supported Credit Guarantee Programmes for SMEs.

OECD (2011) Discussion Paper on Credit Guarantee Schemes.

Oxford Research (2015) Assessing the potential for EU investment in venture capital and other risk capital fund of funds. *Centre for Strategy & Evaluation Services*, European Commission, Brussels.

Robb A. M. and Robinson D. T. (2014) The capital decisions of new firms. *Entrepreneurial Finance and Innovation*, 27(1), 153–179.

Soumaré I. and Lai V. (2016) An analysis of government loan guarantees and direct investment through public-private partnerships. *Economic Modeling*, Elsevier, 59(C), 508–519.

Stiglitz J. and Weiss A. (1981) Credit rationing in markets with imperfect information. *American Economic Review*, 71, 93–410.

Standaert T. (2019) To the rescue: Government intervention in venture capital markets. In *New Frontiers in Entrepreneurial Finance*, World Scientific Publishing.

The World Bank and FIRST Initiative (2015) *Principles for public credit guarantee schemes for SMEs.* World Bank Group, Washington, D.C.

Trujillo P. A., Briozzo A., and Cardone-Riportella C. (2011) What do basel capital accords mean for SMEs? Universidad Carlos III de Madrid, Departamento de Economía de la Empresa.

Ughetto E., Scellato G., and Cowling M. (2017) Cost of capital and public loan guarantees to small firms. *Small Business Economics*, Springer, 49, 319–377.

Zecchini S. and Ventura M. (2009) The impact of public guarantees on credit to SMEs. *Small Business Economics*, 32, 191–206.

Part 2

Fintech Revolution and Entrepreneurial Finance

Chapter 5

New Frontiers in Green Project Financing: Leveraging on the Crowd

Saman Adhami*

Vienna Graduate School of Finance

saman.adhami@vgsf.ac.at

Giancarlo Giudici†

School of Management, Politecnico di Milano

giancarlo.giudici@polimi.it

Huy Pham Nguyen Anh‡

School of Business and Management,
RMIT University (Vietnam)

huy.phamnguyenanh@rmit.edu.vn

*1, Welthandelsplatz, Vienna, 1020, Austria.

†4, Via Lambruschini, Milan, 20156, Italy; Ton Duc Thang University, Ho Chi Mihn City, Vietnam.

‡702, Nguyen Van Linh, Tan Hung, Quan 7, Ho Chi Minh City, 700000, Vietnam.

Abstract

Crowdfunding has become a viable alternative for the financing of sustainability-oriented projects; it allows initiators to collect funds for "green" initiatives and small investors to contribute to the reduction of carbon emissions by accessing investments that are normally open to large investors only. The role of alternative finance is crucial for the continued development of renewable energy projects, given the long-time horizon of such projects, their technological uncertainty and the strong dependence of cleantech investments on political or macroeconomic factors.

We study the determinants of the success of 423 "green" projects published on 27 European crowdfunding platforms specialized in renewable energy with the aim to find the determinants of fundraising success in a business that exhibits such peculiar features.

We find that, consistently with the hypothesis that pledgers are moved by both financial and intrinsic objectives, projects delivering some monetary or tangible benefit to the local community are more likely to reach their funding target. Moreover, we find that investors assign a significant value to being shareholders of "green" projects. On the contrary, we do not find a significant impact of local institutional and environmental factors.

1. Introduction

Alternative finance is an important source of capital for "green" projects (i.e., projects aimed at reducing carbon dioxide emissions through the production of renewable energy, larger energy efficiency and innovation in green technologies) in their quest to overcome the initial financing gap. It has been described by the literature as a primary research goal for the future (Bonzanini *et al.*, 2016; Lam and Law, 2016; Nielsen and Reisch, 2016; Vasileiadou *et al.*, 2016; Krupa and Harvey, 2017; Mazzucato and Semieniuk, 2018). Environmental resources are "public goods" (Baumol and Oates, 1988): consequently, professional investors are less inclined to invest in green projects as they can appropriate just a limited part of the potential benefits. This is why, on the one hand, public authorities typically grant incentives and feed-in tariffs to the producers of green energy, and, on the other hand, impose anti-pollution regulations. Yet the budget troubles and the capital shortage experienced by central governments and local authorities after the Global Financial Crisis, especially in Europe, created a serious threat to the development of green projects. According to the Global Investment Alliance,[1] in 2015 sustainability-themed investments fell in Europe to the lowest level in the decade and in 2016 the fall regarded world-wide investments. National governments in the EU are alleged to have created a booming cycle by initially granting strong support for renewables then rapidly rowing back as they feared about excessive expenses for subsidies and the rise in the price of electricity for traditional industries.[2] The persistently low price of oil also contributed to the reduced appeal of renewables.

Crowdfunding has emerged as an alternative and appealing financing source for both entrepreneurial and no-profit projects, as the volume of investments around the world boomed from virtually zero before 2010 to $34.4 billion in 2015.[3] According to Gerber *et al.* (2012) a number of benefits are expected by initiators of a crowdfunding campaign: fundraising, establishing relationships, receiving legitimacy, replicating successful experiences, and increasing awareness about crowdfunders' work through social media. A better access to customers, more press coverage, and greater interest from potential employees and outside funders are other expected benefits (Mollick and Kuppuswamy, 2014). All of these characteristics make crowdfunding a very valuable financing option for initiators of green projects. Indeed, a number of platforms specialized in green projects have emerged alongside generalist and well-known crowdfunding platforms such as Kickstarter, Indiegogo, Crowdcube, Lending Club and Funding Circle.

In this work, we aim at analyzing the determinants of the funding success of a sample of 423 green projects published on 27 specialized crowdfunding platforms that rose in Europe from 2011 to July 2017.

---

[1] *Source*: Global Sustainable Investment Review 2016, available at: http://www.gsi-alliance.org/members-resources/trends-report-2016/.

[2] https://www.theguardian.com/environment/2016/mar/23/european-clean-tech-industry-falls-into-rapid-decline.

[3] *Source*: Global survey by Crowdsourcing.org.

Our research fills a gap in the literature, since to our knowledge only few studies focus on the peculiarities of crowdfunding in renewable energy projects and no comprehensive analysis has been carried out on the determinants of the fundraising success in such cases.[4]

The topic is relevant and worthy to be analyzed for at least three reasons. First, as highlighted before, in the absence of public subsidies private investors are poorly inclined to fund renewable energy projects as they can appropriate just a limited part of the related benefits; therefore, shedding light on the motivations driving pledgers' choices in "green crowdfunding" is of utmost importance to support entrepreneurship in this industry. Second, many governments and supra-national organizations are making efforts in reducing environmental degradation (OECD, 2015) and the development of crowdfunding for renewable energy projects should be a strategic policy objective to reach the target for the reduction of carbon emissions. Third, investments in renewable energy are typically out of reach of small investors aspiring to contribute to green initiatives; crowdfunding has the potential to increase democratization of entrepreneurial finance (Cumming *et al.*, 2018; Stevenson *et al.*, 2019) mobilizing the crowd and allowing people to share risk, diversify investments and actively contribute to fight climate change.

We find that projects delivering some monetary or tangible benefit to the local community and equity-based projects are more likely to reach the funding target, suggesting that pledgers are moved by both profitability expectations and altruistic motivations, i.e., they appreciate to become "owners" and controllers of the project. We investigate the role of localized factors such as the trust in institutions and quality of public services as well as the intensity of pollution, but we do not find a significant impact on the fundraising success.

The remainder of this chapter is organized as follows. Section 2 explores the existing academic discussion, focusing on the crowdfunding for sustainable and green projects. Section 3 describes the research theoretical framework and the testable hypotheses, while Section 4 presents the

---

[4] An exception is Bonzanini *et al.* (2016) who study a very limited sample made up by 84 campaigns only.

sample. Section 5 contains the empirical analyses and, finally, Section 6 concludes.

2. Literature Review

Crowdfunding can be defined as "the act of acquiring third-party financing from the general public via an intermediary, generally in the form of a web-based platform" (Tomczak and Brem, 2013, p. 339) as opposed to raising money through a small group of specialized investors. More generally, crowdfunding is any open-call on the Internet "for the provision of financial resources either in the form of donation or in exchange for the future product or some form of reward to support initiatives for specific purposes" (Belleflamme *et al.*, 2014, p. 588).

In a market where venture capital investors target a limited number of high-growth start-ups, namely those with the potential to become the next "unicorns", the role of alternative financing mechanisms becomes crucial for a thriving entrepreneurial activity (Bellavitis *et al.*, 2017). The enormous and growing amount of capital raised through crowdfunding around the world in recent years has caught the attention of scholars, who have been investigating several features of this fundraising process and analyzing three group of actors which make a crowdfunding campaign possible: capital seekers (or project initiators), capital providers (or crowdfunders) and intermediaries (namely, the crowdfunding portals). All the possible research questions in the field of crowdfunding can be organized along the three dimensions identified by these three actors, their role, motivations and practices (Moritz and Block, 2016). Through crowdfunding, project initiators do not only meet their vital financing needs but also find, or build, a channel through which they contact potential partners and obtain feedbacks on their project (Bogers *et al.*, 2017). On the other side of the spectrum, crowdfunders can obtain a wide range of different or complementary benefits: social returns, products or services, financial returns or refunds. They are very likely to act similar to conventional investors and evaluate basic venture capital metrics such as quality of product, strength of the entrepreneurial team, and the likelihood of success of the business plan when contributing to projects (Mollick, 2014; Moss *et al.*, 2015). At the same time, crowdfunding platforms act as intermediators between initiators searching for funds and people keen on providing money, and while taking care of the promotion of the campaigns and the modality of contact between different parties, they become the selectors and enablers of a different system of financing flows. The tasks above are carried out in exchange for a fee (usually between 2.5% and 10%). Overall, the contribution of crowdfunding platforms relies in the reduction of information asymmetries and, therefore, of the risks involved for contributors (Allen and Santomero, 1997; Berger and Gleisner, 2010; Haas *et al.*, 2014).

There are different business models in the crowdfunding world, each with their own dedicated web portals and each catering to certain needs of the start-up or project initiator. These models are: (1) donation-based, which creates a donor contract without material rewards, typically adopted to finance a specific project in the social, charitable or cultural field (for collective or personal purposes); (2) reward-based, which determines a tangible gift or pre-selling contract for some type of product or service, perceived as a valuable token of appreciation from the promoters to the supporting investors; (3) lending-based, which creates an actual credit contract committing the borrower to repay the credit plus the interest, based on a rating assessment; and (4) equity-based, which takes the form of a shareholding contract entailing ownership and profit-sharing with the company for the investor and, sometimes, voting rights. While donation, reward and pre-purchase models of crowdfunding are generally admitted in every country, lending and equity crowdfunding must comply with national security compliance rules.

Academic research has shown that social return is present within crowdfunders in all types of contributions, also when the financial component may seem dominant (Allison *et al.*, 2015; Lin *et al.*, 2014). Social return can be defined as the intrinsic motivation of the contributor that wants to see the project realized. In this instance, the reward is the completion and success of the project itself, making this driver the core motive of donation-based crowdfunding. Crowdfunders are typically innovation-oriented and want to be active in the social network created by the campaign (Gerber *et al.*, 2012; Ordanini *et al.*, 2011). Whether the degree of social goodwill created by a project contributes to the success of a campaign has been a focal point in the crowdfunding research. Eventually, Belleflamme *et al.* (2013) provide empirical evidence that companies or projects with a social or non-profit oriented background have a higher probability of receiving financing from the crowd, especially because of the higher credibility that non-profit organizations have in fulfilling the expectation of the project's realization.

For the reasons above, crowdfunding is the ideal source of financing for projects aimed at reducing global greenhouse gas emissions (GHG) through investments in renewable energy plants and technologies (Bonzanini *et al.*, 2016). There is a growing awareness about the dangers of climate change (Pernick and Wilder, 2007) and the protection of the environment is mobilizing people, policymakers and investors around the world (Giudici *et al.*, 2019). Kunze and Becker (2014) identify crowdfunding as a powerful tool of communication and aggregation that can foster and amplify the already ongoing processes of democratization and participation in the energy sector. This, in turn, increases societal support for green projects and forces measures to address climate change through political pressure (Vasileiadou *et al.*, 2016). Moreover, in a decentralized energy generation system, crowdfunding can contribute to reduce the "Not In My Back Yard" (NIMBY) syndrome, maximizing local returns on the investment, fostering local participatory processes and empowering people (Candelise, 2015).

Traditional sources of finance might also fail in supporting green projects because of their risk features (Frankfurt School-UNEP, 2017; Hart and Milstein, 1999). Since the latest financial crisis, a significant gap resulted between supply and demand of financial resources for renewable energy projects across many countries as both governmental funding and bank financing shrank (Creutzig *et al.*, 2014; Eleftheriadis and Anagnostopoulou, 2015; Luthra *et al.*, 2015). In this scenario, where project finance has traditionally been a major means of funding renewable energy projects (Steffen, 2017), crowdfunding presents itself as a very viable and democratic alternative.

Despite the scientific relevance of the topic, academic research on green crowdfunding is still limited (Nielsen and Reisch, 2016). Cumming *et al.* (2017) focus on the crowdfunding of cleantech projects and highlight that it is a more common phenomenon in countries with low levels of individualism (and high long-term orientation) and whenever oil prices are rising. Moreover, the authors find that the success of cleantech projects, compared to other types, is more economically sensitive to the campaign's goal size, being not-for-profit, and having a video pitch. Dilger *et al.* (2017) study German energy cooperatives and find that most have a rather positive attitude towards crowdfunding, with acquisition of capital being the prime advantage they pursued. Calic and Mosakowski (2016) find that sustainability-oriented projects more easily raise money from the crowd, while Hörisch (2015) finds no particular correlation between the green positioning and the success rate.

Donation-based and reward-based crowdfunding have been found to be more suitable for small-scale renewable and sustainable energy and green innovation projects during their inception and prototype stages, which are supported by concerned parties or investors who find a channel for expressing their non-financial, altruistic interest (Lam and Law, 2016). While equity- and lending-based platforms are surely more suitable to support entrepreneurial ventures that have overcome the proof-of-concept phase and can forecast (almost) imminent profitability, there are still many open questions and pitfalls related to possible frauds, valuation issues and lack of secondary markets (Giudici, 2015). Crowdfunders, generally being unsophisticated investors, are unable to replicate screening processes and due diligence carried out by professional investors. Moreover, public market authorities have generally no power to examine any offering memorandum.

While the literature on the determinants of crowdfunding success in general comprises a relevant number of works (see among others Gerber *et al.*, 2014; Colombo *et al.*, 2015; Giudici *et al.*, 2018), there are no comprehensive analyses on the specific dynamics of the fundraising outcome in renewable energy projects posted on crowdfunding platforms. Our research is meant to contribute to fill this gap.

3. Research Questions

We posit that investment projects in the renewable energy field are characterized by specific features, impacting the probability to obtain funding. Nonetheless, they also share features of other crowdfunding projects: the characteristics of the single campaign and of the platform are pointed out by the literature as important determinants of the funding outcome in any crowdfunding deal. For example, there is evidence that crowdfunding campaigns are more likely to succeed when the funding amount or the duration of the campaign are lower, the duration of the project is longer, the minimum contribution allowed is lower (Ahlers *et al.*, 2015; Cordova *et al.*, 2015; Frydrych *et al.*, 2014; Giudici *et al.*, 2018; Kraus *et al.*, 2016; Mollick, 2014). Thus, on the one hand we control for these factors, but on the other hand we introduce three predictions in our empirical analysis, driven by the theory developed in the following.

In particular, we focus on: (i) the role of the benefits granted to local communities, (ii) the security type offered to pledgers, (iii) the impact of localized institutional and environmental variables.

Firstly, contrary to generic crowdfunding projects, aimed at financing the engineering and/or prototyping of a product, or the implementation of a service (Mollick, 2014), renewable energy projects have a strong and visible impact on the local landscape (e.g., the installation of wind mills, water turbines, power stations and all infrastructures needed like access streets, electric cables) which is not always welcomed by local inhabitants. Therefore, we expect a particular sensitivity of pledgers to projects where a part of the benefits and "bounties" is shared with the local community (Bonzanini *et al.*, 2016) as a "compensation" for allowing the exploitation of renewable resources available at the local level and for the tangible impact on the landscape:

> **H1:** *Green projects delivering economic benefits to the local community are more likely to be financed by crowdfunders.*

Secondly, as highlighted by the literature, crowdfunders are motivated by both financial and intrinsic objectives (Allison *et al.*, 2015; Gerber *et al.*, 2012; Lin *et al.*, 2014; Ordanini *et al.*, 2011). We posit that in green campaigns the value attributed to being an *owner* of the project is relevant, compared to simply contributing with funds. This effect is theoretically motivated by the fact that environmental resources are "public goods" (see Section 1): benefits on the reduction of carbon emissions generated by renewable energy projects are shared by everyone in the world and pledgers should be particularly pleased by "owning" a part of the project and having the opportunity to decide on the project management. Therefore, pledgers should be happier to contribute when equity shares of the project are offered:

> **H2:** *Green projects that offer contributors an equity-type stake have better access to crowdfunding vis-à-vis projects offering debt securities.*

Thirdly, contrary to other types of business, renewable energy projects strongly depend on the commitment from public authorities to grant incentives and feed-in tariffs for the production of green electricity in the long run and not to place obstacles to the authorization process *ex ante.* Faith in policy measures has a significant effect in investment decisions regarding renewable energy (Masini and Menichetti, 2013); furthermore, institutional innovation factors (such as policy support and public–private cooperation) are able to reduce the barriers to eco-innovation (Polzin *et al.*, 2016). Early contributors of a crowdfunding project are typically resident in the same area of the initiator (Mollick, 2014), and they have a very powerful impact on campaign success (Colombo *et al.*, 2015). Their willingness to invest might be channeled into green crowdfunding due to the pressure of local institutional or environmental factors increasing pledgers' awareness towards green energy (for example, the level of pollution in the region). Therefore, we posit that:

> **H3:** *Local institutional and environmental factors affect the willingness of crowdfunding investors to finance green projects.*

4. Sample Description

We built a sample of 423 crowdfunding campaigns in the renewable energy sector published on 27 European crowdfunding portals specialized in green projects from 2011 to July 2017. We identified the specialized platforms from their home page on the Internet, checking if the focus on "green" or "sustainable" projects is explicitly mentioned. The list of the platforms and their basic characteristics are presented in Table 1. The projects were manually extracted from the websites of the crowdfunding platforms, including all projects posted since the platform's inception. All the platforms have also been contacted through email for further clarification

Table 1: The sample of European "green" crowdfunding platforms used for the analysis.

CFP	Year founded	Country	Completed projects (as of July 2017)
Panel A: Lending-based platforms			
Abundance Investment	2012	GB	25
Bettervest	2012	DE	54
Coopernico	2013	PT	10
Crowd4Climate	2017	DE	2
Durzaam Investeren	2014	NL	33
Ecco Nova	2015	BE	5
ecoligo	2016	DE	2
Econeers	2014	DE	13
Ecrowd!	2014	ES	44
Enerfip	2014	FR	18
GLS Crowd	2017	DE	4
Green Crowd	2012	NL	37
Greenvesting	2009	DE	7
GreenXmoney	2014	DE	27
Leihdeinerumweltgeld	2011	DE	24
Lendosphere	2014	FR	63
Lumo	2012	FR	29
Trine	2015	SE	13
ZonnepanelenDelen	2012	NL	42
Panel B: Equity-based platforms			
1miljoenwatt	2011	NL	5
Cleantech Investor	2006	UK	3
crowdEner.gy	2011	DE	5
Greenrocket	2013	AT	35
Panel C: Hybrid or various securities			
Goparity	2013	PT	4
Invesdor	2012	FI	81
Trillion Fund	2011	GB	19
Veolis	2014	CH	4

about both criteria for project posting and missing value information. Whenever available, the information was complemented with data from news articles and project aggregator platforms. We selected the single projects if they were primarily related to the production of energy from renewable sources (i.e., photovoltaics, wind, water, biomass) or to any innovative technology or project meant to improve the efficiency of electricity usage. The focus was on European platforms as they are the trend generators in the race towards financing and intermediating clean energy projects, especially given the EU's steady commitment to the Paris Climate agreement of 2015. North America and Asia have, at this stage, very few portals specialized in cleantech and clean energy.

Table 2 reports basic statistics on the campaigns. The great majority of the projects (56.7%) refers to solar energy, then we have wind mills (21.0%) followed by biomass plants (5.2%) and hybrid plants (i.e., plants combining two or more different technologies). Hydropower projects and mixed technologies require generally more funding. The funding rate (i.e., the ratio between the capital raised and the initial target published on the website) is larger for wind turbines and other green projects different from those mentioned before.

The platforms with more projects in our sample are Lendosphere (France, 14.9%) and ZonnepanelenDelen (The Netherlands, 9.7%). The projects published by Abundance (UK) are generally larger in funding mass, while the Dutch GreenCrowd and the German GreenXMoney exhibit lower mean and median values. Interestingly, none of the platforms adopt the donation or reward-based model, meaning that the target pledgers are clearly *investors*. This is useful because it allows us to explore how expected profitability relates with the objective of reducing GHG emissions. Equity-type campaigns account for 6.6% of the project sample; junior debt is issued in 15.1% of the cases while senior debt is the most common security (75.7%). Hybrid financing (i.e., convertible debt, or preferred shares) accounts for 2.6%. Equity projects are characterized by the highest funding rates (which is a first qualitative proof of Hypothesis H2) while hybrid-type campaigns see the largest cumulative amount raised.

Overall, more than one third of the projects have been raising money in 2016, and only 13.7% of the projects in the years from 2011 to 2014.

Table 2: Descriptive statistics on the sampled crowdfunding campaigns.

	Number	Capital Raised (€'000)	Funding Success Rate
Project type			
Solar energy	240 (56.7%)	216.26 (75.00)	115%
Wind energy	89 (21.0%)	485.20 (179.00)	139%
Biomass plants	22 (5.2%)	488.36 (109.00)	98%
Mix of different renewables	22 (5.2%)	3,419.43 (435.00)	119%
Hydro energy	5 (1.2%)	542.64 (683.00)	96%
Other green technologies	45 (10.6%)	169.63 (136.00)	168%
Platform			
Lendosphere (France)	63 (14.9%)	278.22 (125.00)	166%
ZonnepanelenDelen (The Netherlands)	41 (9.7%)	110.72 (74.00)	102%
Durzaam Investeren (The Netherlands)	32 (7.6%)	588.50 (433.00)	100%
Lumo (France)	32 (7.6%)	111.90 (30.00)	86%
GreenCrowd (The Netherlands)	29 (6.9%)	80.32 (45.00)	92%
GreenXmoney (Germany)	26 (6.1%)	29.79 (27.00)	95%
Abundance (UK)	24 (5.7%)	1,836.94 (1,100.00)	173%
Others	176 (41.7%)	566.66 (139.00)	129%
Security type			
Equity	28 (6.6%)	1,513.44 (129.00)	183%
Hybrid Equity	11 (2.6%)	1,538.75 (570.00)	139%
Junior debt	64 (15.1%)	705.33 (361.00)	163%
Senior debt	320 (75.7%)	270.20 (86.00)	112%
Year			
2011–2014	58 (13.7%)	1,352.47 (129.00)	108%
2015	101 (23.9%)	279.57 (80.00)	126%
2016	143 (33.8%)	392.83 (112.00)	121%
2017 (as of July)	121 (28.6%)	235.94 (145.00)	127%
Geographical origin (NUTS2)			
Poitou-Charentes (France)	25 (5.9%)	62.66 (19.00)	86%
Gelderland (The Netherlands)	24 (5.7%)	135.77 (53.00)	96%
Catalonia (Spain)	15 (3.5%)	46.40 (30.00)	100%
Pays de la Loire (France)	12 (2.8%)	188.84 (93.00)	145%
Noord-Holland (The Netherlands)	10 (2.4%)	98.42 (60.00)	104%
Midi-Pyrénées (France)	10 (2.4%)	170.68 (111.00)	139%
Others	327 (77.3%)	553.29 (142.00)	141%
Total Sample	423 (100.0%)	452.49 (111.00)	125%

Notes: In the third column, mean values of the capital raised are reported, while median values are in parentheses. The fourth column presents the mean success rate (ratio between capital raised and initial target capital) for each category.

The average amount of the capital raised seems to be lower from 2015 to 2017 compared to the previous period. The geographical dispersion of the projects is quite high: no single region is associated to more than 6% of the sample. Poitou-Charentes (France) and Gelderland (The Netherlands) account for 25 and 24 projects, respectively.

The total money raised by the 423 projects accounts for €191.4 million (mean value per project €452,491 and median value €111,000). The average funding rate is equal to 125%. Upon request, 75% of the platforms highlighted that they never registered an unsuccessful project. Overall, 90% of the projects were successful and raised the minimum funding goal,[5] which is consistent with what was previously found for other peer samples (e.g., Candelise, 2016).

5. Empirical Analysis

In order to analyze the determinants of the campaign success, our dependent variable (*Funding_ratio*) is the ratio between the capital raised by the project at the end of the campaign and the campaign's funding target level. This variable not only captures whether or not the fundraising had been successful (ratio greater or equal to 1) but it also measures the level of overfunding (i.e., the degree to which a campaign was able to attract funds above the minimum target), which is a common occurrence within our sample.

In order to perform a regression analysis, we introduce a set of independent variables. The project-related variables are extracted directly from the platforms' websites, sometimes complemented by news articles regarding the deal. Firstly, we control for the size of the project

[5]Usually a crowdfunding campaign in the renewable energy sector sets a minimum capital threshold to be raised ("all or nothing"). If the collected funds are lower than the minimum threshold, the offer is withdrawn and the money is paid back to contributors. Sometimes there is also a maximum amount of money that can be collected, especially in equity crowdfunding campaigns, according to the maximum issue size approved by shareholders. The majority of the sample projects are proposed by energy service companies (50% of the sample), then private companies (37%), public entities (6%), cooperative companies (6%) and individuals (1%).

introducing the natural logarithm of the target funding amount (*Target_ln*), and for the minimum investment size allowed in the campaign (*Min_chip*). Moreover, another structural feature of the project is its lifetime or the tenure of the security it offers. The variable *Tenure*, measured in years, proxies the duration of the project but in most cases just represent the investment horizon to which backers adhere. Another independent variable that uniquely characterizes the project is the expected return for investors (*Exp_IRR*). This rate is either stated, in the case of lending-based projects, or computed as the expected return on investment for equity-based campaigns, i.e., ratio between the expected cash flows from the company for the year after the campaign conclusion and the initial valuation of the venture (post-money valuation). For some portals (e.g., Lendosphere in France) a base interest rate is offered to general investors and a larger return is delivered to local investors. In such cases, the floor interest rate is chosen as the representative for the deal. For some other deals, there is an upward sloping yield curve and, in such cases, the average interest rate is used.

It is not uncommon for some projects to have an industrial partner as co-sponsor, or to have already secured some financing (e.g., a bank loan facility) from sources other than the crowd before the start of the campaign. These features were coded by two binary variables, namely *Partner* and *Fin_commitment*.

Despite the focus solely on green crowdfunding portals, some heterogeneity is present among them and it could affect the fundraising of campaigns posted on them. Therefore, we control for the reputation of the crowdfunding platform (proxied by the number of successfully concluded campaigns on the portal) using the count variable *CFP_reputation*, and for the presence of additional services offered by the platform (e.g., credit scoring or secondary trading platforms) using the binary variable *CFP_extra_services*.

The presence of any benefit, other than the return to investors, from the project to the local community is captured by a three-level ordinal variable (*Benefits*). This variable takes the maximum value of two for projects that not only generate a valuable service but also share the profits of the project, at least in part, with the local community. On the other hand, a value of one is assumed if they only share one between economic benefits or valuable services to the local community, and a value of zero if the project provides none of such additional benefits. Under Hypothesis H1, we expect a positive and significant correlation with the dependent variable.

Moreover, some projects offer bonuses or carried interest to local residents in terms of additional economic return on their investment. We coded the presence of such bonuses with a binary variable *Bonus*, inserted in the model alongside an interaction term with the *Exp_IRR* variable to account for the shift in the partial effect of returns once increment yields are also present. We expect a positive relationship between *Bonus* and the funding ratio.

The type of security offered in each project is an information captured by a categorical variable distributed in the regression through a binary variable *Equity_Type*, which takes the value of one if equity or hybrid instruments are offered. Under Hypothesis H2, we expect that equity-based campaigns will attract more funds than debt-based counterparts.

Finally, for each project, the NUTS2 region in which the project is located or will be developed is recorded, thus mapping the whole sample in terms of the EU regions set by Eurostat. A Principal Component Analysis (PCA) was used in order to create a factor capturing the quality of the local institutional environment in terms of economic freedom, trust in institutions and quality of public services (*Factor_GVT*).[6] Moreover, using Eurostat data, regional pollution levels were used to build a continuous variable *Air_pollution,* a proxy for the environmental condition of the region targeted by the campaign as of the beginning of the year when the campaign started. Under Hypothesis H3, we expect both the institutional and the environmental factors to explain variation in the fundraising level.

Table 3 reports the descriptive statistics of the regression variables. As highlighted in Table 2, the mean funding percentage is 125%. The presence of extras in the campaign (benefits, bonuses or external

---

[6]The two metrics identified by the PCA analysis are: "quality and accountability of government services" and "distrust in the legal system"; they are measured at the regional NUTS2 level and are all extracted from the Social Progress Imperative research project (www.socialprogress.org). The variables explain 91.9% of the variance of the PCA model. The estimations of the factor analysis are available from the authors upon request.

Table 3: Variables and descriptive statistics.

Variable	**N**	**Mean**	**St. Dev.**	**Min**	**1st Quartile**	**Median**	**3rd Quartile**	**Max**
Funding_ratio	423	1.251	0.882	0.000	1.000	1.000	1.098	9.996
Project features								
Target_ln	423	11.561	1.439	7.601	10.820	11.513	12.429	16.925
Tenure	421	9.046	7.540	1.000	3.000	7.000	12.000	30.000
Exp_IRR	412	5.319	2.657	0.000	4.000	5.000	6.000	40.853
Min_Chip	420	420.195	2,288.045	5.000	25.000	50.000	250.000	25,000.000
Partner	423	0.504	0.501	0	0	1	1	1
Fin_commitment	423	0.165	0.372	0	0	0	0	1
Crowdfunding platform features								
CFP_reputation	423	17.033	15.010	0	5	13	25	80
CFP_extra_services	423	0.184	0.388	0	0	0	0	1
Benefits for locals								
Bonus	423	0.248	0.432	0	0	0	0	1
Benefits	423	0.326	0.598	0	0	0	1	2
Security type								
Equity_type	423	0.092	0.290	0	0	0	0	1
Regional institutional and environmental factors								
Factor_GVT	402	−0.140	0.902	−3.021	−0.734	−0.247	0.919	2.455
Air_pollution	416	107.265	10.037	81.266	100.142	108.550	115.140	135.380

Notes: The dependent variable is the ratio between the capital effectively raised in the campaign and the initial target amount (*Funding_ratio*), which also accounts for overfunding. All other independent variables are defined in the text. Sample size: 423 green projects published by 27 European platforms from 2011 to 2017.

commitment) is relatively not frequent, while on the contrary the presence of a sponsoring external partner is detected in more than 50% of the cases. The mean (median) expected financial return is 5.3% (5.0%). The minimum investments accepted in the campaigns is considerably variable, from €5 to €20,000; yet the mean (€420.2) and median (€50) values are low enough to attract a wide crowd of investors by allowing them to be a part of the project with relatively small disbursements.

Figure 1 reports the correlation plot for the regressors. Together with other diagnostic tests, the correlation plot confirms that there is no issue of multicollinearity.

Table 4 presents the estimated OLS regression models. Year fixed-effects are introduced in all regressions to account for systematic time-related variability. Model 1 contains the set of controls, i.e., the independent variables related to the project and platform characteristics, alongside the

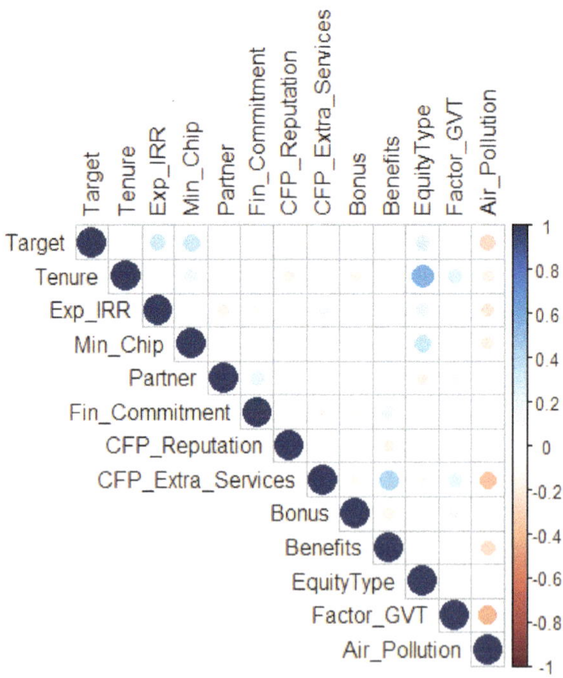

Figure 1: Correlation plot. Only statistically significant correlations have non-empty cells.

Table 4: Determinants of the campaign success: OLS regression results.

	Dependent Variable			
	Funding_Ratio			Amount_Raised_ln
	(1)	(2)	(3)	(4)
Target_ln	0.005	−0.036	−0.051*	0.967***
	(0.027)	(0.026)	(0.030)	(0.018)
Tenure	−0.009	−0.016***	−0.012*	−0.013***
	(0.006)	(0.006)	(0.007)	(0.004)
Exp_IRR	0.024	0.016	0.020	0.020**
	(0.015)	(0.014)	(0.014)	(0.009)
Min_chip	−0.00000	−0.00000	−0.00001	−0.00000
	(0.00002)	(0.00002)	(0.00002)	(0.00001)
Partner	−0.008	0.089	0.088	0.058
	(0.074)	(0.072)	(0.077)	(0.047)
Fin_commitment	−0.067	0.025	0.003	−0.081
	(0.105)	(0.101)	(0.106)	(0.065)
CFP_reputation	0.007**	0.006*	0.003	0.003
	(0.003)	(0.003)	(0.003)	(0.002)
CFP_extra_services	−0.095	−0.190*	−0.190*	−0.105
	(0.104)	(0.104)	(0.110)	(0.067)
Benefits for locals				
Bonus	0.786***	0.885***	1.030***	0.648***
	(0.252)	(0.244)	(0.262)	(0.160)
Bonus x Exp_IRR	−0.094**	−0.101**	−0.120***	−0.088***
	(0.046)	(0.044)	(0.046)	(0.028)

(Continued)

Table 4: (*Continued*).

	Dependent Variable			
	Funding_Ratio			Amount_Raised_ln
	(1)	(2)	(3)	(4)
Benefits	0.212***	0.167**	0.147**	0.091**
	(0.068)	(0.066)	(0.071)	(0.043)
Security type				
Equity_type		0.389**	0.380*	0.284**
		(0.176)	(0.198)	(0.121)
Regional institutional and environmental factors				
Factor_GVT			−0.071	−0.030
			(0.045)	(0.028)
Air_pollution			−0.004	−0.002
			(0.005)	(0.003)
Constant	1.095**	1.333***	1.861**	0.617
	(0.520)	(0.503)	(0.859)	(0.525)
Year fixed effects	Yes	Yes	Yes	Yes
Observations	410	410	393	393
R^2	0.100	0.192	0.203	0.933
Adjusted R^2	0.061	0.152	0.158	0.929
Residual std. error	0.685 (df = 392)	0.651 (df = 390)	0.661 (df = 371)	0.404 (df = 371)
F Statistic	2.557*** (df = 17; 392)	4.868*** (df = 19; 390)	4.490*** (df = 21; 371)	244.948*** (df = 21; 371)

Notes: The dependent variable is the ratio between the capital effectively raised in the campaign and the initial target amount (*Funding_ratio*) for models 1 to 4. Model 5 is a representative robustness check with the natural logarithm of the amount raised (*Amount_raised_ln*) as dependent variable. The independent variables are defined in the text. Standard errors in parentheses. Sample size: 423 green projects published by 27 European crowdfunding platforms from 2011 to 2017. df = degrees of freedom *, **, and *** = statistically different from zero at the 90%, 95%, and 99% confidence levels, respectively variables capturing the different benefits available for locals. We find highly statistically significant coefficients for both *Bonus* and *Benefits*, with positive signs and sizeable effects. In particular, the presence of return bonuses for local investors increases, on average, the funding ratio by about 79 percentage points. On the other hand, the average effect of either social or economic benefits is of 21 percentage points *vis-à-vis* absence of benefits, while the average increase for both types of benefits being simultaneously present is 42 percentage points (*vis-à-vis* the absence case). As it should be expected, there is a downward shift in the partial effect of expected returns on fundraising once return bonuses are introduced, evidenced by the significant coefficient of the interaction term.

Model 2 introduces the nature of the security being offered to potential investors. The coefficient of *Equity_Type* is economically and statistically significant (with a *p*-value lower than 5%), and suggests that, on average, when equity securities are offered the effective funding ratio increases by about 39 percentage points. This confirms our hypothesis that investors do prefer to have an ownership stake in green projects.

Model 3 adds the regional institutional and environmental variables *Factor_GVT* and *Air_pollution*. While there is a slight increase in the explanatory power of the model (i.e., a higher adjusted R-square with respect to Model 2), the coefficients of these variables are not statistically different from zero. Once controlling for local benefits, the institutional factor and pollution level do not appear to influence the fundraising success of green projects.

In addition to the above, various robustness checks were performed (e.g., different policies for influential observations, alternative proxy variables, Logit regressions with a binary variable for success, etc.). An example is the regression of Model 4, were the natural logarithm of the amount raised is used as dependent variable. The statistical significance or the order of magnitude of the coefficients does not change *vis-à-vis* Model 3.

6. Conclusions

Understanding the critical success factors of crowdfunding for green projects is important to address environmental and economic policies in order to favor the achievement of national and global sustainability goals.[7] Crowdfunding is becoming more and more relevant as a source of capital, especially for start-up activities, and this urges for more academic research in this field. Moreover, it allows citizens to access investments which are normally reserved to professional investors, democratizing finance. This aspect is particularly important for green projects: increasing the local awareness (and creating a consensus in order to overcome opposition and distrust about the local impact of renewable energy and green infrastructures) may speed up investments and avoid the NIMBY syndrome.

In this work, we analyze 423 renewable energy projects that raised money on a specialized crowdfunding platform, from 2011 to July 2017. We posit that "green" projects are characterized by peculiar features and specific determinants are able to explain the fundraising success. We find that leaving some benefits to the local community helps to achieve the funding goal. Specifically, as the level of local benefits increases, so does the willingness of investors to fund the project. We also find that potential crowdfunders are very sensitive to the opportunity of receiving an incremental economic return motivated by their being local residents of the region where the project is going to be developed. These results support our first hypothesis.

Our second hypothesis is also confirmed as equity-type campaigns are welcome by investors, showing that they clearly assign a significant value to the possibility of being owners and actively contribute to the management of an environmentally sustainable project.

The level of trust in institutions and quality of public services at the local level, as well as the pollution ratios, do not appear to be relevant for contributors, at least as measured by our proxies. NUTS2 regions are perhaps too large to capture the structural features of the actual communities that (directly or indirectly) shaped the availability of the contributors to invest in green projects. However, given the international coverage of the

[7]The EU Seventh Environment Action Programme (EAP) identifies three key policy objectives: (i) to protect, conserve and enhance the Union's natural capital, (ii) to turn the Union into a resource-efficient, green, and competitive low-carbon economy, (iii) to safeguard the Union's citizens from environment-related pressures and risks to health and well-being.

sample, municipality-level data could not be collected. So, our results could indicate that even more "local" or granular measurement of such features are required.

We underline the relevance of such unprecedented results in the literature for policymakers, sponsors of green energy projects and investors.

Political factors are critical drivers of renewable energy deployment (Cadoret and Padovano, 2016), and thus policymakers should be able to favor the investments on green crowdfunding platforms, as clearly there are substantial benefits in terms of overcoming the funding gap for green projects, increasing the democratization of financial markets and strengthening the local wellbeing and sustainability awareness. Moreover, regulations facilitating crowdfunding activity (especially in the form of equity) can have direct medium-term effects on the reduction of CO_2 emissions at the regional level, which is a very attractive result for European governments given their serious climate change commitments. This adds to the stream of research supporting the argument that financial development plays a crucial role in the deployment of renewable energy resources (Kim and Park, 2016).

Furthermore, our results indicate that sponsors of green projects should care about building an efficient crowdfunding campaign to attract investors, leaving some benefits to the local community and involving the crowd in the ownership of the project. At the same time, pledgers should be aware that investing in green energy projects is a smart way to diversify their portfolio, and to contribute to the reduction of GHG emissions in two ways: providing cash resources to support investments but also improving the local awareness and sensitivity towards environment and sustainability.

Despite being very representative for the phenomenon at hand, the limited number of observations in the sample and the concentration in time (2011–2017) may limit the robustness of the results and leave ample room for improvement in the future. Moreover, wider availability of data may allow future research to employ alternative proxies for regional or local factors that could play a role (either as incentives or as deterrents) for retail investors′ willingness to contribute to a sustainability-related crowdfunding project.

Finally, while the issue of the relevance of local factors on the attractiveness of crowdfunding investments presents many open questions (e.g., which structural community features is the strongest driver for locals to intervene through sustainability-oriented investments?), topics concerning the effects of an increased "green" crowdfunding activity in a region on the local structural characteristics have not been explored so far. We leave this topic for possible future research.

References

Agrawal A., Catalini C., and Goldfarb A. (2011) The Geography of Crowdfunding. NBER working paper. Cambridge, MA. doi: https://doi.org/10.3386/w16820.

Ahlers G. K. C., Cumming D., Günther C., and Schweizer D. (2015) Signaling in equity crowdfunding. *Entrepreneurship Theory and Practice*, 39(4), 955–980. doi: https://doi.org/10.1111/etap.12157.

Allen F. and Santomero A. M. (1997) The theory of financial intermediation. *Journal of Banking and Finance*, 21(11–12), 1461–1485. doi: https://doi.org/10.1016/S0378-4266(97)00032-0.

Allison T. H., Davis B. C., Short J. C., and Webb J. W. (2015) Crowdfunding in a prosocial microlending environment: examining the role of intrinsic versus extrinsic cues. *Entrepreneurship Theory and Practice*, 39(1), 53–73. doi: https://doi.org/10.1111/etap.12108.

Baumol W. J. and Oates W. E. (1988) *The theory of environmental policy*. Cambridge University Press.

Bellavitis C., Filatotchev I., Kamuriwo D. S., and Vanacker T. (2017) Entrepreneurial finance: new frontiers of research and practice: Editorial for the special issue Embracing entrepreneurial funding innovations. *Venture Capital*, 19(1–2), 1–16. doi: https://doi.org/10.1080/13691066.2016.1259733.

Belleflamme P., Lambert T., and Schwienbacher A. (2013) Individual crowdfunding practices. *Venture Capital*, 15(4), 313–333. doi: https://doi.org/10.1080/13691066.2013.785151.

Belleflamme P., Lambert T., and Schwienbacher A. (2014) Crowdfunding: Tapping the right crowd. *Journal of Business Venturing*, 29(5), 585–609. doi: https://doi.org/10.1016/j.jbusvent.2013.07.003.

Berger S. C. and Gleisner F. (2010) Emergence of financial intermediaries in electronic markets: the case of online P2P lending. *BuR Business Research Journal*, 2(1), 39–65. doi: https://doi.org/10.1007/BF03343528.

Bogers M., Zobel A.-K., Afuah A., Almirall E., Brunswicker S., Dahlander L., and Ter Wal A. L. J. (2017) The open innovation research landscape: Established perspectives and emerging themes across different levels of analysis. *Industry and Innovation*, 24(1), 8–40. doi: https://doi.org/10.1080/13662716.2016.1240068.

Bonzanini D., Giudici G., and Patrucco A. (2016) The crowdfunding of renewable energy projects. In: Ramiah, V., Gregoriou, G. (eds.), *Handbook of Environmental and Sustainable Finance.* p. 429. Elsevier, Amsterdam, The Netherlands. doi: https://doi.org/10.1016/B978-0-12-803615-0.00021-2.

Butticè V., Colombo M. G., Fumagalli E., Orsenigo C. (2019) Green oriented crowdfunding campaigns: Their characteristics and diffusion in different institutional settings. Technological Forecasting and Social Change, 141, 85–97. doi: https://doi.org/10.1016/j.techfore.2018.07.047.

Cadoret I. and Padovano F. (2016) The political drivers of renewable energies policies. *Energy Economics*, 56, 261–269. doi: https://doi.org/10.1016/j.eneco.2016.03.003.

Calic G. and Mosakowski E. (2016) Kicking off social entrepreneurship: how a sustainability orientation influences crowdfunding success. *Journal of Management Studies*, 53(5), 738–767. doi: https://doi.org/10.1111/joms.12201.

Candelise C. (2015) *Crowdfunding and the Energy Sector.* Cedro Exchange Empowering Lebanon with Renewable Energy.

Candelise C. (2016) Smart financing and empowerment: the use of crowdfunding in the energy sector. In *the 57th Annual Conference for Italian Economic Association.*

Colombo M. G., Franzoni C., and Rossi-Lamastra C. (2015) Internal social capital and the attraction of early contributions in crowdfunding. *Entrepreneurship Theory and Practice*, 39(1), 75–100. doi: https://doi.org/10.1111/etap.12118.

Cordova A., Dolci J., and Gianfrate G. (2015) The determinants of crowdfunding success: Evidence from technology projects. *Procedia-Social and Behavioral Sciences*, 181, 115–124. doi: https://doi.org/10.1016/j.sbspro.2015.04.872.

Creutzig F., Goldschmidt J. C., Lehmann P., Schmid E., von Blücher F., Breyer C., and Wiegandt K. (2014) Catching two European birds with one renewable stone: Mitigating climate change and Eurozone crisis by an energy transition. *Renewable and Sustainable Energy Reviews*, 38, 1015–1028. doi: https://doi.org/10.1016/j.rser.2014.07.028.

Cumming D. J., Leboeuf G., and Schwienbacher A. (2017) Crowdfunding cleantech. *Energy Economics*, 65, 292–303. doi: https://doi.org/10.1016/j.eneco.2017.04.030.

Cumming D. J., Vismara S., and Meoli M. (2018) does equity crowdfunding democratize entrepreneurial finance? SSRN Working paper.

Dilger M. G., Jovanović T., and Voigt K.-I. (2017) Upcrowding energy co-operatives — Evaluating the potential of crowdfunding for business model innovation of energy co-operatives. *Journal of Environmental Management*, 198, 50–62. doi: https://doi.org/10.1016/j.jenvman.2017.04.025.

Eleftheriadis I. M. and Anagnostopoulou E. G. (2015) Identifying barriers in the diffusion of renewable energy sources. *Energy Policy*, 80, 153–164. doi: https://doi.org/10.1016/j.enpol.2015.01.039.

Frankfurt School-UNEP (2017) *Global Trends in Renewable Energy Investment 2017*. FS UNEP Centre.

Frydrych D., Bock A. J., Kinder T., and Koeck B. (2014) Exploring entrepreneurial legitimacy in reward-based crowdfunding. *Venture Capital*, 16(3), 247–269. doi: https://doi.org/10.1080/13691066.2014.916512.

Gerber E. M., Hui J. S., and Kuo P. Y. (2012, February) Crowdfunding: Why people are motivated to post and fund projects on crowdfunding platforms. In *Proceedings of the International Workshop on Design, Influence, and Social Technologies: Techniques, Impacts and Ethics*, Vol. 2, No. 11. ACM, New York, NY.

Giudici G. (2015) Equity crowdfunding of an entrepreneurial activity. In *University Evolution, Entrepreneurial Activity and Regional Competitiveness*. Springer, Cham, pp. 415–425. doi: https://doi.org/10.1007/978-3-319-17713-7_20.

Giudici G., Guerini M., and Rossi-Lamastra C. (2018) Reward-based crowdfunding of entrepreneurial projects: the effect of local altruism and localized social capital on proponents' success. *Small Business Economics*, 50(2), 307–324. doi: https://doi.org/10.1007/s11187-016-9830-x.

Giudici G., Guerini M., and Rossi-Lamastra C. (2019) The creation of cleantech start-ups at the local level: the role of knowledge availability and environmental awareness. *Small Business Economics*, 52(4), 815–830. doi: https://doi.org/10.1007/s11187-017-9936-9.

Haas P., Blohm I., and Leimeister J. (2014) An empirical taxonomy of crowdfunding intermediaries. In *ICIS 2014 Proceedings*.

Hart S. L. and Milstein M. B. (1999) Global sustainability and the creative destruction of industries. *Sloan Management Review*, 41(1), 23–33.

Hörisch J. (2015) Crowdfunding for environmental ventures: an empirical analysis of the influence of environmental orientation on the success of crowdfunding initiatives. *Journal of Cleaner Production*, 107, 636–645. doi: https://doi.org/10.1016/j.jclepro.2015.05.046.

Kim J. and Park K. (2016) Financial development and deployment of renewable energy technologies. *Energy Economics*, 59, 238–250. doi: https://doi.org/10.1016/j.eneco.2016.08.012.

Kraus S., Richter C., Brem A., Cheng C. F., and Chang M. L. (2016) Strategies for reward-based crowdfunding campaigns. *Journal of Innovation and Knowledge*, 1(1), 13–23. doi: https://doi.org/10.1016/j.jik.2016.01.010.

Krupa J. and Harvey D. (2017) Renewable electricity finance in the United States: A state-of-the-art review. *Energy*. 135(C), 913–929. doi: https://doi.org/10.1016/j.energy.2017.05.190.

Kunze C. and Becker S. (2014) *Energy Democracy in Europe: a survey and outlook*. Rosa-Luxemburg-Stiftung.

Lam P. T. I. and Law A. O. K. (2016) Crowdfunding for renewable and sustainable energy projects: An exploratory case study approach. *Renewable and Sustainable Energy Reviews*, 60, 11–20. doi: https://doi.org/10.1016/j.rser.2016.01.046.

Lin Y., Boh W. F., and Goh K. H. (2014) how different are crowdfunders? examining archetypes of crowdfunders and their choice of projects. *Academy of Management Proceedings*, 2014(1), 13309–13309. doi: https://doi.org/10.5465/AMBPP.2014.209.

Luthra S., Kumar S., Garg D., and Haleem A. (2015) Barriers to renewable/sustainable energy technologies adoption: Indian perspective. *Renewable and Sustainable Energy Reviews*, 41, 762–776. doi: https://doi.org/10.1016/j.rser.2014.08.077.

Masini A. and Menichetti E. (2013) Investment decisions in the renewable energy sector: An analysis of non-financial drivers. *Technological Forecasting and Social Change*, 80(3), 510–524. doi: https://doi.org/10.1016/j.techfore.2012.08.003.

Mazzucato M. and Semieniuk G. (2018) Financing renewable energy: Who is financing what and why it matters. *Technological Forecasting and Social Change*, 127, 8–22. doi: https://doi.org/10.1016/j.techfore.2017.05.021.

Mollick E. (2014) The dynamics of crowdfunding: An exploratory study. *Journal of Business Venturing*, 29(1), 1–16. doi: https://doi.org/10.1016/j.jbusvent.2013.06.005.

Mollick E. R. and Kuppuswamy V. (2014) After the Campaign: Outcomes of Crowdfunding. UNC Kenan-Flagler Research Paper No. 2376997. doi: https://doi.org/10.2139/ssrn.2376997.

Moritz A. and Block J. H. (2016) *Crowdfunding: A Literature Review and Research Directions. In Crowdfunding in Europe*. Springer International Publishing, pp. 25–53. doi: https://doi.org/10.1007/978-3-319-18017-5_3.

Moss T. W., Neubaum D. O., and Meyskens M. (2015) The effect of virtuous and entrepreneurial orientations on microfinance lending and repayment: a signaling theory perspective. *Entrepreneurship Theory and Practice*, 39(1), 27–52. doi: https://doi.org/10.1111/etap.12110.

Nielsen K. R. and Reisch L. A. (2016) Crowdfunding for sustainability - the role of value orientation frames in guiding individual investment behavior. In *Proceedings of the International Conference on Business, Policy and Sustainability*. Copenhagen Business School, 16–17 June, Denmark.

OECD (2015) *Climate Change Mitigation: Policies and Progress*. OECD Publishing, Paris.

Ordanini A., Miceli L., Pizzetti M., and Parasuraman A. (2011) Crowd-funding: transforming customers into investors through innovative service platforms. *Journal of Service Management*, 22(4), 443–470. doi: https://doi.org/10.1108/09564231111155079.

Pernick R. and Wilder C. (2007) *The Clean Tech Revolution: The Next Big Growth and Investment Opportunity*. Collins, New York.

Polzin F., von Flotow P., and Klerkx L. (2016) Addressing barriers to eco-innovation: Exploring the finance mobilisation functions of institutional innovation intermediaries. *Technological Forecasting and Social Change*, 103, 34–46. doi: https://doi.org/10.1016/j.techfore.2015.10.001.

Polzin F., Sanders M., and Stavlöt U. (2018) Do investors and entrepreneurs match? — Evidence from The Netherlands and Sweden. *Technological Forecasting and Social Change*, 127, 112–126. doi: https://doi.org/10.1016/j.techfore.2017.07.016.

Steffen B. (2017) The importance of project finance for renewable energy projects. *Energy Economics*, 69, 280–294. doi: https://doi.org/10.1016/j.eneco.2017.11.006.

Stevenson R. M., Kuratko D. F., and Eutsler J. (2019) Unleashing main street entrepreneurship: Crowdfunding, venture capital, and the democratization of new venture investments. *Small Business Economics*, 52(2), 375–393. doi: http://dx.doi.org/10.1007/s11187-018-0097-2.

Tomczak A. and Brem A. (2013) A conceptualized investment model of crowdfunding. *Venture Capital*, 15(4), 335–359. doi: http://dx.doi.org/10.1080/13691066.2013.847614.

Vasileiadou E., Huijben J. C. C. M., and Raven R. P. J. M. (2016) Three is a crowd? Exploring the potential of crowdfunding for renewable energy in the Netherlands. *Journal of Cleaner Production*, 128, 142–155. doi: https://doi.org/10.1016/j.jclepro.2015.06.028.

Chapter 6

Linguistic Style and Crowdfunding: Moving the Current Debate Forward

Riccardo Maiolini*

Department of Business Administration,
John Cabot University

rmaiolini@johncabot.edu

Francesco Cappa†

Department of Business and Management,
LUISS Guido Carli University

fcappa@luiss.it

Francesco Fasano‡

Department of Business Administration and Law,
University of Calabria

francesco.fasano@unical.it

*233, Via della Lungara, Rome, 00165, Italy.

†12, Viale Pola, Rome, 00198, Italy.

‡Via Ponte Pietro Bucci Cubo 3C, Arcavacata di Rende, 87036, Italy.

Abstract

This chapter provides an overview of the key insights from recent studies concerning the relevance of linguistic style for the success of crowdfunding campaigns, an emerging phenomenon of unconventional financing methods for entrepreneurial projects. In this study, we evidenced how the language used by entrepreneurs to attract funds is crucial for the success of the crowdfunding campaign because it affects the information asymmetries surrounding the project. Additionally, we propose new possible streams of research concerning the role of linguistic style on the success of funding campaigns. We identify promising research directions, based on preliminary results, regarding the influence of repetitive words and different linguistic models on crowdfunding success. Overall, this chapter evidences, based on the state of the art of scientific studies, the importance of considering narrative style when entrepreneurs decide to start a new crowdfunding campaign, and paves the way for interesting future research that may be conducted.

1. Introduction

One of the most important cornerstones of current entrepreneurship research concerns the study of the activities that entrepreneurs undertake to secure the financial resources that are indispensable to bring new products and services into the marketplace (Short *et al.*, 2017). The topic of fund raising is particularly relevant for researchers, entrepreneurs and policymakers, as new ventures represent a major source of new job creation, especially in the recent years after the financial crisis (Fairlie *et al.*, 2015). The successful development of new products and services are strongly dependent on new venture founders' ability to raise financial resources (Bhattacharya, 2017; Rubin *et al.*, 2015; Parhankangas and Ehrlich, 2014; Van Osnabrugge and Robinson, 2000). As a complement to traditional financing methods, crowdfunding is a new method to fund a variety of projects, allowing the collection of small amounts of money from a number of dispersed individuals, in return for some form of reward, property rights, periodic payments, or just for the sake of contributing to a project they like (Mollick, 2014). In the last decade, crowdfunding increasingly helped entrepreneurs to integrate their fundraising based on traditional financing methods or as a stand-alone alternative channel of funding (Block *et al.*, 2017; Butticè *et al.*, 2017; Belleflamme *et al.*, 2014). Crowdfunding draws inspiration from notions like micro-finance (whose importance is evidenced by Morduch, 1999 and Prahalad, 2006) and crowd science (Cappa *et al.*, 2018; Franzoni and Sauermann, 2014; Poetz and Schreier, 2012; Maiolini and Naggi, 2011; Cull *et al.*, 2009) enabled by a small contribution from numerous participants.

In view of the growing diffusion of crowdfunding, scholars and practitioners hold great interest in exploring the successful factors for this means to call for money for new entrepreneurial ventures. Crowdfunding is a promising alternative financing method that overcomes the duties and complexities of other traditional sources of investments (Bi *et al.*, 2017), directly requesting to the general public of Internet for financial help in supporting their innovative idea (Agrawal *et al.*, 2015; Belleflamme *et al.*, 2014; Mollick, 2014). Therefore, the interest resides in determining which factors permit the crowdfunding campaign to be successful in raising the money needed, by motivating the crowd to provide the financial support for the call for funding.

Considering the relevance of crowdfunding on firms' growth, several contributions have examined the success factors of the crowdfunding campaigns from different perspectives. Some of these works focused on the relationship between the type of project and the success of a campaign (Mollick 2014; Belleflamme *et al.*, 2010), while others paid attention to the use of media (e.g., Zheng *et al.*, 2014; Wheat *et al.*, 2013) or social networks (Lu *et al.*, 2014). Other studies concentrate on the role of institutional contexts in the success of crowdfunding campaigns. For instance, Butticè *et al.* (2018) look at the relationship between "green campaigns" and country characteristics, Dushnitsky *et al.* (2016) concentrate on distinct national patterns that emerge in crowdfunding activities; Cholakova and Clarysse (2015) differently observed the motivation for investing in crowdfunding; Colombo *et al.* (2015) remarkably show that backers' contributions in the early stages of a campaign-enhanced crowdfunding success, while Kuppuswamy and Bayus (2017) assert that backers' support increases when the campaign is nearing its target. Some other studies suggest that the crowdfunding platform is relevant for funding success (e.g., Dushnitsky and Fitza, 2018; Fleming and Sorenson, 2016). Butticè *et al.* (2017) found that the experience of serial crowdfunders, entrepreneurs launching crowdfunding campaigns, reduces information asymmetries and enhances the likelihood of success.

Another crucial factor influencing crowdfunding success is the key role of effective communication through the language used during the campaign launch. This essential aspect has not been thoroughly, empirically examined in prior literature, even if it has started to be conceptually theorized (Manning and Bejarano, 2017). Recent papers started studying the impact of language on crowdfunding success. Allison *et al.* (2013) evidence that the language to use depends on country-specific factors. Allison *et al.* (2015) and Moss *et al.* (2015) study the relationship between the language employed and the motivations of backers. From another perspective, Gorbatai and Nelson (2015) interestingly found that the linguistic style to adopt should differ depending on the gender of target backers. Manning and Beiarano (2017) suggest that when the product is intangible entrepreneurs ought to use a future-looking language, while Majumar and Bose (2018) suggest that rational and credible messages favor funding collection. Anglin *et al.* (2018) observe that positive (i.e., optimistic) language increases the likelihood of success. A noteworthy piece of literature suggests that proper communication enhances the success of crowdfunding campaigns, since it reduces asymmetric information between entrepreneurs and backers (Agrawal *et al.*, 2015; Davis and Webb, 2012). Therefore, achieving project goals is influenced by the language used to convince backers about the feasibility of a campaign. Consequently, language represents a key tool to establish a steady relationship between backers and entrepreneurs, especially when lenders face asymmetric-information problems.

In this context, our study aims to highlight the relevance of linguistic style in crowdfunding success by conducting a literature review, examining those contributions that explore the role of narrative style on crowdfunding success in the asymmetric-information context. Moreover, we intend to spur future studies concerning the role of linguistic style on crowdfunding success. In doing so, we shed light on a new possible line of research, whose purpose is to assert that a proper narrative style may favor fund collection. In particular, we observed two particular aspects of narrative style, namely, the use of repetitive words and the distinction between concrete language and linguistic models during the launch of a crowdfunding campaign. Our preliminary findings, which intend to be initial discoveries in this new field of study, show that in the peculiar context of reward-based crowdfunding the repetitiveness of keywords is negatively related to the success rate and that the influence of linguistic models (concrete versus abstract language) depends on the sector in which the crowdfunding is embedded. Therefore, the research here carried out contributes to the crowdfunding literature investigating the role of language on the campaigns' success. Finally, our study possesses essential managerial implications, since entrepreneurs now have further indications about how to narrate their new ideas in order to better promote their campaigns.

The chapter is structured as follows. After an introduction, the origin and the different typologies of crowdfunding are reported. Section 3 is dedicated to the state of the art of research on the success factors in crowdfunding, highlighting the growing importance of both asymmetric information and the language used by entrepreneurs to attract funds. Section 4, after a brief introduction, reports empirical precursor results, while Section 5 concludes the chapter, highlighting possible future research opportunities and entrepreneurial suggestions.

2. The Origin and the Different Typologies of Crowdfunding

2.1. *The origin of crowdfunding*

It is useful to distinguish the origin of the word crowdfunding from the origin of the broadly defined phenomenon. In fact, crowdfunding has an extended and rich history whose origins can even be traced to a time when the term as currently used was not yet coined. In the history, very often it is possible to find examples of fundraising strategies that contain characteristics that we use today to refer to similar crowdfunding-phenomenon campaigns. Some scholars even attribute the origin of the phenomenon of crowdfunding to the financing process of the construction of Saint Peter's Basilica in Rome in the 18th century, when we start to find examples most similar to modern crowdfunding campaigns. For example, in 1713 the poet Alexander Pope asked to pledge money to translate Greek poetry into English promising the backers a shout-out in the acknowledgments of an early edition of the book. After 70 years, in 1783, Mozart advertised an invitation to potential backers to execute three new piano concertos in Vienna. Moving forward to the 19th century, the famous publisher Joseph Pulitzer decided to launch a fundraising campaign to raise $250,000 to build the base for the Statue of Liberty in New York. Jumping forward another century, we moved to 1997 and to the origin of modern crowdfunding, i.e., the one based on online interactions, when a British rock band sponsored their tour through online donations from fans through the (first) ArtistShare (www.artishare.com) platform. Gradually, many other platforms opened and started to use crowdfunding as an innovative method of fundraising.

From a syntactic perspective, the word crowdfunding can be found for the first time only in 2006: Michael Sullivan is ascribed as the coiner of the term (Gobble, 2012). Subsequently he launched Fundavlog, an incubator for videoblog-related projects that includes a simple funding functionality "based on reciprocity, transparency, shared interests and, above all, funding from the crowd." The launch of this platform opened the modern frontier of crowdfunding, paving the way to many other web-based platforms. Nowadays, crowdfunding is well recognized as a two-sided market, binding "together two distinct groups of users in a network" (Eisenmann *et al.*, 2006). Considering the growth of the phenomenon and the managerial implications, scholars started to define the concept of crowdfunding (Belleflamme *et al.*, 2014; Mollick, 2014), sought to understand the theoretical mechanisms behind the process and the actions of the participants (Burtch *et al.*, 2015; Cholakova and Clarysse, 2015; Belleflamme *et al.*, 2014), and especially explored various factors affecting success rates (Agrawal *et al.*, 2015; Zheng *et al.*, 2014). In the following section, we define in detail the different forms of crowdfunding to have a greater understanding of the whole phenomenon, while in section three we review the extant literature on crowdfunding, with an innovative approach based on the analysis of linguistic style in crowdfunding.

2.2. *Different typologies of crowdfunding*

Considering the complexity of the phenomenon, many studies concentrated on distinguishing different forms of crowdfunding, grouping them into four main categories, considering the differences in the nature of the investment and the expectations of would-be investors (Giudici *et al.*, 2018; Assenova *et al.*, 2016; Cholakova and Clarysse, 2015; Colombo *et al.*, 2015). Four types of campaigns can be distinguished, as synthesized in Table 1 and several platforms are continuously spawning worldwide: Kickstarter and Indiegogo from USA, JD Finance from China, Kisskissbankbank and Ulule from France, Becrowdy and Mamacrowd from Italy, Planeta from Russia, Goteo and VErkami from Spain just to name a few.

The focus of our research is mainly on reward-based crowdfunding, since it is the most widespread typology of campaign and the most studied by scholars (Davis *et al.*, 2017; Kraus *et al.*, 2016; Belleflamme *et al.*, 2014), where profit and donation motivations meet each other.

3. Literature Review

This section aims to review the growing literature on crowdfunding and, mostly, the new emerging studies on the role of linguistic style on the success of a crowdfunding campaign, in order to offer some perspectives on how it may evolve in the future. The extant literature on crowdfunding has been documented by several recent reviews (e.g., Buttice *et al.*, 2018; Dushnitsky and Zunino, 2018; Kuppuswamy and Bayus, 2018; Drover *et al.*, 2017; Harvè and Schwienbacher, 2017; Centobelli *et al.*, 2016). However, our work differs from the latter reviews, since it focuses on the literature concerning the role of narrative on crowdfunding success, based on the asymmetric-information framework and signaling theory. Moreover, our work provides interesting preliminary results that pave the way for future research directions about the role of linguistic style for crowdfunding success. In Section 3.1, after a brief, explanatory review of the literature on the determinants of crowdfunding success, we focus on the crucial issue of asymmetric information as a driver to show the importance of linguistic style on a crowdfunding campaign. In Section 3.2, we

Table 1: Different typologies of crowdfunding.

Debt-based crowdfunding	**Equity-based crowdfunding**
Debt-based (or lending-based) crowdfunding allows entrepreneurs to raise funds in the form of loans that they will pay back to lenders over a pre-determined timeline with a set interest rate. Debt-based crowdfunding campaigns are particularly popular with entrepreneurs who do not want to give up equity in their start-up companies immediately and/or do not have access to more traditional types of loan facilities. In debt-based crowdfunding, lenders can earn an interest payment that was contractually agreed upon before the loan was completed (Giudici *et al.*, 2018).	Equity-crowdfunding is based on the exchange of actual shares in a private company for capital (Di Pietro *et al.*, 2018; Block *et al.*, 2017; Agrawal *et al.*, 2016). Such campaigns are the most similar to traditional forms of financing, such as angel investors or venture capital. In this case, in fact, backers are typically individuals who are more informed about the project itself and about the functioning of crowdfunding, than with other forms such as reward-based and donation-based types. The motivational driver of backers, in this case, is more similar to traditional investors, i.e., devoted to obtaining a gain rather than a reward or the pleasure of contributing to a new product/service.
Reward-based crowdfunding	**Donation-based crowdfunding**
In rewards-based crowdfunding, backers typically provide small amounts of money in exchange for a reward. This reward can be a prototype of the item that will be produced, or a gadget like a unique t-shirt, or discount on the product when it will be ready. Reward-based crowdfunding is the most diffused form, in terms of both funds raised and number of financed projects (Davis *et al.*, 2017; Kraus *et al.*, 2016; Belleflamme *et al.*, 2014), and is the focus of the majority of studies.	In donation-based crowdfunding, there is not a reward beyond the gratefulness of the project creator or beneficiary; donors usually contribute with small amounts (typically between $1 and $1,000, but sometimes more) of money as a form of donation, because they like the project or because they want to support a specific cause. Donation-based crowdfunding is typically used to raise money for a non-profit or a social cause (Belleflamme *et al.*, 2014).

broadly review the literature regarding the role of language in the success of crowdfunding, showing how the linguistic content influences fundraising goals and evidencing the key managerial implications.

3.1. *Literature on the success of a crowdfunding campaign*

Understanding why and how some crowdfunding campaigns are successful and others are not, depending on the amount and type of information disclosed, is relevant for both scholars and practitioners (Cumming *et al.*, 2017). Within the vast literature on crowdfunding, campaign success factors received substantial attention, as evidenced by the reviews of Butticè *et al.* (2018) and Centobelli *et al.* (2016). Such success factors studied by the extant literature span across several theoretical backgrounds through which the crowdfunding phenomenon is observed, based mainly in the domains of economics, sociology, psychology and management. Among theoretical theories that have been used to understand and explain crowdfunding in such contexts, the Information-Asymmetry (Agrawal *et al.*, 2015, 2016; Belleflamme *et al.*, 2014) and the Signaling theories (Ahlers *et al.*, 2015) are particularly relevant. The Information-Asymmetry theory refers to the study of decisions in transactions where one party has a greater amount — or better quality — of information than the other. In the context of crowdfunding campaigns, the successful drivers influencing traditional funding cannot directly apply, because backers are moved by different motivations and capabilities than professional investors. Therefore, information asymmetries between crowdfunding backers and entrepreneurs exists and are primarily motivated by a lack of direct face-to-face interaction (Agrawal *et al.*, 2016; Kraus *et al.*, 2016) and by the non-professional character of ordinary backers, who lack the expertise to assess the feasibility and potential profitability of the crowdfunded venture (e.g., lack of initial *ex ante* screening, due diligence and post-investment monitoring). The risk is that crowdfunding investors will devote their money to inconclusive projects because information asymmetries between backers and entrepreneurs are greater (Agrawal *et al.*, 2016; Kraus *et al.*, 2016).

Many of the success factors that have been identified for crowdfunding pertain to the ability of a campaign to overcome such information asymmetries, as evidenced by a noteworthy literature. For instance, Colombo and colleagues (2015) observed the relationship between the *early contributions* shortly after the launch and the success of the campaigns, evidencing how contributions received in the early days of a campaign facilitate its success because they are a "clue about project quality that triggers imitating behavior". Some other studies focused on the positive effects brought about by *media* to communicate the ideas, explaining that videos are important as a "clear signal of at least minimum preparation" (Wheat *et al.*, 2013), or as a good opportunity to introduce the project owner or the team (Cholakova and Clarysse, 2015). Zheng and colleagues (2014) showed that the usage of various media improves the quality of communication and the understanding between the entrepreneurs and the backers. By analyzing the projects updated on Kickstarter, Xu *et al.* (2014) interestingly found that how entrepreneurs communicate with potential backers is more predictive of success than the representation of the project's online campaign page. Moreover, Colombo and his co-authors (2015) studied the relationship between crowdfunding and *social capital* as a component that boosts the probability of successful projects. In particular, they assess that social capital helps to attract backers in the very early days of a crowdfunding campaign, when uncertainty and asymmetric information are relevant. Moreover, Lu and colleagues (2014), found that social networking, particularly in the early stage of the initiative, can raise the probability of obtaining the amount pledged. Kuppuswamy and Bayus (2017) explored that support tends to rise as the project approaches its target goal, for which backers' support changes at different funding timeframes.

Additionally, relevant literature remarks that successful crowdfunding campaigns are strongly determined by entrepreneurs' effective communication (Agrawal *et al.*, 2015; Davis and Webb, 2012), because the proper design of information flows mitigates the strong information asymmetry that characterizes the crowdfunding system and that tends to discourage backers from pledging money. According to Signaling theory (Stiglitz, 1990), information asymmetry is particularly important since the parties do not know each other; no professional scrutiny exists as it does for other types of fund raising and the only way in which the two parties interact is online. Under Signaling theory (Ahlers *et al.*, 2015; Connelly *et al.*, 2011; Spence, 2002, 1973) an effective communication from the entrepreneurs may indicate the quality of the entrepreneurial project. In this way, a proper description of the entrepreneurial project may reduce information asymmetries and provide enough information to reduce the risk of a non-relevant investment or a wrong evaluation of the projects, as evidenced by Moss *et al.* (2015). The authors explain that their study enriches signaling literature regarding the importance of signaling under conditions of information asymmetry in the context of microfinance. Block and colleagues (2018) also evidence the importance of signaling for crowdfunding success in capital markets with asymmetric information. Signaling implicates the agent credibly transferring some information to the principal, highlighting the efforts and costs devoted to transmit the signal of quality of their venture; this theory is useful for describing behavior when two entities have access to different information. As a result, by reducing backers' confidence in the project seeking funding, information asymmetries constitute the most threatening obstacle to crowdfunding success. Therefore, effective communication of project characteristics and achievements constitutes the strongest tool at entrepreneurs' disposal to transmit the quality of the idea and of their commitment (Courtney *et al.*, 2017; Kuppuswamy and Bayus, 2017; Manning and Bejarano, 2017; Parhankangas and Renko, 2017; Moss *et al.*, 2015; Allison *et al.*, 2013; Zhang and Liu, 2012).

This literature also evidences managerial implications, suggesting that entrepreneurs should take into account all the factors influencing a crowdfunding campaign. Nevertheless, several aspects of the crowdfunding phenomenon have not yet been thoroughly explored, for which it is essential to enrich the existing crowdfunding studies (Dushnitsky and Zunino, 2018). In this context, Moritz and Block (2016) evidence several potential research questions to explore. In the light of the above-explained content, the present chapter investigates one important factor which characterizes the information asymmetries, i.e., the linguistic style. Section 3.2 enlightens the extant literature regarding the importance of linguistic style and crowdfunding success.

3.2. *Literature on the importance of linguistic style and crowdfunding success*

In light of the above-explained importance of effective communication in reducing information asymmetries between entrepreneurs and backers, the language used on the campaign deserves specific mention for its importance as a signal of commitment and attention to the message provided to the backers. Therefore, in the following we report the main contributions concerning the impact of language on crowdfunding success, although such a topic has not yet undergone a complete review in the literature. Indeed, literature related to the role of language in the description of crowdfunding campaigns is still scarce and fragmented (Manning and Bejarano, 2017). Former research investigated the role of narratives on consumption experiences (Thompson 1996) and consumption stories (Levy 1981). Gagliardi (1986) found that the use of appropriate language facilitates the connection between entrepreneurs and backers both in terms of reliability that the project will be completed and in terms of emotional involvement. Other previous studies (Semin and Fiedler, 1989) revealed that various linguistic categories, if used effectively, can increase the degree of the relationship between several subjects, by influencing not only the degree of understanding but also the empathic capacity between them.

A first important work arguing that microloan entrepreneurial narratives matter is that of Herzenstein *et al.* (2011). The authors, in their interesting paper "Tell me a good story and I may lend you money: the role of narratives in peer-to-peer lending decisions" focused on peer-to-peer lending decisions, evidencing how narrative, which is a sequentially organized discourse that gives meaning to events, has an impact on backers' choices, since it avoids misleading information and eases the exchange. Herzenstein *et al.* (2011) demonstrate the signalling effect of crowdfundees' narratives. They studied 1,493 loan narratives posted on the peer-to-peer platform Prosper between 2006 and 2007, observing that unverifiable information affects lending decisions more than verifiable information. A couple of years later, Allisson, McKenny and Short (2013) evidenced how the narratives are particularly relevant for microlending policies in developing countries, where language indicating blame and present concern eases funding. Hence, the authors evidence that the institutional context plays a crucial role in determining the relationship between linguistic style and crowdfunding success.

Allison *et al.* (2015) observed a sample of crowdfunding on online platforms containing over 36,000 entrepreneurs in 51 countries. The authors, focusing on the extrinsic and intrinsic motivations of backers, argue that linguistic cues are related to the success of a funding campaign.

They also discover that narratives evidencing pro-social aspects, i.e., improving the societal welfare, rather than business opportunities, are more successful. This evidence is in contrast with that of Cholakova and Clarysse (2015), who assessed that non-financial motivations are not relevant for funding decisions. Moss, Neubaum, and Meyskens (2015), similarly to Allisson *et al.* (2015), found that the narratives emphasizing the opportunity to help others are related to more successful crowdfunding campaigns. The authors investigating a sample of 403,419 contributions from 2006 to 2012 on the Kiva platform suggest that pro-social language, i.e., leveraging social aspects of the crowdfunding project, facilitates the achievement of a campaign. In the same year, Gorbatai and Nelson (2015) observed the role of language in the success of crowdfunding, showing how the linguistic content has an effect on fundraising goals, independently from the type of product or service presented. The authors also underline that men and women use different kinds of language and that entrepreneurs should take into account such differences, trying to decrease gender dissimilarities. Moreover, Manning and Bejarano (2017) studied the narrative style of 54 campaigns launched on the Kickstarter platform during the period 2012–2015, highlighting that future-looking language favors funding of campaigns where the product is intangible, the technology is basic, or the project is socially orientated. Hence, they conceptually stress the importance of using narratives that are coherent with the audience of the campaign, calling for future empirical studies that further validate their assumptions. Furthermore, Parhankangas and Renko (2017) analyzed campaign language, focusing on 656 Kickstarter campaigns between 2013 and 2014 that are video-based rather than textual narratives, interestingly observing that a linguistic style positively influences funding success. Majumdar and Bose (2018) reveal that rational and credible appeals in a message enhance the success rate of crowdfunding. In the context of micro-lending and reward-based crowdfunding, Anglin and colleagues (2018), analyzing 1726 crowdfunding campaigns launched on the platform Kickstarter, interestingly found that positive psychological capital language (based on hope, optimism, resilience, and confidence) is positively related with crowdfunding success.

Focusing on the role of asymmetric information, relevant literature remarks that successful crowdfunding campaigns are strongly determined by the entrepreneurs' effective communication (Agrawal *et al.*, 2015; Davis and Webb, 2012). The latter works highlight how a proper design of narrative style and information flows mitigates the strong information asymmetry that arises between entrepreneurs and backers. Therefore, the success of a crowdfunding project is obtained by the creation of quality content that is able to tell a story and can involve the backers and provide them with enough elements to convince them that the project will be effectively realized. Furthermore, according to Siering, Koch and Deokar (2016), language is also an important driver to detect fraudulent behaviors of funders who provide inaccurate information and try to deceive backers. Cumming *et al.* (2017), documenting new alternative energy technologies crowdfunding, observe that cleantech campaigns are more likely to get their funding target and, among other things, report longer text descriptions. In light of asymmetric information, Cumming and his co-author show that backers face more information problems when investing in alternative energies campaigns, which typically are more risky. For this reason, there are relevant mechanisms, such as narrative descriptions, in order to lessen asymmetric-information problems.

In conclusion, language represents an important tool to facilitate the understanding of projects as well as a signal of commitment of the entrepreneurs, and consequently it increases the ability to build a solid and stable relationship between the promoter of a crowdfunding campaign and its backers. Hence, the relationship between crowdfunding success and linguistic style is a crucial topic, since the effectiveness of a crowdfunding initiative depends on the language used. This is especially valid when backers face asymmetric-information difficulties in obtaining filled information regarding the campaign.

4. Promising Directions of Research and Preliminary Results

Given that the objective of crowdfunding campaigns is the collection of funds requested by the entrepreneurs to start the business project, in the previous section we have seen how academics' interest towards the factors that determine the success of crowdfunding campaigns is constantly growing. Among the success factors, the role of language on crowdfunding campaigns is crucial, for which several studies examined this particular aspect (Manning and Bejarano, 2017; Agrawal *et al.*, 2015; Allison *et al.*, 2015; Gorbatai and Nelson, 2015; Moss *et al.*, 2015; Allisson *et al.*, 2013; Davis and Webb, 2012; Herzenstein *et al.*, 2011). Therefore, language represents an important driver of crowdfunding campaigns, since the success of a project depends on the language used, especially in a context of asymmetric information (Agrawal *et al.*, 2015; Davis and Webb, 2012). In this sense, the project description plays a critical role for convincing the crowd, especially considering that the personal interaction that characterizes traditional financing is lacking in crowdfunding (Butticè *et al.*, 2017; Courtney *et al.*, 2017; Manning and Bejarano, 2017; Parhankangas and Renko, 2017; Hobbs *et al.*, 2016; Kraus *et al.*, 2016). Nevertheless, the topic has not yet been wholly investigated by former papers (Manning and Bejarano, 2017).

In this ongoing stream of studies, we intend to open a new topic, which examines an important aspect of crowdfunding language: i.e., the use of repetitive words, and the use of different linguistic models. Both of these factors might influence the success of a campaign. Our novel approach of investigation is based on the analysis of the repetitiveness of keywords and aims to create an initial conceptualization of the topic. Additionally, this work also aims to be the starting point to develop research regarding another relevant factor in the narrative style of a campaign: the linguistic model, namely the distinction between concrete language and abstract language during the launch of a crowdfunding campaign. In particular, we conducted our research in the context of reward-based crowdfunding collecting data from Kickstarter, the main global crowdfunding platform and a database used by many scientific studies (Butticè *et al.*, 2017; Chan and Parhankangas, 2017; Kaartemo, 2017; Mollick and Nanda, 2016; Colombo *et al.*, 2015; Mollick, 2014).

To the best of our knowledge, no study has yet focused on the effect of repetitive words and linguistic model on the success rate. Thus, the preliminary results reported in this chapter are particularly interesting for doctoral students, researchers, entrepreneurs and policymakers. In our first test, we predict that the use of repetitive words interferes with the success of a campaign, since it indicates that the entrepreneur does not have multiple motivations to explain the feasibility of the project and, therefore, repeats the same words to tell the story. The redundant text might show a scarce mastery of the initiative and the entrepreneur resorts to duplication of words when narrating the campaign. Hence, we foresee a negative effect between recurrent words and crowdfunding success. The second test scrutinizes the influence of linguistic models (concrete versus abstract language) on crowdfunding success, predicting that the typology of the campaign has an impact on the narrative style to employ, since each campaign has its own backer addressees, who report different backgrounds (social, cultural and economic) and, as such, are likely to prefer different linguistic styles.

We also suggest that these new streams of research have important managerial implications, since they satisfy the need for guidance to non-professional investors in a context of asymmetric information. Backers are not professional investors and no additional information is available other than the project description and entrepreneurs' brief profile available in the web-based platform. Therefore, entrepreneurs should take into account the language to use during their campaign and will benefit from the enrichment of the extant literature studying the impact of linguistic style on crowdfunding success. Hence, through our forerunning results, as well as through future research, we aim to spur crucial guidelines for entrepreneurs who intend to launch new crowdfunding campaigns.

4.1. *Data and variables*

As mentioned above, this chapter investigates the role of linguistic style *vis-à-vis* crowdfunding success with a novel approach, with the purpose of urging future research in this field. To do this, we collected approximately 93,000 crowdfunding projects from the Kickstarter platform. Kickstarter is one of the most popular platforms around the world. Many firms and start-ups world-wide promote their projects through Kickstarter, where a considerable amount of projects covering different sectors were launched. Each project we analyzed contains a written description of the project, a title and a series of variables containing information on the geographical location of the project, information on the promoter of the initiative (number of projects already proposed) total amount of money requested and total harvest, number of backers who participated in the project, and the start and end date of the campaign. The total amount of money harvested as a percentage of the money requested is our main variables of interest, named "success rate." This variable represents, in terms of percentages, the capability of obtaining the amount requested (when the value is equal to one) or a greater amount (values higher than one) or a failed campaign (with a value lower than one). The success rate ratio varies from 0 to 144 and the average value is 0.51.

The analysis of the narrative was done through the semantic analysis tool Word Frequency Counter (Available for free from the website www.writewords.org.uk). After obtaining the list of the most commonly used words in the dataset, those repeated words that were not meaningful for analysis purposes were excluded (such as articles, repetitions of the DB categories, auxiliary verbs, adjectives, adverbs, etc.). We eliminated the latter words since they do not add value to our research. After having eliminated the commonly used words, we calculated the frequency (ratio between the number of the words' use and the total number of words found) and the cumulative frequency of the remaining keywords. A total of 87,513 keywords were identified within the entire sample, with a total of 1,495,885-word appearance in the text. Of these 87,000 words, 4,191 appear with a frequency of more than 50 times. Subsequently, the most frequently cumulated keywords were subdivided by campaign category collected in order to explore characteristics of products and campaigns that could attract backers interested in certain types of products. Moreover, each of the project descriptions was assigned to one linguistic model, based on the most recurring typology of word used, following indications in the paper by Semin and Fiedler (1989).

4.2. *The effect of commonly used words: Preliminary results*

A first unique perspective we observe regarding the role of narrative style is the effect of repetitive words on the success rate. In this first study, we explore the use of repetitive words used by the entrepreneurs in the collected crowdfunding campaigns. The research question is: Can repetitive words negatively influence the success of crowdfunding campaigns? Based on Signaling Theory, we expect that the use of recurrent words is a signal of scarce quality of the project description and therefore of commitment by the entrepreneurs. A proper use of linguistic style may represent a cost and effort for the venture, which may be translated into a positive signal of quality and commitment for the investors to convince them to provide their money.

Data analyzed with the Word Frequency Counter tool showed that there are 533,707 words in the total titles of the dataset, from which it was possible to extract the most commonly used ones, eliminating prepositions, articles and abbreviations. In greater details we focused on the top 20% words used from the total sample (around 92,000 keywords). Examples of the most recurrent words are "needs" (19.4%), "fund" (18.9%), "work" (18.6%), "old" (18.4%), "unique" (17.7%), as reported in Table 2.

Then, to assess the impact of recurrent words on the success of a crowdfunding campaign we run a linear regression (OLS) whose dependent variable is the "success rate", that is, the amount of funds collected as a share of those intended as an objective (Josefy *et al.*, 2017). The independent variable used for the analysis of commonly used words was created according to the keyword count distribution, i.e., the top 20% count of the words used in the description of the crowdfunding campaign. Starting from the observation of the results of the frequency of the keywords (Table 2), we note that many words are specific to some sectors. Therefore, sector controls were included in the analysis.

Table 2: Examples of keywords for the top 20% of the total sample.

Needs	**Stories**
Fund	Adventure
Work	Family
Old	Production
Unique	Home
Time	Community
People	Fun
Feature	Great
Novel	Journey
Original	Release

Table 3: OLS, with the "success rate" as dependent variable and "top 20% word count" as independent variable.

Number of Observations	**92328**
Prob > *f*	0.000
R^2	0.1091
	Coefficient
Top 20% word count	−0.0055206*

Notes: The model employs the following control variables: Backers Count, Campaign Duration, Start Year, Sector Dummy Variables (Art, Book, Crafts, Design, Fashion, Film, Food, Games, Graphic design, Hardware, Journalism, Mixed media, Music, Open software, Product design, Technology, Video games) and dummy variables for the continents where the business projects take place. *stands for $p < 0.10$.

Source: Our processing.

The results of the linear regression reported in Table 3 show that the repetitiveness of the keywords present in the top 20% of our sample leads to a lower success rate (p-value = 0.06). The reason behind this result lies in the logic according to which the use of extremely recurrent words leads to a lower possibility of catching the lenders' attention and therefore of reaching the fundraising goal. In greater detail, the use of recurrent words decreases the success rate by 0.5%, which, although not representing a crucial aspect, it may be relevant for entrepreneurs who aim to maximize fund raising. Moreover, as stated, this preliminary study is intended as a starting point for future advancements that may consider also variables such as additional moderation and mediation effects to our results.

With this study, we contribute to the research stream that analyzes the impact of linguistic styles on crowdfunding success, by evidencing the negative effect brought about by recurrent words in the description of the project in terms of funds collected. Hence, as expected, recurrent words might be signals of scarce mastery of the project. The result obtained can be crucial, given the opportunity to start a new line of studies, which could empirically test the impact of repetitive words on crowdfunding success from different viewpoints.

4.3. *The effect of the linguistic model: Preliminary results*

The main objective of the second piece of research is to explore the different forms of linguistic models used for crowdfunding campaigns, to understand if there is a positive relationship between narrative forms of project descriptions and crowdfunding success. As demonstrated in previous studies (Semin and Fiedler, 1989), various linguistic categories, if used effectively, can increase the degree of relationship between several subjects, by influencing not only the degree of understanding but also the empathetic capacity between them and the perceived quality. In fact, linguistic style, if properly implemented by devoting internal resources to it, may represent a signal of quality and commitment of the entrepreneurs. Therefore, the research question we have analyzed in this study is: Can different linguistic models influence the success of crowdfunding campaigns?

In particular, the attention is focused on the semantic classifications concerning the distinction between concrete language and abstract language, called the "Linguistic Category Model" (Semin and Fiedler, 1989). In the LCM, distinctions are made between four categories of words (including adjectives and three types of verbs), to distinguish adjectives, i.e., devices used to describe properties, from verbs that refer to specific actions (speaking, calling, etc.), verbs concerning interpretive actions and verbs referring to psychological states. It is possible to identify these four types of linguistic categories defined as follows:

(1) Descriptive Action Verbs (Acronym DAV: Descriptive Action Verbs);
(2) Interpretative Action Verbs (IAV Acronym: Interpretative Action Verbs);
(3) State Verbs (SV Acronym: State Verbs);
(4) Adjectives (Acronym ADJ: Adjectives).

The four categories are organized along a continuum of abstract concreteness. At the one extreme of the continuum are the DAVs, verbs that indicate an immediate reference to events and behaviors, and at the other extreme the ADJs, which instead designate an abstract reference to the psychological properties of a person. With regard to this classification scheme, in investigating the psychological implications, the abstractness of a category implies less information about the project. This taxonomy subdivides words according to a dimension of concreteness/abstractness, as follows: the first two categories correspond to a higher level of concreteness, while the second two categories have a greater abstraction. The more abstract the information is, the more it is informative and lasting, but also debatable and less verifiable. On the other hand, as the concreteness of the word increases, controllability increases, as does the ease with which an imperative is formed to specify a behavioral prescription (Semin and Fiedler, 1989). As for the intermediate categories, the theory states that the IAVs imply a low consensus and a low specificity; while the SV imply a high consensus and a high specificity. Examples of words divided into linguistic categories are available in Table 4.

A relational analysis was carried out among the types of linguistic categories and the success rate of the crowdfunding campaign. In this case, we conducted two OLSs with respect to two different macro sectors, i.e., the "Tech & Innovation" and "Art" groups. We expected that the linguistic category model would differently impact the funds raised depending on these two sectors, as the backers providing money were different and may have been affected by the words used to dissimilar extents. As control variables, we included the total number of previous projects as a proxy of entrepreneurial experience and number of backers as a proxy of social capital of that particular crowdfunding project.

Observing, in the first instance, the projects related to the "Tech & Innovation" category, we relied on 17,780 observations to perform the linear regression whose output is shown in Table 5. Concerning the independent variables, we have four different variables counting the number of

Table 4: List of words divided into four categories.

Category 1: DAV	Category 2: IAV	Category 3: SV	Category 4: ADJ
Create	Help	Love	New
Making	Need	Like	Short
Play	Support	Fun	Young
Come	Needs	Free	Original

Table 5: OLS regression for "Tech and Innovation" projects.

Number of observations	**17880**
p-value Fisher test	0.00
R^2	0.08
Adjusted R^2	0.08
	Coefficient
Sum of DAV words	0.090*
Sum of IAV words	–0.028
Sum of SV words	–0.022
Sum of ADJ words	0.05
Intercept	0.630**

Notes: Success Rate is the dependent variable. Control variables are considered: total number of previous projects as a matter of entrepreneurial experience and number of backers as a matter of social capital of that particular crowdfunding project. *stands for $p < 0.10$; **stands for $p < 0.05$.

words belonging to each of the linguistic categories, i.e., DAV, IAV, SV and ADJ. Among them, we evidence that DAV positively affects the success rate of crowdfunding by 9% (p-value = 0.098). In greater detail, if the sum of DAV words is equal to 1, the success rate increases by 9%; if the sum is 2, the success rate will increase by 9% × 2; and so on. Moreover, the success rate is also influenced by "Number of backers" and the "Total number of previous projects." In fact, both the control variables show a p-value < 0.001 as expected from previous results.

We carried out the same analysis for the second category of projects, i.e., "Art" campaigns. As shown in Table 6, the number of projects is equal to 75,370 and we confirm that the success rate is influenced by the control variables "Number of backers" and "Total number projects" p-value < 0.001 as expected. In this case, the IAV variable has a significant (p-value = 0.006) negative effect of 1.5% and consequently the success rate is dependent on the absence of the IAV language entry. More specifically, if the IAV sum is equal to 1, the success rate decreases by 1.5%; if the sum is 2, the success rate will decrease by 1.5% × 2; and so on.

Table 6: OLS regression for "Arts" projects.

Number of observations	**75370**
p-value Fisher test	0.00
R^2	0.08
Adjusted R^2	0.08
	Coefficient
Sum of DAV words	−0.007
Sum of IAV words	−0.015*
Sum of SV words	−0.002
Sum of ADJ words	0.005
Intercept	0.593*

Notes: Success rate is the dependent variable. Control variables are considered: total number of previous projects as a matter of entrepreneurial experience and number of backers as a matter of social capital of that particular crowdfunding project. *stands for $p<0.01$.

Therefore, the impact of linguistic models differs depending on the sector to which the crowdfunding campaign belongs, providing useful insights to increase the funds raised. In these cases, the magnitude of the effect is lower than the previous study, i.e., 0.1% but it may still be interesting for practitioners looking to maximizing the funds raised. The different purposes that characterize diverse sectors also have varying implications for the design of crowdfunding projects. Therefore, our research offers some interesting implications, suggesting that entrepreneurs should firstly analyze the sector in which their projects take place and, then, launch a campaign using a proper language according to the addressees.

In conclusion, in the present work we highlighted two promising future directions that can be analyzed more deeply in future studies, which integrate the literature conducted in the previous sections. Our evidence aims to be the starting point of a new stream of research and to stimulate subsequent literature to develop this new framework of investigation.

5. Conclusions and Future Research Opportunities

This chapter aims to review and stimulate the emerging new stream of research about narrative style and crowdfunding success. After recapping the major findings in this field, our research highlights the importance of repetitive words and linguistic models on crowdfunding success in order to inspire future and promising empirical studies as well as to provide implications to practitioners, entrepreneurs and policymakers. In greater detail, we provided a snapshot of the existing understanding about crowdfunding in the entrepreneurial financing landscape, and we reported the state of the art regarding the main contributions of the extant literature regarding factors influencing crowdfunding success.

After this introduction, we conducted an original-literature review, studying those papers that observe the key role of linguistic style-based on the theoretical framework of asymmetric information and signaling theory. Previous analysis showed that the main aspects accessible to backers, which may influence their willingness to provide funds, are entrepreneurs' characteristics and project descriptions on the online platforms (Kuppuswamy and Bayus, 2017; Agrawal *et al.*, 2016; Belleflamme *et al.*, 2014; Schwienbacher and Larralde, 2010). The importance of the project description is exacerbated by the absence of face-to-face interaction between entrepreneurs and backers that can be crucial in motivating the crowd (Cappa *et al.*, 2016) and by asymmetric information present in such novel financing mechanisms that involves non-expert investors (Agrawal *et al.*, 2015; Davis and Webb, 2012). These aspects distinguish crowdfunding from traditional financing and for these reasons the linguistic style of crowdfunding appears to play a growing and significant role for the financing of new ventures and projects. Indeed, in the absence of previous track records, linguistic style may represent the main signal of quality and commitment to the entrepreneurial project (Ahlers *et al.*, 2015; Block *et al.*, 2018; Connelly *et al.*, 2011; Spence, 2002, 1973).

In this stream of research, our work observed a different and original aspect of linguistic style of crowdfunding campaigns, finding that the use of repetitive words negatively influences the amount of financial resources collected. Moreover, we also found that the linguistic models (concrete versus abstract language) that are advisable to use depends on the context and where the campaign is launched. For instance, we observed that in the "Tech & Innovation" sector it is preferable to use Descriptive Action Verbs while in the "Arts" sector Interpretative Action Verbs should be avoided. Entrepreneurs should thus avoid using recurrent words and take into account the sector in which the campaign is embedded. Therefore, with this chapter we enrich the existing literature, evidencing future research opportunities to investigate how linguistic style influences the success rate of collecting money and thus contributing to a better academic understanding of the crowdfunding phenomenon.

From a managerial point of view, our research has crucial implications. Firstly, it is possible to rethink the concept of crowdfunding as a form of marketing of a new generation, where the difference depends on the narrative style of the entrepreneurs. Crowdfunding should not be considered just as a method of alternative financing, but a new method of communication that allows the dissemination of new ideas that should convince backers of the feasibility of the project while leveraging their emotions in order to receive funding. Entrepreneurs who plan to start a new crowdfunding campaign should design their project considering the advantages of avoiding the excessive use of repetitive words and employing either concrete or abstract language, depending on the sector where the campaign is launched. These considerations represent interesting implications of our research and are essential to efficiently collect funds through crowdfunding.

Future research should further explore the impact that linguistic style may have on crowds' tendency to respond to calls for money, also considering video content rather than just written description of the project. Especially in the current informational arena where we are offered with a multitude of stimuli, entrepreneurs must be able to deliver the right message to widely dispersed individuals and properly design the narrative of the crowdfunding campaign. In our opinion, the new pattern of study evidenced in this chapter provides fascinating hints for future investigations. It is possible to deepen the analysis of the distinct effect that linguistic style has on different crowdfunding sectors, as we started to differentiate the projects in the "Arts" and "Tech & Innovation" sectors, also considering more detailed categorizations. Another possible interesting trajectory could be to understand the narrative dynamics that impact on no-profit projects (distinguishing for example among social enterprises, voluntary projects and philanthropic initiatives) and the difference with respect to traditional for-profit crowdfunding projects. Moreover, another future development that can stem from the empirical outcomes of our study is the analysis of the impact brought about by the mostly used words with respect to social media and the World Wide Web in general, rather than relying on those used in other crowdfunding projects. In addition, while our study focused on Kickstarter platform, future studies may consider other platforms to compare the effects of different culture and institutions where the crowdfunding platform resides. Furthermore, as the empirical setting of our analyses is represented by reward-based crowdfunding, future studies should also consider other typologies of crowdfunding, i.e., debt-based, equity-based and donation-based to highlight whether there are differences among them about the effect brought about by different narratives. Overall we believe that our study paves the way for several future developments, evidencing that the stream of research about the impact of narrative style and crowdfunding success is particularly interesting and potentially flourishing for both students and researchers.

Acknowledgments

Francesco Cappa would like to gratefully acknowledge Ermenegildo Zegna, who supported this research, thanks to the EZ Founder's Scholarship 2017–2018 and 2018–2019. Francesco Cappa and Riccardo Maiolini would also like to thank the Walliance Crowdfunding Platform and Gruppo Bertoldi for the "Best Paper on Crowdfunding" prize, awarded during the Third Entrepreneurial Conference held in Milan in June 2018, which has further inspired us to continue our scientific focus towards linguistic-style impact on crowdfunding.

References

Agrawal A., Catalini C., and Goldfarb A. (2016) Are Syndicates the killer app of equity crowdfunding? *California Management Review*, 58, 111–124. doi:10.1525/cmr.2016.58.2.111.

Agrawal A., Catalini C., and Goldfarb A. (2015) Crowdfunding: Geography, social networks, and the timing of investment decisions. *Journal of Economics and Management Strategy*, 24, 253–274. doi:10.1111/jems.12093.

Ahlers G. K. C., Cumming D., Günther C., and Schweizer D. (2015) Signaling in equity crowdfunding. *Entrepreneurship: Theory and Practice*, 39, 955–980. doi:10.1111/etap.12157.

Allison T. H., McKenny A. F., and Short J. C. (2013) The effect of entrepreneurial rhetoric on microlending investment: An examination of the warm-glow effect. *Journal of Business Venturing*, 28, 690–707. doi:10.1016/j.jbusvent.2013.01.003.

Assenova V., Best J., Cagney M., Ellenoff D., Karas K., Moon J., Neiss S., Suber R., and Sorenson O. (2016) The present and future of crowdfunding. *California Management Review*, 58, 125–135. doi:10.1525/cmr.2016.58.2.125.

Belleflamme P., Lambert T., and Schwienbacher A. (2014) Crowdfunding: Tapping the right crowd. *Journal of Business Venturing*, 29, 585–609. doi:10.1016/j.jbusvent.2013.07.003.

Belleflamme P., Lambert T., and Schwienbacher A. (2010) Crowdfunding: An industrial organization perspective. *Business*, 25–26. doi:10.1.1.416.4643.

Bhattacharya A. (2017) Innovations in new venture financing: Evidence from Indian SME IPOs. *Global Finance Journal*, 1–17. doi:10.1016/j.gfj.2017.02.001.

Bi S., Liu Z., and Usman K. (2017) The influence of online information on investing decisions of reward-based crowdfunding. *Journal of Business Research*, 71, 10–18. doi:10.1016/j.jbusres.2016.10.001.

Block J. H., Colombo M. G., Cumming D. J., and Vismara S. (2018) New players in entrepreneurial finance and why they are there. *Small Business Economics*, 50, 239–250. doi:10.1007/s11187-016-9826-6.

Block J. H., Colombo M. G., Cumming D. J., and Vismara S. (2017) New players in entrepreneurial finance and why they are there. *Small Business Economics*, 1–12. doi:10.1007/s11187-016-9826-6.

Burtch G., Ghose A., Wattal S., and Burtch G. (2015) The hidden cost of accommodating crowdfunder privacy preferences: A randomized field experiment the hidden cost of accommodating crowdfunder privacy preferences: A randomized field experiment. *Management Science*, 61, 949–962.

Butticè V., Franzoni C., Rossi-Lamastra C., and Rovelli P. (2018) The road to crowdfunding success: A review of extant literature. *Creating and Capturing Value Through Crowdsourcing*. Oxford University Press, Oxford.

Butticè V., Colombo M. G., and Wright M. (2017) Serial crowdfunding, social capital, and project success. *Entrepreneurship Theory and Practice*, 41, 183–207. doi:10.1111/etap.12271.

Cappa F., Laut J., Nov O., Giustiniano L., and Porfiri M. (2016) Activating social strategies: Face-to-face interaction in technology-mediated citizen science. *Journal of Environmental Management*, 182, 374–384. doi:10.1016/j.jenvman.2016.07.092.

Cappa F., Laut J., Porfiri M., and Giustiniano L. (2018) Bring them aboard: Rewarding participation in technology-mediated citizen science projects. *Computers in Human Behavior*, 89, 246–257. doi:https://doi.org/10.1016/j.chb.2018.08.017.

Cholakova M. and Clarysse B. (2015) Does the Possibility to make equity investments in crowdfunding projects crowd out reward-based investments? *Entrepreneurship Theory and Practice*, 39, 145–172. doi:10.1111/etap.12139.

Colombo M. G., Franzoni C., and Rossi-Lamastra C. (2015) Internal social capital and the attraction of early contributions in crowdfunding. *Entrepreneurship: Theory and Practice*, 39, 75–100. doi:10.1111/etap.12118.

Connelly B. L., Certo S. T., Ireland R. D., and Reutzel C. R. (2011) Signaling theory: A review and assessment. *Journal of Management*, doi:10.1177/0149206310388419.

Courtney C., Dutta S., and Li Y. (2017) Resolving information asymmetry: Signaling, endorsement, and crowdfunding success. *Entrepreneurship: Theory and Practice*, 41, 265–290. doi:10.1111/etap.12267.

Cull R., Demirgüç-Kunt A., and Morduch J. (2009) Microfinance meets the market. *Contemporary Studies in Economic and Financial Analysis*, 92, 1–30. doi:10.1108/S1569-3759(2009)0000092004.

Cumming D. J., Leboeuf G., and Schwienbacher A. (2017) Crowdfunding cleantech. *Energy Economics*, 65, 292–303. doi:10.1016/j.eneco.2017.04.030.

Davis B. C., Hmieleski K. M., Webb J. W., and Coombs J. E. (2017) Funders' positive affective reactions to entrepreneurs' crowdfunding pitches: The influence of perceived product creativity and entrepreneurial passion. *Journal of Business Venturing*, 32, 90–106. doi:10.1016/j.jbusvent.2016.10.006.

Davis B. C. and Webb J. W. (2012) Crowd-funding of entrepreneurial ventures: Getting the right combination of signals. *Frontiers of Entrepreneurship Research*, 32, 16.

Di Pietro F., Prencipe A., and Majchrzak A. (2018) Crowd equity investors: An underutilized asset for open innovation in startups. *California Management Review*, 60, 43–70. doi:10.1177/0008125617738260.

Eisenmann T., Parker G., and Alstyne M. W. Van (2006) Strategies for two- sided markets. *Harvard Business Review*, 84, 12. doi:10.1007/s00199-006-0114-6.

Fairlie R., Reedy E., Morelix A., and Russell J. (2015) *Kauffman Startup Activity Index 2015*, Ewing Marion Kauffman Foundation. doi:10.1002/352760362X.

Franzoni C. and Sauermann H. (2014) Crowd science: The organization of scientific research in open collaborative projects. *Research Policy*, 43, 1–20.

Gagliardi P. (1986) The Creation and change of organizational cultures: A conceptual framework. *Organization Studies*, 7, 117–134. doi:10.1177/017084068600700203.

Giudici G., Guerini M., and Rossi-Lamastra C. (2018) Reward-based crowdfunding of entrepreneurial projects: The effect of local altruism and localized social capital on proponents' success. *Small Business Economics*, 50, 307–324. doi:10.1007/s11187-016-9830-x.

Gobble M. A. M. (2012) Everyone is a venture capitalist: The new age of crowdfunding. Research *Technology Management*, 55, 4–7. doi:10.5437/08956308X5504001.

Hobbs J., Grigore G., and Molesworth M. (2016) Success in the management of crowdfunding projects in the creative industries. *Internet Research*, 26, 146–166. doi:10.1108/IntR-08-2014-0202.

Josefy M., Dean T. J., Albert L. S., and Fitza M. A. (2017) The role of community in crowdfunding success: Evidence on cultural attributes in funding campaigns to "save the local theater." *Entrepreneurship: Theory and Practice*, 41, 161–182. doi:10.1111/etap.12263.

Kraus S., Richter C., Brem A., Cheng C.-F., and Chang M.-L. (2016) Strategies for reward-based crowdfunding campaigns. *Journal of Innovation & Knowledge*, 1, 13–23. doi:10.1016/j.jik.2016.01.010.

Kuppuswamy V. and Bayus B. L. (2017) Does my contribution to your crowdfunding project matter? *Journal of Business Venturing*, 32, 72–89. doi:10.1016/j.jbusvent.2016.10.004.

Lu C.-T., Xie S., Kong X., and Yu P. S. (2014) Inferring the impacts of social media on crowdfunding. In *Proceedings of the 7th ACM International Conference on Web Search and Data Mining — WSDM '14,* pp. 573–582. doi:10.1145/2556195.2556251.

Maiolini R. and Naggi R. (2011) Crowdsourcing and SMEs: Opportunities and challenges, in: Information technology and innovation trends in organizations. *Physica* — Verlag HD, Heidelberg, pp. 399–406. doi:10.1007/978-3-7908-2632-6_45.

Manning S. and Bejarano T. A. (2017) Convincing the crowd: Entrepreneurial storytelling in crowdfunding campaigns. *Strategic Organization*, 15, 194–219. doi:10.1177/1476127016648500.

Mollick E. (2014) The dynamics of crowdfunding: An exploratory study. *Journal of Business Venturing*, 29, 1–16. doi:10.1016/j.jbusvent.2013.06.005.

Moss T. W., Neubaum D. O., and Meyskens M. (2015) The effect of virtuous and entrepreneurial orientations on microfinance lending and repayment: A signaling theory perspective. *Entrepreneurship Theory and Practice*, 39, 27–52. doi:10.1111/etap.12110.

Parhankangas A. and Ehrlich M. (2014) How entrepreneurs seduce business angels: An impression management approach. *Journal of Business Venturing*, 29, 543–564. doi:10.1016/j.jbusvent.2013.08.001.

Parhankangas A. and Renko M. (2017) Linguistic style and crowdfunding success among social and commercial entrepreneurs. *Journal of Business Venturing*, 32, 215–236. doi:10.1016/j.jbusvent.2016.11.001.

Poetz M. K. and Schreier M. (2012) The value of crowdsourcing: Can users really compete with professionals in generating new product ideas? *Journal of Product Innovation Management*, 29, 245–256.

Rubin T. H., Aas T. H., and Stead A. (2015) Knowledge flow in Technological business incubators: Evidence from Australia and Israel. *Technovation*, 41, 11–24. doi:10.1016/j.technovation.2015.03.002.

Schwienbacher A. and Larralde B. (2010) Crowdfunding of small entrepreneurial ventures. *Handbook of Entrepreneurial Finance*, 2010, 1–23. doi:10.2139/ssrn.1699183.

Semin G. R. and Fiedler K. (1989) Relocating attributional phenomena within a language-cognition interface: The case of actors' and observers' perspectives. *European Journal of Social Psychology*, 19, 491–508. doi:10.1002/ejsp.2420190602.

Short J. C., Ketchen D. J., McKenny A. F., Allison T. H., and Ireland R. D. (2017) Research on Crowdfunding: Reviewing the (very recent) past and celebrating the present. *Entrepreneurship: Theory and Practice*, 41, 149–160. doi:10.1111/etap.12270.

Spence M. (2002) Signaling in retrospect and the informational structure of markets. *American Economic Review*, 92, 434–459. doi:10.1257/00028280260136200.

Spence M. (1973) Job market signaling. *The Quarterly Journal of Economics*, 87, 355. doi:10.2307/1882010.

Van Osnabrugge M. and Robinson R. J. (2000) Angel Investing: Matching startup funds with startup companies — the guide for entrepreneurs and individual investors, San Francisco, CA: Jossey Bass.

Wheat R. E., Wang Y., Byrnes J. E., and Ranganathan J. (2013) Raising money for scientific research through crowdfunding. *Trends in Ecology and Evolution*, doi:10.1016/j.tree.2012.11.001.

Zhang J. and Liu P. (2012) Rational Herding in microloan markets. *Management Science*, 58, 892–912. doi:10.1287/mnsc.1110.1459.

Zheng H., Li D., Wu J., and Xu Y. (2014) The role of multidimensional social capital in crowdfunding: A comparative study in China and US. *Information and Management*, 51, 488–496. doi:10.1016/j.im.2014.03.003.

Chapter 7

An Introduction to Blockchain, Cryptocurrency and Initial Coin Offerings

Pierluigi Martino*
Department of Economics and Management, University of Pisa
pierluigi.martino@ec.unipi.it

Kevin Jue Wang†
Auckland Business School, Auckland University
jy02749974@hotmail.com

Cristiano Bellavitis†
Auckland Business School, Auckland University
c.bellavitis@auckland.ac.nz

Carlos M. DaSilva‡
HEG School of Management Fribourg/HES-SO//University of Applied Sciences Western Switzerland
Carlos.dasilva@hefr.ch

*10, Via Cosimo Ridolfi, Pisa, 56124, Italy.
†12, Grafton Road, Auckland, 1010, New Zealand.
‡Chemin du Musée 4, 1700 Fribourg, Switzerland.

Abstract

Blockchain is a revolutionary technology that allows people to record transactions on a digital, decentralized, distributed ledger, without any central authority. Some consider this technology as "the trust machine" and cryptocurrency is without doubt the most notable by-product of the blockchain revolution. Initial coin offering (ICO) is a new way to raise entrepreneurial finance, newly created cryptocurrencies are being sold to the public by start-ups in exchange of capital. This chapter intends to clarify this phenomenon by explaining the concepts of blockchain technology, cryptocurrency and ICO, in order to provide valuable insights into this new trend of entrepreneurial finance.

1. Introduction

The technology boom felt over the past few years has led to new forms of entrepreneurial finance (Bruton *et al.*, 2014). Specifically, new players and new means of financing entrepreneurial firms have recently emerged (Block *et al.*, 2018). A central innovation to these advances is blockchain technology, acknowledged as a disruptive technology with the potential to transform our society and economy (McKinsey, 2016; OECD, 2018). Born as the foundational technology underlying cryptocurrencies, blockchain has progressively found applications well beyond its original purpose (Tapscott and Tapscott, 2017).

One such application is capital fundraising. As Tapscott and Tapscott (2017) reveal, Blockchain enables companies of any size to raise money via peer-to-peer financing through globally distributed share offerings and open a new array of possibilities for entrepreneurs to finance their business. Through initial coin offerings (ICOs) mechanism, new fundraising blockchain-based models allow companies to raise capital from the general public by issuing their own cryptocurrencies. Today, ICOs are considered an alternative to traditional financing such as venture capital (VC) or angel investors (SEC, 2017). Such offer entrepreneurs an array of possibilities, but also pose strategic, economical and regulatory challenges (Philippon, 2016; Bellavitis *et al.*, 2017;

Block *et al.*, 2018). While ICOs have the potential to revolutionize the way firms raise capital, create and deliver products, the literature is still fuzzy on the potential of blockchain and ICOs to entrepreneurial finance.

The objective of this chapter is to investigate and clarify the uses and challenges associated with blockchain technology, cryptocurrencies and ICOs in the context of entrepreneurial finance. The chapter is then structured as follows: first we provide an overview of blockchain technology, highlighting its key features, archetypes, benefits and disadvantages; second, we explore the topic of cryptocurrencies in the context of entrepreneurial finance; third, we explore the process of ICO, exposing its advantages and disadvantages *vis-á-vis* other traditional forms of financing available to entrepreneurs and corporations; fourth, we offer concluding remarks and suggestions for further research on the topic.

2. Blockchain

Blockchain technology was introduced in 2008 by "Satoshi Nakamoto". It represents the foundation of the digital peer-to-peer cash "Bitcoin" (Nakamoto, 2008). Bitcoin originated as a means of independence from government control and central authority, and aimed at drastically reduce transaction costs by cutting costly middle-men. It represented a means for otherwise excluded individual (i.e., due to cost, regulation, governmental restrictions) to have a decentralized bank account accessed via a wallet from the internet. From these original motivations, the blockchain technology evolved beyond cryptocurrencies to a wide range of applications in both financial and non-financial industries, from money transfers to securing digital music sales (Crosby *et al.*, 2016; Pierro, 2017).

In a nutshell, blockchain is a digital, decentralized, distributed ledger that records transactions (Adhami *et al.*, 2018; Gatteschi *et al.*, 2018; Niranjanamurthy *et al.*, 2018; Siba and Prakash, 2016; Swan, 2015). Its name originally comes from the "block" and "chain" where transactions are grouped in blocks as a data package and also chained sequentially with each block linked to the previous one. Thus, a blockchain represents a complete ledger of the transaction history (Nofer *et al.*, 2017). In addition, blockchain is a distributed system that requires more than one node to be fully functional, but, at the same time, it is also decentralized so that no individual node can fully control the whole network. Hence, no central authority is required. Furthermore, transparency is guaranteed in blockchain as the complete transaction history is stored by all participants on the network (Bhaskar and Chuen, 2015).

In blockchain, each block not only stores the transaction's detail and timestamp, but also saves the hash values (numeric value of a fixed length that uniquely identifies data) of the previous block with a nonce (a random number). Figure 1 is a typical example of a basic blockchain. When storing transaction details, blockchain technology employs the nonce for verifying the hash to ensure the integrity of the entire blockchain (Gatteschi *et al.*, 2018; Nofer *et al.*, 2017; Pierro, 2017). A hash value is produced by the cryptographic hash function that maps a given set of data to a fixed-size string of numbers and letters (Drescher, 2017). For example, the hash value of a single word "hello" and the hash value of a sentence with 10 words will be two unique values but exactly the same size and length. In addition, transactions of a block are hashed through the Merkle root, which is already the hash of all the transaction hashes in the block. As a result, hashing a block with 100 transactions takes exactly the same

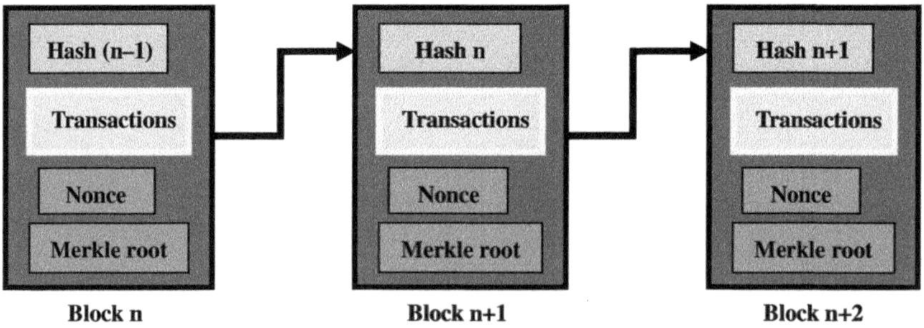

Figure 1: Basic blockchain.

amount of effort as hashing a block with only one transaction (Bhaskar and Chuen, 2015). In addition, fraudulent transactions can be effectively prevented since any change in a block would also change the respective hash value.

A new block will only be added to the chain when the majority of nodes in the network were agreed by a consensus mechanism on both validities of transactions in a block and the block itself (Nofer *et al.*, 2017). This consensus mechanism is a process to ensure the information of a newly added block is valid and it records the latest transaction. It ensures the majority of network validators agree on the state of the ledger. It is also a set of rules and procedures between multiple participating nodes to ensure the validity of the ledger (Swanson, 2015). In addition, new transactions will be stored in a block for a particular period by the consensus process (time may vary depending on the blockchain, for example, 10 mins in Bitcoin blockchain) before added to the ledger. After such period, the information can no longer be changed (Nofer *et al.*, 2017).

Proof of Work (PoW) is the first and also the most popular blockchain consensus mechanism. HashCash is a PoW based algorithm that is used by many cryptocurrencies, including Bitcoin for block generation (Siba and Prakash, 2016). New blocks will only be validated and added through the "mining process", which the protocol rewards the first node (miner) that solves a complex mathematical problem with the newly created coin unit (Nofer *et al.*, 2017). Hence, the probability for mining a new block depends on the miner's ability to solve the mathematical problem. According to Gatteschi *et al.* (2018), this process requires "nodes to find a random value that, combined with the hash of transactions and of the previous block header, produces a given result. When a node identifies a possible solution, it broadcasts the result to the others nodes, which check it. If the majority of the nodes agree on the result, the block is considered valid and it is added to the blockchain, making each node update its local copy (the winner can also receive a reward; for example, in the form of a transaction fee)" (p. 63). However, in PoW, the difficulty level of mining increases as more blocks are solved, meaning it only gets harder and harder for miners to obtain a new coin unit. Moreover, PoW also comes with high costs for miners, as better mining hardware with high electricity costs are required in order to win the mining competition (Bhaskar and Chuen, 2015).

Besides Bitcoin, there are several types of PoW, and token-based or blockchain inspired consensus protocols have been developed. For instance, both BitShares and Peercoin are great examples of Proof of Stake (PoS) consensus protocols. In PoS, the mining power (or the ability to validate block transactions) depends on the miner's ownership stake of that cryptocurrency (Bhaskar and Chuen, 2015; Lai and Chuen, 2018). Therefore, unlike PoW (where the protocol rewards miners depending on their ability to solve mathematical problems in order to create and validate new blocks); in PoS, the node with more coins (stake) simply has a higher mining power. For example, a user holding 1% of the total coins can mine 1% of the PoS blocks (Bhaskar and Chuen, 2015).

2.1. *Asymmetric cryptography*

In addition to all the unique features of blockchain mentioned above, asymmetric cryptography also has been utilized in blockchain technology. It is also known as public-key cryptography which helps users protect their digital property and enhance user security. This function enables information to be encrypted, then transferred through a combination of public and private keys. A public key can be seen by anyone freely; it represents an individual's account address. On the other hand, a private key restricts the account ownership access only to the private key/account holder. For example, the public key in the Bitcoin blockchain resembles an email address, and the private key resembles a password that logs in to the email address. By simply having an email address, people can send and receive emails after they login. Similarly, with Bitcoin, people can send and receive Bitcoins with their private keys (Swan, 2015). Note that it is nearly impossible to derive a private key only based on its paired public key. Moreover, a "digital signature" is created when any account holder authorizes transactions, in order to ensure the integrity of the data. It is done by using a mathematical algorithm, combining users' private key with the data that they would like to transfer. Therefore, the accuracy and completeness of the transferred data are guaranteed since the user's private key is now part of the data (Drescher, 2017).

2.2. *Advantages and disadvantages of blockchain technology*

Blockchain technology brings several advantages as follows:

(1) decentralization (it cannot be controlled by any central authority and is not dependent on a third party to function);
(2) transparency (the complete transaction history is visible to everyone);
(3) automation (by automating parts of organizations' business process, blockchain may reduce the costs associated with areas such as compliance — reducing the time and effort spent on regulatory reporting;
(4) better fault tolerance and attack resistance (due to the nature of its distribution that relies on multiple individual components making it hard to fail or to be targeted by a cyber attack);
(5) potentially lower transaction costs and faster transaction (for example, Banco Santander launched in April 2018 the first blockchain-based international money transfer service that makes it possible for customers to complete international transfers on the same day) (Niranjanamurthy *et al.*, 2018).

However, blockchain technology also presents a series of challenges as follows:

(1) When compared to the traditional banking system, higher transaction costs and slower transaction time might occur due to its high power consumption and hardware requirements. Since the mining process is more like a competition among nodes where only the quickest wins, modern and up to date hardware equipment with higher hash rate will do better. (Adhami *et al.*, 2018; Niranjanamurthy *et al.*, 2018; Gatteschi *et al.*, 2018).
(2) Blockchain comes with potential environmental issues due to its vast power consumption requirements and frequent hardware update

requirements. As a peer-to-peer network, multiple running nodes/computers are needed in order to maintain the functionally, as well as modern hardware to run it.

(3) Security issues, risks of theft activity and cyber attack are still present (Niranjanamurthy *et al.*, 2018). For example, the "51% vulnerability" is one of the most known risks in blockchain technology — where a malicious minor gains control of over 50% of the network's hashrate. As the blockchain consensus mechanism itself has 51% vulnerability, it can be exploited by hackers to control the entire blockchain (Li *et al.*, 2017). Another major risk is the security of private key. A private key is considered as the identity and security credential of a user in blockchain. Therefore, if the user's private key is stolen by a hacker, the user's account will face the risk of being tampered. Furthermore, it is difficult to recover the modified blockchain information on hacked accounts, since blockchain technology is based on a decentralized network.

(4) Full transparency may lead to privacy concerns as everyone can access the whole blockchain; as De Filippi (2016) notes, if not properly accounted for, the transparency inherent to blockchain technology is such that anyone can retrieve the history of all transactions executed on a blockchain and rely on big data analytics in order to retrieve potentially sensitive information.

(5) Smart contracts[1] are vulnerable and might lead to cyber attacks as they cannot be modified (Gatteschi *et al.*, 2018). In traditional systems, security vulnerabilities can be fixed by patching. In fact, when there is a bug in a system, users can deploy a patch that fixes the problem and prevents future exploits of that specific bug. Conversely, once a contract is published on the blockchain, it can no longer be modified due to the immutable nature of smart contracts. Therefore, if a contract contains a bug, there is no direct way to fix it (Atzei *et al.*, 2017).

According to Weaver (2018), cryptocurrency risks associated with the blockchain technology can manifest in the following ways: first, there are technical risks to participants as anyone can access cryptocurrencies and

[1]Smart contracts, enabled by blockchain, fundamentally are programmable contracts that automatically execute when certain pre-defined conditions are met.

move money once the private key has been stolen or hacked. Even if cryptocurrencies are stored on participant's system, the nature of cryptocurrencies are "internet of money". It is not entirely safe as theft is possible over the internet. The second risk is about economic risks to participants. Since the actual value of cryptocurrencies is only based on the price somebody is willing to pay for, the price that reflects the actual value of cryptocurrencies is volatile and vulnerable to collapse. Thirdly, systemic risks exist in the cryptocurrency ecosystem from government intervention, central authorities, exchanges, and worms. While cryptocurrency claims that central authorities and governments cannot censor cryptographic transactions, the rules of cryptocurrency exchange can be changed by the authorities' intervention in a response to possible theft, fraud or financial crimes aimed at avoiding regulatory supervision via cryptocurrency exchange. Furthermore, due to peer-to-peer systems, worms can easily spread globally in a matter of seconds.

2.3. *Types of blockchain*

Depending on the nature of the ledger, blockchains can be classified into three categories as shown in Figure 2, which are the public, private and hybrid blockchains. The ledger of a public blockchain is completely decentralized, and any internet user can access it. Public blockchains are usually based on the PoW consensus mechanism as explained above. For example, Bitcoin blockchain is a public blockchain since it allows

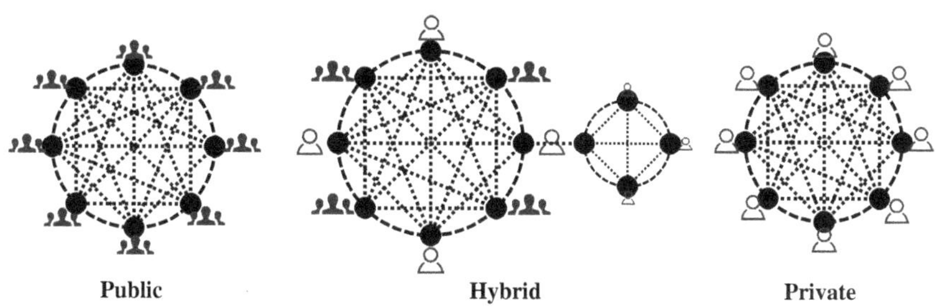

Figure 2: Types of blockchain.

anyone to: (a) run Bitcoin full node and mine Bitcoins; (b) check and review the whole ledger; and (c) make transactions on the blockchain.

On the other hand, an entirely private blockchain is monitored by the creator of the blockchain in question, or by network participants, who designates who can participate in the network. Thus, authentication of participant identities and authorization are required for access (Lai and Chuen, 2018). A well-known example of the private blockchain is the Hyperledger Fabic by The Linux Foundation. It has been designed as a permission network of only known participants that is mainly used by enterprises. For example, the digital identity function can benefit the healthcare industry by providing secure data exchange for service providers or patients (Jayachandran, 2017).

The hybrid blockchains are between the two extremes, which are those "partially decentralized" blockchains, also called as "consortium blockchains", that "constitute a hybrid between the low-trust and the single highly-trusted entity model" (Niranjanamurthy *et al.*, 2018; Siba and Prakash, 2016, p. 31). The XDC hybrid blockchain developed by XinFin is a typical example of a hybrid blockchain. Part of its network is accessible for any participant, which allows retail users to trade freely. However, at the same time, institutional participants can also create their private sub-networks, which are not visible by everyone (XinFin, 2018).

2.4. *The evolution of blockchain*

As the blockchain technology is developing rapidly, the evolution of blockchain technology can be acknowledged in three different categories: blockchain 1.0, 2.0 and 3.0. Blockchain 1.0 is currency, the development of cryptocurrencies that are related to cash or payments, such as Bitcoin. Blockchain 2.0 is about the functionalities that lie beyond a "currency", especially smart contracts. A smart contract is a piece of code that is stored on the blockchain. It can be executed automatically without control of a third party, but only when certain conditions are met. Thus, different types of application can be built on blockchains through this kind of "contract". Ethereum — an open source blockchain platform supporting smart contracts, which allows developers to write smart contracts and decentralized applications, is a prime example of the blockchain 2.0. Its blockchain can empower Dapps (decentralized applications that run on the peer-to-peer computer network instead of an individual computer) and smart contracts. It allows for the creation of different market and financial applications on top of its blockchain protocol (Gatteschi *et al.*, 2018; Swan, 2015). "The DAO" project was one of the most well-known examples of blockchain 2.0. Just like its name suggests, it was a digital decentralized autonomous organization (what DAO stands for) that was built as a smart contract, on top of the Ethereum blockchain. It was also considered as a form of investor-directed VC fund without any central authority. Investors of the DAO received voting rights by purchasing the DAO digital token, in order to vote on different project proposals as an investment. Unfortunately, this project failed in a matter of months due to its flawed smart contract. It allowed hackers who exploited a bug to steal a third of the DAO's fund (approximately US $50 million) (Murck, 2017). However, this project is still an amazing real-world example of the blockchain technology, and it expresses well the potential flaws of smart contracts.

Blockchain 3.0 is all about applications. Blockchain is no longer limited to finance and transactions due to the further development and application of smart contracts. This technology has the potential to be merged into various sectors, such as government, education and more (Gatteschi *et al.*, 2018; Swan, 2015). In addition, some studies share a similar view of blockchain 3.0, also suggesting that blockchain technology can be beneficial for both financial and non-financial industries. Crosby *et al.* (2016) claim that rather than considering blockchain technology as a threat to traditional business models, big financial institutions are looking for opportunities to integrate this technology into their business. Scholars (Crosby *et al.*, 2016; Siba and Prakash, 2016) and practitioners (CB Insights, 2018) reveal that applications for non-financial industries are endless.

EXAMPLE 1: MYCELIA

In the music industry, companies such as Mycelia are building an ecosystem with smart contracts that can help artists sell directly to consumers without going through a third party company (Tapscott and Tapscott, 2016). Mycelia's "Creative Passport" can serve as a peer-to-peer verified digital identity and "container" for all music makers. Based on the blockchain technology, it not only holds the musician's verified profile, works and acknowledgments, but also provides quick and easy direct payment mechanisms between the musician and related business or consumers (Mycelia, 2018).

EXAMPLE 2: WALMART

The supply chain industry is another notable example of blockchain technology in action where it is possible to attach invisible tracking tokens to products. This can help users "to intermediate goods as they progress along the production, shipping, and delivery phases of a supply chain and as title to them passes between different players" (Casey and Wong, 2017, p. 4). For example, in December 2017, Walmart, JD.com (a Chinese online retailer and also a Fortune Global 500 Company), IBM and Tsinghua University announced that they would work together to launch a Blockchain Food Safety Alliance in China. They have traced pork in China and mangoes in the US through the supply chain to store shelves, suggesting that this technology can provide real-time traceability (IBM, 2017).

EXAMPLE 3: BITGIVE FOUNDATION

When making a charitable donation, transparency as to where the funds are heading is crucial. Blockchain allows the tracking of donations from the moment they are given to the moment they are used for good allowing for accountability and transparency in the process. The BitGive Foundation uses blockchain's secure and transparent distributed ledger in order to give greater visibility concerning donor's funds receipt and use. Its platform allows for the transfer, tracking and permanent record of charitable financial transactions allowing for greater trust the cooperation from donors worldwide.

3. Cryptocurrency

Cryptocurrency is a pioneering application of the blockchain technology, and is considered a financial instrument. Thanks to the blockchain technology, cryptocurrencies can generate a distributed system with certification and integrity once a payment transaction is made on the internet.

In contrast to the traditional fiat currency which always required a central trusted party (for example, central bank) to guarantee the value of the national currencies or transaction, cryptocurrencies that are based on the blockchain technology create a digital online distributed system of certification for payment transactions without any central authority involved (Adhami *et al.*, 2018).

Looking back at history, people have been looking for alternative payment solutions for decades. Back in the 1990s, eCash was introduced by DigiCash Inc, which can be considered as the first digital currency similar to the current cryptocurrencies. However, eCash did not survive the 2000 Internet bubble (Frunza, 2016). Since then, numerous digital payment solutions such as Apple Pay, Google Wallet, and PayPal have been introduced. However, digital currencies are still based on fiat currency and mainly used for e-commerce. Cryptocurrency's promise is to offer a new type of currency rooted on blockchain technology and supported by cryptographic proof instead of trust. Some consider blockchain technology as "the trust machine" and cryptocurrency is most notable example (*The Trust Machine*, 2015). It solved the issue of a third party requirement when using an alternative payment solution instead of traditional cash (Nian and Chuen, 2015). There are currently more than a thousand types of cryptocurrencies (Alina *et al.*, 2017). Among all of them, Bitcoin is to date the most popular and also the pioneer to be rooted on blockchain technology (Frunza, 2016).

Bitcoin was first introduced as a medium of exchange (Elbahrawy *et al.*, 2017). In 2008, Satoshi Nakamoto published a paper on the internet to introduce Bitcoin as a peer-to-peer electronic cash system to the world. This paper was never submitted to an academic journal, and the actual identity of Satoshi Nakamoto remains anonymous (Pierro, 2017). It described Bitcoin as a digital cash system that can issue digital currency and allows direct payments or transactions between two individuals without going through any central authority (Iansiti and Lakhani, 2017). A few months after this paper's publication, an open source program implementing the blockchain technology was released. People who installed this program have become part of the Bitcoin peer-to-peer network (Crosby *et al.*, 2016). In 2009, Bitcoin trading platforms emerged, the initial rate was 1309.03 Bitcoin in exchange for one US

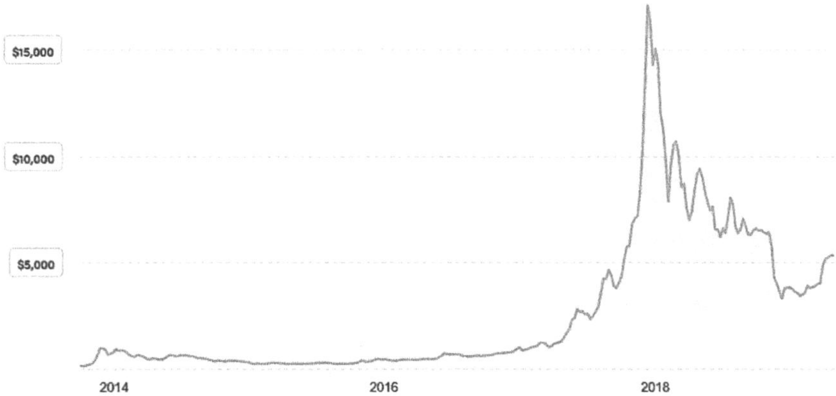

Figure 3: Bitcoin price index in USD, data source: Coindesk.

dollar. The first transaction of Bitcoin was completed by buying two pizzas at a price of 10,000 Bitcoins in 2010. Referring to Figure 3, Bitcoin rose up to US $1,000 per Bitcoin in 2013 and finally reached a peak exchange rate of US $19,000 per Bitcoin in 2017, making it the most common cryptocurrency to date (Alina *et al.*, 2017). Nevertheless, Figure 3 shows that the Bitcoin price has also been very volatile with several large falls. A study by Ciaian *et al.* (2016) on the determinants of Bitcoin price formation reveals that both the traditional determinants of currency price (e.g., market forces of supply and demand) and digital currencies (e.g., news events, high speculation and users sentiments) have significantly impacted Bitcoin's price.

Although many cryptocurrencies have only been created as a simple clone of Bitcoin with minimal changes, some were created with significant improvements and pushed further the development of cryptocurrency in general. Here are some examples:

(1) Ether (ETH) which is arguably the second most commonly used cryptocurrency. It is used as a form of payment in the Ethereum

platform.[2] The Ethereum blockchain is the most well-known blockchain that introduces smart contracts and Dapps (Elendner *et al.*, 2017);

(2) Dash, which is a cryptocurrency-based on Bitcoin with advanced modifications that solve many of the shortcomings inherent in Bitcoin. In particular, Masternodes were introduced in this cryptocurrency. They are distinct from normal nodes (miners), which only perform specialized transactions, in order to provide functions, such as instant transactions and enhanced anonymous transactions;

(3) LiteCoin was introduced in 2011 and considered as one of Bitcoin's leading rivals. It not only enables faster transaction confirmation time but also comes with potentially better mining energy efficiency;

(4) Ripple was designed as a real-time gross settlement system (RTGS), which aims to provide secure real-time financial transactions across the globe. Unlike many cryptocurrencies that are built on blockchain technology which relies on nodes with the mining process, Ripple is built on a unique, rather "centralized" blockchain in order to improve the reliability and transaction speed. Ripple has already used by many financial companies, such as UBS, Santander, and Standard Chartered (Chan *et al.*, 2017).

In May 2018, the valuation of all cryptocurrencies was estimated at US $350 billion. Unlike national currencies, who are backed by faith, economic power, gold reserves and tax revenue of a nation, cryptocurrencies derive their real economic value from the following sources: (1) being universal currencies which can be transferred at low cost (without foreign exchange transaction fees charged by banks) and at high speed; (2) financial inclusion as it allows populations without bank accounts to leverage cryptocurrencies due to their low charges and simplicity; and (3) trust from users on the underlying technologies behind cryptocurrencies (Jacobs, 2018).

---

[2] Basically, Ether is the underlying token powering the Ethereum blockchain. Although it is traded on public markets like bitcoin, Ether's main purpose is to serve as the "fuel" that powers the Ethereum network.

Recent research suggest that cryptocurrencies should be divided into two major categories: coins and tokens. Massey *et al.* (2017) define coins as a cryptocurrencies' native to a particular blockchain. The sole purpose of these cryptocurrencies is to exchange value, and have limited functionality beyond that. Tokens are the result of developments in the blockchain technology, as it allowed the creation of Dapps and smart contracts, such as Ethereum. They allow logic to be coded into the blockchain, such as a process that executes automatically only if certain conditions are met. This functionality also allows users to create different tokens on top of a blockchain protocol. A token is normally used as a medium to execute a smart contract. Hence, a token not only can serve as a medium of exchange (as a coin) but can also represent the functionality desired by its creator (Massey *et al.*, 2017). Ethereum is the most common blockchain platform for the creation of new tokens; the majority of which are ERC20[3] standard compliant tokens. Thus, tokens can easily be exchanged and recognized from one to another by using the same standard. The market value of a token usually depends on the services or benefits that it can provide in addition to its exchange value (Chen, 2018). For example, Binance platform is a cryptocurrency exchange with a capacity of processing 1,400,000 orders per second. Its token, Binance Coin (BNB), is also based on the Ethereum blockchain with ERC20 standard. People can use BNB to pay for services, such as exchange or listing service on the platform (Binance, 2017).

4. Initial Coin Offering

Given the increasing popularity of cryptocurrency as a new means of payment, many start-ups are launching their own cryptocurrencies through a mechanism called ICO. This new method of fundraising has become the most popular fundraising solution for companies operating in the blockchain industry, and has the potential to reach traditional business as well (ESMA, 2017).

---

[3] ERC20 is a technical standard used for smart contracts on the Ethereum blockchain for implementing tokens. It defines a common list of rules that tokens on Ethereum have to implement.

An ICO can be described as an event where a start-up or project sells its new cryptocurrency for the first time to the public in order to raise capital (Chen, 2018; Dhillon *et al.*, 2017; Hill, 2018; Rogers, 2018). A new type of cryptocurrency is then created on an existing blockchain protocol, such as Ethereum or its own protocol during an ICO. The project team who initiates the ICO will determine the initial selling price. Depending on the nature of the project, investors might use these cryptocurrencies as coins or tokens that can be exchanged for future products of the company. Meaning that these coins or tokens may serve to access or purchase a service or product that the issuer develops using the proceeds of the ICO; may provide voting rights or a share in the future revenues of the issuing venture; or may be traded and/or may be exchanged into fiat or virtual currencies at specialized coin exchanges after issuance (European Securities and Market Authority, 2017). The price of the specific cryptocurrency is settled through supply and demand in the market, rather than by a central authority (Kastelein, 2017). Although the name ICO is similar to initial public offering (IPO), in most cases an ICO does not grant the ownership of the company to the investors like an IPO does (Dhillon *et al.*, 2017; Massey *et al.*, 2017). Specifically, ICOs represent a new funding model based on blockchain and related cryptocurrencies, with strong similarities to crowdfunding (Arnold *et al.*, 2018; Bellavitis *et al.*, 2017). However, it sells instruments of a different nature — i.e., tokens (which are cryptographically secured digital assets) — and use blockchain technology for verification instead of crowdfunding platforms. Similarly to crowdfunding, it allows early stage start-ups and projects to raise financial capital without using traditional fundraising options, such as angel investors or venture capitalists (VCs). The difference is participants receive the project's cryptocurrencies in exchange (Chen, 2018; Hill, 2018).

To start an ICO, the start-up or project team will usually publish a document called a "whitepaper" which describes the details of the project and the cryptocurrencies that they are going to offer. Therefore, the people who are interested in the project can understand what they are going to invest or participate in. In general, the whitepaper contains the following information:

(1) the details of the project, such as a description of the project, business plan, amount of required funds, development roadmap, and project milestones with the project progress schedule;
(2) the technical specifications, such as the mechanism and the adopted blockchain protocol of the project;
(3) ICO details including terms and conditions, start and end dates of the ICO, total cryptocurrency supply, team allocation and initial pricing of the cryptocurrency (Adhami *et al.*, 2018; Chen, 2018).

An ICO fundraising usually begins at a given time mentioned in the whitepaper. It ends as soon as all the cryptocurrencies are sold out or at a given time set previously in the whitepaper. The number of the cryptocurrencies within a project is usually limited, and the project team might reserve part of them as rewards (Chen, 2018). Early participants usually receive extra rewards or early bird discounts as it is done in reward crowdfunding. Most of the campaigns only accept the major cryptocurrencies (such as Bitcoins and Ethers) as payments. However, some ICOs do accept fiat currency via other financial institutions. Tezos ICO for example accepted fiat currency through a financial institution, Bitcoin Suisse AG. In general, due to smart contracts technology, the actual offering procedure in an ICO is secure and safe (Adhami *et al.*, 2018). Typically, the Ethereum protocol is used in ICOs given its easy-to-use smart contract functionality. In addition, smart contracts also work as an escrow agreement where invested Bitcoins or Ethers are only released to the project team when the agreed amount of newly issued coins are delivered in the backer's digital wallet (Adhami *et al.*, 2018).

ICO is a popular phenomenon these days, but it did not come into the public eye until recently. The first ICO in record was held by Mastercoin back in 2013. The project collected approximately 5,000 BTC, which represented approximately $500,000 at that time (Shin, 2017). Since then, hundreds of ICOs have been launched. Recent research conducted by Shifflett, Jones and Sender (2018) reveals that there were close to 2000 cryptocurrency projects that announced an ICO from 2013 to early 2018 (their data were collected from three major websites: Coinmarketcap.com, Tokendata.io, and ICORating.com). Hill (2018) also found that ICOs were scheduled to collect an estimated amount of $2.5 billion in 2017 alone.

Furthermore, the OECD (2018) reveals cumulative ICO funding has grown from marginal in 2014 to $5 billion in 2017[4] and is expected to reach $12 billion by early 2019.

To date, ICO has become a popular fundraising method, surpassing traditional funding options for blockchain-related companies. According to Nolan, Dartley, Baker, ReVeal, and Rinearson (2018), $350 million of traditional VC money was invested in the first three-quarters of 2017 versus $2 billion raised via ICOs in the same period. ICOs are shaping the future of entrepreneurial finance (Block *et al.*, 2018; Howell *et al.*, 2018; Bellavitis *et al.*, 2017). The distributed ledger technology of blockchain, on which ICOs work, enables new ventures to have access to a wider pool of investors all over the world, and to conduct operations in a decentralized peer-to-peer network (Tapscott and Tapscott, 2017), eliminating the need for the middlemen (such as financial institutions) to verify the integrity of transactions. Specifically, since companies have the possibility to issue securities directly on the ledger, they have access to a wider pool of investors (European Central Bank — ECB, 2016). The cross-border nature of blockchain technology means also that private investors around the world are able to participate in an ICO, thus increasing the number of potential investors in the company and, consequently, the potential amount of capital raised. Previous research suggests that, investors in early stage entrepreneurial ventures tend to be located in close proximity of their investees (e.g. Sorenson and Stuart, 2001; Agrawal *et al.*, 2011). With blockchain technology and its decentralized and accurate record-keeping capabilities, improvement of information flows and accurate tracking of asset reduce investor's monitoring costs (Block *et al.*, 2018; Huang *et al.*, 2018). As a result, it increases transparency, accountability and control over how funds are used. This means that ICOs may prove to overcome the market frictions associated with geographic distance, usually linked to financing entrepreneurial ventures. Another strength of ICOs is that blockchain enables operations in a decentralized peer-to-peer (P2P) network, where transactions are verified by a network-wide

[4] By comparison, in 2017 blockchain equity funding was about only $1 billion, via IPO's or private equity, while VC in blockchain development companies reached a cumulative level of about $2.5 billion in 2017.

consensus mechanism, thus eliminating the need for the middlemen (Arnold *et al.*, 2018). Furthermore, since ICOs do not have a standard regulatory framework, it allows greater flexibility from entrepreneurs and enables them to raise capital with minimal effort by avoiding costs of compliance and intermediaries associated with traditional means of fundraising (Fisch, 2018). This means that ICOs may improve the efficiency in raising capital from early stage entrepreneurs as it is faster and provides a low cost way alternative to other traditional mechanism. Finally, ICOs may provide advantages for investors as well. As Tapscott and Tapscott (2017) claim, ICOs may democratize participation in global capital markets by allowing anyone to invest any amount in a company, thus dramatically reducing entry barriers to participate financially in the successes of start-up companies.

Nevertheless, ICOs do come with both pros and cons. The following are some potential drawbacks to ICOs. First, potential taxation. ICOs, considered as cryptocurrency investments, may suffer from tax treatments in some countries. For example, according to Nolan *et al.* (2018), the US Internal Revenue Service (IRS) has already characterized cryptocurrencies as property for tax purposes. They also stated that "for issuers and investors, the tax treatment of transactions involving ICOs will vary depending on the facts of each ICO, including whether the tokens being issued are equity, security or utility tokens" (p. 5). Second, ICOs are not always a better means of fundraising. The project team usually has to sell a significant portion of tokens to attract investors, whereas traditional early stage equity financing usually required a much smaller portion on the company. Third, ICOs are facing regulatory uncertainty. In the US, Securities and Exchange Commission (SEC) has already considered some of the tokens that are offered in ICOs as securities. Both China and South Korea government issued an ICO Ban in 2017. Most countries seem to be attempting to regulate ICOs. Thus, companies who are planning to start an ICO might also face a lot of uncertainties (Chen, 2018). In fact, the current lack of regulation represents in itself an investment risk subject to fraud, which is not always clear in the whitepapers read by potential investors (European Securities Markets Authority — ESMA, 2017). Fourth, there are also risks of thefts and hacking in ICOs. As EY (2018) reported, more than 10% of ICO funds are lost or stolen in hacker attacks (nearly $400 million). One notable example is the DAO hack in 2017. The hacker was able to steal nearly 3.6 million Ethers due to the flawed smart contract, which was worth around $50 million at that time (Murck, 2017). Lastly, the project itself might represent significant risks for all investors. For instance, amateurs might launch an ICO with a project that is born to be a failure, or the project might take an extended period of time to accomplish its goals (Dhillon *et al.*, 2018). As a result, high price volatility exposes investors to a major risk of not being able to redeem their coins or tokens for a prolonged period of time ... possibly never (ESMA, 2017).

5. Conclusions

The advantages of blockchain technology, cryptocurrencies and ICOs are becoming increasingly apparent to entrepreneurship and the broader economy. Scholars and practitioners have both acknowledged the potential of these innovations in shaping the entrepreneurial finance landscape of the future (Block *et al.*, 2018; Howell *et al.*, 2018). Nevertheless, research on the topic is still at its infancy (Bellavitis *et al.*, 2017; Block *et al.*, 2018). This chapter provided an overview on the potential of blockchain technology and ICOs in the context of entrepreneurial finance. In particular, it outlined the potential advantages and challenges of blockchain technology, cryptocurrencies and related ICOs mechanism for practitioners. In particular, this chapter brings light to the ICO process of fundraising and compares it with traditional forms of financing. It also opens several avenues for future research. In particular, since the majority of studies on this topic are theoretical or descriptive, it encourages researchers to bring more empirical studies and case studies on the topic. For instance, the investigation of the effectiveness of ICOs in terms of their returns post-offering, and their ability to foster entrepreneurship. Furthermore, research still lacks empirical studies that identify what are the critical success factors of an ICO campaign, as well as the what kind of new business models have emerged for entrepreneurial firms using this means of fundraising.

References

Adhami S., Giudici G., and Martinazzi S. (2018) Why do businesses go crypto? An empirical analysis of Initial Coin Offerings. *Journal of Economics and Business*. doi: 10.1016/j.jeconbus.2018.04.001.

Agrawal A. K., Catalini C., and Goldfarb A. (2011) *The Geography of Crowdfunding* (No. w16820). National bureau of economic research.

Alina C., Cerasela S. E., and Gabriela G. (2017) Cybercurrencies. *Ovidius University Annals, Economic Sciences Series*, 17(2), 514–518. Retrieved from https://econpapers.repec.org/article/ovioviste/v_3axvii_3ay_3a2017_3ai_3a2_3ap_3a514-518.htm.

Arnold L., Brennecke M., Camus P., Fridgen G., Guggenberger T., Radszuwill S., Rieger A., Schweizer A., and Urbach N. (2019) Blockchain and Initial Coin Offerings: Blockchain's Implications for Crowdfunding. In *Business Transformation through Blockchain*, Palgrave Macmillan, Cham, pp. 233–272.

Atzei N., Bartoletti M., and Cimoli T. (2017) A survey of attacks on ethereum smart contracts (sok). In *Principles of Security and Trust*. Springer, Berlin, Heidelberg, pp. 164–186.

Bellavitis C., Filatotchev I., Kamuriwo D. S., and Vanacker T. (2017) Entrepreneurial finance: new frontiers of research and practice: Editorial for the special issue Embracing entrepreneurial funding innovations.

Bhaskar N. D. and Chuen D. L. K. (2015) Bitcoin mining technology. In Chuen D. L. K. (eds.), *Handbook of Digital Currency*, pp. 45–65. doi: 10.1016/B978-0-12-802117-0.00003-5.

Binance. (2017) Binance exchange whitepaper. Retrieved from https://www.binance.com/resources/ico/Binance_WhitePaper_en.pdf.

Block J. H., Colombo M. G., Cumming D. J., and Vismara S. (2018) New players in entrepreneurial finance and why they are there. *Small Business Economics*, 50(2), 239–250.

Bruton G., Khavul S., Siegel D., and Wright M. (2015) New financial alternatives in seeding entrepreneurship: Microfinance, crowdfunding, and peer-to-peer innovations. *Entrepreneurship Theory and Practice*, 39(1), 9–26.

Casey M. and Wong P. (2017) Global supply chains are about to get better, thanks to blockchain. *Harvard business review*. Retrieved from https://hbr.org/2017/03/global-supply-chains-are-about-to-get-better-thanks-to-blockchain.

CB Insights. (2018) Banking is only the beginning: 42 big industries blockchain can transform. Retrieved from https://www.cbinsights.com/research/industries-disrupted-blockchain/.

Chan S., Chu J., Nadarajah S., and Osterrieder J. (2017) a statistical analysis of cryptocurrencies. *Journal of Risk and Financial Management*, 10(2), 12. doi: 10.3390/jrfm10020012.

Chen Y. (2018) Blockchain tokens and the potential democratization of entrepreneurship and innovation. *Business Horizons*, 61, 567–575. doi: 10.1016/j.bushor.2018.03.006.

Ciaian P., Rajcaniova M., and Kancs D. A. (2016) The economics of BitCoin price formation. *Applied Economics*, 48(19), 1799–1815.

Coindesk. (2018) Bitcoin price index. Retrieved from: https://www.coindesk.com/price/.

Crosby M., Pattanayak P., Verma S., and Kalyanaraman V. (2016) Blockchain technology: Beyond bitcoin. *Applied Innovation*, 2, 6–10. Retrieved from https://j2-capital.com/wp-content/uploads/2017/11/AIR-2016-Blockchain.pdf.

De Filippi P. (2016) The interplay between decentralization and privacy: the case of blockchain technologies. *Journal of Peer Production*, (7).

Dhillon V., Metcalf D., and Hooper M. (2017) Blockchain enabled applications: Understand the blockchain ecosystem and how to make it work for you. doi: 10.1007/978-1-4842-3081-7.

Drescher D. (2017) Blockchain basics: A non-technical introduction in 25 steps. doi: 10.1007/978-1-4842-2604-9.

Elbahrawy A., Alessandretti L., Kandler A., Pastorsatorras R., and Baronchelli A. (2017) Evolutionary dynamics of the cryptocurrency market. *Royal Society Open Science*, 4(11), 170623. doi: 10.1098/rsos.170623.

Elendner H., Trimborn S., Ong B., and Lee T. M. (2017) The cross-section of crypto-currencies as financial assets: Investing in crypto-currencies beyond bitcoin. In Chuen D. L. K and Deng, R (eds.), *Handbook of Blockchain, Digital Finance, and Inclusion*, Vol. 1, pp. 145–173. doi: 10.1016/B978-0-12-810441-5.00007-5.

ESMA (2017) ESMA highlights ICO risks for investors and firms. Available at: https://www.esma.europa.eu/press-news/esma-news/esma-highlights-ico-risks-investors-and-firms.

European Central Bank (2016) *Distributed Ledger Technology*, Issue 1, 2016.

EY. (2018) Big risks in ICO market: flawed token valuations, unclear regulations, heightened hacker attention and congested networks. Retrieved from https://www.ey.com/en_gl/news/2018/01/big-risks-in-ico-market--flawed-token-valuations--unclear-regulations-heightened-hacker-attention-and-congested-networks.

Frunza M. (2016) Solving modern crime in financial markets. doi: 10.1016/C2015-0-02293-6.

Gatteschi V., Lamberti F., Demartini C., Pranteda C., and Santamaría V. (2018) To blockchain or not to blockchain: That is the question. *IT Professional*, 20(2), 62–74. doi: 10.1109/MITP.2018.021921652.

Hill J. (2018) Fintech and the remaking of financial institutions. doi: 10.1016/C2016-0-03863-9.

Howell S. T., Niessner M., and Yermack D. (2018) Initial coin offerings: Financing growth with cryptocurrency token sales (No. w24774). National Bureau of Economic Research.

Huang W., Meoli M., and Vismara S. (2018) The geography of initial coin offerings. *Small Business Economics*, 1–26.

Iansiti M. and Lakhani K. R. (2017) The truth about blockchain. *Harvard Business Review*. Retrieved from https://hbr.org/2017/01/the-truth-about-blockchain.

IBM. (2017, December 14). Walmart, JD.com, IBM and Tsinghua University Launch a Blockchain Food Safety Alliance in China [Press release]. Retrieved from https://www-03.ibm.com/press/us/en/pressrelease/53487.wss.

Jacobs G. (2018) Cryptocurrencies and the challenge of global governance. *Cadmus*, 3(4), 109–123. Retrieved from http://cadmusjournal.org/.

Jayachandran P. (2017) The difference between public and private blockchain. IBM Blockchain Blog, May, 31. Retrieved from https://www.ibm.com/blogs/blockchain/2017/05/the-difference-between-public-and-private-blockchain/.

Kastelein R. (2017) What initial coin offerings are, and why VC firms care. *Harvard Business Review*. Retrieved from https://hbr.org/2017/03/what-initial-coin-offerings-are-and-why-vc-firms-care.

Lai R. and Chuen D. L. K. (2018) Blockchain — from public to private. In Chuen D. L. K. and Deng, R. (eds.), *Handbook of Blockchain, Digital Finance, and Inclusion*, Vol. 2, pp. 145–177. doi: 10.1016/B978-0-12-812282-2.00007-3.

Li X., Jiang P., Chen T., Luo X., and Wen Q. (2017) A survey on the security of blockchain systems. *Future Generation Computer Systems*. doi: 10.1016/j.future.2017.08.020.

Massey R., Dalal D., and Dakshinamoorthy A. (2017) Initial coin offering: A new paradigm. Retrieved from https://www2.deloitte.com/content/dam/Deloitte/us/Documents/process-and-operations/us-cons-new-paradigm.pdf.

McKinsey&Company (2016) How blockchains can change the world. Available at: https://www.mckinsey.com/industries/high-tech/our-insights/how-blockchains-can-change-the-world.

Murck P. (2017) Who controls the blockchain? *Harvard Business Review*. Retrieved from https://hbr.org/2017/04/who-controls-the-blockchain.

Mycelia. (2018) CREATIVE Passport. Retrieved from http://myceliaformusic.org/creative-passport/.

Nakamoto S. (2008) Bitcoin: A peer-to-peer electronic cash system. Retrieved from https://bitcoin.org/bitcoin.pdf.

Nian L. P. and Chuen D. L. K. (2015) Introduction to bitcoin. In Chuen D. L. K. (ed.), *Handbook of Digital Currency*, pp. 5–30. doi: 10.1016/B978-0-12-802117-0.00001-1.

Niranjanamurthy M., Nithya B. N., and Jagannatha S. (2018) Analysis of blockchain technology: pros, cons and SWOT. *Cluster Computing*, 1–15. doi: 10.1007/s10586-018-2387-5.

Nofer M., Gomber P., Hinz O., and Schiereck D. (2017) Blockchain. *Business & Information Systems Engineering*, 59(3), 183–187. doi: 10.1007/s12599-017-0467-3.

Nolan A. R., Dartley E. T., Baker M. B., ReVeal J., and Rinearson J. E. (2018) Initial coin offerings: Key US legal considerations for ICO investors and sponsors. *Journal of Investment Compliance*, 19(1), 1–9. doi: 10.1108/JOIC-02-2018-0016.

OECD (2018) Blockchain Technology and Corporate Governance.

Philippon T. (2016) The fintech opportunity (No. w22476). National Bureau of Economic Research.

Pierro M. D. (2017) What is the blockchain? *Computing in Science & Engineering*, 19(5), 92–95. doi: 10.1109/MCSE.2017.3421554.

Rogers Z. (2018) Blockchain and the state: Vehicle or vice? *AQ — Australian Quarterly*, 89(1), 3–9. Retrieved from http://go.galegroup.com.ezproxy.auckland.ac.nz/ps/i.do?id=GALE%7CA523889354&v=2.1&u=learn&it=r&p=AONE&sw=w.

Securities and Exchange Commission (SEC) (2017) Investor Bulletin: Initial Coin Offerings.

Shifflett S., Jones C., and Sender H. (2018) Buyer beware: Hundreds of bitcoin wannabes show hallmarks of fraud; A wall street journal analysis of 1,450 cryptocurrency offerings reveals rampant plagiarism, identity theft and promises of improbable returns. *Wall Street Journal (Online)*. Retrieved from http://ezproxy.auckland.ac.nz/login?url=https://search-proquest-com.ezproxy.auckland.ac.nz/docview/2039959824?accountid=8424.

Shin L. (2017) Here's the man who created ICOs and this is the new token he's backing. *Forbes*. Retrieved from https://www.forbes.com/sites/laurashin/2017/09/21/heres-the-man-who-cre-ated-icos-and-this-is-the-new-token-hes-backing.

Siba T. K. and Prakash A. (2016) Block-chain: An evolving technology. *Global Journal of Enterprise Information System*, 8(4). doi: 10.18311/gjeis/2016/15770.

Sorenson O. and Stuart T. E. (2001): "Syndication Networks and the Spatial Distribution of Venture Capital Investments," *American Journal of Sociology*, 106(6), 1546–1588/.

Swan M. (2015) Blockchain: Blueprint for a new economy. Retrieved from https://www.safaribooksonline.com/library/view/blockchain/9781491920480/?ar.

Swanson T. (2015) Consensus-as-a-service: A brief report on the emergence of permissioned, distributed ledger systems. Retrieved from http://www.ofnumbers.com/wp-content/uploads/2015/04/Permissioned-distributed-ledgers.pdf.

Tapscott A. and Tapscott D. (2017) How blockchain is changing finance'. *Harvard Business Review*, 1.

Tapscott D. and Tapscott A. (2016) The impact of the blockchain goes beyond financial services. *Harvard Business Review*. Retrieved from https://hbr.org/2016/05/the-impact-of-the-blockchain-goes-beyond-financial-services.

The Trust Machine (2015) The promise of the blockchain. *The Economist*, 417, 13. Retrieved from http://ezproxy.auckland.ac.nz/login?url=https://search-proquest-com.ezproxy.auckland.ac.nz/docview/1728728650?accountid=8424.

Weaver N. (2018) Risks of cryptocurrencies. *Communications of the ACM*, 61(6), 20–24. doi: 10.1145/3208095.

XinFin. (2018) XDC PROTOCOL. Retrieved from https://www.xinfin.org/xdc-protocol.php.

Chapter 8

Mini-Bonds: An Emerging Link in the Intermediation Chain in Europe

Luisa Anderoni*

Milan State University, Università degli Studi di Milano

luisa.anderloni@unimi.it

Maria Debora Braga†

SDA Bocconi School of Management

mariadebora.braga@sdabocconi.it

Abstract

Mini-bonds represent a financial innovation aimed at filling a gap in the offer of funding for SMEs. While there is a long tradition of specialized markets and intermediaries for SMEs access to equity financing, the bond segments is still underdeveloped. In this chapter, we focus on a new form of bonds targeted to SMEs: mini-bonds, which were developed in the context of programs aimed at promoting economic growth and innovation leveraging on SMEs. Analyzing and comparing the mini-bonds markets in

*7, Via Festa del Perdono, Milan, 20122, Italy.

†8, Via Bocconi, Milan, 20136, Italy; University of Valle d'Aosta, Aosta, Italy.

Europe, (France, Germany, Italy, Spain and the United Kingdom) we find two emerging market models. In the model adopted in Italy and Spain, the issues are reserved to institutional and professional investors, well equipped to manage the risks related to the mini-bonds, and the trading is on a dedicated stock exchange market segment. In these cases, SME issuers benefit from simpler and less expensive issuing procedure and lower periodical information and regulatory requirements. The other model is the one adopted in France and, to some extent, in the United Kingdom: here the mini-bonds are sold through crowdfunding platforms to retail investors. New rules and regulations have been set up in order to balance the needs of investors — disclosure and protection — and issuers — easy procedures and low-issuing costs. In the United Kingdom and Germany, also dedicated retail bond markets for SMEs have been opened, complementing the alternative equity markets for SMEs. Mini-bonds and the innovations they triggered enrich the chain of financial intermediation. Due to the novelty of these financial instruments and markets, the topics deserve further research and empirical analysis.

1. Introduction

Mini-bonds represent a financial innovation aimed at filling a gap in the offer of funding for SMEs.

According to the life cycle paradigm, banks, financial intermediaries, and markets interact in order to complement firms' financial structure along the stages of their financial growth cycle (Berger and Udell, 1998). Each stage in a firm's life cycle has its own financing needs in terms of instruments, volume, and related advice services and its own requirements regarding collateral, creditworthiness, economic prospects, and risk profile.

As a direct result of the complementary nature of the role of banks and other financial intermediaries and that of financial markets, well-functioning equity and debt markets are needed both for balanced and efficient firm financing, especially in a firm's early stages. Financial markets and their intermediaries have strong interconnections, and alternative markets and specialized intermediaries usually meet the financial needs of start-ups and SMEs better than traditional intermediaries.

Traditional debt financing like bank loans, overdrafts, and credit lines are the most common sources of external financing for many SMEs, entrepreneurs' working capital needs and sometimes capital investments. However, banking sources are often not adequate to finance SMEs and start-ups' growth projects as a result of issues that constrain credit availability, such as information opacity, asymmetric information, principal/agent problems, lack of credit history, and lack of collateral (Berger and Udell, 1998, 2006, Bhaumik *et al.,* 2015, Mitter and Kraus, 2011). Assessment and monitoring of credit risk for such enterprises is disproportionally more difficult and riskier than for larger, well-rooted companies. In addition, in entrepreneurial companies, the owner's finances and those of the business are often not clearly separated, which increases the overall risks. It is widely recognized that the reasons for the financial market's failure to provide the necessary credit in these cases relate to both insufficient supply of capital and inadequate demand.

Alternative debt instruments that are available from investors in the capital market, other than banks, are often a missing or weak link in the intermediation chain of European countries because of high costs, minimal market size, complicated procedures and regulations.

In the aftermath of the 2008–2009 global financial crisis, the credit crunch hit SMEs particularly hard, especially those with high risk/return profile, such as start-ups, fast-growing SMEs, and highly innovative SMEs, deepening a longstanding financial gap (Artola and Genre, 2011; Casey and O'Toole, 2014; Drakos, 2012). This problem fueled theoretical studies and empirical analyses regarding SMEs' and entrepreneurial companies' financing and a renewed interest in alternative debt instruments that could provide a solution (Altman *et al.*, 2018; Block *et al.*, 2018; Collins *et al.*, 2013; Cusmano, 2018; Kaousar Nassr and Wehinger, 2014; Sunak, 2017; British Business Bank — IPSOS MORI, 2018). Studies conducted by public authorities and international institutions on the funding difficulties for SMEs highlighted the underdevelopment of bond markets. Instruments and initiatives created to facilitate SMEs debt financing have been used mainly by mid-cap firms, large and listed companies (European Commission, 2017; European Investment Bank, 2018; OECD, 2015, 2016).

As part of the disintermediation process, private debt offered in the form of bonds, frequently called mini-bonds, is a recent financial innovation that addresses this credit crunch. This innovation lies in the broad context of innovations concerning the use of internet platforms with a variety of finance-related functionalities (Boschmans and Pissareva, 2017; Wardrop *et al.*, 2015; Ziegler *et al.*, 2017; Zhang, 2018).

A single definition of the new instrument is not possible, but considering the common feature in the various contexts, we identify them as "the issue of debt securities with low face value by companies, mainly SMEs and start-ups". Placement can take place via crowdfunding platforms, be addressed to retail investors, or be offered exclusively to professional investors.

In some countries, alternative markets have been created *ad hoc* for the negotiation of these financial instruments. These bonds may benefit from the risk-mitigation instruments (public or mixed and/or on a cooperative basis) that are typically applied to bank loans.

Basket bonds — that is, those that pool mini-bonds in aggregate vehicles — have also been created as an extension of this innovation, as have multi-originator (consortia) deals to reach the scale of issuance required to be attractive to investors, diversify risk, and benefit from asset managers' expertise.

Another innovation linked to mini-bonds is specialized institutional debt funds created by institutional investors who invest in mini-bonds (exclusively or with other debt instruments). Investors buy units of these funds to benefit from attractive returns, diversified portfolios, the umbrella of fund regulation, and secure access to the SME asset class, which can be difficult to tap. Fund managers are sometimes part of a private equity fund that leverage on their expertise of identifying target companies. According to EIF (Kramer-Eis *et al.*, 2014). only a minority of debt funds invest in SMEs: most of them chose mezzanine or mid-cap companies.

Considering these trends, the issuance of debt securities on the market from smaller enterprises (direct channel) is clearly an emerging link in the chain of intermediation. Until recently, this link was lacking or weak in continental Europe even though financial intermediaries (sponsors, institutional investors, basket bond creators, and private debt funds) have generated market demand for these bonds, especially in Italy and Spain where mini-bonds are exclusively offered to institutional and professional investors. As theoretically stated, sometimes these intermediaries address the opacity problem suffered by SMEs with soft information gathered scouting for private equity opportunities instead of relying on typical benefits of relationship lending and contribute to transmit positive signals to the markets.

Furthermore, it is well known that financial innovations often feature a trade-off between two different goals: on one side there is the willingness to leave the market free to experiment new design issues that meet both issuers and investors requests, and, on the other side, the necessity to set regulatory requirements that provide a solid and protected institutional framework. Therefore, the matter of whether the existing regulation is adequate also to these instruments and markets is emerging at both national and European level.

In the light of this, this chapter is aimed at analyzing mini-bonds as an innovation for SMEs and start-up debt financing in Europe and their potential to fill the above-mentioned financial gap.

The rest of the chapter is organized as follows. Section 2 presents the institutional framework and the market features of the main European experiences with mini-bonds issues. Section 3 deals with pricing and Section 4 provides an analysis of the theoretical and factual benefits of mini-bond issues for smaller firms and investors. In conclusion, Section 5 suggests avenues for further research.

2. Institutional Framework and Market Experience in Europe

The main experiences with mini-bonds issued and traded in Europe have been in France, Italy, Germany, Spain and the UK (Eisele and Novak, 2018). These experiences have followed different paths, models, and regulation approaches and have raised different levels of market interest as well.

As previously mentioned, the term "mini-bond" refers to several types of securities, so a comparative analysis necessitates the consideration of a broader jurisdictional framework by identifying the legitimate issuers of mini-bonds, their legal features (e.g., coupon, maturity, transferability, seniority, covenants, callability), and their possible investors.

In the perspective of the issuing firms, it is also useful to determine any other intermediaries or subjects that play roles in the initial offer and/

or the secondary market for mini-bonds. Other elements include the nature of any secondary markets (regulated or multilateral trading facilities and their special segments), their rules, and their efficiency. In addition, we should consider the cases in which placement and/or trading has been done via websites (crowdfunding platforms).

In order to provide a snapshot of the instruments in the different markets, Table 1 summarizes their characteristics and facilitates the understanding of heterogeneous experiences we discuss.

2.1. *Italy*

The Italian experience is often mentioned as one of the most promising example of mini-bonds issuing. In Italy, this innovation has been supported by regulatory reform and favorable fiscal treatment for SMEs, along with the creation of a specialized trading facility.

Although the term mini-bonds was not officially used till 2014, the changes in legal and fiscal contexts to favor such bonds started in 2012. Specifically, the new laws and regulations were part of a set of initiatives for boosting the country's economic growth.[1] Limits to bond issues by unlisted companies were relaxed and then cancelled for bonds negotiated in a regulated market or in a multilateral trading facility. In addition, the tax treatment of unlisted companies' bond issuances and interest expense was aligned to that of the listed companies, provided that the bonds are traded in a multilateral trading facility and placed with institutional or qualified investors that are not direct or indirect stockholders of the issuing companies.

In February 2013, a new specialized trading facility, ExtraMot Pro, was launched in the Italian Stock Exchange for the listing of commercial papers, bonds, and notes to help Italian firms take the opportunity and the fiscal benefit offered by mini-bonds. ExtraMot Pro is a market segment reserved for professional investors, and the infrastructure offers easy and efficient first access to capital markets: since retail investors are excluded, consumer protections do not apply, and listing requirements are softened.

[1] All legislative and regulatory references are provided in the appendix.

Table 1: Main features of mini-bonds experiences in Europe.

	Italy		France	United Kingdom		Germany	
	Mini-bond	Spain	Mini-bond	Bond	Retail bonds	Schuldschein	(SMEs) Corporate bonds
ISSUER	Joint stock companies and limited liabilities companies	Joint stock companies and limited liabilities companies	Joint stock companies and limited liabilities companies	Joint stock companies and limited liabilities companies	Joint stock companies and limited liabilities companies	Companies	Joint stock companies and limited liabilities companies
	At least two audited annual reports	At least two audited annual reports	At least two approved annual reports		At least two audited financial statements		Company history of at least 2 years (last audited financial statement)
	In order to benefit from Italian Central Guarantee Scheme: – micro firms, SMEs and their consortia – firms investing in entrepreneurial projects						At least three out of six criteria fulfilled on EBITDA interest coverage, EBITD interest coverage, debt/EBITDA, net debt/EBITDA, risk bearing capital and debt/capital

(*Continued*)

Table 1: *(Continued)*

	Italy		France	United Kingdom		Germany	
	Mini-bond	Spain	Mini-bond	Bond	Retail bonds	Schuldschein	(SMEs) Corporate bonds
Type of Instrument	Bond	Bond	Interest bearing notes or short-term bonds	Bonds, sometimes with voucher for non-cash rewards	Bond	Bilateral loans, privately placed.	Bearer bonds
Main Technical Characteristics	No minimum size	Minimum size of €100.000	Maximum issued by an issuer €2.5 million in 12 months		Minimum tradable value £100–1,000 Minimum volume £ 25,000	Deals run from €10 to €500 million and recently 1 billion	Placed volume of at least €20 million Denomination up to a maximum of €1.000
	Both amortizing and bullet bonds		Amortizing bonds Fixed interest rates		Mainly bullet bonds. Both fixed and floating (less common) interest rates	Often fixed rates for long-dated tranches and floating rates for shorter tranches	
	Both rated and unrated bonds	Minimum rating of BB- or a credit-solvency assessment				Syndicated loans, with different tranches divided up into various-sliced slices	Corporate or bond rating

	Maturity ranging from less than 1 year to 10 years, with an average maturity of 5 years		Maximum maturity 5 years	Maturity around 3–5 years	Maturity 5–12 years with cases of 30 years	Maturity longer than 5 years Freely transferable in whole or in part	
Trading Venues or Platforms	ExtraMotPro	MARF	Crowdfunding platforms and blockchain	Crowdfunding platforms	ORB	= = = Only OTC transferable	SCALE
	Private placements to institutional/ qualified investors	Private placements to institutional/ professional investors				Private placements	
Investors	Only institutional/ qualified investors	Only institutional/ professional investors	No limits	No limits	Both retailer and institutional investors	Buy and hold investors, as banks, savings banks and institutional investors.	No limits
Other Players		Registered advisor	Investment service providers IFP and Crowdfunding investment advisor — CIP		Committed market maker	Arranger Guarantor (if any)	Deutsche Borse Capital market partner

In the meantime, the international brand of the market helps Italian SMEs to gain visibility and credibility. The only listing requirements are the publication of annual financial statements for the past two years, the second of which has been audited, and the provision of an admission document with some essential information. After the admission to listing, the issuer must publish audited financial statements, disclose the bond rating if a public rating is assigned, and provide price-sensitive information, and any technical information related to the instrument's characteristics (e.g., payment dates, interest coupons, sinking schedule). Although it is not mandatory, a specialist may support the instrument's liquidity.

In 2013, a new legislative act increased the liberalization of mini-bonds. The new regulation governing securitization processes allowed special-purpose vehicles to acquire corporate bonds, including mini-bonds. As a consequence, credit funds were created with the purpose of aggregating in a portfolio a number of mini-bonds issued by various firms by relying on institutional investors' ability to screen, monitor, and diversify risk.

In 2014, the Italian Central Guarantee extended its guarantees to investments made in mini-bonds. It covers both single investments and portfolio investments (that is, packages of mini-bonds with the same technical features), invested by banks, financial intermediaries, or asset managers. In this framework, the term "mini-bonds" was used for the first time in the Italian law to refer to notes/bonds and similar securities issued by final investing firms classified as micro firms, SMEs, and their consortia (art. 32 Legislative Decree 83/2012). The requirements for single or portfolios of mini-bonds to be included in the guarantee program, include the following: the funding is for an entrepreneurial investment; it cannot be used to refund previous debt; the bond maturity is between 36 and 120 months; and other guarantees (collateral or insurance) do not cover the same portion of credit risk that is covered by the fund. The amount of the guarantee for amortizing mini-bonds must be no more than 50% of the nominal value and the maximum amount for each firm is €1.5 million. On the whole, these requirements channel mini-bond funding to new investments undertaken by SMEs and promote investments by institutional investors like private debt funds.

In the same year, 2014, a new agreement was signed by The European Investment Fund and the Italian Investment Fund to support the development of Italian SMEs. It foresaw a close cooperation between the two institutions aimed at co-investing between €500 and €600 million in private equity and private debt funds — including those investing in mini-bonds.

Additional fiscal benefits were introduced in 2016 on interest and revenue to mini-bonds, even if they are not traded in multilateral trading facilities as long as they are in qualified investors' portfolios.

Overall, the Italian legislature promoted a market for mini-bonds that is open only to institutional investors. This has benefits for SMEs, as the informational documentation is simple and no sponsor is needed to provide liquidity to the market. On their side, institutional and professional investors are well-equipped to select investments and evaluate proposals and to monitor risks over time.

Issuers and investors have positively evaluated the Italian institutional framework for mini-bonds, and a market of about 321 issues raised about €15,736 million at the end of 2017. The first issues date back to November 2012 (Politecnico di Milano, 2015). As of December 2017, about 83.5% of the issues are less than €50 million in size (11.7% of the money raised), and only 11.2% exceed €150 million in size (78.4% of the money raised) (Politecnico di Milano, various years). About 51% of Italian mini-bonds are amortizing bonds and 49% are bullet bonds; 77% are without guarantees and 23% have guarantees; and 14% are rated. The average maturity is 5 years.

The number of interventions from the Italian Guarantee Fund for SMEs is low for the mini-bond market, with only one intervention in 2015, seven in 2016, and four in 2017 (Fondo di garanzia per le PMI, 2015, 2016, 2017). By the end of June 2018, 201 mini-bonds were listed in ExtraMot Pro, issued by 153 companies for a face value of €11,418 million.

Another experience in the Italian mini-bond market is Elite basket bonds. This is the international platform set up in 2012 by the Italian Stock Exchange in partnership with the Italian association of manufacturing and service companies (Confindustria) and an investment bank acting as arranger in most mini-bond issues (Finint). Through a Special Purpose Vehicle (EBB1 s.r.l.), a 10-year bond (December 2017–2027) consisting of ten well-performing and innovative Italian companies was issued with a successful closing of €122 million raised. The notes are backed by mini-bond issues from €8 to €18 million and have a credit enhancement for 15% of the total amount raised. The resulting asset-backed securities were underwritten by the European Investment Bank (50%), the Italian State (33%), and institutional and professional investors targeted though an ELITE Club deal, a private placement platform dedicated to elite companies.

Finally, it is worth mentioning the role of private debt funds. In only 4 years (2014–2017), there were 24 active operators, of which eight were international, dealing with fund-raising or investment transactions. The funds are close funds managed by adopting a buy-and-hold approach. Although the capital raised by the Italian funds is under €2 billion, these bonds represent an important emerging link in the chain of intermediation that can contribute to the functioning of the whole system. In 2017, one out of four private debt investments referred to private-equity-backed firms, so venture capitalists and private equity fund managers have begun to play an important role in scouting and networking activity. The State, too, contributes to this chain through its financial arms, Cassa Depositi e Prestiti and Fondo Italiano d'investimento, which manage the "Fund of Funds Private Debt."

2.2. *Spain*

The Spanish experience is similar to the Italian one.

In 2013, the Spanish stock exchange, Bolsa y Mercados Espanoles (BME), set up an alternative market dedicated to SMEs, where both commercial paper and bonds are traded. This market, the Mercado Alternativo de Renta Fija (MARF) is a multilateral trading facility that is open only to professionals, insurance companies, pension funds, investment funds, asset managers, banks, and other investment service entities. Bonds have a minimum size of €100.000 and can be issued by joint-stock companies and limited liability companies. This market is regulated in part by a set of reforms that seek to reduce the Spanish economy's dependence on bank intermediations.

As an alternative market, MARF provides issuers with access to capital markets under more flexible conditions than those of more traditionally regulated markets (Guijarro and Manueco, 2013). Requirements for issuers include at least two audited annual reports, but the annual accounts do not have to be presented under international accounting standards, so the issuers can present accounts according to local accounting standards, and it is not necessary to get approval of the Spanish National Competent Authority (the CNMV) for the prospectus to be published. The necessary requirements are a rating from a rating agency or a credit or solvency assessment report issued by an entity certified and registered with ESMA. BME currently requires a minimum rating of BB- or a credit or solvency-assessment report issued by a certified agency that concerns risks and solvency. Price sensitivity information must also be provided.

MARF caters especially to SMEs, offering access to the market for relatively small issuances and enabling a first contact with capital markets while diversifying non-bank financing. As is usual in alternative markets, the companies that access MARF benefit from a simplified process and lower costs. One important player is the Registered Advisor, whose function is to provide advice to companies that use this market regarding the regulatory requirements and other aspects of the issuance when it is prepared and throughout its life.

In the recent context of low interest rates, institutional investors have been attracted to the higher yields offered by MARF. Since its establishment, MARF has handled more than €7.57 billion of funding through new issuances, and it had an outstanding balance at the end of 2017 of €2.26 billion, (+40.2%), of which 60.4% corresponded to medium- and long-term assets (Figures 1(a) and 1(b)), and 41 companies have been directly financed through the market.

2.3. *France*

A completely different model followed the French experience.

Mini-bonds were introduced in France in 2016 with a new section ("Le minibon") in the Monetary and Financial Code in the asset class of interest-bearing notes. Mini-bonds offer a way to modernize the instrument "bon de caisse", which were created in 1937 and since the 1980s have gradually fallen out of use. French mini-bonds are interest-bearing notes or short-term bonds that are offered with the support of registered

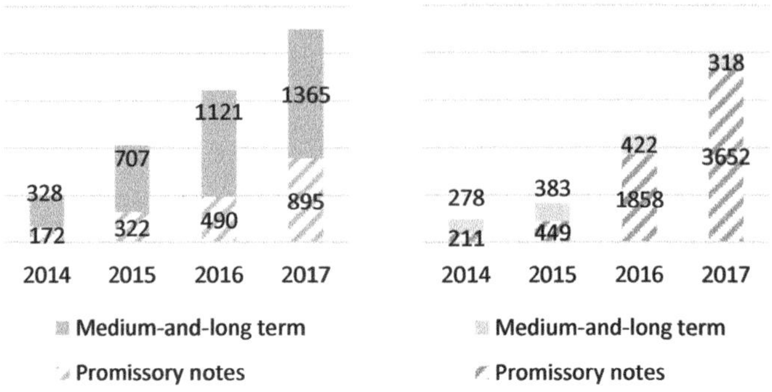

(a) (b)

Figure 1: (a) New issues on MARF (€ million). (b) Outstanding balance (€ million).
Source: BME.

intermediaries via a website. Intermediaries include investment services provider (prestataire de services d'investissement — IFP) but also crowd-funding investment adviser (conseiller en investissements participatifs — CIP). This modernization process is part of a policy to spur the digital economy and financial markets.

Because the law is new, the market is thin, and we have only a few experiences with a fair track record to analyze. However, the regulatory framework appears to be effective, well designed, and able to meet demand, as testified by the number of issues and the reactions to the consultative process.

Mini-bonds must fulfill the conditions laid down by the General Rules of Financial Market Authority (AMF). Only public limited companies or limited liability companies, whose capital is fully paid, can issue mini-bonds. Issuing firms must have at least three approved annual reports, which are made available to investors. The maximum face amount of mini-bonds issued by each issuer cannot exceed €2.5 million in any 12-month period. The nominal value and interest rate of each mini-bond are subject to regular repayments by the issuer at a frequency that may not exceed one per quarter throughout the mini-bond's duration. Interest rates are fixed and capped to anti-usury rates. Fixed interest rates make it easier to evaluate the expected return and risk exposure at the interest rate risk. Mini-bonds' duration must not exceed 5 years, and notes must be issued to a named person and are not negotiable. They are entered in the name of their owners in a register kept by the issuer. The underwriting document is generated at the end of issue process — if the target amount has been reached — and available for download in the personal space of each investor.

Sometimes, the issuance of mini-bonds is recorded in a blockchain via hyperlink. In this case the transfer of ownership occurs when the disposal is recorded in the blockchain, which removes the need for a document between the seller and the buyer and effects the transfer of the mini-bond's ownership. This additional feature of this innovation is a nod to the digital economy. This approach simplifies the information that must be disclosed by the issuer and the providers to investors prior to subscription of notes, which may be communicated by email.

The key regulatory information for mini-bonds covers the issue (duration, interest rate, amortization terms, rights attached to mini-bonds), the project (with a description of the risks), the service provider managing the website (legal data, fees), and information on how the subsequent resale of the mini-bond is to be dealt with. A template is provided that prescribes not only the detailed structure of the information document but also sentences to be used, specific wording, and the maximum number of words to be used.

The marketing of crowdfunding offers is also regulated by the AMF: it needs to be clear, balanced, and not misleading. Such rules apply to both the webpage (home page, project pages, FAQ page) and other channels, such as the follow-up emails the platform sends to the investors and the search engine's indexing paragraph. The platforms are obliged to publish default rates of the mini-bonds on the market every quarter.

As for the secondary market, because these securities are non-negotiable, they are not traded in regulated markets or multilateral trading facilities. Secondary markets can develop only after adopting a blockchain process.

In less than 2 years since mini-bonds were first issued, they have raised €10.8 million, equal to 5.5% of all the loans raised via crowdfunding platforms' loans (Association Financement Partecipatif France and KPMG, 2017). An average of 122 investors invest in each mini-bond issue, which is close to that of bonds (131) but far below that of loans (447). The size of funding provided by each investor per project is about half that provided by bonds (€2,368 versus €5,896) and about seven times that of loans (€310). As expected, the money raised via mini-bonds (€198,608 on average) is smaller than that raised from bonds (€487,395) but greater than that collected via simple loans (€121,706) (Association Financement Participatif France and KPMG, 2017).

The inclusion of limited liability companies among the issuers of mini-bonds opens the door to SMEs for this form of financing, but the requirement of at least three approved annual reports limits start-ups' access in their early stages.

2.4. *The United Kingdom*

The British model shares various features of both the Italian and of French models.

In the UK's common law context, a legal definition of "mini-bonds" does not exist. However, in economic literature and on the market, this term generally refers to bonds that are targeted to retail investors and are small in size, such as between £100 and £10,000, and are placed/traded through two markets: the Order Book for Retail Bonds (ORB) and crowdfunding platforms via the Internet.

The ORB is an official market that the London Stock Exchange set up in 2010 with the aim of opening up new sources of capital for companies that were looking to diversify their funding, establish a primary market to distribute retail bonds, and develop a secondary market for trading activities (corporate bonds and gilts). Unlike the Italian experience, the UK market is open to both retail and institutional/professional investors. It is a regulated market in which rules concerning the prospectus (the offering document), the information booklet, and the pricing supplement apply. The company that issues the bonds must have 2 years of audited financial statements prepared in accordance with International Financial Reporting Standards, and there must be a committed market maker on ORB that provides two-way on-screen prices throughout the trading day. Retail bonds are characterized by simple structures and are mainly fixed or floating bonds and rarely index-linked bonds.

Considering the costs of compliance with listing and disclosure obligations at issuance and over time, the economic minimum size of these bonds is estimated to be around £25 million. Clearly, only well-organized companies can face this cost, so mini-bonds issued on the ORB look to be best suited for mid-cap companies.

The second channel, crowdfunding via Internet platforms, dates back to the early 2000s but saw exponential growth in 2016. On this channel, mini-bonds are sometimes issued by well-known consumer businesses, such as food and beverage, leisure, and large retail companies, which offer non-cash rewards like free or discounted products that are designed to attract loyal customers. For instance, the London-based Mexican fast food chain Chilango launched the "Burrito bonds" in Crowncube. They offer investors an 8% annual return over a 4-year term. Added benefits are free burrito vouchers for all investors and a VIP bondholder party for the first 100 investors. Hotel Chocolat in 2010 raised £3.7 million selling "Chocolate Bonds" in multiples of either £2,000 or £4,000. The return to investors was around 5%.

As a result of stringent and restrictive regulations, these mini-bonds are not suitable to be issued on the exchange, so they are not freely tradeable or transferable like typical corporate bonds are; on the contrary, they are marketed directly to individuals.

The regulation of crowdfunding lies in the frame of The Financial Services and Markets Act 2000 (Regulated Activities), as amended by Order 2013 and 2014 and regulated by the Financial Conduct Authority (FCA). In this framework, mini-bonds are recognized as a type of debt security with a maturity of around three to 5 years that is typically issued by small businesses and offered on crowdfunding platforms or in direct marketing. The FCA surveyed that in the last 3 years, the interest rate was between 6% and 8% a year.

Mini-bonds are not protected by the Financial Services Compensation Scheme (FSCS) if the issuer fails. Concerns about the marketing of these instruments regard the fact that the firms (and the platforms) fail to make clear that mini-bonds are investments that place investors' capital at risk and they are not deposit-based or capital-protected products. Promotion is not balanced and the risk-return profile is not highlighted. Mini-bonds are generally illiquid, so investors should be aware that their investments are locked in until maturity.

Regulation for securities that are not "readily realizable" (i.e., unlisted) offered on crowdfunding or other media says that they can be promoted only to certain types of "expert/sophisticated" investors, that is, those who understand the inherent risks or have the financial capacity to bear eventual losses. In addition, where no advice is provided, firms must check that their clients have the knowledge and experience they need to understand the risk involved before being invited to respond to an offer.

As for the tax treatment and exemptions, since 2016, peer-to-peer loans and crowdfunding debentures (including crowdfunded debt securities issued by companies and bonds issued by registered charities), are eligible for the Innovative Finance ISA-IFISA (a new tax-free savings account), provided that they are transferable, create indebtedness, are facilitated by an authorized person, and are made through an electronic system in the European Economic Area. The new IFISA offered new opportunities for investors and will contribute to the development of crowdfunding placements, including mini-bonds.

The UK market of investment crowdfunding is highly dynamic. The market for debt-based securities is still small compared to other models of alternative finance peer-to-peer (P2P) lending, equity financing, and invoice financing, but it is growing quickly (Table 2).

The increase in market volume is partly due to the entry of new providers of this type of alternative financing, with several new platforms

Table 2: UK debt-based securities/debentures in comparison with other finance instruments (£ million).

	2013	2014	2015	2016
Debt-based securities	2.7	4.4	6.2	79.2
Equity-based crowdfunding	28	84	245	272
P2P business lending	139	749	881	1,232
P2P consumer lending	287	547	909	1,169
Invoice financing	97	270	352	472

Source: Cambridge Center for Alternative Finance, University of Cambridge (2017).

offering corporate bonds. The most attractive sectors are Food and Beverage, which generate 36% of the subscriptions; Renewable Energy, with 27% of the subscriptions; and Community and Social Enterprises, which accounts for 14% of the subscription. These leading sectors suggest that investors are attracted to well-known brands and projects that contribute to green economy and local development. Institutional investors are only moderately interested in this type of financing, and are responsible for only 8% of total investment. Such investors spend considerable time performing their own due diligence, rather than relying on that done by the platform or co-investors.

2.5. *Germany*

In Germany, mini-bonds have been issued through two different instruments: Schuldscheine (Figure 2) and bonds listed on the Scale segment.

Schuldscheine (SSD) is sometimes translated as "certificate of indebtedness", but they are not quite a loan, nor a bond. They are bilateral loans, privately placed, unlisted and unregistered. They are not securities as the debt is legally constituted by the underlying loan agreement, rather than by the certificate of indebtedness itself. Lenders or investors are

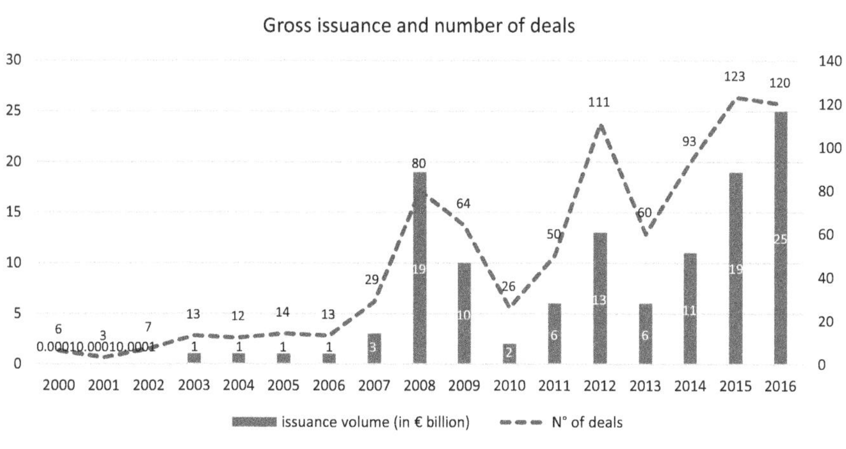

Figure 2: Schuldscheine: Gross issuance and number of deals.
Source: Loan Market Association.

mainly professional investors (credit institutions such as banks, and institutional investors such as insurance companies, investment management companies and pension funds). This instrument offers a great flexibility: SSD can carry varying maturities of typically between 2 and 10 years, with different types of interests; it also uses denomination in different currencies. The issuing costs are fairly lower than those for corporate bonds are.

SDD success is partly due to the fact that it does not need to be assessed on a mark-to-market basis, thus limiting volatility impact on the financial statement and results. Furthermore, since 2007, SSD has been deemed suitable for refinancing with BCE. Another advantage is the possibility for the company to raise capital with discretion and confidentiality, from outside its core banking group (Loan Market Association, 2016; European Commission, 2017).

The SSD market dates back to the beginning of this century and presents some waves: a surge in the year of the acute crisis (2008), and again in 2012. Since 2014, there was a steady growth in issuance volumes and in numbers of deals.

The other phenomenon that favored mini-bonds in Germany is the creation of a new segment market at Deutsche Stock exchange for SMEs corporate bonds, called Deutsche Börse Cash Market (Scale for corporate bonds). It is a regulated unofficial market based on private law. Companies are included in trading at fewer formal requirements (see below) and lower costs (inclusion fees of €10,000 and quotation fees for calendar quarter of €2,500). As the information requirements for the issuers are low, the market is targeted to qualified and experienced investors. The Scale Market follows the unsuccessful experience of other markets for SMEs, such as Mittelstand Market in Dusseldorf, m:access in Munich and Mittelstandsborse in Hamburg-Hannover (Metzner *et al.*, 2017).

Bonds issued on the Scale Market can be considered as mini-bonds as the issuer is required to have only a 2-year company history, adopting national accounting standards and last one annual financial statement audited and place at least €20 million with corporate bonds denominated up to a maximum of €1,000.

At least three out of six performance criteria have to be met: EBIT Interest Coverage ≥ 1.5; EBITDA Interest Coverage ≥ 2.5; Total

Debt/EBITDA ≤ 7.5; Total Net Debt/EBITDA ≤ 5; Risk Bearing Capital ≥ 0.20; Total Debt/Capital ≤ 0.85. These performance requisites are meant to limit the risk of an overoptimistic evaluation about the growth and success of the issuing company, as experienced by the number of defaults on the first wave of mini-bond issues in 2010–2014, rated by smaller local agencies. On a sample of 118 issues, 24 resulted non-performing and 40 raised more than €200 million by large companies, not classified as SMEs (Mietzner *et al.*, 2018). The failure of previous experiences is partly due to the narrow segmentation of those markets and to the over-optimism of local rating agencies and investors.

The dimension of the Scale market is still small: at the end of 2018 only 14 bonds were listed from 10 issuers. These are plain vanilla issues with a fixed coupon and defined maturity redeemed at face value. The coupon rate varies from 4.5% to 8% with a yield to maturity of between 1.71% and 3.58%. It is necessary to underline that there is a limited number of bonds active on the market, the others are part of investment portfolios and are subject to buy and hold policy: such yields mature when the exchange value is slightly higher for a final volume that is only scarcely significant.

The German experience regarding mini-bonds has changed over time as a result of default and recent market revitalization. Thus, it would be interesting to verify the success and capability of the market to attract emissions pertaining to SMEs in the near future.

3. Valuation of Mini-bonds

In order to have a successful placement of mini-bonds, an issuer cannot disregard the evaluation from the investor's point of view. While the issuer is mainly concerned about the cost and the outflows structure of its debt financing, the investor pays attention to the expected return and risk of his investment. Therefore, it becomes clear that the evaluation of cost and expected return are two sides of the same coin.

The key features associated with mini-bonds (lighter issuing regulation, absent or limited negotiability, issuance by small and medium size firms typically less established than companies that offer conventional bonds) are inherent sources of risk (market risk, credit risk, liquidity risk).

With reference to mini-bonds, it is therefore reasonable to state that investors will value the bond at a price that allows for the inclusion of an additional compensation relative to the "promised" ones by the Treasury spot rate curve in the role of benchmark curve. The value of a default free bond, can be obtained as the sum of discounted values of future cash flow using the risk free spot rate as discount rates. This leads to apply Z-spread as a tool of comparative analysis in this field. Z-spread is a constant or static spread to add over each maturity of the entire spot rate curve that makes the present value of cash flows from the mini-bond, obtained with risk free spot rates plus the spread as discount rates, equal to the mini-bond's market price. As highlighted by Choudry *et al.* (2005), the computation of Z-spread is more realistic and a useful spread (than a standard yield to maturity spread) when a bond carries certain additional risks. As was said, this is exactly the case for mini-bonds for which we recognize not only the existence of a credit/default risk, but also an illiquidity risk and a size risk as well.

Formally, Z-spread (z_s) is derived by solving the following equation[2]:

$$P = \sum_{t=1}^{T} \frac{C_t}{(1+r_{0,t}+z_s)^t} + \frac{NV}{(1+r_{0,T}+z_s)^T},$$

where P is the bond price; C_t is the coupon payment in t; $r_{0,t}$ ($r_{0,T}$) is the spot rate for maturity t (T); NV is the nominal (face) value of the bond.

For an amortizing bond, the above equation would change and be expressed thus:

$$P = \sum_{t=1}^{T} \frac{E(NV)_t i_c + E(NV)_{t-1} - E(NV)_t}{(1+r_{0,t}+z_s)^t},$$

where $E(NV)_t$ is the estimated residual nominal (face) value of the bond in t; i_c = coupon rate adjusted for the frequency of coupon payments.

[2] While regarding this equation it is important to keep in mind that if we had considered a default free bond, the equation would have been as follows:

$$P_{\text{Default free}} = \sum_{t=1}^{T} \frac{C_t}{(1+r_{0,t})^t} + \frac{NV}{(1+r_{0,T})^T}$$

using the above notation.

To solve the above equations for z_s, a trial-and-error procedure is required.

To illustrate this, we refer to a real euro denominated mini-bond issued at par on April 15, 2015 with maturity on April 15, 2020 (so it is a 5-year bond) with a rating coming exclusively from a local (e.g., Italian) agency. The issuer is Ferrarini S.P.A., a medium unlisted company active in the food sector. The coupon rate is 6.375% and coupon payments are semi-annual. The principal is repaid only at maturity and there are no embedded options. At the time of issue (but also in the following years), due to the combined effect of the obvious high credit worthiness of AAA government rated bonds and especially the ECB's very accommodative monetary policy (including unconventional measures), the benchmark term structure exhibits negative rates approximately up to 5 years.

Table 3 shows the payments "promised" by the mini-bond under consideration at the time of its issuance at par, its payments dates, the risk free spot rates corresponding to these dates, the Z-spread obtained by solving the 1st equation and the proof that the sum of discounted cash flows in the last column is equal to the issue's price.

Table 3: Determination of implicit Z-spread at time of issuance for a mini-bond.

Cash flow dates	Days	Years	Spot rates (%)	Cash flows	Z-spread	Spot rates + Z-spread (%)	Discounted cash flows
15/04/2015					**6.62%**		
15/10/2015	183	0.501	−0.318	3.1875		6.301	3.091
15/04/2016	366	1.003	−0.282	3.1875		6.337	2.997
15/10/2016	549	1.504	−0.250	3.1875		6.369	2.905
15/04/2017	731	2.003	−0.238	3.1875		6.381	2.816
15/10/2017	914	2.504	−0.234	3.1875		6.385	2.730
15/04/2018	1096	3.003	−0.225	3.1875		6.394	2.646
15/10/2018	1279	3.504	−0.212	3.1875		6.407	2.564
15/04/2019	1461	4.003	−0.192	3.1875		6.427	2.484
15/10/2019	1644	4.504	−0.168	3.1875		6.451	2.405
15/04/2020	1827	5.005	−0.139	103.1875		6.480	75.361
							100

Therefore, 662 basis points is the implicit Z-spread at the issuing date. It represents the compensation for additional credit risk and liquidity risk the market participants were exposed to by subscribing to the mini-bond rather than investing in a government bond issued by, for example, Germany or Luxembourg. In other words, Z-spread is the return the investors want to earn besides the base interest rate demanded in an economic area just for waiting, i.e., for time.

The same bond was priced 94 on September 12, 2018. Both the (remaining) cash flow profile of the bond at this time and the current risk free spot rate curve are shown in Table 4.

The significant increase is clearly visible in the Z-spread (more than doubled) when only a year and a half remains at the natural redemption date. At this time the Z-spread embodies mainly credit risk, while liquidity risk is much less relevant. Having used the spot rates of AAA government rated bonds, also the country risk affects the Z-spread.

It must be observed that, at least from a theoretical point of view, Z-spread is a flexible tool so, even if it is typically calculated using, as it was just noted, the spot rates for AAA rated government bonds as benchmark curve, it can also be computed selecting a different benchmark curve. For example, if it was possible to have, as benchmark, a spot rate curve for issuers similar to the one in the above example (with the same credit rating), the calculated Z-spread would be mainly attributable to the liquidity risk.[3]

However, one must acknowledge that Z-spread can be quite unreliable or biased in the case of non-bullet bonds. Quite frequently, mini-bonds are non-bullet-bonds as they include embedded options. Indeed, they are often callable bonds as the issuer has the discretionary power to call (buy) the mini-bonds from the bondholders before the stated maturity. From the investors' point of view, it is like saying they have a financial security

---

[3]Ratings for mini-bonds usually come from local rating agencies so they may be difficult to "reconcile" with the rating scales adopted by the "Big Three" (Fitch, Moody's and Standard & Poor). This would be necessary to identify the spot rate curve related to a large population under observation by the "Big Three" with the same rating of the mini-bond issuers under analysis. A difficulty or a problem in doing this is that mini-bond ratings are prone to rating inflation as observed by Mietzner *et al.* (2017).

Table 4: Z-spread determination for the mini-bond at an intermediate date.

Cash flow dates	Days	Years	Spot rates (%)	Cash flows	Z-spread	Spot rates + Z-spread (%)	Discounted cash flows
12/09/2015					**13.55%**		
15/10/2018	33	0.090	-0.200	3.1875		13.28	3.152
15/04/2019	215	0.589	-0.627	3.1875		12.86	2.968
15/10/2019	398	1.090	-0.633	3.1875		12.85	2.794
15/04/2020	581	1.592	-0.600	103.1875		12.88	85.086
							94

containing a long position in a traditional bullet bond and a short position in a call option.

The shortcoming of Z-spread to assess the relative value of the mini-bonds in these cases is attributable in essence to the assumption of a static interest rate environment; that's why it is also called zero-volatility spread. It is easy to understand it is not plausible to ignore the fact that interest rates are volatile when analyzing such mini-bonds. Interest rate changes affect the cash flows from an investment in mini-bonds because they influence the issuer's decision about an earlier redemption.[4] This circumstance makes the mini-bond profile uncertain; the issuer can alter the cash flows for the investors.

In this context, instead of referring to the (static) Z-spread, it is more appropriate to refer to the option adjusted spread (OAS). Logically it corresponds to the Z-spread after subtracting for the option value and expresses the return investors would demand if the bond did not include embedded options.

In practice, the procedure for evaluating the OAS consists of a technique that works by simulating many scenarios of future interest rate paths and by taking into account the cash flow payments that would occur with these paths. It represents a quantity (exactly a spread) to be added to all the

[4]The issuer reasonably would call the bond when the decrease in interest rates allows the issuer to save on the issue of new debt with a maturity equal to the residual life of the callable bond.

spot rates within all interest rate paths such that the average discounted value of the paths is equal to the current market price of the mini-bond. In this way, a demanded return (for inherent credit risk and liquidity risk) is available for comparative analysis also for mini-bonds with embedded options.

4. Why Issue and Invest in Mini-Bonds?

This study on the principal European experience of mini-bond issues allows us to identify factors that determine the attractiveness of these new instruments for smaller companies that want to finance their projects and reduce their dependence on banks, and for investors that want to participate in a new market to diversify their investments at a desirable risk-return level.

The underlying process of financial innovation has been supported and also sometimes led by governments as part of industrial policy to promote the growth of SMEs and facilitate their access to financial markets.

From the issuers' standpoint, mini-bonds broaden the available financing alternatives and shift the sources of financing from banks and financial intermediaries to alternative markets. Thus, smaller firms can diversify their financial sources, gain experience with financial markets' dynamics and evaluation criteria, and interact with the financial intermediaries that advise and assist companies in accessing capital markets. Mini-bonds should provide SMEs with an opportunity to settle into financial markets and open doors to further developments. Alternative markets have fewer regulatory hurdles to be met (as no prospectus is required) and lower requirements with which to comply, so they provide a faster and more flexible way for companies to raise financing. It is also much cheaper for SMEs to issue mini-bonds to the market, but experience is still too limited to find empirical evidence on the effective level of interest rates and compare it to more traditional banking instruments.

The specifics of each institutional framework and of the market features in different countries call for additional comments.

The Italian and Spanish experiences have seen only institutional/professional investors as investors and a dedicated market infrastructure, promoted in both cases by the national stock exchange, as the trading venue. In these models, the purpose of promoting a learning process is evident, as is the desire to enrich a chain of intermediation with new, specialized markets and new types of institutional investors.

In the French experience, mini-bond issuers target the retail investor market via investment crowdfunding platforms. Such platforms offer the opportunity to use this instrument to raise money to finance "green" projects funded by public–private-partnerships that involve the local population by leveraging their desire to belong to the local community and support a green project. Some offers have been earmarked for families living in the area of the green project with interest rates offered differentiated based on the distance from the family's home to the wind farm or photovoltaic plant the project supports. In these cases, mini-bond pricing rely not only on economic and financial variables but also on the promotion of the whole project.

The UK case stands in the middle of these experiences. Here we find traditional bond structures that contain traditional financial elements, but also mini-bond offers that combine the objectives of both raising money and increasing customer awareness and loyalty. Companies that are in the retail Food and Beverage sector and others that have direct contact with consumers can issue mini-bonds as part of campaigns to promote their brands and enhance customer loyalty.

The German experience is more complex to evaluate. SSDs are, by their nature, undisclosed transactions and we have only positive figures on the market growth. The other mini-bonds segment, the Scale market, is still a young, very thin market and it follows some failures in other local experiences of SMEs dedicated markets.

From the investors' standpoint, the low interest rates offered nowadays by other investments have pushed investors to look for more profitable investments with an appropriate balance between risk and expected return. On the demand side, there is an opportunity for financial operators to create new financial instruments, such as investment funds, and special purpose vehicles (SPVs) that specialize in mini-bond investing either in renewable or energy-efficiency projects funded by mini-bonds. Crowdfunding platforms also see the opportunity to enrich their portfolio of offerings by adding securities to peer-to-peer lending or less risky investments than equity investments.

Financial regulators and authorities have paid attention to this innovation and undertaken to provide a legal and regulatory framework that balances the need to promote clear, non-misleading sales while not nipping this innovation in the bud.

The passage of time will offer additional experiences and data with which to evaluate mini-bonds' performance or failures and determine whether this innovation is sufficiently resilient and able to enrich the chain of financial intermediation to meet the financial needs of SMEs.

5. Conclusions and Avenues for Future Research

As previously said, mini-bonds have a potentially key role in the financing of SMEs, filling a gap in debt financing. Despite this, the academic studies on mini-bonds are virtually absent. Most of the existing works on mini-bonds are reports analyzing the market developments (as the repeatedly mentioned Politecnico di Milano, various years, the UK Alternative Finance Industry Report, various years, and the Association Financement Participatif-KPMG, Baromètre du crowdfunding en France 2017) or are comments on specific experiences, often now out-of-data. Therefore, the lack of studies is probably due to the relatively recent nature of mini-bonds and the shortage of data. At this stage, a literature review would probably provide no added value.

Based on our analysis of mini-bonds experiences in Europe, we identify some matters that deserve further research and empirical analysis. Significant opportunities for further investigation exist both in microeconomic perspectives and in macroeconomic ones.

In the first area, considering the operational performances of firms issuing mini-bonds, a further interesting research direction is to verify whether, thanks to the relaxation of financial constraints, firms issuing mini-bonds improve their operational performance in the medium-run and to ascertain whether they have specific characteristics in terms of size, growth, internationalization, industry, financing patterns or other key variables (Feihle and Lawrenz, 2017, Moritz *et al.*, 2015). As shown by Feihle and Lawrenz (2017), from a practical point of view this requires the availability of a significant sample of mini-bonds issuers with a long enough track record.

Considering both perspectives, with reference to those markets where mini-bonds are traded on stock exchanges or multilateral trading facilities, an interesting research question relates to the significance of trades in terms of liquidity and traded volume in order to understand if we can expect from those markets a price discovery function.

It can be seen as related to the same stream of analysis, an extensive investigation throughout different countries of underpricing phenomenon for mini-bonds. Following Allen and Faulhaber (1989), an empirical test can be conducted to understand if underpricing is a signal for differentiation for the quality of the issuers. To be more precise, the hypothesis to test consists of a positive correlation of the issuing firm quality with mini-bonds underpricing.

With a view to the functioning of markets and instruments, it seems interesting to verify in a just time-frame, if instruments and markets originally set up to provide SMEs with new opportunities to access capital markets have actually been used — and perhaps jeopardized — by larger companies. Should that be proved, a further research question refers to the origins of this double market failure: on one side the SMEs displacement in that should have been their dedicated market, on the other side the main market failure if large companies prefer to migrate to or also use other market segments.

Finally, it seems interesting to verify empirically, in the next future with a growing track record of mini-bond experiences, how the lifecycle paradigm works, following Berger and Udell (1998, 2006) clarifications to their model — which includes more variables than age, dimension and information transparency — and the evidence of Gregory *et al.* (2005).

Appendix — Legislative and Regulatory References

Italy

- Civil Code art. 2412, point 5. as amended by Legislative Decree no. 83/2012.
- Legislative Decree no. 83/2012, art. 32 "Interventions for promoting economic growth" (Decreto Crescita) and Legislative Decree no. 179/2012, art. 36.

- Legislative Decree no. 145/2013, art. 12 concerning "Measures aimed at facilitating credit access to SMEs, in the context of Promoting Italian economy (Decreto Destinazione Italia).
- Legislative Decree 91/2014 (Decreto Competitività), art. 21 "Measures aimed at promoting corporate bond issues".
- Decree March 6, 2017 of Minister for Economic Development concerning "New forms of firm evaluation in order to benefit of insurance from the Guarantee fund for SMEs and loss protection".

Spain

- MARF-BME, The Alternative Fixed Income Market, MARF, Regulating, April 17, 2018.

France

- Code monétaire et financier, articles L.223-6 to L-223-13 as added by Order no. 2016-520, April 28, 2016, pursuant to Law August 6, 2015 for the Growth, activity and levelled play field for equal economic opportunities, also known as "Macron Law".
- Civil Code, III, Section I, Chapter II, Title IV.
- AMF, DOC 2014-12, "Information to be provided to investors by the issuer and the crowdfunding investment adviser or the investment services provider within the framework of crowdfunding".
- AMF Instruction DOC-2014-12, "Information to be provided to investors by the issuer and crowdfunding investment adviser or investment services provider within the framework of crowdfunding".
- AMF Position-Recommendation DOC-2018-02, "Marketing of crowdfunding offers, calculation of default rates and run-off management of platforms".
- Order no. 2016-520, April 28, 2016.

Great Britain

- The Financial Services and Markets Act 2000.

- Financial Conduct Authority, Consultation Paper CP13/13, "The FCA's regulatory approach to crowdfunding (and similar activities), October 2013.
- Financial Conduct Authority, Consultation Paper CP16/4, "Loan-based crowdfunding platforms and segregation of client money", January 2016.
- Financial Conduct Authority, Discussion Paper DP15/6, "Possible FCA Handbook changes to reflect the introduction of the Innovative Finance ISA and the regulated activity of advising on peer-to-peer agreements", November 2015.
- Financial Conduct Authority, Consultation paper CP16/5, "Possible FCA Handbook changes to reflect the introduction of the Innovative Finance ISA and the regulated activity of advising on peer-to-peer agreements", February 2016.
- Financial Conduct Authority, Consultation paper CP18/20, "Loan-based ("peer-to-peer") and investment-based crowdfunding platforms: Feedback on our post-implementation review and proposed changes to the regulatory framework", July 2018.
- Financial Conduct Authority, Policy statement PS14/4, "The FCA's regulatory approach to crowdfunding over internet, and the promotion of non-readily realizable securities by other media. Feedback to CP13/13 and final rules", March 2014.
- Financial Conduct Authority, Policy Statement PS16/8, "FCA Handbook changes regarding the segregation of client money on loan-based crowding platforms, the Innovative Finance ISA, and the regulated activity on peer-to-peer agreements", March 2016.
- Financial Conduct Authority, "A review of the regulatory regime for crowdfunding and the promotion of non- readily realizable securities by other media", February, 2015.
- Financial Conduct Authority, "Call for input to the post-implementation review of the FCA's crowdfunding rules", July 2016.

Germany

- Deutsche Börse, General Terms and Conditions for Participation in the Prime Standard for Corporate Bonds, April 2017.

References

Allen F. and Faulhaber G. (1989) Signalling by Underpricing in the IPO market, *Journal of Financial Economics*, 23, 303–323.

Altman E. I., Esentato M., and Sabato G. (2018) Assessing the credit worthiness of Italian SMEs and mini-bond issuers, *Global Finance Journal*, September.

Artola C. and Genre V. (2011) Euro Area SMEs Under Financial Constraints: Belief or Reality? CESifo Working Paper Series No. 3650.

Association Financement Partecipatif France — KPMG (2018) Baromètre du crowdfunding en France 2017, January.

Baeck P., Collins L., and Zhang B. (2014) Understanding Alternative Finance. The UK Alternative Finance Industry Report 2014, Nesta, University of Cambridge.

Berger A. N. and Udell G. F. (1998) The economics of small business finance: The roles of private equity and debt markets in the financial growth cycle, *Journal of Banking and Finance*, 22, 613–673.

Berger A. N. and Udell G. F. (2006) A more complete conceptual framework for SME finance, *Journal of Banking and Finance*, 30, 2945–2966.

Bhaumik S. K., Fraser S., and Wright M. (2015) What do we know about entrepreneurial finance and its relationship with growth? *International Small Business Journal*, 33, 70–88.

Block J. H., Colombo M. G., Cumming D. J., and Vismara S. (2018) New players in entrepreneurial finance and why they are there, *Small Business Economics*, 50, 239–250.

Boschmans K. and Pissareva L. (2017) Fostering Markets for SME Finance. Matching Business and Investors Needs, OECD SME and Entrepreneurship Papers, no. 6. OECD Publishing, Paris.

British Business Bank — IPSOS MORI (2018) 2017 Business Finance Survey: SMEs, February.

Cambridge Centre for Alternative Finance — University of Cambridge (2017) Entrenching Innovation. The 4th Alternative Finance Industry Report, Cambridge Centre for Alternative Finance — University of Cambridge, December.

Casey E. and O'Toole C. (2014) Bank Lending Constraints, Trade Credit and Alternative Financing during the Financial Crisis: Evidence from European SMEs, *Journal of Corporate Finance*, 27, 173–193.

Collins L., Swart R., and Zhang B. (2013) The Rise of Future Finance, The UK Alternative Finance Benchmarking Report, Cambridge Centre for Alternative Finance, University of Cambridge, December.

Cusmano L. (2018) SME and Entrepreneurship Financing. The Role of Credit Guarantee Schemes and Mutual Guaranties in supporting finance for small and medium-sized enterprises, OECD SME and Entrepreneurship Papers, no. 1, OECD Publishing, Paris.

Drakos K. (2012) Bank loan terms and conditions for eurozone SMEs, *Small Business Economics*, 41, 717–732.

Eisele A. and Novak E. (2018) Market innovations for (non-bank) financing of SMEs in light of the crisis and new regulation: A policy perspective. In *Finance and Investment: The European Case*, Mayer, C., Micossi S., Onado M., Pagano M., and Polo A. (eds.). Oxford University Press.

European Commission (2017) Analysis of European Corporate Bond Markets, Analytical report supporting the main report from the Commission Expert Group on Corporate Bonds, November.

European Commission (2016) Crowdfunding in the EU Capital Markets Union, Brussels, May.

European Commission (2015) European Crowdfunding Stakeholders Forum — Third meeting, March.

European Investment Bank (2018) From Recovery to sustainable growth. Investment report 2017/2018.

Feihle P. C. and Lawrenz J. (2017) the issuance of german sme bonds and the impact on operating performance, *Schmalenbach Business Review*, 18, 227–259.

Financial Conduct Authority (2018) Investment Platforms Market Study. Interim report. Market Study MS17/1.2, July.

Fondo di garanzia per le PMI (2015) Report Nazionale 2015.

Fondo di garanzia per le PMI (2016) Report Nazionale 2016.

Fondo di garanzia per le PMI (2017) Report Nazionale 2017.

Gregory B. T., Rutherford W., Oswald S., and Gardiner L. (2005) An empirical investigation of the growth cycle theory of small firm financing, *Journal of Small Business Management*, 43, 382–392.

Guijarro P. and Manueco P. (2013) MARF: Perspectives and risks for Spain's new alternative fixed income market, *Spanish Economic and Financial Outlook*, 2(6).

Kaousar Nassr I. and Wehinger G. (2014) Unlocking SME finance through market-based debt: Securitisation, private placements and bonds, *OECD Journal: Financial Market Trends*, 2014(2).

Kramers-Eis H., Bottazzi F., Charrier R., Natoli M., and Squilloni M. (2014) Institutional non-bank lending and the role of Debt Funds, European Investment Fund, Working paper 2014 4/25.

Loan Market Association (2016) Schuldscheindarlehen — LMA Product Guide, London.

Mietzner M., Proells J., and Schweizer D. (2017) Hidden champions or black sheep? The role of underpricing in the German mini-bond market, *Small Business Economics*, 50, 375–395.

Mitter C. and Kraus S. (2011) Entrepreneurial finance — issue and evidence, revisited, *Int. J. Entrepreneurship and Innovation Management*, 14, 132–150.

Moritz A., Block J. H., and Heinz A. (2015) Financing Patterns of European SMEs: An Empirical Taxonomy, European Investment Fund, Working Paper 2015/30.

OECD (2015) New Approaches to SME and Entrepreneurship Financing: Broadening the Range of Instruments, OECD Publishing, Paris.

OECD (2016) G20/OECD Support note on diversification of financial instruments for SMEs, OECD Publishing, Paris, July.

Politecnico di Milano (2015) Osservatorio Mini-Bonds, 1 Report Italiano sui Mini-bonds, Milano, February.

Politecnico di Milano (2016) Osservatorio Mini-Bonds, 2 Report Italiano sui Mini-bonds, Milano, February.

Politecnico di Milano (2017) Osservatorio Mini-Bonds, 3 Report Italiano sui Mini-bonds, Milano, February.

Politecnico di Milano (2018) Osservatorio Mini-Bonds, 4 Report Italiano sui Mini-bonds, Milano, February.

Sunak R. (2017) A New Era for Retail Bonds. How our savings could help SMEs grow, Centre for Policy Studies, London, November.

Wardrop R., Zhang B., Rau R., and Gray M. (2015) Moving Mainstream. The European Alternative Finance Benchmarking Report, University of Cambridge.

Zhang B., Baeck P., Ziegler T., Bone J., and Garvey K. (2016) Pushing Boundaries. The 2015 UK Alternative Finance Industry Report, Cambridge Centre for Alternative Finance, University of Cambridge, February.

Ziegler T., Shneor R., Garvey K., Wienzlaff K., Yerolemou N., Hao R., and Zhang B. (2017) Expanding Horizons. The 3rd European Alternative Finance Industry Report, Cambridge Centre for Alternative Finance, University of Cambridge.

Part 3

Soft Characteristics and Entrepreneurial Finance

Chapter 9

Construed Shared Expectations: Facilitating Access to Early-Stage Equity Financing in Developing Countries

Carlos Martínez*
University of St. Gallen
carlosroberto.martinezromero@student.unisg.ch

Abstract

This chapter aims to understand how "disconnected entrepreneurs" access early-stage financing in non-developed countries. Previous studies have pointed out that due to the weak institutional environment in such contexts, investors have had to replace formal institutions with networks and other informal institutions. For this reason, connections and trust are particularly relevant for accessing entrepreneurial funding in non-developed countries. However, previous research has not explained how disconnected entrepreneurs from the lower social classes generate such trust and connections with business angels (BAs). The grounded theory

*50, Dufourstrasse, St. Gallen, 9000, Switzerland.

method was used to analyze 33 semi-structured interviews with Central American actors related to entrepreneurial financing. Based on the grounded evidence and the social capital dimensions framework, the study proposes a model explaining how former investors, businesspersons, and other institutional actors improved access to entrepreneurial financing in developing countries by building shared expectations and serving as a bridge between BAs and disconnected entrepreneurs. The chapter contributes to the entrepreneurial financing literature by explaining the effect of the cognitive social capital dimension on access to early-stage financing. The study has practical implications for organizations interested in promoting entrepreneurship in developing countries.

1. Introduction

This chapter investigates access to early-stage equity financing in developing countries. In some of these countries, entrepreneurial equity financing works as "Closed Clubs" to which only the closest to the wealthy families have access. In Central America for instance, the colonial heritage, class struggles during the Cold War, and current situation of gangs and organized crime have generated a barrier among actors from different social classes. Such barrier hinders access to early-stage equity financing for those low and middle-class entrepreneurs away from the trust circles of the wealthy families (from now on "disconnected entrepreneurs"). Government agencies that promote entrepreneurship have tried to bring disconnected entrepreneurs and business angels (BAs) closer through business plan competitions and other programs. However, such initiatives have failed because of the discrepancy in expectations between BAs and disconnected entrepreneurs. On the one hand, entrepreneurs do not understand how the BAs model works and believe that it is similar to a bank loan. Also, they are afraid that investors will steal their ideas or take full control of the start-up due to previous bad experiences with "not-so-angel" investors. On the other hand, BAs complain that entrepreneurs lack a scaling-up mindset and a culture of accountability. BAs said that the latter had been promoted by the government programs that grant seed capital without requiring anything in return.

The structural and cognitive barriers described above undermine the explanatory power of previous research related to early-stage financing in environments where entrepreneurs and investors are disconnected. Previous studies have pointed out that due to the weak institutional environment in non-developed countries, investors have had to replace formal institutions with networks and other informal institutions (Ahlstrom and Bruton, 2006; Bruton and Ahlstrom, 2003). For this reason, connections and trust are particularly relevant for accessing entrepreneurial funding in such contexts (Batjargal and Liu, 2004; Talavera *et al.*, 2012). However, previous research has not explained how disconnected entrepreneurs generate trust and connections with the members of the "Closed Clubs." This research seeks to answer the questions: *Which are the barriers restricting access to early-stage equity financing in developing countries? Moreover, how have such barriers been addressed?*

The current study proposes a model explaining how some wealthy businesspersons interested in developing the economy of their countries through entrepreneurship improved access to early-stage equity financing. Firstly, they reconciled the expectations of the previously disconnected actors by inducing a scaling-up and accountability mindset in entrepreneurs and by forming a network of BAs committed to the economic development of their nations. Secondly, they served as mediators of the nascent bond of trust between the mentioned actors.

This chapter contributes to the entrepreneurial financing literature by explaining the effect of the cognitive social capital dimension on access to early-stage financing. According to Jonsson and Lindbergh (2013), the cognitive dimension has received considerably less attention than the other social capital dimensions in the entrepreneurial financing literature. The chapter proposes the concept "construed shared expectations" defined as the development of a common understanding of critical aspects that make actors believe that counterparts will act for mutual benefit. Such tacit reciprocal commitment allows the creation of trust bonds between BAs and disconnected entrepreneurs. In addition to the theoretical contribution, the study has practical implications for investors, government agencies, and other organizations interested in the development of high-growth entrepreneurship in developing countries.

This chapter is organized as follows: Section 2 presents the research method, including data collection and analysis. Following this, Section 3 proposes a grounded model of access to entrepreneurial financing in developing countries. Finally, Section 4 presents the theoretical contribution and practical implications, describes limitations of the research design, and suggests areas for further investigation.

2. Method

Within the entrepreneurial financing literature, several authors have addressed a "funding gap" issue from a positivist approach, assuming that a shortage of supply "exist out there" "waiting to be filled" (Lam, 2010, p. 269). In contrast, this chapter addresses the research question from a grounded theory approach, reconstructing reality from the perspective of the "knowledgeable agents" at the supply and demand sides (Gioia *et al.*, 2013).

2.1. *Data collection*

The primary source of data was 33 semi-structured interviews with agents related to entrepreneurial financing in the Central American countries: Guatemala, El Salvador, Honduras, Nicaragua, Costa Rica, and Panama. The interviewees were directors of entrepreneurship centers and university incubators, VCs, BAs, entrepreneurs, government officials, and an executive of a second-tier development bank. Interviews were carried out between June 2017 and May 2018. Table 1 presents some characteristics of the data sample. Other sources of qualitative data were the documents provided by the interviewees (e.g., "maps" of local entrepreneurial support organizations, program evaluation reports) and direct observation at events organized by the interviewees (e.g., business plan contests and entrepreneurial "retreats").

The mentioned Central American countries provide an ideal "laboratory" to address the research question. Firstly, these countries are in low positions in the VC/PE attractiveness ranking prepared by IESE Business

Table 1: List of interviewees.

ID	Description	Primary Country of Operation	Contacted via	Date
1	Consultant of an International Cooperation Agency	El Salvador	Skype	20/09/17
2	Consultant of a seed-capital Program	El Salvador	Skype	13/09/17
3	Deputy Minister of Economy	Guatemala	Skype	12/09/17
4	Entrepreneurship Center former director	El Salvador	Skype	22/08/17
5	Entrepreneurship Center director	Costa Rica	Face-to-face	16/08/17
6	Entrepreneurship Professor and Consultant	Guatemala	Skype	23/08/17
7	Entrepreneur	El Salvador	Face-to-face	26/10/17
8	Government BA network consultant	Guatemala	Skype	06/12/17
9	Government seed-capital program consultant	Guatemala	Skype	19/09/17
10	Second-tier development bank executive	Costa Rica	Telephone	30/08/17
11	Stock Exchange Executive (SMEs securitization program)	Costa Rica	Skype	06/09/17
12	Entrepreneur and IE (Coworking)	Honduras	Skype	18/08/17
13	Entrepreneur and IE (Coworking)	Panama	Skype	25/08/17
14	IE (accelerator and BA network) and Broker	Costa Rica	Skype	14/12/17
15	IE (accelerator and BA network) and Broker	Guatemala	Telephone	01/09/17
16	IE (incubator) and Broker (impact investment funds)	Guatemala	Skype	07/12/17
17	IE (incubator and BA network) and Broker	Honduras	Telephone	08/09/17
18	IE (incubator)	Honduras	Skype	12/09/17
19	IE (incubator) and former VC	Nicaragua	Skype	14/12/17
20	IE (BA network) and Broker	Panama	Telephone	18/09/17

(*Continued*)

Table 1: (*Continued*)

ID	Description	Primary Country of Operation	Contacted via	Date
21	IE (coworking, incubator, BA network) and Broker	El Salvador	Telephone	21/09/17
22	IE (coworking, accelerator) and VC	Guatemala	Skype	30/08/17
23	IE (coworking, accelerator) and VC	Guatemala	Skype	28/11/17
24	BA, Broker, and former social entrepreneur	Guatemala	Skype	29/11/17
25	BA and former PE associate	El Salvador	Skype	28/08/17
26	BA and former M&A/PE associate	Costa Rica	Telephone	06/09/17
27	M&A/PE Managing Partner	Panama	Telephone	12/09/17
28	VC/PE Managing Partner	Costa Rica	Telephone	29/08/17
29	VC/PE Managing Partner	Costa Rica	Telephone	18/08/17
30	VC/PE Managing Partner	Costa Rica	Skype	28/01/18
31	VC/PE Managing Partner	Guatemala	Skype	28/08/17
32	SMEs financial provider	El Salvador	Face-to-face	22/09/17
33	Entrepreneur	Costa Rica	Skype	04/05/18

Note: IE: Institutional Entrepreneurship actor; M&A: Merger and Acquisition; PE: Private Equity.

School (Groh *et al.*, 2018). Secondly, they have weak institutional environments. According to the Global Competitiveness Report, these countries have a lack of formal institutions providing reliable information, embryonic stock markets and investor networks, weak regulatory frameworks, high wealth concentration in a few powerful and politically connected families, and low level of property rights (WEF, 2016).

As researchers, we experienced first-hand the difficulties of accessing potential early-stage investors, because we did not have close ties to approach them, and further we could not find from public sources who they were. Consequently, interview candidates were identified and approached through a snowball sampling technique (Biernacki and Waldorf, 1981). The research began by contacting the directors of the entrepreneurship center of the leading business school in Central America, who provided contacts within the school's alumni network. The preliminary analysis and selection of interviewees were conducted concurrently and iteratively, consistent with the grounded theory methodology (Corbin and Strauss, 1990; Suddaby, 2006). Initially, we were looking for BAs, VCs, and entrepreneurs who had received financing. However, based on the findings of the first interviews, we noticed a common pattern in different countries: former investment banking associates and wealthy businesspersons were developing entrepreneurial support organizations and BAs networks and linking disconnected entrepreneurs to such networks. We asked our first interviewees to introduce us to these actors in order to interview them.

The interviews were conducted based on a narrative semi-structured technique (Spradley, 1979). Interviewees were encouraged to provide "thick" descriptive data: As they made observations, we asked them questions to elicit rich details in order to help explain how such observations were important (Isabella, 1990). The interviews were conducted in Spanish, audiotaped with the consent of the interviewees, and transcribed verbatim. We conducted all the interviews, and a research assistant with experience in qualitative methods transcribed them. After each interview, we immediately made annotations and prepared a summary. Data collection ended at saturation, namely, when the interviews stopped providing new insights.

2.2. *Data analysis*

The transcripts were analyzed using Corbin and Strauss' (1990) three-stage coding. The process was done in Spanish. In the open coding, transcripts were analyzed without any theoretical guidance looking with an open mind for those extracts that were interesting to understand the issues that restricted the access to financing and the actions carried out for addressing such issues. The selected extracts were summarized in 949 open codes, using words similar to those said by the interviewees trying to keep these labels as close to the ground as possible. Examples of these codes are: "How do you contact investors if they do not have a label on their heads?" and "For security reasons, wealthy people only invest in their relatives' startups."

In the axial coding, 33 first-order categories were established by gathering several of the open codes into labels that summarized similar issues or activities, without making significant conceptual abstractions.

Examples of these subcategories are: "The worlds of entrepreneurs and investors are disconnected" and "Closed Clubs: Financing restricted to startups in the family circle." Before moving on to selective coding, we iterated between the analysis of grounded evidence and the search for theoretical and conceptual lenses that would help us to transform static subcategories into a dynamic grounded theory model (Gioia *et al.*, 2013).

Nahapiet and Ghoshal's (1998) framework was selected from the mentioned iterative process as the "substantive theory" which would help to "lift the data" (Suddaby, 2006, p. 634). According to such framework, social capital is comprised of three dimensions: structural, namely, the overall pattern of connections between actors (Burt, 1992); relational, referring to strong ties agents develop through a history of interactions (Granovetter, 1992); and cognitive relating to those resources providing shared representations, interpretations, and systems of meaning among parties (Cicourel, 1981).

The social capital dimensions served as the "theoretical glue" among the second-order themes. Based on the substantive theories, we grouped the first-order categories into eight second-order themes and connected them accordingly. Table 2 provides transparency to the study by presenting the data structure. The second-order themes include three barriers restricting access to entrepreneurial financing and three institutional activities to address such barriers, each one of them related to a social capital dimension. For instance, the categories for the structural dimension are "Disconnection between entrepreneurs and BAs" and "Bridging brokerage across BAs and disconnected entrepreneurs" The two remaining second-order themes are the mechanisms that facilitate access to entrepreneurial financing, each of which is related to two social capital dimensions. Finally, a preliminary version was presented to two of the capital providers interviewed (ID# 23 and 24) for obtaining their feedback.

3. Results

From the grounded evidence and substantive theories, we propose a model explaining access to entrepreneurial financing in developing countries. Figure 1 presents the relationships among the second-order

Table 2: Data structure.

1st Order Categories	2nd Order Themes	Aggregate Dimensions
The worlds of entrepreneurs and investors are disconnected Entrepreneurs need financing but cannot find investors Investors with appetite but cannot find entrepreneurs Investors remain anonymous for security reasons Closed Clubs: Financing restricted to start-ups in the family circle	Disconnection between entrepreneurs and BAs	Barriers that restrict access to entrepreneurial financing
Lack of an entrepreneurial financing network Lack of regulatory frameworks and policies to support ent. financing Lack of articulation among the nascent entrepreneurial support org.	Disarticulated entrepreneurial financing network	
Entrepreneurs do not understand BAs' business model Poor education in business and finance Subsistence start-ups without innovation or scaling-up potential Seed-capital programs foster a culture of lack of accountability	Discrepancy in the expectations of entrepreneurs and BAs	
An actor with a motivation beyond profit-seeking An actor with strong ties to the wealthy families An actor with contacts within the entrepreneurial community Linkage between non-elite entrepreneurs and wealthy individuals	Bridging brokerage between disconnected entrepreneurs and investors	Institutional work

(*Continued*)

Table 2: (*Continued*)

1st Order Categories	2nd Order Themes	Aggregate Dimensions
Development of BAs networks with friends and acquaintances Members are interested in their nations economic development Not only investors but business coaches and networking enhancers Local network grows through references among members IDB supports the creation of a regional network of BAs References through regional network increase investment matching	Development of network of committed bas with a motivation beyond for profit	
Pipeline development as there are not "investment ready" ent Institutional ent. create incubators, accelerators, co-working spaces Mentoring for the development of a scaling-up mindset Development of accountability culture	Development of entrepreneurs' scaling-up and accountability culture	
Wealthy individuals have a close relationship with the broker Ent. recognize that broker has good intentions and wants to help Brokers mediation creates a trusted environment for wealthy ind.	Trust bonds between investors and disconnected entrepreneurs	Mechanisms that facilitates access to entrepreneurial financing
Entrepreneurs understand BAs´ entrepreneurial financing model Entrepreneurs recognize the high risk of early-stage investment BAs are willing to coach, provide networking, and face a potential loss Brokers link parties only until entrepreneurs "are ready"	Construed shared expectations	

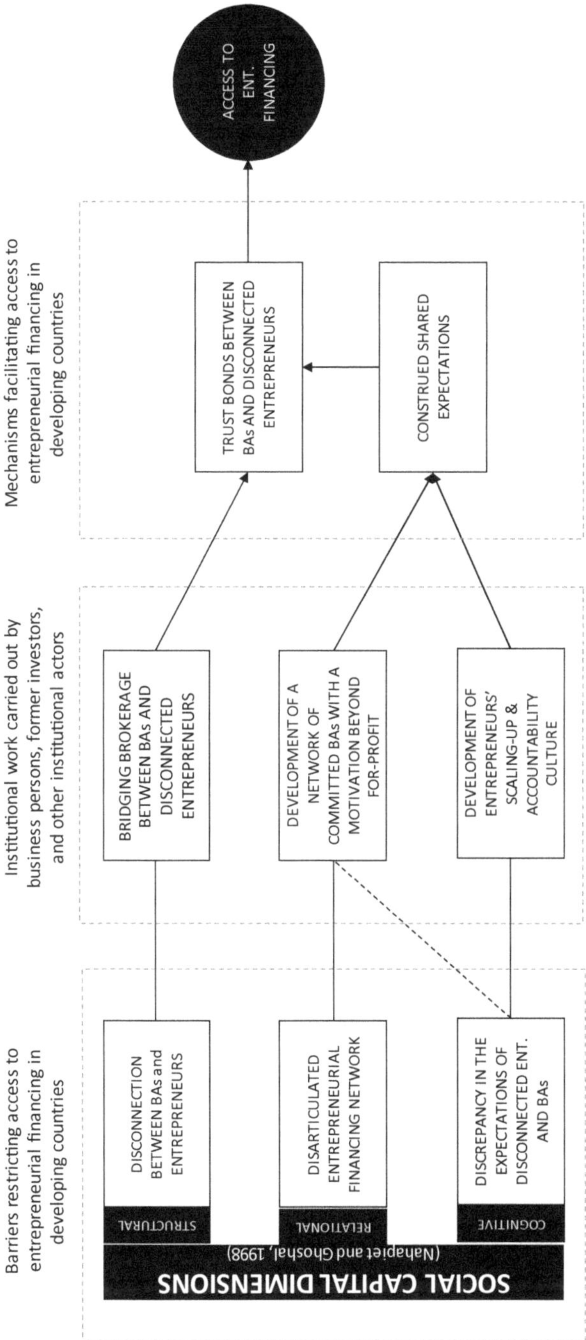

Figure 1: Model of entrepreneurial financing access in developing countries.

themes connected using the social capital dimensions as "theoretical glue." The model helps to explain how investors and other actors addressed three barriers restricting access to entrepreneurial financing through three activities that enabled two mechanisms that facilitated the linkage between BAs and disconnected entrepreneurs.

3.1. *Barriers restricting access to entrepreneurial financing in developing countries*

3.1.1. *Disconnection between entrepreneurs and BAs*

The first barrier is related to the structural dimension of social capital. Various interviewees highlighted the disconnection between entrepreneurs and investors as one of the leading barriers for obtaining funding. The interviews provide evidence that there is as much need for financing as appetite for investment, but the "worlds" of entrepreneurs and investors are disconnected.

The interviewees said that there were BAs in Central America; however, only entrepreneurs close to the wealthy families could reach them. According to the interviewees, BAs only invested in ventures of acquaintances due to security reasons, given the extortion and organized crime situation in Central America. Interviewee #6 mentioned that entrepreneurial financing in Central America worked as "Closed Clubs" where only young generations of wealthy families can enter. According to him, there was not a bridge between such families and disconnected entrepreneurs.

3.1.2. *Disarticulated entrepreneurial financing network*

The second barrier is related to the relational dimension of social capital. Some interviewees asserted that due to the embryonic state of the ecosystems, there was no entrepreneurial financing network linking BAs, VCs, and incubators/accelerators. Interviewee #14 mentioned that there were several institutional deficiencies, such as the lack of regulatory frameworks and policies, which hindered the creation of an entrepreneurial financing market.

> *(Program's name) sought to address some voids in the Costa Rican entrepreneurial ecosystem and was financed by the (second-tier development bank) investment fund. One of those voids was the lack of a BAs network* (Interviewee #14).

The interviewees asserted that different support programs for entrepreneurs were emerging from both public and private initiatives; however, there was a lack of articulation between the different initiatives, a role in which government agencies could help:

> *In El Salvador, there are outstanding entrepreneurs, but there is not an entity that articulates and creates synergy among all the emerging initiatives* (Interviewee #21).

3.1.3. *Discrepancy in the expectations of BAs and disconnected entrepreneurs*

The third barrier is related to the cognitive dimension of social capital. One of the problems that restricted access to entrepreneurial financing was that entrepreneurs did not understand BAs expectations and business model. According to the investors, most of the start-ups in Central America did not have the scaling-up potential they were looking. Furthermore, they said that some entrepreneurs thought that BAs worked like banks and failed to understand the specialized language used by investors (e.g., exit, due diligence, teaser).

The interviewees suggested three causes for the mentioned barrier. The first one was the entrepreneurs' poor education. According to the interviewees, the entrepreneurs had severe deficiencies in accounting, finance, human resources, and time management. Some of the capital providers asserted that they had to invest significant time in training entrepreneurs. However, in their opinion, tertiary education providers should address that deficiency.

Secondly, interviewees asserted that most entrepreneurs did not have a scaling-up mindset. According to them, entrepreneurs did not have a global approach but instead focused on the small local markets. Also, the projects lacked innovation and were related to basic industries such as handicrafts.

Thirdly, interviewees asserted that government agencies and organizations that promote social entrepreneurship foster an unaccountability culture. They affirmed that some government programs provide seed capital without demanding anything in return. Moreover, some social entrepreneurship programs foment the misconception that social impact is a sufficient argument for obtaining financing:

Some interviewees argued that investors also have a misconception about early-stage financing. According to Interviewee #6, some investors sought to obtain full control of the companies, and in extreme cases steal the business idea of the entrepreneurs. Such attitude had generated an atmosphere of distrust among the entrepreneurs, many of whom avoided business model competitions for fear that investors would take away their ideas. An official of the Ministry of Economy of Guatemala commented on how a government initiative failed precisely due to entrepreneurs and BAs' misconception of entrepreneurial financing:

> *In 2011, we carried out a program of BAs that unfortunately did not work because there was ignorance on that part of investors and entrepreneurs. On the one hand, the entrepreneurs did not know the different types of investment vehicles and capital structures that could be used to incorporate investors in the business. On the other hand, many of the BAs turned out to be not-so-angels: they acquired large equity stakes, with unfavorable valuations for entrepreneurs. Moreover, several of them ended up taking over the whole business. Investors failed to fully understand what it means to be an angel* (Interviewee #8).

3.2. *Institutional work addressing the entrepreneurial financing barriers*

The interviews provided evidence of three institutional activities addressing the entrepreneurial financing barriers in Central America. Such institutional work was carried out by former investment bankers and wealthy businesspersons who sought to improve the economy of their countries by supporting high-growth entrepreneurship. Initially, they sought to invest in local ventures but then realized that they had arrived too early. Given their motivation beyond profit-seeking, they "rolled up their shirts" and decided to carry out activities aimed at strengthening the institutions related to entrepreneurial financing. Firstly, they created entrepreneurial support organizations where they induced in entrepreneurs a scaling-up and accountability culture. Secondly, they fostered the creation of local BAs networks. Thirdly, they served as bridging brokers to connect disconnected entrepreneurs with BAs.

3.2.1. *Development of entrepreneurs' scaling-up and accountability culture*

Several of the interviewees affirmed that initially, they had been investors attracted by the idea that in Central America many start-ups could not scale-up due to lack of financing. After looking for investment opportunities, the former-investors realized that there was not such a pipeline of ventures with scale-up potential ready to receive investment. Those agents with a motivation beyond profit-seeking decided to develop the pipeline, creating entrepreneurial support organizations.

> *Finding a pipeline in the region is complicated because in Central America there are few companies ready to receive investment [...] We are investors, and we do many activities to strengthen the entrepreneurial ecosystem to have more startups in which to invest eventually. In 2012 and 2014, we opened two coworking spaces [...] In 2016, we started working on 'bootcamps' and an acceleration program for early-stage entrepreneurs* (Interviewee #22).

According to the interviewees, the entrepreneurial support organizations sought to address two deficiencies. The first one was the lack of a scaling-up mindset. The mentioned initiatives sought to improve business models and train entrepreneurs in matters of strategic planning and sales. Interviewees mentioned that these programs also sought to fill the educational deficiencies of the entrepreneurs and induce on them an accountability culture. For that reason, they trained entrepreneurs in accounting, legal, fiscal, and corporate governance issues.

3.2.2. *Development of a network of committed BAs with a motivation beyond for-profit*

Some interviewees mentioned that before connecting entrepreneurs with investors, they used their family and professional networking with wealthy people to form local BAs networks. A second-tier development bank also noted the lack of an entrepreneurial financing network in Central America and has encouraged the creation of local BAs networks and the articulation of such networks in a regional platform. This platform sought that BAs shared knowledge and investment opportunities:

> *(Interviewee #14) participates in one of our programs, called 'Platform to catalyze early-stage investments.' It is a Latin American platform where we work with different national and regional networks of angel investors, mainly to share lessons learned and investment projects* (Interviewee #10, Executive of a second-tier development bank).

Interviewees provided evidence of an incipient network of accelerators and capital providers that begins to derive investment opportunities among members.

> *We are part of different organizations and have partnerships with accelerators and other investment funds, so we are part of this network of networks that are constantly sending us investment opportunities. We analyze them, and when we find something that is convenient for us, we contact them. Then, there is a constant flow of ventures looking for investment* (Interviewee #22).

3.2.3. *Bridging brokerage across disconnected entrepreneurs and investors*

Interviews provided evidence of seven bridging brokers connecting entrepreneurs with BAs networks (Interviewees #14, 15, 16, 17, 20, 21, and 24).

We found a pattern among these agents: Firstly, these brokers had a beyond profit-seeking motivation and were interested in improving the economies of their respective countries by fostering high-growth entrepreneurship. Secondly, they had strong ties with the wealthy families of the region, either because they were members of these families or because of professional/business relationships. Thirdly, they were directly or indirectly connected with the community of entrepreneurs. The brokers interviewed asserted that after helping to create networks of BAs, they connected them with the entrepreneurs who had already gone through an incubation/acceleration program. In most of the cases, brokers asserted they were directly related to such programs. In other cases, they made partnerships with actors related to entrepreneurial support organizations. The Interviewee #33 commented on how the organization of Interviewee # 14 connected him to a network of BAs who invested in his company. He also provides evidence about the generation of a direct link between the entrepreneur and the BA:

> *Accessing investors is difficult for a middle-class entrepreneur who is just beginning. Now, entrepreneurship is in vogue, and there are accelerators like (Organization of Interviewee #14). However, some years ago the investor ecosystem was not as organized as it is now [...] (Organization of Interviewee #14) supported me before introducing me to investors. They significantly helped me with the ´pitch´ and business model. I 'pitched' to their BAs network, and some of them invested in my project. (Organization of Interviewee #14) got some shares as compensation for their work. I keep contacting them when I have doubts about strategic issues, and occasionally, I still use their offices* (Interviewee #33).

3.3. *Mechanisms that facilitate access to entrepreneurial financing*

The three activities described enabled two mechanisms that facilitated access to entrepreneurial financing: construed shared expectations and trust bonds between BAs and disconnected entrepreneurs. In the following section, we explain and provide evidence on how these mechanisms improve access to entrepreneurial financing.

3.3.1. *Construed shared expectations*

The first mechanism, "construed shared expectations", is related to the cognitive and relational dimensions of social capital. The mechanism is defined as the development of a common understanding of critical aspects that make actors believe that counterparts will act for mutual benefit. Such tacit reciprocal commitment allows the creation of trust bonds between BAs and disconnected entrepreneurs. The critical aspects include an accountability and scaling-up mindset from the side of the disconnected entrepreneurs and a genuine interest in support start-ups as a minority investor from the side of the BAs.

The institutional work described above helped to construct such shared expectations on BAs and disconnected entrepreneurs. The entrepreneurial support organizations fostered the culture of accountability and scaling-up mindset of disconnected entrepreneurs. The change of mindset allowed entrepreneurs to understand the level of risk assumed by the BAs when investing in their start-ups.

At the same time, the institutional work helped to construct a tacit reciprocal commitment from the side of investors. The BAs network was formed only with those investors who fulfilled a specific profile: they must have financial resources, have a genuine interest in supporting entrepreneurs, and feel comfortable in a minority investor position. Such characteristics were aimed at generating trust in entrepreneurs. Interviewee #14 explains the characteristics that he looked for in the potential BAs of the network that he formed:

> *A network of angel investors in an emerging market is something completely new. We look for investors with sufficient assets so that such a risky investment would not significantly impact their finances. They must have experience in high-risk investments such as startups or private equity, or at least as minority investors. They must feel comfortable not having total control over the firm. Also, they must have a genuine interest in supporting startups in commercial aspects and networking. They have to be willing to coach entrepreneurs in order to increase their investment's value and mitigate risks in areas in which they have expertise* (Interviewee #14).

Some interviewees asserted that the necessary conditions for linking disconnected entrepreneurs with investors were generated only until the institutional actors aligned the expectations of both groups:

> *We could not find entrepreneurs with high-growth potential, so we had to develop their ideas from scratch before introducing them to investors* (Interviewee #15).
> *After addressing the problems of entrepreneurs and earn their trust, we were ready for the next phase: integrate investors and mentors in our model. If you only have the entrepreneurs without the committed investors, the model does not work* (Interviewee #19).

3.3.2. *Trust bonds between BAs and disconnected entrepreneurs*

The second mechanism is related to the relational and structural dimensions of social capital. The construction of this bridge of trust between BAs and disconnected entrepreneurs was possible thanks to the previous institutional work. The bridging brokers built bonds of trust between BAs and disconnected entrepreneurs and then used this close ties to foster a nascent link between the actors of such groups. On the investors' side, the brokers already had strong ties within the network as in most cases they were wealthy individuals. In one of the cases (e.g., Interviewee #14), the broker acquired such strong ties from his previous job interactions as an investment banker.

Brokers also established strong ties within the disconnected entrepreneurs′ network. They directly collaborated in the formation of co-working spaces, accelerators, and incubators and gained the entrepreneurs' trust. Many of the entrepreneurs distrusted in participating in business plan contests for fear that the investors would steal their ideas. However, the brokers managed to demonstrate to the entrepreneurs their good intentions, and their implicit socio-economic development motivation in supporting potential successful ventures.

Once brokers established strong links within the disconnected entrepreneurs and BAs networks they served as a bridge of trust to generate a nascent link between actors from such networks. One of the interviewees, a broker, BA, and former social entrepreneur mentioned that both investors and entrepreneurs felt trust when she established the link between both parties. Such feeling was so due to the bonds of trust that she had built in both networks:

> *Entrepreneurs trust me because they know that I was an entrepreneur and understand them. Also, investors believe me when I present them an investment opportunity because they know me. So, I believe that this bridge generates trust between people from two disconnected worlds* (Interviewee #24).

4. Discussion

The primary purpose of this study was to understand the barriers restricting access to entrepreneurial financing in developing countries. The characteristics of some developing countries, such as disconnection among people from different social classes (Woolcock and Narayan, 2000) and weak institutional environments that foster necessity entrepreneurship (Amorós *et al.*, 2017), represent barriers in the structural and cognitive dimensions of social capital. Such barriers reduce the explanatory power of previous studies in the entrepreneurial financing literature, which assume that entrepreneurs have access to a well-structured network of close and weak ties (Seghers *et al.*, 2012; Shane and Cable, 2002; Uzzi, 1999). Even studies in developing countries fail to explain access to financing for disconnected entrepreneurs without connections (Batjargal and Liu, 2004; Talavera *et al.*, 2012). Previous authors have highlighted the institutional entrepreneurship role assumed by venture capitalists in developing countries, but without explaining how their institutional work improved access to entrepreneurial financing (Bruton *et al.*, 2009).

The study identified three main barriers that hinder access to early-stage funding in developing countries: Disconnections between BAs and entrepreneurs; disarticulated entrepreneurial financing networks; and discrepancies in the expectations of the mentioned actors. This chapter describes three activities carried out by wealthy businesspersons, former investors, and other institutional actors to address the mentioned issues. These actors sought the economic development of their countries through the spillover effect of entrepreneurship. Due to the institutional deficiencies in their countries, they assumed an institutional entrepreneurship role

(Bruton *et al.*, 2009), developing entrepreneurial support organizations, BAs networks, and bridging brokerage firms.

The study explains how the mentioned institutional activities enabled two mechanisms that improved different social capital dimensions, facilitating access to entrepreneurial financing (Nahapiet and Ghoshal, 1998). In the cognitive dimension, the institutional work fostered the construction of shared expectations between disconnected entrepreneurs and BAs. The shared understanding facilitated the linkage of actors who previously distrusted one another. In the structural dimension, investors and businessperson assumed a bridging broker role, fostering the formation of strong ties between BAs and disconnected entrepreneurs.

The proposed concept "construed shared expectations" adds to the entrepreneurial financing literature by illuminating the effects of the cognitive social capital dimension on access to early-stage financing. As noted by Jonsson and Lindbergh (2013), scholars have investigated in depth the relational dimension, but our understanding of the cognitive one needs further development. The findings of this chapter indicate that a shared understanding of the entrepreneurial financing's key concepts and a tacit reciprocal commitment are prerequisites for the formations of trust bonds between entrepreneurs and investors from different social classes. The suggestion is a causal relationship between the cognitive dimension and another form of social capital classified by Nahapiet and Ghoshal (1998) in the relational dimension: obligations and expectations (Coleman, 1988).

This study proposes an explanation for the creation of expectations and trust among BAs and disconnected entrepreneurs, which differs from the established theory. According to Coleman (1988, p. 107), network closure is instrumental for the existence of norms and trustworthiness that allow "the proliferation of obligation and expectations." Instead, this study argues that in the case of BAs and disconnected entrepreneurs, the causal relationship between expectations and trust goes in the opposite direction. That is to say; the construed shared understanding lays the foundations for a reciprocity commitment that precedes the formation of the bond of trust (see Figure 2).

The grounded evidence underpins the argument above: As BAs and entrepreneurs were disconnected, there were no norms, trust, or common

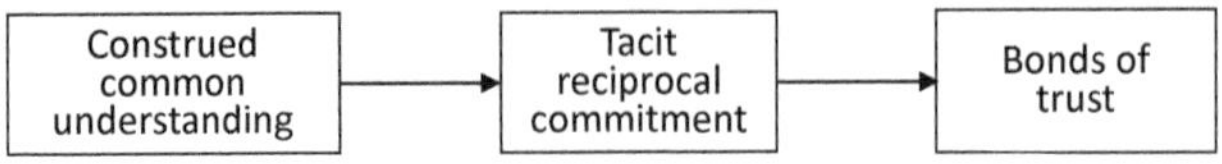

Figure 2: Effects of cognitive social capital in the formation of relational social capital between investors and disconnected entrepreneurs.

understanding between them. An external actor was required to reconcile the misconceptions and *construct a common understanding*. On the one hand, after their training in the entrepreneurial support organizations, disconnected entrepreneurs understood the level of risk associated with start-ups and the high return rate expected by the BAs. In exchange for such rate, they expected that the BAs would support them without attempting to take full control of the start-up. BAs networks were formed exclusively with wealthy individuals interested in the economic development of their countries and willing to add value to the entrepreneurs without taking full control of the start-up. In exchange for their financial resources and coaching, the BAs expected that the disconnected entrepreneurs would be accountable and develop scalable business models that would compensate for the level of risk assumed. The evidence suggests a *tacit reciprocal commitment* that was absent prior to the institutional work carried out by investors and businesspeople. The necessary conditions for the construction of the *bond of trust* between BAs and disconnected entrepreneurs were generated only until both parties perceived that their counterparts were willing to meet their expectations.

4.1. *Limitations and implications for future research*

Although this study is based on rich qualitative data, it has a geographic focus limited to Central America. The disconnection between entrepreneurs and investors' networks in several of the Central American countries can be stronger than in other non-developed countries due to the colonial heritage, processes of class struggle, and the current situation of gangs and organized crime in some of the mentioned countries. Another limitation of the study is related to the snowball sampling process. This process began with the director of an entrepreneurship center at a business school, who then provided contacts from the Alumni network. Although 19 of the

33 interviewees were outside of this Alumni network, we recognize that the mentioned starting point may have biased the results. Future studies could address these limitations and investigate similar research questions in other developing countries in Asia and Eastern Europe, starting their snowball sampling with root-level actors.

Previous entrepreneurial financing research emphasized the relational dimension of social capital and assumed that entrepreneurs could access distant nodes in a well-structured network, notwithstanding their social status (Seghers *et al.*, 2012; Shane and Cable, 2002; Uzzi, 1999). Even research in non-developed countries emphasized the explanatory power of connections ("guanxi") and trust, but without explaining how disconnected entrepreneurs obtained such social capital (Batjargal and Liu, 2004; Talavera *et al.*, 2012).

This study explains how the disconnection among social classes in developing countries, limit access to financing especially for those disconnected entrepreneurs without connections in the isolated networks of wealthy families, the potential BAs. Such explanation is instrumental given the importance of the bonds of trust in the BAs' decision-making process (Bammens and Collewaert, 2014; Maxwell and Lévesque, 2014). Future research could test the explanatory power of this extended mechanism by comparing the effect of bridging brokers on BAs' deal selection in subsamples of developed and developing countries.

Due to their restricted perspectives, previous studies addressing similar questions from the supply and demand side overlooked the marked cognitive barrier in developing countries between necessity entrepreneurs and "not-so-angel" investors. According to Lam (2010), scholars have explored access to entrepreneurial financing focusing on the supply side and from a positivist perspective, assuming that the "funding gap" is something that exists out there and must be filled. An exception to this trend is the study of Mason and Harrison (2001), who explained the shortcomings in demand for entrepreneurial capital, arguing that many of the entrepreneurs lack "investment readiness". The proposed construct offers an explanation that takes into account the cognitive discrepancies between both parties.

Future research in developing countries could apply the proposed cognitive-relational mechanism in entrepreneurial financing topics. The effects of government programs aimed at economic development through entrepreneurship have been sharply criticized (Shane, 2009). The proposed mechanism could explain why some of these programs are successful and others are not. Future research could test the explanatory power of the proposed concept as a mediator between the mentioned programs and access to early-stage financing. Moreover, "construed shared expectations" could underpin hypotheses related to the effects of accelerators and incubators on investment matching in developing countries, extending the findings of previous research (Dutt *et al.*, 2016; Gonzalez-Uribe and Leatherbee, 2017).

4.2. *Implications for practice*

In addition to the theoretical contributions, the current study has practical implications for various actors interested in improving access to financing in developing countries. Previous authors have framed the problem of the equity gap as a lack of investment supply and "investment readiness". Contrarily, this study makes a call for the construction of a common understanding on key entrepreneurial financing issues that lay the foundations of trust bonds between investors and entrepreneurs. Such a call is addressed to government agencies, university entrepreneurship centers, international cooperation agencies, incubators, and other organizations interested in the development of high-growth entrepreneurship.

Government agencies and international cooperation agencies should refocus programs towards the construction of a culture of accountability. The evidence gathered in the interviews indicates that many of such programs have given seed capital without demanding anything in return, fostering a lack of accountability contrary to the expectations of investors. The mentioned agencies should provide technical assistance programs and release the seed capital through staggered disbursements with strict monitoring of the funds granted. Also, they must request a report of accountability of such funds and include clauses obliging recipients to return the money when it is used in assets or expenses different from those established in the business plan. These actions will reinforce the culture of accountability expected by investors, facilitating entrepreneurs' access to sources of equity financing.

Secondly, the university entrepreneurship centers and incubators must promote among the (potential) entrepreneurs a scaling-up mindset. Due to their socioeconomic conditions, most Central American entrepreneurs still have a necessity entrepreneurship mindset, which has been reinforced by government programs aimed at self-employment and SMEs. Universities and incubators should encourage among their students and mentees a mindset oriented towards scalable business models correlated with attractive returns for investors.

Thirdly, individuals with strong ties within networks of local wealthy individuals could encourage the creation of BAs networks. The potential investors should not only have financial resources but also be committed to the development of local economies. They must be willing to give part of their time to coach entrepreneurs and feel comfortable as minority investors. Government agencies and second-tier development banks could encourage the formation of regional BAs networks, facilitating the connection between the local networks through meetings and online platforms. Such regional network could facilitate the sharing of best practices and investment opportunities, creating an aggregate demand and increasing the investment matching likelihood.

5. Conclusion

The current study contributes to the theoretical development of entrepreneurial financing in contexts with weak institutions and disconnected entrepreneurs. From a dual supply/demand and social construction perspective, this study has illuminated the effect of the cognitive social capital dimension on access to early-stage financing. Such contribution has implications for the entrepreneurial financing literature, opening promising research opportunities.

References

Ahlstrom D. and Bruton G. D. (2006) Venture capital in emerging economies: Networks and institutional change. *Entrepreneurship: Theory and Practice*, 30(2), 299–320.

Amorós J. E., Ciravegna L., Mandakovic V., and Stenholm P. (2017) Necessity or Opportunity? The Effects of State Fragility and Economic Development on Entrepreneurial Efforts. *Entrepreneurship Theory and Practice*. doi: https://doi.org/10.1177/1042258717736857.

Bammens Y. and Collewaert V. (2014) Trust between entrepreneurs and angel investors: Exploring positive and negative implications for venture performance assessments. *Journal of Management*, 40(7), 1980–2008.

Batjargal B. and Liu M. (Manhong). (2004) Entrepreneurs' access to private equity in china: The role of social capital. *Organization Science*, 15(2), 159–172.

Biernacki P. and Waldorf D. (1981) Snowball sampling: Problems and techniques of chain referral sampling. *Sociological Methods and Research*, 10(2), 141–163.

Bruton G. D. and Ahlstrom D. (2003) An institutional view of China's venture capital industry: Explaining the differences between China and the West. *Journal of Business Venturing*.

Bruton G. D., Ahlstrom D., and Puky T. (2009) Institutional differences and the development of entrepreneurial ventures: A comparison of the venture capital industries in Latin America and Asia. *Journal of International Business Studies*, 40(5), 762–778.

Burt R. S. (1992) *Structural Holes: The Social Structure of Competition*, Vol. 58. Harvard University Press, Cambridge MA.

Cicourel A. V. (1981) The role of cognitive-linguistic concepts in understanding everyday social interactions. *Annual Review of Sociology*, 7, 87–106.

Coleman J. S. (1988) Social capital in the creation of human-capital. *American Journal of Sociology*, 94, S95–S120.

Corbin J. and Strauss A. (1990) Grounded theory research: Processes, canons, and evaluative criteria. *Qualitative Sociology*, 19(6), 418–427.

DiMaggio P. J. (1988) Interest and agency in institutional theory. In Zucker L. (Ed.), *Institutional Patterns and Culture*. Cambridge, MA: Ballinger, 3–22.

Dutt N., Hawn O., Vidal E., Chatterji A., McGAHAN A., and Mitchell W. (2016) How open system intermediaries address institutional failures: The case of business incubators in emerging-market countries. *Academy of Management Journal*, 59(3), 818–840.

Gioia D. A., Corley K. G., and Hamilton A. L. (2013) Seeking qualitative rigor in inductive research: Notes on the gioia methodology. *Organizational Research Methods*, 16(1), 15–31.

Gonzalez-Uribe J. and Leatherbee M. (2017). The effects of business accelerators on venture performance: Evidence from start-up chile. *The Review of Financial Studies*, 31(4), 1566–1603.

Groh A., Liechtenstein H., Lieser K., and Biesinger M. (2018) The venture capital and private equity country attractiveness index 2018. Retrieved from IESE Business School. https://blog.iese.edu/vcpeindex/files/2018/02/report2018.pdf.

Isabella L. A. (1990) Evolving interpretations as a change unfolds: How managers construe key organizational events. *Academy of Management Journal*, 33(1), 7–41.

Jonsson S. and Lindbergh J. (2013) The development of social capital and financing of entrepreneurial firms: From financial bootstrapping to bank funding. *Entrepreneurship Theory and Practice*, 37(4), 661–686.

Lam W. (2010) Funding gap, what funding gap? Financial bootstrapping. *International Journal of Entrepreneurial Behavior and Research*, 16(4), 268–295.

Mason C. M. and Harrison R. T. (2001) Investment readiness: A critique of government proposals to increase the demand for venture capital. *Regional Studies*, 35(7), 663–668.

Maxwell A. L. and Lévesque M. (2014) Trustworthiness: A critical ingredient for entrepreneurs seeking investors. *Entrepreneurship: Theory and Practice*, 38(5), 1057–1080.

Nahapiet J. and Ghoshal S. (1998) Social capital, intellectual capital, and the organizational advantage. *The Academy of Management Review*, 23(2), 242.

Seghers A., Manigart S., and Vanacker T. (2012) The impact of human and social capital on entrepreneurs' knowledge of finance alternatives. *Journal of Small Business Management*, 50(1), 63–86.

Shane S. (2009) Why encouraging more people to become entrepreneurs is bad public policy. *Small Business Economics*, 33(2), 141–149.

Shane S. and Cable D. (2002) Network Ties, reputation, and the financing of new ventures. *Management Science*, 48(3), 364–381.

Spradley J. P. (2016). *The ethnographic interview*. Waveland Press.

Suddaby R. (2006) What grounded theory is not. *Academy of Management Journal*, 49(4), 633–642.

Talavera O., Xiong L., and Xiong X. (2012) Social capital and access to bank financing: The case of chinese entrepreneurs. *Emerging Markets Finance and Trade*, 48(1), 55–69.

Uzzi B. (1999) Embeddedness in the making of financial capital: How social relations and networks benefit firms seeking financing. *American Sociological Review*, 64(4), 481.

WEF (2016) The Global Competitiveness Report 2016–2017. *World Economic Forum Reports 2016.*

Woolcock M. and Narayan D. (2000) Social Capital: Implications for development theory, research, and policy. *The World Bank Research Observer*, 15(2), 225–249.

Chapter 10

Financial Literacy and Entrepreneurship

Riccardo Calcagno*

emlyon **business school**

calcagno@em-lyon.com

Yan Alperovych*

emlyon **business school**

alperovych@em-lyon.com

Anita Quas†

University of Milan and emlyon **business school**

anita.quas@unimi.it

Abstract

The measurement, drivers and outcomes of financial literacy for individuals and households received substantial academic attention in the recent years.

*23, Avenue Guy de Collongue, Ecully, 69134, France.

†7, Via Conservatorio, Milan, 20122, Italy; 23, Avenue Guy de Collongue, Ecully, 69134, France.

In this chapter, we focus on entrepreneurs' financial literacy. Entrepreneurs are renowned sources of innovation and growth but their ability to achieve such outcomes is fundamentally intertwined with their ability to take correct financial decisions. Despite the fact that financial literacy is arguably essential for entrepreneurs to take such decisions, empirical evidence on this topic is scarce. This chapter reviews the few academic studies that preliminarily investigate the degree of financial literacy of entrepreneurs. More importantly, we highlight relevant avenues for future research aimed at understanding how to measure financial literacy for (potential) entrepreneurs, and what is the impact of such construct on entrepreneurial outcome.

1. Introduction

In 2014, the OECD included "lack of financial literacy" as one of the most important challenges faced by micro, small and medium enterprises (MSMEs) and potential entrepreneurs, that may prevent them from starting a business, reduce their chance of survival or slow the growth of their business (OECD, 2015).

But what is financial literacy? Although the debate on a unique and accepted definition has been fierce (Remund, 2010), most commonly, financial literacy is viewed as the ability to process economic information in order to make good financial decisions (Lusardi and Mitchell 2014) and it is considered "an essential tool for anyone who wants to be able to succeed in today's society" (Lusardi, 2011). Conceptually, financial literacy refers to a skill, i.e., the ability to manage financial affairs successfully, and consequently can be considered as a component of human capital (Lusardi *et al.*, 2017).

Most of the existing theoretical and empirical research has focused almost exclusively on financial literacy as the ability of households to manage their personal finance in a healthy way (e.g., Lusardi and Mitchell, 2007). Other studies target more specific populations, such as students (Ansong and Gyensare, 2012), women (Lusardi and Mitchell, 2008), employees (Bayer *et al.*, 2009) or investors (Müller and Weber, 2010).

In this chapter, we focus on a special case: The degree of financial literacy of (potential) entrepreneurs.

The degree of financial literacy of entrepreneurs has important policy implications because of the substantial role entrepreneurs play in promoting innovation and generating growth and employment

(Palacín-Sánchez *et al.*, 2013; Puri and Zarutskie, 2012). In an average OECD country about 61% of all jobs in 2016 were concentrated within firms with less than 250 employees; firms with less than 50 employees accounted for 33% of the overall number of jobs (*Source*: OECD Statistics, 2016). Entrepreneurs are therefore the backbone of the modern economic landscape yet they also operate under important long- and short-term financial constraints (Cassar, 2004; Robb and Robinson, 2014) which could impair their growth and survival.

Financial literacy is particularly relevant for entrepreneurs because, on top of taking care of their personal finance effectively, they also have to make good financial decisions when managing their business activity. The OECD has provided a definition of financial literacy for entrepreneurs as *the combination of awareness, knowledge, skills, attitudes and behavior that a potential entrepreneur or an owner or manager of a micro, small or medium sized enterprise should have in order to make effective financial decisions to start a business, run a business, and ultimately ensure its sustainability and growth* (OECD, 2018).

This lays down the general necessity to understand whether entrepreneurs have or can access the skills/ability to make "effective financial decisions". Such decisions may regard the deployment of the short- and long-term capital of their ventures (working capital and investment decisions), and the access to the funding for the latter (financing decisions).

Investment decisions rely on relatively simple but fundamental concepts like the net present value (NPV), which takes into account the magnitude and the risk of the projects' future cash flows. Working-capital decisions include the management of short-term assets and liabilities in a way that ensures the adequacy of liquid financial resources for company operations. Although these concepts are covered in a standard business education curriculum, it is not obvious to assume that all entrepreneurs master them properly. Shepherd *et al.* (2015) recently reviewed various aspects of entrepreneurial decision-making studied by the academic community. Surprisingly, none of the examined studies explicitly focused on the questions pertaining to the efficient capital allocation decisions by entrepreneurs. Still, Salazar *et al.* (2012) provide some relevant evidence. They studied financial decisions made by small businesses in Mexico, finding that bad financing decisions represent a central problem that detriments small business' development and survival.

Financing decisions, that is the decisions about the funding and the capital structure of entrepreneurial opportunities, are much better explored by the vast academic literature on entrepreneurial finance. The cornerstones in these decisions are the severe information asymmetries, potential agency issues, and important transaction costs surrounding the entrepreneurial ventures (Binks *et al.*, 1992; Harris and Raviv, 1991; Jensen and Meckling, 1976; López-Gracia and Sogorb-Mira, 2008; Van Auken, 2005). Because of these market imperfections, entrepreneurs encounter substantial rejection rates and worse credit conditions than large companies when applying for the outside capital needed to cover capital expenditures (Cosh *et al.*, 2009; Cowling *et al.*, 2012). At the same time, the human capital of entrepreneurs, and in particular their education level, affects the entrepreneurs' access to external finance. More educated entrepreneurs are more likely to seek external finance and, if they do so, to obtain it (Colombo *et al.*, 2019; Cosh *et al.*, 2009; Eckhardt *et al.*, 2006; Mina *et al.*, 2013; Seghers *et al.*, 2012).

Furthermore, the frequency at which entrepreneurs should make financial decisions, either because of the changing external business conditions or for the sake of better management of their firm, is in fact substantial. For instance, while the most common form of financing seems to be debt capital (Robb and Robinson, 2014), much of it is not necessarily linked with the long-term needs for capital expenditures but with short term-financing of operations (Cosh *et al.*, 2009). In this sense, entrepreneurs are akin repeated borrowers, which opens yet another interesting perspective — that of the role, relationships and networks in entrepreneurial financing (Berger and Udell, 1995; Bird *et al.*, 2018).

Financial literacy could therefore be an important driver of entrepreneurial outcome. Arguably, more financially literate individuals can take better financing, investing and working capital decisions. Ultimately, individuals with a high degree of financial literacy might be less reluctant to become entrepreneurs, because of their high comprehension of the alternative financial sources on the market, and of a superior ability to talk with banks or other financial intermediaries. They could even be more successful entrepreneurs, if they are able to secure and wisely manage the financial resources a start-up needs in the first phases of its development.

These are the reasons why a better understanding of the degree of financial literacy of entrepreneurs is an important priority for policy makers interested in spurring innovation and growth in their jurisdictions (OECD, 2015). Surprisingly, in contrast to the case of households, there is very little empirical evidence on the degree of financial literacy of self-employed and small entrepreneurs, and on the relation between financial literacy and the likelihood to start a company, or the business performance (Ćumurović and Hyll, 2018; Dahmen and Rodríguez, 2014; Lusardi *et al.*, 2016; Trombetta, 2016). We believe that the effect of financial literacy on entrepreneurial outcome deserves much more academic attention.

The aim of this chapter is therefore manifold. First, we will elaborate on the interest that entrepreneurs' degree of financial literacy raised among policy makers, followed by the calls for more academic studies on this topic. Second, we will discuss the problems related to the measure of financial literacy in the whole population and specifically for entrepreneurs. For each issue, we will highlight interesting avenues for future research in that direction. As there is virtually no research measuring explicitly the effects of the degree of entrepreneurs' financial literacy, in this chapter we take inspiration from the much broader literature on financial literacy in other contexts, mainly households.

2. Policy and Academic Interest for Financial Literacy and Entrepreneurship

The OECD Governments officially recognized the importance of financial literacy in 2002 with the launch of the first financial education project. In 2008, the project was further enhanced through the creation of an International Network on Financial Education (INFE) a network of over 240 public institutions — including central banks, financial regulators and supervisors, ministries of finance and ministries of education — in over 110 countries. In 2014, the INFE Advisory Board and its Technical Committee agreed that the INFE should focus on financial education for potential entrepreneurs and MSMEs through a dedicated Expert Subgroup.

Since then, the INFE has been studying what financial literacy may mean for MSMEs and potential entrepreneurs, providing a formal definition to it (as mentioned above) in 2018.

In 2018, the INFE also published a core competencies framework on financial literacy for MSMEs and potential entrepreneurs (OECD 2018).

The framework is a tool that local policy makers can adapt to the context of their economies. The objective of the framework is to design some concrete survey-based measures of financial literacy for entrepreneurs, although to the best of our knowledge the results of these surveys are not yet known. The final aim is to complement or to improve the financial literacy of owners and managers of MSMEs and of potential entrepreneurs in their experience of starting, running or growing a business. Figure 1 summarizes the framework elaborated by the OECD, which is articulated into "Areas of competency", "Dimensions of financial literacy" and

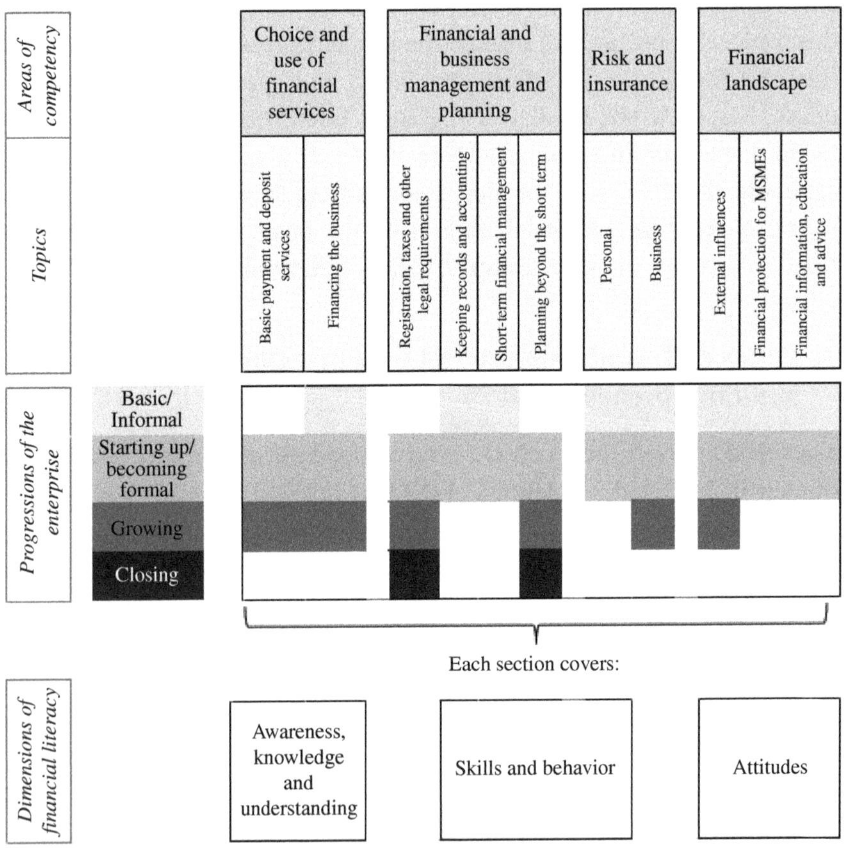

Figure 1: Structure of the core competencies framework on financial literacy for MSMEs and potential entrepreneurs.
Source: OECD (2018).

"Progressions of the enterprise". The areas of competency are: the choice and use of financial services; financial and business management and planning; risk and insurance; financial landscape. Within each area, competencies encompass three dimensions: awareness, knowledge and understanding; skills; and behavior and attitudes. In each area of competence and for each dimension, the competencies are ordered across the main stages of development of the firm (or life stages): basic, starting up, growing and closing. To give few examples, knowing how much money will be needed to start the business and become operational pertains to the "awareness, knowledge and understanding" of entrepreneurs in the area of the "choice and use of financial services", necessary in the starting up phase of development. Having a plan for dealing with unexpected business expenses is a "skill or behavior" the entrepreneur must have in the basic/informal stage of development, related to the area of "risk and insurance".

At the national level, many governments have a strategy to increase the levels of financial literacy in their own nation, but only recently they started to focus specifically on entrepreneurs and small business owners. The Netherlands and Canada are good examples.

Aware of the difficulties that the Dutch entrepreneurs were facing when confronted by financial problems, in 2016 the Netherlands Chamber of Commerce launched a survey to 4,000 registered members representative of the Dutch SMEs sector, to enquire about their level of financial literacy (Utrecht Chamber of Commerce, 2017). The survey was based on a self-assessment of financial literacy and highlighted that while many business owners think that they know about the financial issues required to run a business, they are less proficient with regard to matters that are more future-oriented, such as knowledge of profitability forecasts.

In October 2017, the Business Development Bank of Canada (BDC) partnered with the Telfer School of Management at the University of Ottawa to measure the degree of financial literacy of Canadian business owners (BDC, 2017). The objective was to better understand the business owners' mindset regarding finances in general, as well as this mindset effects for the business, with the final aim of developing content and tools for business leaders and future entrepreneurs across Canada. The survey was sent online to business owners who are members of the BDC and 892 answers were collected.

These initiatives show that policy makers currently are trying to identify the areas in which entrepreneurs feel less knowledgeable and consequently need more professional help. Specifically, these studies allow to adjust the professional advice to the entrepreneurs' needs and also to predict the mistakes that entrepreneurs are more likely to do when managing the finances of their businesses. For example, if entrepreneurs admit to have difficulties in formulating a long-term strategy for their business, and are not able to interpret profitability forecasts, they are prone to react too slowly to changes in the business environment. Academics might also get relevant information from this kind of studies. Investing in projects that pay off in the short-term but with uncertain long-term potential could provoke a serious inefficiency in the resources allocation, damaging the growth potential of small businesses. It is reasonable to expect more national initiatives along these lines in the coming years.

In parallel with the policy interest, the academic interest for financial literacy (in general) has gained momentum in recent years, as shown by the skyrocketing number of citations on the subject (see Figure 2). Such attention is driven by the fact that financial literacy can explain various financial or economic behaviors, especially relevant given the increased responsibility of individuals for their own financial planning (Aren and Dinç Aydemir, 2014).

The literature of financial literacy is complex, and several researchers recently tried to review and make sense of the different theoretical studies and empirical results (Aren and Dinç Aydemir, 2014; Lusardi and Mitchell, 2014; Stolper and Walter, 2017). From these reviews, a framework seems to emerge, according to which the literature can be classified in three main research streams, addressing (1) how to measure financial literacy, (2) what factors influence and improve financial literacy, and (3) what are the outcomes of financial literacy.

The answers to these research questions strongly depend on the population targeted by the study. The vast majority of papers analyze the general population, either at individual or at household level. In the following, we focus on each of the three research streams, summarize findings based on households, and try to elaborate research questions addressing financial literacy for potential entrepreneurs.

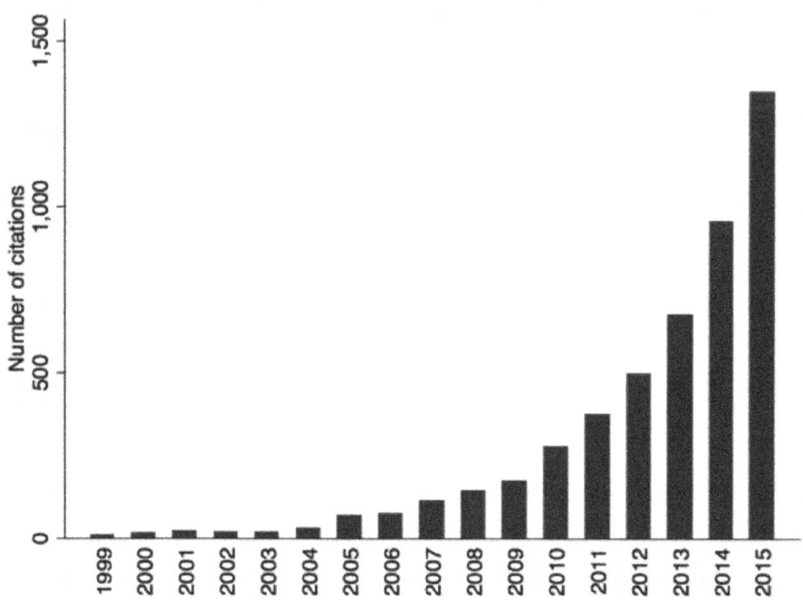

Figure 2: Number of citations of published items with the keyword "financial literacy" per year.
Source: SSCI, Kaiser and Menkhoff (2017).

3. How to Measure the Degree of Financial Literacy of Entrepreneurs

In the academic literature studying financial decision-making, financial literacy has been measured in different ways. A first distinction concerns the specific competences that have been considered as part of financial literacy (Hastings *et al.*, 2012): from knowledge of basic concepts (like inflation, interest compounding and diversification), to knowledge of the main financial products (stocks, bonds, mutual funds).[1]

[1] An interesting view is the one by Lusardi *et al.* (2017), who see financial literacy as a type of investment in human capital. According to their framework, individuals that invest more in their financial literacy can earn above average expected returns on their investments, yet there will still be some optimal level of financial ignorance.

The second distinction can be made between the objective and subjective measures of financial literacy.

Test-based approaches have become prevalent in order to objectively capture financial literacy (Hung *et al.*, 2009). In their pioneering work on the measurement of financial literacy, Lusardi and Mitchell (2008) developed a test-based methodology to measure the level of basic financial literacy based on three simple questions suitable of being included in national surveys of the population, the so-called "Big Three":

1. Suppose you had $100 in a savings account and the interest rate was 2% per year. After 5 years, how much do you think you would have in the account if you left the money to grow?
   Possible answers: More than $102 (correct); Exactly $102; Less than $102; Do not know/Refuse to answer.
2. Imagine that the interest rate on your savings account was 1% per year and inflation was 2% per year. After 1 year, how much would you be able to buy with the money in this account?
   Possible answers: More than today; Exactly the same; Less than today (correct); Do not know/Refuse to answer.
3. Please tell me whether this statement is true or false. "Buying a single company's stock usually provides a safer return than a stock mutual fund."
   Possible answers: True; False (correct); Do not know/Refuse to answer.

Such questions address individuals' numeracy and knowledge of the inflation, compounding and risk diversification concepts. They are considered to be the golden standard in measuring individuals' financial literacy and they have been incorporated in many household surveys around the world, although very often several other questions are added. For instance, for the 2012 PISA assessment (OECD, 2014), the OECD designed a survey with 40 finance-related questions as well as questions in the areas of mathematics and reading abilities to capture financial literacy in students.

The alternative subjective approach to measure financial literacy is based on self-assessment, in which respondents are asked to assess their own financial literacy on a scale.

Interestingly, test-based and self-assessment-based measures of financial literacy do not always correlate strongly (Parker *et al.*, 2012), and there is evidence that individuals tend to overestimate their financial literacy. For instance, in the 2009 US Financial Capability Study, 70% of respondents gave themselves a score of 4 or higher (out of 7), but only 30% of the sample could answer the factual questions correctly (Lusardi, 2011). Individuals sometimes rely on what they think they know, rather than on what they actually know. This suggests there could be a relation between perceived rather than actual financial literacy and financial behavior. Allgood and Wallstad (2016) argue that it is important to measure both test-based and the self-assessed financial literacy. This is because a combined measure of the two dimensions provides a better understanding of the link between financial literacy and financial choices. Measuring both the objective and the subjective measure of financial literacy also allows to determine the degree of overconfidence of the individual. Given that overconfidence is associated with a higher propensity to engage in risky financial behaviors (Barber and Odean, 2000), with a lower willingness to rely on experts (Guiso and Jappelli, 2006) and with improper financial planning (Rooij *et al.*, 2011), the need to measure both dimensions of financial literacy becomes clear.

So far, the number of studies that measure financial literacy for entrepreneurs is extremely limited. Two recent surveys investigate the subjective degree of financial literacy of self-employed and business owners in general, one in the Netherlands (Utrecht Chamber of Commerce, 2017) and the other one in Canada (BDC, 2017). In both surveys the respondents are asked to self-assess their own knowledge in the field of financial management. Moreover, the Canadian survey also included 10 questions aimed at objectively measuring financial literacy. These covered very basic concepts such as unit price, interest rates, ATM cards, credit rating, cost of house, bond pricing, the determination of the price of a good or service. Up to our knowledge, Dahmen and Rodríguez (2014) and Trombetta (2016) are the only academic studies based on test-based surveys conducted on the specific group of entrepreneurs. Dahmen and Rodríguez (2014) conducted an in-depth interview with 14 small businesses requesting growth acceleration consulting services from the Florida Small Business Development Center at the University of South Florida. During the interview, the researchers enquired about: the company's financial positioning for growth; financial difficulty; financial statements; role of business owner in financial matters. Further questions were asked in case of financial difficulty. Trombetta (2016) proposes a questionnaire of eight questions on accounting and finance concepts, which he tested on a sample of 400 self-employed Spanish. Besides the three basic questions ("Big Three"), the other five advanced questions tackle the following issues: perception of debt as a financing tool; evaluation of growth opportunities; cash vs accrual financial performance measurement; depreciation; and economic vs financial profitability.

Still, no consensus has been reached yet on this basic "financial toolkit" most relevant for entrepreneurs and self-employed. As previously mentioned, only very recently the OECD has detailed a framework of financial concepts that are considered important for this target group. These cover basic financial planning, access to finance for their business, together with some accounting and finance basic knowledge. To fine-tune measures of financial literacy for small entrepreneurs, further empirical academic work is needed.

4. Factors Affecting Financial Literacy

Existing research consistently found low levels of financial literacy for individuals, when measured objectively. In the 2004 Health and Retirement study, the Big Three were administered to a representative sample of US citizens aged 50 or older: only one third could answer the three questions correctly (Lusardi and Mitchell, 2014). Moreover, there is a large evidence that households are bad in planning and suffer many biases in decision-making (inertia, e.g., Calvet *et al.*, 2009a; use of rules of thumbs, e.g., Barber and Odean, 2013; hyperbolic discounting, e.g., Laibson, 1997, among others).

4.1. *Socio demographic factors*

While the level of financial literacy is on average low, research highlighted that several individual-level factors affect financial literacy. Not surprisingly, economically vulnerable groups are placed at further disadvantage by their lack of financial literacy: individuals that are very young or very old, women, less educated, unemployed, lower paid, ethnic minorities, more geographically isolated individuals systematically obtain lower financial literacy scores than their counterparts, at least in the US (Lusardi and Mitchell, 2014).

Interestingly, it is well known that factors such as age, gender, race or ethnicity, income, employment status and level of education also matter for entrepreneurial outcome (Reynolds, 1997; Storey, 1994). For instance, on a representative sample representative of US adults (18 and older) in 1993, Reynolds (1997) finds that nascent entrepreneurs are more likely to be men, aged 25–34, with higher educational attainment, longer residence in the US, self-employed, unemployed or students and located in the West and Northeast.

One wonders to what extent such differences across categories of individuals in their propensity to become entrepreneurs can be explained by differences in financial literacy. For instance, let us focus on the role of gender on entrepreneurial outcome and financial literacy. Gender studies in entrepreneurship have been booming in recent years (e.g., Markussen and Røed, 2017). It has been shown that women are less likely to become entrepreneurs virtually in all industrialized countries (Kelley *et al.*, 2012) and their businesses tend to have lower growth than male-owned businesses (Kalnins and Williams, 2014). Interestingly, human capital obtained through education (i.e., average years of education and tertiary education) is a fundamental factor in explaining the gender differences in entrepreneurial activity (Dilli and Westerhuis, 2018). This might imply that financial literacy could play a role in explaining gender gap in entrepreneurship. According to test-based assessment of financial literacy, men are more financially knowledgeable than women on both basic and more sophisticated literacy questions. Such differences are present not only in a sample of adults, but also among students (Lusardi and Mitchell, 2014). Additionally, not only women are less likely to answer financial literacy questions correctly than men, but they are also far more likely to admit they 'do not know' an answer to a question. Several partial explanations have been raised for gender differences in financial literacy, including differing levels of confidence (Bucher-Koenen *et al.*, 2017), and diverging interests in financial matters (Brown and Graf, 2013). However, none of the approaches can entirely explain the gender gap, thus making the issue a promising avenue for further research, especially in the context of entrepreneurship.

Similar emphasis could be put in uncovering the complex relationship between financial literacy and entrepreneurial outcomes for other categories of individuals, such as ethnic minorities, unemployed, uneducated or geographically isolated people.

4.2. *Financial education programs*

The "lack of financial skills" (or too low financial human capital) highlighted by studies of financial literacy has been a serious concern to regulators and other public institutions. In response to the diffuse presence of biases in households' financial decision process, governments have launched several interventions across many different countries targeting the general population. The most famous intervention is probably the creation of the Consumer Financial Protection Bureau (CFPB) in the US. Many OECD countries and even companies launched strategies for Financial Education after the last global financial crisis. In Germany, for instance, employees of Deutsche Bank deliver financial training directly to schools through its Financial Literacy initiative and employee engagement.[2] The Netherlands launched its "Money Wise Action Plan" in June 2008 and have revised it with a new timeframe 2014–2018 (OECD, 2016).

Although financial education is considered as one of the main instruments to improve financial behavior, research evaluating the impact of financial education programs aimed to improve financial literacy and financial behavior found rather disappointing results. Some meta-analysis conclude that financial education can improve financial behavior (Collins and O'Rourke, 2010; Gale *et al.*, 2012), but this impact is very small (Kaiser and Menkhoff 2017; Stolper and Walter 2017). Some other meta-analyses that specifically consider studies with more rigorous designs, such as randomized or natural experiments (Fernandes *et al.*, 2014; Hastings *et al.*, 2012) conclude that the effect is negligible. Since the

[2] *Source*: https://www.db.com/cr/en/concrete-financial-literacy-initiative.htm.

overall effect of education interventions on actual financial decisions is, at best, very small on average, it is important to identify which elements are critical for the success of a program. It is possible that these factors will depend not only on the content of the programs alone but also on the ability of these programs to induce participants to act upon the content learned.

Research has highlighted some of these elements. First, education programs are more efficient when the participants have the possibility to apply what they learnt in a concrete case of interest to them (Fernandes *et al.*, 2014). One reason for the decrease in efficiency is that the intervention effects decay over time (Lusardi and Mitchell, 2014, among many others). Second, mandatory initiatives have a lower impact than non-mandatory initiatives, probably because people who self-select in a voluntary educational program are more motivated and interested in the topics. Third, the channel of the intervention (e.g., classroom, online, individual counseling) matters: one of the most effective channels has proven to be individual counseling (Carpena *et al.*, 2017). Fourth, more intense interventions, focused on a single, concrete issue, rather than a more general behavior, are more effective (Kaiser and Menkhoff, 2017). Lastly, the quality of the teachers or the design of the intervention is extremely important (Lusardi and Mitchell, 2014). A general lesson we can draw from the literature is that one-size does not fit all in financial education.

Some academic papers studied education interventions with entrepreneurs as target group, but they all focused on the special case of emerging countries. The rationale for these interventions is that "managerial capital" or business skills are an important driver of firm growth and a key determinant of productivity in these countries. Such interventions are not specifically targeted to the improvement of financial literacy, but financial literacy is often a key component. Bjorvatn and Tungodenn (2010) evaluate a business training program in Tanzania. They find that entrepreneurs who reported less interest in participating in training, with lower business knowledge, and less financial education, were the ones to gain the most from the program. Karlan and Valdivia (2011) focus instead on the effect of business training for a Peruvian group lending program for female micro-entrepreneurs. The treatment effect of program participation on business revenue, profits, or employment is not significant, although the business knowledge of micro-entrepreneurs improved. Similarly, Bruhn and Zia (2013) find that a comprehensive business and financial literacy program in Bosnia-Herzegovina did not influence business survival, but it significantly improved business practices, investments, and loan terms for surviving businesses. Entrepreneurs with higher *ex ante* financial literacy further exhibited some improvements in business performance and sales. Drexler *et al.* (2014) show that a basic rules-of-thumb-based training, but not formal business training, leads to improvements in business outcomes for micro-entrepreneurs in the Dominican Republic.

To our knowledge, no country-wise initiatives have been launched to improve the financial literacy of a specific sub-group of entrepreneurs in developed countries. Nevertheless, national and international policy and private interest for such issue has recently started to manifest (BDC, 2017; OECD, 2018; Utrecht Chamber of Commerce, 2017) and it will possibly result in further initiatives of this sort. An evaluation of the impact of such initiatives will therefore be needed.

A low level of financial literacy does not necessarily imply that entrepreneurs are bound to take poor financial decisions concerning their business. Especially in developed countries, where professional financial advice is easily accessible, they can seek guidance from advisors, or directly hire some financial manager in their organizations. Several problems may undermine this argument.[3] First, entrepreneurs may not demand advice when they would need the most.[4] This would be the case if the entrepreneur does not realize he (she) does not know enough about the topic. Second, just as households, entrepreneurs might not act on advice (Fernandes *et al.*, 2014), especially if they do not trust the source (Gennaioli *et al.*, 2015), or if they do not agree with the proposed solutions. Moreover, the cost of external professional financial advice may be prohibitive for many entrepreneurs.

---

[3] Referring to households seeking advice for their financial decisions, another problem arises: the fact that professional advice is often biased. For a discussion on this, see Calcagno and Monticone (2015).

[4] Referring to households' decisions, there is a large debate whether financial literacy and demand for advice are substitutes or complements. For example, see Stolper and Walter (2017).

5. Outcomes of Financial Literacy

Several papers studied financial literacy as an antecedent to various healthy households' financial behaviors. Financial literacy is positively correlated with planning for retirement, savings and wealth accumulation (Lusardi and Mitchell, 2007; Rooij *et al.*, 2011), to stock market participation (van Rooij *et al.*, 2011), to better portfolio diversification (Calvet *et al.*, 2009b) and to choosing a low fee investment portfolio (Hastings *et al.*, 2012), while it is negatively correlated with debt accumulation and high-cost borrowing (Lusardi and Tufano, 2009) and mortgage delinquency and home foreclosure (Gerardi *et al.*, 2010).

It is difficult to conclude, however, that there is a causal relation between the objective degree of financial literacy and financial behavior. This is because many other individual traits correlated with financial literacy have proved important to determine households' financial behavior in addition to financial literacy (Fernandes *et al.*, 2014). Among the ones which have been most investigated, are mathematical skills and numeracy, the general cognitive ability, the propensity to plan for the use of money (Lusardi *et al.*, 2009) and the need for cognition (Epstein *et al.*, 1996).

It remains to be assessed whether financial literacy has any impact on entrepreneurial outcome beyond the already known factors. As previously mentioned, we are aware of very few studies that specifically addressed this question. Moreover, most of such studies present clear methodological limitations. Lusardi *et al.* (2016) base their results on the US Health and Retirement Study (HRS). Using two different definitions of entrepreneurship (being self-employed and being a business owner), they show that entrepreneurs present significant differences from the rest of the Baby Boomers population, being more highly educated, healthier and wealthier, which are all characteristics related to higher financial literacy. Nevertheless, they do not test financial literacy differences explicitly. Cumurovic and Hyll (Ćumurović and Hyll, 2018) study the relationship between financial literacy and self-employment in Germany. They use the German SAVE study on financial literacy for households, which also enquires about whether respondents are self-employed. Therefore, their measures of financial literacy are quite standard and not fine-tuned for entrepreneurs. They address the direction of causality by applying instrumental variable techniques and provide support that financial literacy positively affects the probability of being self-employed. Ad-hoc measures of financial literacy for entrepreneurs were instead used by Dahmen and Rodríguez (2014) and Trombetta (2016). The former study, based on 14 small businesses requesting growth acceleration consulting services from the Florida Small Business Development Center at the University of South Florida, highlights a strong association between the businesses' financial strength and the business owners' habits of mind with regard to their financial statements. Nevertheless, the sample size limits the generalizability of the results. Trombetta (2016) is based on a Spanish sample of 400 self-employed individuals and 100 individuals who are not entrepreneurs. The author uses eight questions to capture financial literacy for entrepreneurs, and finds that the overall level of basic financial literacy of Spanish self-employed individuals is quite low and does not differ across entrepreneurs and non-entrepreneurs. He also explores differences in financial literacy across categories based on age and industry of the business or whether individuals were serial successful entrepreneurs or not. The (working) paper is promising although the analysis is still quite preliminary.

Such early stage studies open the way for further work on the impact of financial literacy on entrepreneurial outcome. First, once measures for financial literacy of entrepreneurs are established, researchers should focus on how such measures affect *entrepreneurial intentions, or the probability of founding a start-up*. The main challenge of such studies is the necessity to control for a vast array of confounding factors, such as sociodemographics, family background, experience and personality traits, all of which are important drivers of entrepreneurial activity (Butler and Herring, 1991; Reynolds, 1997; Robinson *et al.*, 1991; Shinnar *et al.*, 2012) and to collect samples of both entrepreneurs and other individuals. Second, it would be interesting to study how financial literacy affects entrepreneurs' ability to take good financial decisions, which in turn improve *entrepreneurial performance*, in terms of start-ups' survival, performance and growth (Cassar, 2004; Salazar *et al.*, 2012; Seghers *et al.*, 2012). While qualitative approach would probably suit better the analysis of financial literacy impact on financial decisions, the effect on performance is more easily tested with a quantitative approach. Therefore, mixed methods studies are probably the most appropriate tools for this type of study.

6. Conclusions

In this chapter, we present a "state of the art" view on financial literacy, with a particular focus on entrepreneurs. In general, the issue of financial literacy attracted a growing interest from policy makers, international institutions such as OECD, and academics. It is surprising that although financial literacy has been largely studied in the context of households and personal finance, almost no attention at this point has been devoted to the case of entrepreneurs. Yet, the latter are bound to make financial decisions on almost an everyday basis. Basic understanding of the functioning of accounting and finance may therefore prove vital for them, especially in their interactions with the providers of capital (banks and equity investors), tax authorities, clients and suppliers. In this chapter we used as a starting point the definition of financial literacy for entrepreneurs provided by the OECD, as the *the combination of awareness, knowledge, skills, attitudes and behavior that a potential entrepreneur or an owner or manager of a micro, small or medium sized enterprise should have in order to make effective financial decisions to start a business, run a business, and ultimately ensure its sustainability and growth* (OECD, 2018). Then, we try to make room for inquiries in the matter by taking inspiration on the broader extant findings on financial literacy.

Existing literature on financial literacy resolves itself into several sub-fields. The first sub-field deals with the question of how to measure financial literacy. Evaluators of financial literacy in the general population often resort to the use of survey tests or questionnaires with the aim to obtain respectively the objective or the self-evaluated levels of financial literacy in respondents. The second sub-field investigates the socio-demographic factors that explain differences in financial literacy, and those that help improving the level of financial literacy like schooling and/or coaching in schools and in certain policy initiatives. The third sub-field analyzes the extent to which financial literacy affects the ability of individuals to take savvy financial decisions.

The overall conclusion of the studies we have reviewed is that the level of financial literacy is low, although a heterogeneity exists within the various studied groups (e.g., elderly people, students, investors, employees). Clear differences in the levels of financial literacy were observed among individuals in terms of their overall degree of income, education, gender, race, ethnicity, etc. All these gaps exist in the entrepreneurial activity as well, yet more effort is certainly needed to understand the sources of these gaps and/or biases. Such an understanding would definitely help identifying the possible remedies.

The degree of financial literacy can be improved, yet despite a considerable effort delivered by various state and private initiatives, but the overall effect of the programs remains almost insignificant. It is also important to note that, to the best of our knowledge, none of the programs have been targeted to the entrepreneurs in the developed countries.

Likewise, in terms of outcomes of financial literacy, most of the existing evidence is based on the studies of individuals and/or households, rather than (potential) entrepreneurs. While it seems fair to conclude that higher financial literacy positively affects the outcomes of financial decision-making, such a shortcut conclusion must be avoided when one transposes this evidence on the entrepreneurs. First, entrepreneurs are advised by experts in their financial choices much more intensely than households, or they partly delegate these decisions to an employee. Second, self-employed and company founders have to make financial decisions more frequently, often on a daily basis. Such greater intensity may help identifying the causal effect of literacy. However, the objectives and outcomes for individuals and households are not the same as for the entrepreneurs. Entrepreneurial outcomes may be related to securing long-term financing sources, short-term working capital management, none of which is of any concern to an individual or a household. Therefore, more careful assessment of these issues is required to provide a clear understanding of the overall causal effect of financial literacy on entrepreneurial outcomes.

That is the reason why with this chapter we try to pave a road to the future research investigating financial literacy in an entrepreneurial framework. The first important challenge is to measure such a construct. Few scholars tried to design ad hoc questionnaires to capture financial literacy for entrepreneurs, but we are still far from having a "golden standard" to measure it. The first step in this direction was taken by the OECD, which in 2018 published a definitional framework for financial literacy for entrepreneurs. Such framework could be used as reference for the development of a standard methodology to measure financial literacy for (potential) entrepreneurs. Once a measure of financial literacy for entrepreneurs has been established, future research should tackle the important relationship between it and entrepreneurial outcome, in terms of probability to become entrepreneurs, and later to take savvy entrepreneurial financial decisions. Ultimately, financial decisions should influence entrepreneurial success, in terms of survival and growth. Importantly, such studies will need to take into account factors that can simultaneously affect financial literacy and entrepreneurial outcome, such as socio-demographic factors, family background and other established drivers of entrepreneurial activity.

References

Allgood S. and Walstad W. B. (2016) The effects of perceived and actual financial literacy on financial behaviors. *Economic Inquiry*, *54*(1), 675–697. doi:10.1111/ecin.12255.

Ansong A. and Gyensare M. A. (2012) Determinants of University Working-Students' Financial Literacy at the University of Cape Coast, Ghana. *International Journal of Business and Management*, *7*(9). doi:10.5539/ijbm.v7n9p126.

Aren S. and Dinç Aydemir S. (2014) A literature review on financial literacy. *Finansal Araştırmalar ve Çalışmalar Dergisi*, *6*(11). doi:10.14784/JFRS.2014117326.

Barber B. M. and Odean T. (2000) Trading is hazardous to your wealth: the common stock investment performance of individual investors. *The Journal of Finance*, *55*(2), 773–806. doi:10.1111/0022-1082.00226.

Barber B. M. and Odean T. (2013) The Behavior of individual investors. *Handbook of the Economics of Finance*, 2, 1533–1570. doi:10.1016/B978-0-44-459406-8.00022-6.

Bayer P. J., Bernheim B. D., and Scholz J. K. (2009) The effects of financial education in the workplace: evidence from a survey of employers. *Economic Inquiry*, *47*(4), 605–624. doi:10.1111/j.1465-7295.2008.00156.x.

BDC (2017) Financial literacy among Canadian entrepreneurs and business owners, (December), 1–15.

Berger A. N. and Udell G. F. (1995) Relationship lending and lines of credit in small firm finance. *The Journal of Business*. The University of Chicago Press. doi:10.2307/2353332.

Binks M. R., Ennew C. T., and Reed G. V. (1992) Information asymmetries and the provision of finance to small firms. *International Small Business Journal, 11*(1), 35–46. doi:10.1177/026624269201100103.

Bird A., Karolyi S. A., and Ruchti T. G. (2018) Information sharing, holdup and external finance: evidence from private firms. *The Review of Financial Studies*. doi:10.1093/rfs/hhy110.

Bjorvatn K. and Tungodden B. (2010) Teaching business in Tanzania: Evaluating participation and performance. *Journal of the European Economic Association*, *8*(2–3), 561–570. doi:10.1111/j.1542-4774.2010.tb00526.x.

Brown M. and Graf R. (2013) Financial literacy and retirement planning in Switzerland. *Numeracy*, *6*(2). http://scholarcommons.usf.edu/numeracy/vol6/iss2/art6/. Accessed 10 October 2018.

Bruhn M. and Zia B. (2013) Stimulating managerial capital in emerging markets: the impact of business training for young entrepreneurs. *Journal of Development Effectiveness*, *5*(2), 232–266. doi:10.1080/19439342.2013.780090.

Bucher-Koenen T., Lusardi A., Alessie R., and van Rooij M. (2017) How financially literate are women? an overview and new insights. *Journal of Consumer Affairs*, *51*(2), 255–283. doi:10.1111/joca.12121.

Butler J. S. and Herring C. (1991) Ethnicity and entrepreneurship in America: toward an explanation of racial and ethnic group variations in self-employment. *Sociological Perspectives*, *34*(1), 79–94. doi:10.2307/1389144.

Calcagno R. and Monticone C. (2015) Financial literacy and the demand for financial advice. *Journal of Banking and Finance*, 50, 363–380. doi:10.1016/j.jbankfin.2014.03.013.

Calvet L. E., Campbell J. Y., and Sodini P. (2009a) Fight or flight? portfolio rebalancing by individual investors. *Quarterly Journal of Economics*, *124*(1), 301–348. doi:10.1162/qjec.2009.124.1.301.

Calvet L. E., Campbell J. Y., and Sodini P. (2009b) Measuring the financial sophistication of households. *American Economic Review*, *99*(0214061), 393–398. doi:10.1257/aer.99.2.393.

Carpena F., Cole S., Shapiro J., and Zia B. (2017) The ABCs of financial education: experimental evidence on attitudes, behavior, and cognitive biases. *Management Science*, (September), mnsc.2017.2819. doi:10.1287/mnsc.2017.2819.

Cassar G. (2004) The financing of business start-ups. *Journal of Business Venturing*, *19*(2), 261–283. doi:10.1016/S0883-9026(03)00029-6.

Collins J. M. and O'Rourke C. M. (2010) Financial education and counseling — still holding promise. *Journal of Consumer Affairs*, *44*(3), 483–498. doi:10.1111/j.1745-6606.2010.01179.x.

Colombo M. G., D'Adda D., and Quas A. (2019) The geography of venture capital and entrepreneurial ventures' demand for external equity. *Research Policy*, *48*(5), 1150–1170. doi: https://doi.org/10.1016/j.respol.2018.12.004.

Cosh A., Cumming D. J., and Hughes A. (2009) Outside entrepreneurial capital. *Economic Journal*, *119*(1), 494–533. doi:10.1111/j.1468-0297.2009.02270.x.

Cowling M., Liu W., and Ledger A. (2012) Small business financing in the UK before and during the current financial crisis. *International Small Business Journal*, *30*(7), 778–800. doi:10.1177/0266242611435516.

Ćumurović A. and Hyll W. (2018) Financial literacy and self-employment. *Journal of Consumer Affairs* November, 1–33. doi:10.1111/joca.12198.

Dahmen P. and Rodríguez E. (2014) Financial literacy and the success of small businesses: an observation from a small business development center. *Numeracy*, *7*(1), 3. doi:10.5038/1936-4660.7.1.3.

Dilli S. and Westerhuis G. (2018) How institutions and gender differences in education shape entrepreneurial activity: a cross-national perspective. *Small Business Economics*, *51*(2), 371–392. doi:10.1007/s11187-018-0004-x.

Drexler A., Fischer G., and Schoar A. (2014) Keeping it simple: financial literacy and rules of thumb. *American Economic Journal: Applied Economics*, *6*(2), 1–31. doi:10.1257/app.6.2.1.

Eckhardt J. T., Delmar F., and Shane S. (2006) Multistage selection and the financing of new ventures. *Management Science*, *52*(2), 220–232. doi:10.1287/mnsc.1050.0478.

Epstein S., Pacini R., Denes-Raj V., and Heier H. (1996) Individual differences in intuitive-experiential and analytical-rational thinking styles. *Journal of Personality and Social Psychology*, *71*(2), 390–405. doi:10.1037/0022-3514.71.2.390.

Fernandes D., Lynch J. G., and Netemeyer R. G. (2014) Financial literacy, financial education, and downstream financial behaviors. *Management Science*, *60*(8), 1861–1883. doi:10.1287/mnsc.2013.1849.

Gale W. G., Harris B. H., and Levine R. (2012) Raising household saving: does financial education work? *Social Security Bulletin*, *72*(19), 39–48. https://heinonline.org/HOL/Page?handle=hein.journals/ssbul72&id=173&div=&collection=. Accessed 10 October 2018.

Gennaioli N., Shleifer A., and Vishny R. (2015) Money doctors. *Journal of Finance, 70*(1), 91–114. doi:10.1111/jofi.12188.

Gerardi K., Goette L., and Meier S. (2010) Financial literacy and subprime mortgage delinquency: evidence from a survey matched to administrative data — Federal Reserve Bank of Atlanta. Federal Reserve Bank of Atlanta Working Paper Series, 10 (April), pp. 1–53. https://www.frbatlanta.org/research/publications/wp/2010/10.aspx.

Guiso L. and Jappelli T. (2006) Information acquisition and portfolio performance. CEPR Discussion Paper No. 5901. https://papers.ssrn.com/sol3/papers.cfm?abstract_id=954121. Accessed 17 December 2018.

Harris M. and Raviv A. (1991) The theory of capital structure. *The Journal of Finance, 46*(1), 297–355. doi:10.2307/2328697.

Hastings J. S., Madrian B. C., and Skimmyhorn W. L. (2012) Financial literacy, financial education and economic outcomes. *National Bureau of Economic Research Working Paper 18412, 5*(1), 1–42. doi:10.1146/annurev-economics-082312-125807.NBER.

Hung A., Parker A. M., and Yoong J. K. (2009) Defining and measuring financial literacy. RAND Working paper series, no. 708, pp. 1–28. https://www.rand.org/pubs/working_papers/WR708.html. Accessed 9 October 2018.

Jensen M. C. and Meckling W. H. (1976) Theory of the firm: Managerial behavior, agency costs and ownership structure. *Journal of Financial Economics, 3*(4), 305–360. doi:10.1016/0304-405X(76)90026-X.

Kaiser T. and Menkhoff L. (2017) Does financial education impact financial literacy and financial behavior, and if so, when? *The World Bank Economic Review, 31*(3), 611–630. doi:10.1093/wber/lhx018.

Kalnins A. and Williams M. (2014) When do female-owned businesses out-survive male-owned businesses? A disaggregated approach by industry and geography. *Journal of Business Venturing, 29*(6), 822–835. doi:10.1016/j.jbusvent.2013.12.001.

Karlan D. and Valdivia M. (2011) Teaching entrepreneurship: Impact of business training on microfinance clients and institutions. *Review of Economics and Statistics, 93*(2), 510–527. doi:10.1162/REST_a_00074.

Kelley D. J., Singer S., and Herrington M. (2012) Global Entrepreneurship Monitor 2011 Global Report. Babson College, p. 39. doi:10.1017/CBO9781107415324.004.

Laibson D. (1997) Golden eggs and hyperbolic discounting. *The Quarterly Journal of Economics, 112*(2), 443–478. doi:10.1162/003355397555253.

López-Gracia J. and Sogorb-Mira F. (2008) Testing trade-off and pecking order theories financing SMEs. *Small Business Economics*, 31, 117–136. doi:10.1007/s11187-007-9088-4.

Lusardi A. (2011) Economic and personal finance education in our nation's schools. *Council for Economic Education.*

Lusardi A., Christelis D., and de Bassa Scheresberg C. (2016) Entrepreneurship among baby boomers: recent evidence from the health and retirement study. *Global Financial Literacy Excellence Center, 4*(September), 1–58. doi:10.2139/ssrn.2898910.

Lusardi A., Michaud P.-C., and Mitchell O. S. (2017) Optimal financial knowledge and wealth inequality. *Journal of Political Economy, 125*(2), 431–477. doi:10.2139/ssrn.2585222.

Lusardi A. and Mitchell O. S. (2007) Baby Boomer retirement security: The roles of planning, financial literacy, and housing wealth. *Journal of Monetary Economics, 54*(1), 205–224. doi:10.1016/j.jmoneco.2006.12.001.

Lusardi A. and Mitchell O. S. (2008) Planning and financial literacy: how do women fare? *American Economic Review, 98*(2), 413–417. doi:10.1257/aer.98.2.413.

Lusardi A. and Mitchell O. S. (2014) The economic importance of financial literacy: theory and evidence. *Journal of Economic Literature, 52*(1), 5–44.

Lusardi A., Mitchell O. S., Lusardi A., and Mitchell O. (2009) How ordinary consumers make complex economic decisions: financial literacy and retirement readiness. https://econpapers.repec.org/paper/nbrnberwo/15350.htm. Accessed 9 October 2018.

Lusardi A. and Tufano P. (2009) Debt literacy, financial experiences, and overindebtedness. https://ora.ox.ac.uk/objects/uuid:57fe97be-d8fa-4290-b101-1b70360bf81d. Accessed 9 October 2018.

Markussen S. and Røed K. (2017) The gender gap in entrepreneurship – The role of peer effects. *Journal of Economic Behavior & Organization, 134*(201336), 356–373. doi:10.1016/j.jebo.2016.12.013.

Mina A., Lahr H., and Hughes A. (2013) The demand and supply of external finance for innovative firms. *Industrial and Corporate Change, 22*(4), 869–901. doi:10.1093/icc/dtt020.

Müller S. and Weber M. (2010) Financial literacy and mutual fund investments: who buys actively managed funds? *Schmalenbach Business Review, 62*(April 2010), 126–153. http://ssrn.com/abstract=1093305.

OECD (2014) PISA 2012 Results: Students and Money: Financial Literacy Skills for the 21st Century. *PISA, OECD Publishing, 6.* doi: http://dx.doi.org/10.1787/9789264208094-en.

OECD (2015) OECD / INFE Progress report on financial education for MSMEs and potential entrepreneurs, (September), pp. 1–25. http://g20.org.tr/wp-content/uploads/2015/11/OECD-INFE-Progress-Report-on-Financial-Education-for-MSMEs.pdf.

OECD (2016) *Financial Education in Europe: Trends and Recent Developments*. OECD Publishing, Paris. doi:10.1787/9789264254855-en.

OECD (2018) OECD/INFE Core Competencies Framework on Financial Literacy for MSMEs, (July), 1–36.

Palacín-Sánchez M. J., Ramírez-Herrera L. M., and di Pietro F. (2013) Capital structure of SMEs in Spanish regions. *Small Business Economics, 41*(2), 503–519. doi:10.1007/s11187-012-9439-7.

Puri M. and Zarutskie R. (2012) On the lifecycle dynamics of venture-capital and non-venture-capital financed firms. *Journal of Finance, 67*(6), 2247–2293. doi:10.1111/j.1540-6261.2012.01786.x.

Remund D. L. (2010) Financial literacy explicated: The case for a clearer definition in an increasingly complex economy. *Journal of Consumer Affairs, 44*(2), 276–295. doi:10.1111/j.1745-6606.2010.01169.x.

Reynolds P. D. (1997) Who starts new firm? Preliminary explanation of firm-in-gestation. *Small Business Economics, 9*(5), 449–462.

Robb A. M. and Robinson D. T. (2014) The capital structure decisions of new firms. *Review of Financial Studies, 27*(1), 153–179. doi:10.1093/rfs/hhs072.

Robinson P. B., Stimpson D. V., Huefner J. C., and Hunt H. K. (1991) An Attitude approach to the prediction of entrepreneurship. *Entrepreneurship Theory and Practice, 15*(4), 13–32. doi:10.1177/104225879101500405.

Salazar A. L., Soto R. C., and Mosqueda R. E. (2012) The impact of financial decisions and strategy on small business competitiveness. *Global Journal of Business Research, 6*(2), 93–104. doi:10.1016/j.techfore.2013.05.008.

Seghers A., Manigart S., and Vanacker T. (2012) The impact of human and social capital on entrepreneurs' knowledge of finance alternatives. *Journal of Small Business Management, 50*(1), 63–86. doi:10.1111/j.1540-627X.2011.00344.x.

Shepherd D. A., Williams T. A., and Patzelt H. (2015) Thinking about entrepreneurial decision making. *Journal of Management, 41*(1), 11–46. doi:10.1177/0149206314541153.

Shinnar R. S., Giacomin O., and Janssen F. (2012) Entrepreneurial perceptions and intentions: the role of gender and culture. *Entrepreneurship: Theory and Practice, 36*(3), 465–493. doi:10.1111/j.1540-6520.2012.00509.x.

Stolper O. A. and Walter A. (2017) Financial literacy, financial advice, and financial behavior. *Journal of Business Economics, 87*(5), 581–643. doi:10.1007/s11573-017-0853-9.

Storey D. J. (1994) *Understanding The Small Business Sector*. Routledge. doi:10.4324/9781315544335.

Trombetta M. (2016) Accounting and finance literacy and self-employment: an exploratory study. Working Paper (May), pp. 1–32.

Utrecht Chamber of Commerce. (2017) In control of the company: Entrepreneurs on their financial literacy. *Kamer van Koophandel, November,* 1–27.

Van Auken H. E. (2005) A model of small firm capital acquisition decisions. *The International Entrepreneurship and Management Journal, 1*(3), 335–352. doi:10.1007/s11365-005-2599-z.

van Rooij M., Lusardi A., and Alessie R. (2011) Financial literacy, retirement planning, and household wealth. DNB working paper, August (313), pp. 1–49.

van Rooij M., Lusardi A., and Alessie R. (2011) Financial literacy and stock market participation. *Journal of Financial Economics, 101*(2), 449–472. https://ideas.repec.org/a/eee/jfinec/v101y2011i2p449-472.html. Accessed 9 October 2018.

Chapter 11

Social Entrepreneurship Competitions: Hoping for Funding and Gaining Valuable Experience in the Process — An Exploratory Study

Moriah Meyskens*

University of San Diego

mmeyskens@sandiego.edu

Rachel Christensen*

University of San Diego

rchristensen@sandiego.edu

Patricia Márquez*

University of San Diego

pmarquez@sandiego.edu

*5998, Alcala Park, San Diego, CA 92110, USA.

Abstract

The purpose of this study is to better understand the role of social entrepreneurship competitions in the start-up process through implementation of pre and post surveys. Our exploratory research suggests that many students join these competitions seeking mentors and funding, but during the process of the competition, some elements of self-efficacy are actually reduced as a result of participation. Since competitions enable participants to experience first-hand the different layers of complexity of starting a venture, participants realize how challenging the process is and thus might have less confidence in starting a venture. Participants also suggest that the competition helped them better understand the needs of the society they are focusing on and that the mentorship gained through the competition is apparently more valuable than funding. In summary, although individuals might join competitions motivated by funding opportunities, they finish the process actually saving resources in the long term because through experiential learning they experience how difficult it is to actually start a venture. This insight can be used by competition organizers to better design social entrepreneurship competitions, so that participants might experience during the competition cycle even more of the complexities of starting a venture. At the same time, academics and doctoral students might conduct future studies with a larger sample size to better understand other types of knowledge gained through these competitions as well as which competition activities lead to the greatest levels of transformation and learning in participants.

1. Introduction

Social entrepreneurship has rapidly become commonplace in universities around the world. An Ashoka study found that the number of social innovation educational offerings (co-curricular and curricular programs) worldwide grew from 7 in 1991 to 34 in 2000 to 199 in 2008 to 598 in 2013 (Ashoka, 2014). A 2013 Ashoka study found that the number of social innovation majors grew 60% and minors 81% from 2009 to 2013. Most students today (72%) want to have a job "where they can make a difference" and many (65%) expect to "make a social or environmental impact through their work" (Zukin and Szeltner, 2012).

As part of this trend, and recognizing the applied nature of social entrepreneurship, universities offer a range of experiential learning tools, including social entrepreneurship competitions (Dumaine and Pofeldt, 2007). Many universities sponsor a competition that focuses entirely on social entrepreneurship or has a social venture track (Brock and Ashoka, 2008; Ashoka, 2013). These competitions offer a broad range of workshops, mentors, funding opportunities and other facets of support to their participants. Universities host these competitions hoping to help their students launch their ventures. Although many students are motivated by potential financial prizes to join these competitions, they actually gain many other important start-up resources in the process.

Our study focuses on better understanding the role of social entrepreneurship competitions in helping participants learn and experience the start-up process. Particularly we focus on how self-efficacy, attitude toward helping society and entrepreneurial intentions are impacted as a result of participating in this competition. Although the number of competitions has grown exponentially in recent years as a mechanism for start-up support, few studies analyze the impact of these competitions in student learning and in what ways these competitions help shape their attitudes towards solving problems via venture creation.

Research in entrepreneurship education analyzing competitions evaluates the influence of business planning on venture success (Delmar and Shane, 2003; Honig and Karlsson, 2004; Lange *et al.*, 2007), and how competitions provide an opportunity for participants to network, gain feedback, obtain future investment capital, and learn about social issues (Gupta and York, 2009; Kwong *et al.*, 2012; Russell *et al.*, 2008). Little academic research has provided insight into the impact of these social entrepreneurship competitions (Meyskens and Auch, 2013). This lack of attention is somewhat perplexing given the amount of resources (financial and other) expended by universities on these competitions and the potential these competitions have to assist in shaping entrepreneurial attitudes and ensuing the creation of ventures that generate social value. This study aims to fill the gap in the literature, by assessing social venture competitions impact on participants learning outcomes. Through this study, educators and competition sponsors can gain further insights into how to develop more effective learning experiences so that students wanting to become entrepreneurs emerge prepared to make informed decisions regarding their career paths, in alignment with their interests and capabilities. Similarly, better understanding the learning outcomes of providing the start-up experience for students can lead to new competition designs, where funding and human resources are best allocated.

2. Literature Review

2.1. *Social entrepreneurship competitions*

As the number of programs and courses in the area of social entrepreneurship grow, so do the number of experiential activities like social entrepreneurship competitions. These competitions gave out combined award money of more than $1 million per year in 2008 (Brock and Ashoka, 2008). By 2017, the most endowed social venture competition alone, The Hult Prize, annually gave away one million dollars (http://www.hultprize.org/). Not surprisingly, many students or aspiring entrepreneurs are told to join a competition as a first place to seek potential funding for their venture. The Mentor Capital Network gathers information regarding these competitions worldwide and in 2016 they had 140 competitions listed that are sponsored both by non-profit entities as well as universities. This number grew from 45 in 2009 (Meyskens, 2010). However, we expect the number to be much greater as many university competitions are not included in the Mentor Capital Network list (as of 2018 they only had 27 competitions on their website (https://web.archive.org/web/20180928140838/). Most larger universities nowadays have entrepreneurship competitions and most of these have a prize focusing on social ventures.

Social venture competitions focus on developing initiatives that create solutions to social and environmental problems, and have social or environmental impact, rather than financial impact, as their primary judging criteria. They vary in form, scope and purpose. Some social venture competitions are hosted by business schools and focus only on business students, whereas others are offered by specific university centers, or are collaborations organized by a variety of schools and/or departments within a University (Schlee *et al.*, 2008). Generally, both undergraduate and graduate students can participate in these competitions. Some competitions are just for internal university participants and others are open to students or alumni nationally and worldwide, and/or the community outside the university. The ventures developed as part of these competitions must focus on addressing social and/or environmental problems and are generally at the start-up phase. Sponsoring institutions offer workshops and technical assistance during the competition cycle (usually the academic year if at a university) to assist participants in developing their ventures.

In terms of the deliverables some competitions require participants to develop detailed venture plans through a comprehensive and sometimes lengthy process. Other competitions are focused more on the initial proposal or concept stage, and create a platform to unlock and jumpstart innovative thinking with low barriers to entry. Regardless of format and goal, all of these competitions have been designed as experiential learning opportunities for participants. The universities sponsoring these competitions hope that they have both pedagogical benefits by impacting participant's skills, attitudes, intentions and ability to launch their social venture, as well as result in the creation of more social ventures. Evidence of the impact of the competitions mostly focuses on the numbers of overall participants or submissions and anecdotal stories highlighting few participants. Previous studies have assessed the value of this impact at the individual, venture and societal level through surveys conducted after the competition (Meyskens and Auch, 2013). However, research has not systematically analyzed the resources and knowledge gained through this experiential learning initiative.

2.2. *Impact of entrepreneurship education and competitions*

The impact of entrepreneurship education has been analyzed in different settings. Jensen (2014) conducts a case study of social entrepreneurship in the Humanities in Denmark. The study suggests that students develop a holistic dynamic understanding of social entrepreneurship through different entrepreneurial experiences in their daily life and through their different courses. Stamboulis and Barlis (2014) conducted a paired samples test of 169 University students before and after attending an entrepreneurship class to assess how economic, social, psychological, environmental, demographic, and cultural factors impact the pursuit of entrepreneurial endeavors. They find that participating in a course changes students' perception and increases their knowledge of starting a venture. In another study by Kadir, Salim and Kamarudin (2012) they find that educational support contributed towards entrepreneurial intent of students. Tshikovhi and Shambare (2015) find that being part of a specialized group (like www.enactus.org) increases entrepreneurial intentions. Thus, entrepreneurship education provides an opportunity for the individual to gain a holistic understanding of the topic so that they better understand how to and are more likely to start a venture (e.g., Kirkwood, 2009; Ioannou, 2001).

In prior studies, entrepreneurship competitions have also been found to have an impact at the institutional and individual level. Early research in this area suggests that business plan competitions were initially conducted by some schools to establish the legitimacy of their entrepreneurial programs following isomorphic pressures (Honig 2004; Meyer and Rowan, 1977). Thus their pedagogical value in such instances is secondary. More recent research suggests that competitions serve as an important opportunity for participants to network, gain feedback, and obtain future investment capital (Gupta and York, 2009). In addition, they help participants develop skills, increase self-confidence, enhance risk-taking propensity, gain access to mentors who provide valuable feedback, and create opportunities for networking (Russell *et al.*, 2008). Kwong *et al.* (2012) suggests that social business plans and participation in their corresponding competitions enable students to gain awareness of social and civic matters in addition to developing an in-depth understanding of managing organizations in a social economy. Meyskens and Auch (2013) suggest that social entrepreneurship competitions influence career choices of past participants and venture development as well as have an impact on society. Huster *et al.* (2016) find that networking and mentoring are key benefits of participating in social entrepreneurship competitions. Oluwatobi *et al.* (2018) looked at the Hult Prize (www.hultprize.org) finals in Nigeria to discover that students were primarily motivated to solve practical global problems rather than to start a business venture. Competitions provide an opportunity for participants to experience the process of business planning and the different aspects of venture development in a structured learning environment. The process of business planning is extremely valuable for new venture development (Carsrud and Brännback, 2007; Cooper and Vlaskovits, 2010; Vendel and Brown, 2012).

The current state of research regarding the impact social entrepreneurship competitions is thus far scant and primarily focuses on outputs. Even though existing research point at the relevance of the process in a competition or business planning process, more research is required to know how these affect individual participants. Thus, this study tries to better understand how participation in these competitions has an effect at the individual level.

3. Hypothesis Development

In order to measure the impact of these competitions, we assess how different individual attributes (those that are important in the entrepreneurial process) might be changed as a result of participation in a competition. These attributes are recognized in research as important to venture development and include: self-efficacy, attitude toward helping society and entrepreneurial intentions (Mair and Noboa, 2003, 2005, 2006). Each of these is discussed in the following section.

3.1. *Self-efficacy*

Self-efficacy measures a person's belief in their ability to successfully launch an entrepreneurial venture (Bandura, 1997; McGee *et al.*, 2009). The concept takes into account both the personality of the potential entrepreneur as well as environmental factors affecting the decision to become an entrepreneur (Bird, 1988). The concept is similar to *perceived behavioral control* which refers to the perceived ease or difficulty of acquiring the resources needed for exploitation as well as anticipated impediments and obstacles (Ajzen, 1991). Many researchers include perceived behavioral control as one of the motivational antecedents affecting entrepreneurial intentions (Fitzsimmons and Douglas, 2011; Krueger *et al.*, 2000; Liñán and Chen, 2009).

Entrepreneurship is a process whereby start-ups and their founders marshal resources and organize for continued growth. Obstacles and impediments naturally occur during this process and without a certain level of perceived control entrepreneurs are less likely to embark on the process. The literature has consistently indicated that self-efficacy, the self-perception of one's competence in given domains, has indicated a strong relationship between self-efficacy and career choice (Bandura *et al.*, 2001).

In other words, we tend to show the strongest interest in careers for which we feel that we have the abilities to succeed. Beliefs such as "I am confident that I can start a new venture" and "I can control the creative process of starting a new venture" are essential qualities that will fortify an individual's intention in starting a social venture. Thus, individuals with high social entrepreneurial self-efficacy are more likely to pursue and then persist in starting a venture than those individuals who possess low social entrepreneurial self-efficacy (Bandura, 1997).

Research suggests that an individual's self-efficacy is enhanced in a number of ways. Bandura (1992) outlines four key sources: mastery experiences, modeling, social persuasion, and judgments of our own physiological states. Mastery experiences (often referred to "learning by doing") (Florin *et al.*, 2003) appear to be an important antecedent of self-efficacy in future-related tasks (Cox *et al.*, 2002). Social entrepreneurship competitions, through providing opportunities to better understand the market, develop business plans, and get feedback from mentors and judges, provide a mastery experience for participants. Thus, these competitions can therefore potentially play an important role in developing social entrepreneurial self-efficacy. Social entrepreneurship competitions also frequently have guest speakers and successful social entrepreneurs as judges, and these can also provide role models. These in turn help individuals form judgments of their own capabilities by comparing themselves to others (Cox *et al.*, 2002). The literature also suggests that self-efficacy can also be enhanced through social persuasion, from the positive encouragement and feedback that individuals are given by mentors (professors and community mentors) and coaches in social entrepreneurship competitions.

In summary, participation in a competition with the corresponding workshops, mentors, and idea development, provides an opportunity to gain important skills and insight into the entrepreneurial start-up process. As a result, this experiential learning provides participants a means to enhance their competencies and knowledge of starting a venture. Thus, a participant's belief and confidence that they will successfully be able to launch a venture increases. Thus:

> **H1:** *Participation in a social entrepreneurship competition positively influences an individual's social entrepreneurial self-efficacy.*

3.2. *Attitude toward helping society*

Behavioral *attitude* suggests that an individual finds starting a social venture to be an attractive career option (Ajzen, 1991). Such beliefs predispose individuals on a particular career path. In the commercial entrepreneurship setting, such attitude might be related to one's attitude towards monetary rewards, status or the professional freedom that can be associated with a successful entrepreneurial career. In the social entrepreneurship setting, the behavioral attitude, similar to the concept termed as "perceived desirability" (Mair and Noboa, 2003), may however, be quite distinct. The positive attitude and perceived desirability of a social entrepreneurial career might be motivated by empathy towards the less fortunate or a disadvantaged group in society as well as a desire to help them. At the same time, individuals with higher levels of moral judgment seem to have a higher tolerance towards minority or disadvantaged groups, altruistic orientations and pro-social activities. Craving social justice, these individuals may be possessed by a need to be loyal to their principles, to be socially responsible and to assist vulnerable populations (Mair and Noboa, 2003, 2005, 2006).

Individuals with a predisposition to social and environmental causes are more likely to be attracted to enter a social venture competition. However, it is also likely, that through participation in a social venture competition the motivations or commitment of participants to these issues be reinforced through speakers, mentors and activities that focus on the impact of social innovations in helping society. In addition, most competitions focus on helping participants better empathize and understand the needs of the society they are trying to help. This exposure will likely appeal to the emotional side of an individual and increase their passion about helping society. Thus:

> **H2:** *Participation in a social entrepreneurship competition positively influences an individual's attitude toward helping society.*

3.3. *Entrepreneurial intentions*

At a fundamental level, entrepreneurial behaviors (i.e., launching a social venture) are preceded by intentions to become an entrepreneur. According to the theory of planned behavior, human behavior is guided by three motivational antecedents which influence an individual's intention towards start-up. The three types of considerations are categorized as: (1) *behavioral attitude*- referring to favorable or unfavorable attitude towards the likely consequences of the behavior; (2) *subjective norm* — referring to how the decision maker perceives the expectations of others important to them regarding the behavior; and (3) *perceived behavior control (self-efficacy)* — as discussed above, referring to how the decision maker perceives the presence of favorable circumstances or obstacles that affect the control the decision maker has of the behavior (Ajzen, 2001). The theory suggests that the stronger the behavioral attitude, the subjective norms, and the perceived behavior control, the stronger the behavioral intentions towards entrepreneurship, and in turn, the more likely that someone will become an entrepreneur. Research has shown that individuals assign different levels of importance to these three motivational antecedents and that the weight of such predictors may differ depending on the culture in which individuals operate (Finlay *et al.*, 1997, 1999; Trafimow and Finlay, 1996).

Numerous studies assess entrepreneurial intentions in the commercial entrepreneurship setting (Autio *et al.*, 2001; Fitzsimmons and Douglas, 2011; Kolvereid, 1996; Krueger, 1993; Krueger and Brazeal, 1994; Krueger *et al.*, 2000; Lee and Wong, 2004; Liñán and Chan, 2009; Liñán *et al.*, 2010; Moriano *et al.*, 2011). However, few have empirically analyzed social entrepreneurial intentions (Mair and Noboa, 2005; Nga and Shamuganathan, 2010). Most of these existing studies focus on evaluating the different factors impacting the intentions of individuals to start a new venture, but not necessarily a social venture that seeks to help society in some way (Dees, 1998; Mair and Marti, 2006).

Entrepreneurial intentions assess an individual's aspirations and interest in starting a venture. Participation in a social entrepreneurship competition exposes students to new ideas on ways to develop a new venture and resources to do so. In addition to exposure, the students participating in a competition undergo a process experience designed to instill greater confidence in starting a venture; that is, they hear all along they can translate their ideas into action. At the same time, through mentors and networking in competitions, participants get additional insight into how they might start their venture, thus increasing their interest in starting a venture. Thus:

> **H3:** *Participation in a social entrepreneurship competition positively influences an individual's social entrepreneurial intentions.*

4. Methodology

4.1. *Sample*

In order to assess the benefits of this experiential learning initiative to understanding the start-up process, we conducted a pre and post survey of the Social Innovation Challenge (SIC) at the University of San Diego (USD) during the 2015–2016 academic year. In total, 205 individuals took the pre-survey and 39 individuals took the post survey. Of these, 25 individuals completed both the pre and post surveys. We also include student testimonials from the competition in 2017 and 2018. The sample size of participants who took both the pre and post survey in 2017 and 2018 was even lower (n = 15 and n = 2, respectively) and is not included.

The SIC is led by the Center for Peace and Commerce, a joint venture between the School of Business Administration and the Kroc School of Peace Studies. The competition started in 2011 with 16 applicants (it includes individuals and teams) and four awardees winning a total of $11,000 in seed funds. By 2016 the SIC had expanded to include six other local universities and a total of 296 participants, 101 applicants, 52 semi-finalists and 15 finalists. Of the 15 finalists, two were from a University in Baja California, Mexico, five were from neighboring San Diego County universities and eight were USD student-led initiatives.

The competition cycle runs from September to May with "Idea lab" workshops in the fall and spring. The 2016 SIC included a general track, a women innovators track and a mobile-tech track as allocated by sponsors. That year SIC culminated in the final pitches in mid-April and an award ceremony in early May. The competition was open to all students at USD and these six local universities, regardless of their area of study. Every team participating in the competition had to be led by a student. Initial applicants completed six questions regarding their social project. Semi-finalists had to write a more detailed summary of their idea, a roadmap and make a two-minute video highlighting the key attributes of their idea. Finalists were provided coaching and mentorship from successful entrepreneurs, alumni, community experts and faculty and then they pitched their idea to judges in six minutes. During the final awards ceremony the 15 finalists provided a one-minute summary of their idea, the audience picked a $1,000 live audience choice award via a cellular phone poll and judges announced the teams which earned a cash or in-kind prize. In 2016, nine winning teams were awarded a total of $50,000 in seed funding and in-kind prizes including incubator space, pro-bono consulting and legal support.

4.2. *Survey instrument*

The survey instrument assesses the impact of participating in a social venture competition at the individual level. The survey has 23 questions total. The first section assesses self-efficacy, general attitude toward helping society and the entrepreneurial intentions of participants. The first section is composed of 12 questions and is measured on a 5-point Likert scale. The second section is composed of 11 demographic questions. The survey instrument has approval from the Institutional Review Board and is included in the Appendix.

This survey instrument has been under development since 2009. A previous study on the value of social entrepreneurship competitions by one of the same authors as this study included only a post survey of 2012 and 2013 SIC participants as well as a different post survey on a random sample of social entrepreneurship competitions from 2005 to 2009 (Meyskens and Auch, 2013; Meyskens, 2010). In 2014, pre and post-surveys with 74 questions were also implemented at USD but the response rate was low (26 participants total) and no participant took both the pre and post survey. In order to increase participation in 2015 we decreased the survey to 23 questions, offered an incentive to those who participated in the survey (enter a raffle to win a $25 Amazon Gift Card), and the authors were more proactive in encouraging participants to take the survey by attending idea labs. This resulted in the completion of 61 pre-surveys and 15 post-surveys in 2015, but only two individuals completed both the pre and post surveys. With lessons learned in the previous year, in 2016 we collaborated more closely with SIC organizers and made participation an integral part of participating in the competition. Competition organizers integrated the survey into the application and also followed up with participants to complete post-surveys by sending several personalized email reminders.

4.3. *Variables*

Self-efficacy: These are assessed on a 5-point Likert scale: (1) Strongly Disagree; (2) Disagree; (3) Neutral; (4) Agree; and (5) Strongly Agree. These questions include: I am confident in my ability to: (1) identify (come up with) a new idea to solve a social problem; (2) design a product or service that will alleviate a social problem; (3) develop a budget that estimates the amount of start-up funds and working capital necessary to start my social initiative; (4) lead others who identify with and believe in my vision for a new social venture; (5) clearly and concisely explain my social venture (in written form); (6) clearly and concisely explain my social venture (in verbal form); (7) develop a strong network of individuals with the skills to help me with my social venture; and (8) develop a plan for implementing my venture.

Attitude toward helping society: These are assessed through two questions on a 5-point Likert scale. These questions include: (1) I am strongly committed to helping society in some way; and (2) I deeply understand the needs of the community that I want to create solutions for.

Entrepreneurial intentions: These are assessed through three questions on a 5-point Likert scale: (1) I am likely to start a social venture on my own or with others in the next 12 months; (2) I am likely to start a social venture on my own or with others in the next 5 years; and (3) I see myself working at a social venture at some point in my career.

Demographic questions: The demographic section of the survey includes questions that might provide additional insight into the results. These include gender, education level, participant area of study, experience with a family business or start-up, and what participants hope to gain from participation in the competition.

5. Results

In order to assess the hypotheses we conducted a paired samples t-test of the matched participants. Table 1 shows the results from the participants who took both the pre-survey and post-survey. These results as well as the qualitative data from participants suggest some exploratory insight into the value of social entrepreneurship competitions and their impact on participants.

Table 1: Pre-post survey — Exploratory results.

	Matched Pre	Matched Post
Self Efficacy ... I am confident in my ability to ...		
Come up with new idea	4.64	4.47
Design product or service	4.56	4.28
Develop a budget	4.12*	3.68
Lead others	4.48	4.32
Explain social venture (written)	4.40	4.16
Explain social venture (verbal)	4.38	4.35
Develop a strong network	4.36	4.16
Develop a plan	4.52**	4.29
Attitude Toward Helping Others		
I am strongly committed to helping society in some way		4.64
Understand needs of community	4.28	4.41
Entrepreneurial Intentions ... I am likely to ...		
Start a social venture in 12 months	4.00	3.80
Start a social venture in 5 years	4.30	4.24
Work at a social venture sometime	4.50	4.28
Venture Participation Goals		
Hope to gain a mentor in competition	4.44	

Note: $n = 25$; $*p < 0.05$; $**p < 0.10$.

The results suggests that Hypotheses 1 is partially supported as two of the questions were significant at the 0.05 and 0.10 levels. This suggests that participating in the competition actually reduces some elements of self-efficacy. Although at first apparently disappointing and contrary to theory, this trend is actually in line with the point that by participating in experiential learning activities like a social entrepreneurship competition, students learn that starting a venture is actually much more difficult than it seems. Participants see that developing a budget and a plan is a lengthy difficult process and confidence in their ability to do these activities decreases. This extremely valuable lesson suggests that students should take the opportunity to learn in an educational setting. In fact, most students indicated in either the pre and/or post survey that they were excited about the *experience* of participating in the process of starting a social venture and the opportunity to learn.

Particularly, student testimonials discuss the importance of this experience and the practical skills gained:

- I hoped to learn what it takes to actually have an actual social impact. People don't really talk about what has to happen after you say you want to make a change just the beginning and the end (2016 Student Participant).
- We hoped to learn about our team, the unknown that existed in the company, and how best to complete our project. We hoped to gain valuable connections and mentors along the way. We accomplished all of this (2016 Student Participant).
- I didn't have any expectations going into the SIC but I was extremely excited about being surrounded by like-minded individuals wanting to create grand change in the world. It was definitely more than I would have ever hoped for and I made the most of it. The extensive amount of work done for the proposals made it that *much more difficult but in a great way* (since it was passion driven). *It taught me about the realities of building a company in a field I knew nothing about going in.* I just knew there was a problem that needed to be fixed; bigger than myself (2016 Student Participant)
- The Social Innovation Challenge allowed me to better present our idea and foster our plans for further development of our idea and product.

Not only did it allow us to present our passion and care for women with postpartum depression, but also bring together so many other companies and ideas with their own inspiring passion for social change. I was very inspired in such an environment and am more motivated than ever before! (2017 Student Participant).

- I enjoyed practicing each of the components (problem/solution landscape, infographic, business model canvas and roadmap, 2 min video and 90s pitch) of the SIC. Each provided real-world skills that are applicable to any setting (2018 Student Participant).

The student participant quotes indicate the importance of this experience and all the knowledge gained which could be incorporated into their ventures. Entrepreneurship is a complex process. The competition process provides an opportunity for participants to acquire certain types of knowledge and skill-sets in an experiential setting, rather than in the real world where they could spend their savings or invest a lot of time in launching a misguided venture. Thus, this exploratory analysis suggests that the competition provides an opportunity for students to learn and experience the realities of starting a social venture.

Hypothesis 2 was not supported. In addition, the question relating to *attitude toward helping others* was only complete in the post survey. One of the goals of competition organizers is that students gain deeper knowledge of the population they are focusing on. Often students are eager to come up with ideas or solutions, with only a superficial understanding of the problem. Although Hypothesis 2 was not supported, student testimonials suggest that the competition provided the platform to examine and try to better understand the customer's needs:

- I hoped to gain the means necessary to help the Navajo people with their current water situation. This competition helped shed some light on other community problems and demonstrate to other schools that they are capable of tackling these problems even if they believe that they do not have the resources to do so (2016 Student Participant).
- SIC moved our venture along in development and critical thinking. The questions posed made us truly think about the impact we were intending to create and how to best suit our model to societies/customers needs (2016 Student Participant).

Although Hypothesis 3 is not supported as it is not statistically significant, the averages between the pre and post survey decreased. Given the findings in previous research that self-efficacy often leads to greater entrepreneurial intentions (Bandura, 1997), we hope that academics assess these findings in a larger sample size in future research. If the self-efficacy of individuals is actually reduced by participating in competitions, their intent to start a venture might be reduced as well.

Finally, the open-ended question regarding what students hope to gain in the competition suggests that mentoring is often the aspect of the competition that is most valued by participants. This finding regarding the importance of mentoring has been consistent across previous post-surveys and other studies (Hester *et al.*, 2008; Meyskens and Auch, 2013; Russell *et al.*, 2008). Although many students went into the competition seeking both funding and a mentor, student testimonials indicated that the most valuable aspect of the competition was gaining a mentor, feedback and advice:

- We developed lasting relationships with key figures in business, education, and non-profit sectors. This is continuing to be highly valuable to us (2016 Student Participant).
- The support, ideas, and mentorship of the SIC really helped us turn our idea into something tangible (2017 Student Participant).
- I enjoyed being able to sit down with the coaches, who offered some great insights as to how to proceed. They really encouraged my team to think outside the box, which strengthened our social innovation (2018 Student Participant).

In addition, students particularly thought speed coaching was a valuable component which should be integrated more into future competitions.

- One of my favorite events was the speed coaching because that allowed me to feel pressured in a quick pitch type setting but then I still had plenty of time to elaborate on what I needed clarity on and the coaches showed great knowledge and patience. Even if they had no idea since it wasn't their field, they were still able to provide objective information on business strategy/planning to give me a good foundation. It allowed me to strategize how I would explain it to someone with no prior knowledge at all. Simplifying complicated concepts seemed to be the theme throughout the entire experience. A big culture shock for me was the fact that in the social entrepreneurship realm people are willing to connect/want to help you. Since I had experience otherwise in business where everyone is trying to help themselves or own self-gain, it was refreshing. That is when I knew I belonged in social entrepreneurship being surrounded by good-hearted individuals fighting for problems bigger than themselves (2016 Student Participant).

One student recommended a murder board as a way to get more constructive feedback in future competitions:

- I was hoping for more constructive feedback during the dry run. Something our team did which was immensely valuable was a "murder board" dry run with professionals from our office. We gathered experts in business development, marketing, and presentation skills; pitched to them; then let them rip in to us with everything that was wrong and didn't make sense (2016 Student Participant).

Other suggestions from student comments included integrating the competition into university classes and having a business development session at the beginning of the competition cycle so that people from different backgrounds and education levels could be on the same page.

Overall, these student testimonials suggests that competition organizers should be sure to continually integrate longer speed networking meetings, more fast-pitch competitions and generally more interaction with mentors and community members into all aspects of the competition.

6. Discussion

The purpose of this study is to better understand the role of social entrepreneurship competitions in helping participants learn and experience the start-up process. More and more universities around the world are allocating resources (both time and money) to these contests. However, thus far there is little evidence on their impact on preparing cadres of social entrepreneurs. Assumptions about their worth stem from anecdotal stories of relatively few individuals as well as post-surveys which do not assess how participation can lead to individual changes. These success stories support efforts for further creating and sustaining competitions, but do not clearly show their effect on participating students.

This exploratory study makes three contributions to our understanding of the pedagogical value of social entrepreneurship competitions. First, the results partially suggest that participation in a competition reduces some elements of the self-efficacy of individual participants. Second, comments from participants suggest that the SIC experience enables students to gain a deeper understanding of the communities they are focusing on and the social issues they want to address. Finally, as seen in previous studies (Hester *et al.*, 2008; Meyskens and Auch, 2013; Russell *et al.*, 2008) mentoring is highly valued by participants (more so than funding) and needs to be more thoroughly integrated into these competitions.

Regardless of the relatively small scale of the sample, a most revealing insight meriting further research is that participation in a competition actually reduces some elements of self-efficacy. Although this at first might seem contrary to expectations, this is actually an extremely valuable lesson in entrepreneurship education. Competitions such as the SIC provide a means for participants to immerse themselves in the levels of complexity involved in developing and sustaining a viable venture focused on helping society. A competition provides a structure and a safe space for participants to develop a venture and receive guidance at every point during the process. However, the results suggests that some participating students might find the process overwhelming to the point of reducing levels of confidence to develop a budget or plan for a potential start-up. The number of components that need to come together to develop a successful social venture is often much more complex than students might realize when first seeking to solve a social problem. Students are often passionate about the prospect of helping a marginalized population and "being the change" and "making a difference." However, by participating in a competition, students experience first-hand that identifying an idea is only one part of the process. Actually, working with a team, defining a clear value proposition, pulling together different resources, determining assessment metrics of social impact and putting it all together to actually develop a budget and plan for a real venture is not easy. The initial enthusiasm that participants feel about the prospect of helping society through venture creation can be diminished by experiencing the reality of the process. Having the opportunity to go through the learning experience offered by the SIC in a safe space with guidance offers an opportunity for students to learn.

The fact that the results suggest that some elements of self-efficacy (confidence in the ability to develop a budget and plan) was reduced by participation in the SIC competition is actually an extremely powerful learning outcome that requires further research. If these results hold within a larger sample size, it might invite even more reflection on what exactly should be the goals of a social entrepreneurship competition in the context of the university.

Second, participants in the study suggest that the social entrepreneurship competition enables them to better understand the communities they are focusing on. Often students become enamored with their solution without adequate knowledge of the problem or without any type of experience with the population that they seek to assist. Many attempts have been made to address this through learning tools such as design thinking, lean start-up and the impact gap canvas which focus on gaining customer/beneficiary feedback as part of an iterative process in developing solutions. Competition organizers design the process in ways that encourage participants to better understand the populations they are focusing on and the potential social impact of their ideas offering idea labs or workshops. The application to the competition requires participants to make more explicit what they actually know regarding their beneficiary. For example, in round 1 of the SIC, questions like "Who benefits from your social innovation" or "What is your success" help students engage with understanding the needs of the population they are addressing. In the final round participants are further required to reflect on the "social, environmental or peace impact" of their idea. Thus, throughout the process participants are moved to conduct some type of research to better understand the needs of the community they are focusing on.

Finally, as seen in previous studies mentoring is highly valued by participants (more so then funding in the end) and needs to be more carefully integrated into these competitions. As noted earlier the authors of this study have been engaged in assessing the value of social entrepreneurship competitions since 2009, and mentoring has consistently been highlighted as one of the most important aspects of the competition by participants (Meyskens and Auch, 2013). As a result, competition organizers have moved to continually integrate mentors into different layers of the competition over the last few years: first at idea lab workshops, then for semi-finalists, and in 2016 for finalists. In addition, finalists are encouraged to engage with their mentors even after the competition ends. The continued emphasis on mentors suggests that competition organizers should continue to integrate mentors into the competition as much as possible. Student testimonials suggest murder boards and more fast pitched competitions as potential ways to do this. Not only are these a means to fully engage competition participants, but also they provide an opportunity to excite qualified alumni and community members who want to be more actively involved in the university.

In summary, our findings suggest that although social entrepreneurship competitions are most often seen as a vehicle to provide funding, resources and tools to the best venture proposals so that they can develop, grow and help society, it is actually the process of the competition that might provide the most value. Our results are similar to studies on business plans in the sense that it is not the plan itself that provides the most value, but rather the process of writing the business plan (Delmar and Shane, 2003). Our empirical findings on the pedagogical impact of competitions at the individual level are interesting, but exploratory. Further research is warranted both at USD as well as other universities and institutional settings, as well as on other types of competitions (not necessarily social) to assess the generalizability of these findings.

7. Limitations

The purpose of this study is to better understand the role of social entrepreneurship competitions in helping participants learn and experience the start-up process, however it has many limitations. First, this study only assesses the impact on 25 participants who took the pre and post-tests. Many of these were semi-finalists. In addition, there was some missing data. Although this study provides some exploratory insight into the impact of social entrepreneurship competitions on participants, these variables should be analyzed in a larger sample size in future research. In addition, further studies should assess whether these findings hold across different types of participants. Is there a particular workshop that is extremely valuable in impacting entrepreneurial intentions, self-efficacy or attitude toward helping others? Are competition applicants and finalists experiencing the same level of impact? Second, this study is only assessed at one university. Further research would need to evaluate whether these findings are generalizable across competitions at other universities or other institutional settings. In competitions where participants have more entrepreneurial experience (outside universities) or more at stake (they are no longer students) these findings might not hold. Finally, this study only assesses three individual outcomes related to self-efficacy, entrepreneurial intentions and attitude. Future studies could assess other outcomes at the individual as well as the venture and societal level. Regardless of these limitations, this paper is a step forward in assessing the effectiveness and impact of social entrepreneurship competitions and we look forward to seeing more research in this area.

8. Practitioner Recommendations

This study provides important insight for the leaders of the Social Innovation Challenge that can be applied at other institutions with social entrepreneurship competitions. These practical applications revolve around (1) greater problem analysis at the beginning of the competition; (2) tailoring mentoring programs to the needs of participants; (3) helping participants understand their own personal role in changemaking and providing insight into different types of changemaking opportunities; and (4) implementing competition participant and alumni surveys. First, we encourage other competitions to provide opportunities for participants to "apprentice with the problem" with tools like the Impact Gap Canvas early on in the competition cycle. The SIC has embedded a deeper study of the selected social or environmental challenge into the competition so that round one starts with a map of the problem's context rather than a solution. This provides students the opportunity to understand the problem at a deeper level. At the same time, it encourages students to be committed to the problem beyond the length of the competition and regardless of their pitch's success.

Second, we encourage competition organizers to tailor mentoring programs to the needs of their participants. The SIC has implemented mentoring programs that help students work with mentors to identify their own "theory of change" which may include "pivoting" to a different personal strategy to make an impact. As part of this mentoring process the SIC partners participants with individuals in the community who make change within an organization. At the same time, the SIC has integrated mentoring into every level of the competition process.

Third, we recommend that other competitions integrate more workshops into their competition cycle so that participants better understand their own personal changemaking goals as well as other types of changemaking opportunities. The Transformative Action Institute has a Story of your Life exercise with questions exploring an individual's past, present and future that can assist with participants better understanding their own personal role in changemaking. The SIC also hosts seminars and workshops to introduce students to other types of changemaking opportunities so that they can find out ways to guide their passion for change into paths they had not previously considered such as being "entrepreneurial" within an existing organization (intrapreneurial).

Finally, we recommend that competition organizers conduct robust surveys of competition participants and alumni. The SIC recently started a study to follow the alumni of the program, following their shifts and pivots to understand trends in how students continue to engage with their areas of passion for social impact beyond the competition and their time at USD. As an example, one student participant incorporated her venture as a 501(c)(3), built a board of directors and had initial customer traction after participating in the SIC but then decided to wind it down because she felt collaborating in between organizations was a better way to achieve her aims of youth empowerment through theater. Through the experience, her commitment to social impact deepened and now she works full time for venture capital fund committed to social impact organizations.

Other insight from the alumni survey indicates that financing is not the only constraint that entrepreneurs face. In fact, alumni:

- often have frustrating co-founder relationships,
- often are discouraged/feel alone/need encouragement,
- often need legal advice (incorporation, IP),

- find mentoring and coaching and connections more important than seed funding,
- desire more time to network with other teams,
- often find co-working spaces or other community spots to be very helpful as they kept going,
- sometimes abandon ventures because they got full time jobs or because their idea wasn't working.

This insight can be used to integrate workshops into the competition cycle that might address some of these issues and allow competition participants an opportunity to work through these in an experiential school setting. For example, a workshop or activity that deals with team conflict, might help alumni with future tensions between co-founders.

In summary, we recommend that competition organizers integrate additional resources into studying the problem a venture focuses on, tailoring the mentoring program and competition workshops to be more inclusive of pivots, and increase student/alumni follow up and measurement.

9. Conclusion

This study illustrates the pedagogical value of the social entrepreneurship competition process at the individual level in different ways. Although funding promises might initially entice students to join a competition, the learning gained through participation in the competition has far greater value than the funding alone. We encourage competition organizers to continue to focus efforts in improving the semester or year-long experiential learning process, rather than focusing mostly on the number of participants and the winning proposals. We also believe there are many opportunities for researchers to further analyze different elements of entrepreneurship competitions to better understand best practices in entrepreneurship education.

Acknowledgments

The authors would like to thank the competition organizers Nadia Auch, Grace Michael, Amit Kakkad, as well as assistants Johanna Wagner and

Rui Yang for their continual support in developing the ideas, as well as collecting and analyzing the data needed for this study. In addition, Fiona Wilson has worked with the authors on previous versions of this study and provided valuable insight particularly regarding self-efficacy. Special thanks for research funding from the University of San Diego to develop this study.

Appendix: Assessing the Impact of the USD Social Innovation Challenge

The survey aims at assessing the impact on individuals of participating in the USD Social Innovation Challenge. When filling out this survey, please read each statement carefully and answer all questions by choosing a number from the scale below.

1 = "Strongly Disagree" (SD); 2 = "Disagree" (D); 3 = "Neutral" (N)
4 = "Agree" (A); 5 = "Strongly Agree" (SA)

Thank you for taking the time to fill out this survey. The results are anonymous and strictly confidential. Please note that there is no right or wrong answer.

When did you first come up with your social innovation idea?	>1 year ago	7–12 months ago	3–6 months ago	1–2 months ago	<1 month ago
Questions	**(SD)**	**(D)**	**(N)**	**(A)**	**(SA)**
A1. I am likely to start a social venture on my own or with others in the next 12 months.	1	2	3	4	5
A2. I am likely to start a venture on my own or with others in the next 5 years.	1	2	3	4	5
A3. I see myself working at a social venture at some point in my career.	1	2	3	4	5
B4. I am confident in my ability to identify (come up with) a new idea to solve a social problem.	1	2	3	4	5

(*Continued*)

(Continued)

When did you first come up with your social innovation idea?	>1 year ago	7–12 months ago	3–6 months ago	1–2 months ago	<1 month ago
Questions	**(SD)**	**(D)**	**(N)**	**(A)**	**(SA)**
B5. I am confident in my ability to design a product or service that will alleviate a social problem.	1	2	3	4	5
B6. I am confident in my ability to develop a budget that estimates the amount of start-up funds and working capital necessary to start my social initiative.	1	2	3	4	5
B7. I am confident in my ability to lead others who identify with and believe in my vision for a new social venture.	1	2	3	4	5
B8. I am confident in my ability to clearly and concisely explain my social venture (in written form).	1	2	3	4	5
B9. I am confident in my ability to clearly and concisely explain my social venture (in verbal form).	1	2	3	4	5
B10. I am confident in my ability to develop a strong network of individuals with the skills to help me with my social venture.	1	2	3	4	5
B11. I am confident in my ability to develop a plan for implementing my venture.					
B12. I deeply understand the needs of the community that I want to create solutions for.					
B13. Through participation in the competition I hope to gain a mentor (level of mentor benefit in post survey).					
B14. What specifically do you hope to gain from participation in the competition?					

C. Demographic Questions

Please provide the following information:

1. Email Address ______________________________
2. First & Last Name ______________________________
3. Name of Venture/Initiative ______________________________

	Male	**Female**	**Other/Decline to State**
4. Gender	1	2	3

	Undergraduate degree	**Masters degree**	**Doctoral Degree**
5. Education Completing Currently	1	2	3

	2015	**2016**	**2017**	**2018**	**2019**
6. Expected Graduation Year If already graduated, what year?	1	2	3	4	5

	Business	**Arts & Science**	**Engineering/ Computer Science**	**Health**	**Other**
7. What is your area of study? More open ended..	1	2	3	4	5

8. Someone in my family has started their own business	Yes	No
9. I have worked for a start-up company before.	Yes	No
10. I have started a venture or initiative before.	Yes	No

Other potential demographic questions: Berkeley include first 3

D. If you have any further comments about the impact of the Social Innovation Challenge, please provide them here.

*Thank you for taking the survey ** Date Survey was Taken ___________

References

Autio E., Keeley R. H., Klofsten M., GC Parker G., and Hay M. (2001) Entrepreneurial intent among students in Scandinavia and in the USA, *Enterprise and Innovation Management Studies*, 2(2), 145–160.

Ajzen I. (1991) The theory of planned behavior, *Organizational Behavior and Human Decision Processes*, 50(2), 179–211.

Ashoka (2014). Chapter 3: The Global Landscape & Field-Level Trends, *Trends in Social Innovation Education*. page 26. https://ashokau.org/trends/.

Bandura A. (1992) Exercise of personal agency through the self-efficacy mechanism. *Self-Efficacy: Thought Control of Action*. Hemisphere, Washington, DC.

Bandura A. (1997) *Self-Efficacy: The Exercise of Control*, W. H. Freeman, New York.

Bandura A., Barbaranelli C., Caprara G., and Pastorelli C. (2001) Self-efficacy beliefs as shapers of children's aspirations and career trajectories, *Child Development*, 72(1), 187–206.

Bird B. (1988) Implementing entrepreneurial ideas: The case for intention, *Academy of Management Review*, 13(3), 442–453.

Brock D. and Ashoka's Global Academy for Social Entrepreneurship (2008) *Social entrepreneurship teaching resources handbook*, Retrieved October 22, 2009, from http://www.universitynetwork.org/sites/universitynetwork.org/files/files/Soc%20Ent%20Handbook%20March%202008%20Final.pdf.

Carsrud A. L. and Brännback M. (2007) *Entrepreneurship*. Greenwood Press, Westport, CT.

Cooper B. and Vlaskovits P. (2010) *The Entrepreneur's Guide to Customer Development*. Cooper-Vlaskovits, Lexington, KY.

Cox L., Mueller S., and Moss S. (2002) The impact of entrepreneurship education on entrepreneurial self-efficacy, *International Journal of Entrepreneurship Education*, 1(2).

Dees J. G. (1998) The meaning of social entrepreneurship, Stanford University: Draft Report for the Kauffman Center for Entrepreneurial Leadership. Retrieved October 22, 2009, from http://www.caseatduke.org/documents/dees_sedef.pdf.

Delmar F. and Shane S. (2003) Does business planning facilitate the development of new ventures? *Strategic Management Journal*, 24, 1165–1185.

Dumaine B. and Pofeldt E. (2007) Best colleges for aspiring entrepreneurs, *Fortune Small Business*, 17, 60.

Finlay K. A., Trafimow D., and Jones D. (1997) Predicting health behaviors from attitudes and subjective norms: Between-subjects and within-subjects analyses, *Journal of Applied Social Psychology*, 27(22), 2015–2031.

Finlay K. A., Trafimow D., and Moroi E. (1999) The importance of subjective norms on intentions to perform health behaviors, *Journal of Applied Social Psychology*, 29(11), 2381–2393.

Fitzsimmons J. R. and Douglas E. J. (2011) Interaction between feasibility and desirability in the formation of entrepreneurial intentions, *Journal of Business Venturing*, 26(4), 431–440.

Gupta V. K. and York A. S. (2009) Determinants of participation in business plan competitions: An attribution theory perspective, Paper presented at the *USASBE Conference*, Anaheim, CA, January.

Honig B. (2004) Entrepreneurship education: Toward a model of contingency based planning, *Academy of Management Learning and Education*, 3, 258–273.

Honig B. and Karlsson T. (2004) Institutional forces and the written business plan. *Journal of Management*, 30, 29–48.

Huster K., Petrillo C., O'Malley G., Glassman D., Rush J., and Wasserheit J. (2016) Global entrepreneurship competitions: Incubators for innovations in global health? *Journal of Management Education*, 41(2), 249–271.

Ioannou K. (2001) *The Guide of the New Entrepreneur*. Papasotiriou, Athen.

Jensen T. L. (2014) A holistic person perspective in measuring entrepreneurship education impact — Social entrepreneurship education at the Humanities. *International Journal of Management Education*, 12(3), 349–364.

Kadir M. B., Salim M., and Kamurudin H. (2012) The relationship between educational support and entrepreneurial intentions in Malaysian higher level institution. *Procedia*, 69, 2164–2173.

Kirkwood J. (2009) Motivational factors in a push-pull theory of entrepreneurship. *Gender in Management: An International Journal*, 24(5), 346–364.

Kolvereid L. (1996) Prediction of employment status choice intentions, *Working Paper Series Henley Management College HWP*, 21(1), 47–58.

Krueger N. F. (1993) The impact of prior entrepreneurial exposure on perceptions of new venture feasibility and desirability, *Entrepreneurship Theory and Practice*, 18(1), 5–21.

Krueger N. F. and Brazeal D. V. (1994) Entrepreneurial potential and potential entrepreneurs, *Entrepreneurship Theory and Practice*, 18, 91–91.

Krueger N. F., Reilly M. D., and Carsrud A. L. (2000) Competing models of entrepreneurial intentions, *Journal of Business Venturing*, 15(5), 411–432.

Kwong C. C. Y., Thompson P., and Cheung C. W. M. (2012) The effectiveness of social business plan competitions in developing social and civic awareness and participation. *Academy of Management Learning and Education*, 11, 324–348.

Lange J. E., Mollov A., Pearlmutter M., Singh S., and Bygrave W. D. (2007) Pre-startup formal business plans and post-startup performance: A study of 116 new ventures. *Venture Capital Journal*, 9, 1–20.

Lee S. H. and Wong P. K. (2004) An exploratory study of technopreneurial intentions: A career anchor perspective, *Journal of Business Venturing*, 19(1), 7–28.

Liñán F. and Chen Y. W. (2009) Development and cross-cultural application of a specific instrument to measure entrepreneurial intentions, *Entrepreneurship Theory and Practice*, 33(3), 593–617.

Mair J. and Marti I. (2009) Entrepreneurship in and around institutional voids: A case study from Bangladesh', *Journal of Business Venturing*, 24(5), 419–435.

Mair J. and Noboa E. (2003) Social entrepreneurship: How intentions to create a social enterprise get formed, IESE Business School Working Paper: D-521-E.

Mair J. and Noboa E. (2005) How intentions to create a social venture are formed: A case study, IESE Business School Working Paper No. 593.

Mair J. and Noboa E. (2006) Social entrepreneurship: How intentions to create a social enterprise get formed, in J. Mair J. R. and K. Hockerts (eds.), *Social Entrepreneurship.* Palgrave, London, pp. 121–135.

Meyer J. and Rowan B. (1977) Institutionalized organizations: Formal structure as myth and ceremony. *American Journal of Sociology*, 83, 340–363.

Meyskens M. and Auch N. (2013) *An Exploratory Study of Social Venture Competitions: Value Creation at the Individual, Venture and Societal Levels.* Theory and Empirical Research in Social Entrepreneurship, Edward Elgar.

Moriano J. A., Gorgievski M., Laguna M., Stephan U., and Zarafshani K. (2012) A cross-cultural approach to understanding entrepreneurial intention, *Journal of Career Development*, 39(2), 162–185.

Ndivhuho Tshikovhi and Richard Shambare (2015) Entrepreneurial knowledge, personal attitudes and entrepreneurship intentions among South African Enactus students. *Problems and Perspectives in Management*, 13(1–1), 152–158.

Nga J. K. H. and Shamuganathan G. (2010) The influence of personality traits and demographic factors on social entrepreneurship start up intentions, *Journal of Business Ethics*, 95(2), 259–282.

Oluwatobi, Stephen and Oshokoya, Damilare and Atayero A. A., and Oludayo O. Olumuyiwa and Nsofor, Colette and Oyebode, Adeola (2018) Students' participation in Hult Prize and their decision for entrepreneurship: Data gathered from Hult Prize 2018 regional finals in Nigeria. Data in Brief, 19, pp. 693–699.

Russell R., Atchison M., and Brooks R. (2008) Business plan competitions in tertiary institutions: Encouraging entrepreneurship education, *Journal of Higher Education Policy and Management*, 30, 123–138.

Stamboulis Y. and Barlas A. (2014) Entrepreneurship education impact on student attitudes, *International Journal of Management Education,* 12(3), 365–373.

Trafimow D. and Finlay K. A. (1996) The importance of subjective norms for a minority of people: Between subjects and within-subjects analyses, *Personality and Social Psychology Bulletin*, 22(8), 820–828.

Vendel M. and Brown T. (2012) Serial entrepreneurs: Alternatives to traditional business plans. Paper presented at the annual *Babson Entrepreneurship Research Conference.*

Zahra S. A., Gedajlovi E., Neubaum D. O., and Shulman J. M. (2009) A typology of social entrepreneurs: Motives, search processes and ethical challenges. *Journal of Business Venturing*, 24(5), 519–532.

Zhao H., Seibert S. E., and Hills G. E. (2005) The Mediating Role of Self-Efficacy in the Development of Entrepreneurial Intentions, *Journal of Applied Psychology*, 90(6), 1265–1272.

Zukin C. and Szeltner M. (2012) Talent report: What workers want in 2012. Prepared for Net Impact. http://netimpact.org/docs/publications-docs/NetImpact_WhatWorkersWant2012.pdf.

Index

A
abstract language, 153
abstractness, 169
access to entrepreneurial financing, 244, 246, 250, 252, 254–255, 259, 262–263, 265
access to external finance, 274
accountability culture, 244, 256–258, 260, 266
accountability mindset, 245
accounting and finance, 289
accrual, 282
active involvement, 14, 28–29, 31–32
additionality, 114
addressees, 164
adjectives, 168
adverse selection, 94
age, 283
agency costs, 110
alternative debt instruments, 209
alternative finance, 122
alternative financing method, 151
alternative market, 218, 232
American Research & Development (ARD), 3
American SBIC system, 6
analysis of linguistic style, 154
angel, 13–21, 23–37
angel-backed, 16, 23, 35
angel investors, 5, 8
appropriate language, 160
Ashoka, 300
asymmetric cryptography, 186
asymmetric information, 94
asymmetric-information problems, 162
ATM cards, 281
attitude toward helping others, 312, 314
attitude toward helping society, 311
attract backers, 158
awareness, 277

B
backers, 160
bank loan, 135
banks, 289
Basel regulations, 97
basic, 289
basket bond, 210, 217

BAs network, 249, 254–255, 257–259, 261, 264, 267
behavioral attitude, 307
behavioral attitude-referring, 308
Berger, A. N., 208
biases, 282
Big Three, 280
biomass, 132
bitcoin, 7, 189, 193
blockchain, 7, 182–184, 187–188, 190
Blockchain 3.0, 191
blockchain technology, 190
bond of trust, 245, 265
bond pricing, 281
bonds, 279
business angels, 5, 14–15, 25, 93
business environment, 278
business management, 277
business owner, 287
business planning, 125, 301, 304
business practices, 286
business skills, 285
business survival, 286
business training program, 285

C

capital expenditures, 274
capital markets, 94
carbon accessing, 122
carried interest, 112
category of projects, 170
central American, 8
chain of intermediation, 210, 233
cleantech, 122
cleantech campaigns, 162
climate change, 124
coaching in schools, 289
cognitive, 260, 262
cognitive social capital, 245, 250, 255, 263, 267
co-investment, 26–28, 33, 36
collateral, 97
commonly used words, 165
competences, 279
competition, 299–301, 304, 309, 316–317
competition sponsors, 301
concept of crowdfunding, 173
concrete language, 153
concreteness, 169
confidence, 283
connections and trust, 245
constrain credit availability, 209
construction of Saint Peter's Basilica in Rome, 154
construed shared expectations, 245, 259–260, 263
Consumer Financial Protection Bureau (CFPB), 284
corporation, 3
counseling, 285
co-working spaces, 2
credit guarantee schemes, 98
credit rating, 281
crowd, 163
crowdfunding, 6, 93, 122, 154, 221–224
crowdfunding campaign, 151
crowdfunding-phenomenon, 153
crowdfunding platforms, 233
crowdfunding studies, 159
crowding-out, 54, 57
cryptocurrencies, 7, 189, 192, 195

cryptocurrency is a pioneering, 192
cryptocurrency risks, 188

D
Dash, 195
debt-based crowdfunding, 156
debt capital, 274
debt funds, 210
debt securities, 210
default ratio, 97
demand advice, 286
democratization, 127
depreciation, 282
descriptions, 168
Descriptive Action Verbs, 168
design of narrative style, 162
developing countries, 7
different linguistic models, 150
different motivations, 157
digital assets, 7
dimensions of financial literacy, 276
disconnected entrepreneurs, 244–245, 249–250, 254–255, 257–261, 263–264
dissemination, 173
diversification, 279
donation-based crowdfunding, 156
Doriot, G., 3
driver of crowdfunding campaigns, 163
due diligence, 128

E
eagerness to invest, 114
early contributions, 157
early-stage equity financing, 244–245
early-stage financing, 8, 256
eco-innovation, 130
economic freedom, 136
education, 274, 283
effective communication, 152, 158
effective financial decisions, 273, 289
Eisele, A., 211
electricity, 132
employees, 290
employment, 272
employment status, 283
energy cooperatives, 128
entrepreneurial, 158
entrepreneurial activity, 291
entrepreneurial finance, 2, 4, 6–7, 124
entrepreneurial financing, 246, 250, 256, 274
entrepreneurial firms, 2
entrepreneurial funding, 5
entrepreneurial intentions, 288, 301, 307–308, 311–312
entrepreneurial outcome, 283
entrepreneurial performance, 288
entrepreneurial success, 291
entrepreneurial team, 125
entrepreneurial ventures, 274
entrepreneurs, 2, 7–8, 250
entrepreneurs' financial literacy, 272
entrepreneurship competitions, 304
entrepreneurship education, 303
environmental degradation, 124
equity-based crowdfunding, 156
equity gap, 51, 53, 76–77, 96
equity investors, 289
Ether (ETH), 194
Ethereum blockchain, 191
ethnic minorities, 283
EU invest program, 104

European Fund for Strategic Investments, 111
European Scale-Up Action for Risk Capital, 110
experience, 288, 313–314
experiential learning, 301, 303
experts, 290
extant literature on crowdfunding, 155
ExtraMot Pro, 212

F

face-to-face interaction, 157
family background, 291
feed-in tariffs, 130
financial behavior, 284
financial constraints, 234, 273
financial decisions, 272
financial difficulty, 282
financial education programs, 284
financial education project, 275
financial human capital, 284
financial innovation, 211, 232
financial landscape, 277
financial literacy, 7, 272
financial literacy for (potential) entrepreneurs, 291
financial planning, 278, 281
financial products, 279
financial statements, 282, 288
financial toolkit, 282
financial training, 284
financing gap, 122
fintech, 6
firm performance, 59, 69–70, 73, 75
forms, 168
four main categories, 155
fragmented capital market, 98
France, 211, 213–214, 219, 236
free-rider, 103
fund, 166
fund collection, 153
funding decisions, 161
funding gap, 246, 265
fund raising, 150
fundraising goals, 156
future-looking language, 161

G

gender, 283
gender dissimilarities, 161
gender gap, 283
Germany, 211, 213–214, 225, 237
Global Financial Crisis, 123
government limited partner, 58–59, 73–79, 81–84
governments, 5
government GVC, 5, 58–59, 69–73, 76–79, 81–82
Great Britain, 236
green infrastructures, 142
green projects, 6
grounded theory, 246, 249
growth, 272, 289, 291
growth potential, 278
guarantees, 6, 93

H

habits of mind, 288
Health and Retirement Study (HRS), 287
Herfindahl, 96
high-cost borrowing, 287
home foreclosure, 287
households, 272, 289
Hult Prize, 302, 304

human capital, 272, 274
hydropower, 132
hyperbolic discounting, 282

I
impact gap canvas, 318
impact of linguistic models, 171
impact of these competitions, 301
improve financial literacy, 278
incentives, 130
income, 283
industrial revolution, 3
inertia, 282
inflation, 279
information asymmetries, 6, 126, 152, 274
Information-Asymmetry theory, 157
information disclosed, 157
initial coin offerings (ICOs), 4, 7, 182–183, 196–199
initial public offering (IPO), 197
initiative, 164
innovation, 2–3, 212, 234, 272
institutional contexts, 151
institutional work, 251, 256, 260–264
insurance, 277
interest compounding, 279
interest rate, 135
interests of politicians or interest groups, 57
International Network on Financial Education (INFE), 275
investment, 273, 286
investment patterns, 59, 69, 72–74, 77, 81
investment schemes, 98
investment ticket, 99
investors, 5, 290
Italy, 211–214, 235

K
keywords, 163
Kickstarter, 155, 161

L
launch a campaign, 171
learning outcomes, 301
legislation, 7
leverage, 108
likelihood of success, 152
linguistic models, 153
linguistic style, 150
linguist models, 7
liquidity, 94
LiteCoin, 195
loan gap, 96
local awareness, 142
local community, 122, 135
long-term financing sources, 290
low-carbon economy, 142

M
managerial capital, 285
mandatory initiatives, 285
market-conform, 113
market failure, 100, 235
measure financial literacy, 278
mechanism, 183
media, 158
mentor, 301, 306, 315
Mentor Capital Network, 302
mentoring, 318, 320–322
mentorship, 300
meta-analysis, 284
mezzanine, 93

micro-entrepreneurs, 285
microfinance, 159
microloan, 160
micro, small and medium enterprises (MSMEs), 272
mini-bond, 7
mining process, 187
money, 165
moral hazard, 93
mortgage delinquency, 287
motivations of backers, 152
Mozart, 154
multilateral trading facilities, 235
mutual funds, 279

N

Nakamoto, S., 183
narratives, 160
natural experiments, 284
need for cognition, 287
needs, 166
negative effect, 167
net present value, 273
network of BAs, 245
networks, 274
new technologies, 2
new ventures, 2, 4
NIMBY syndrome, 142
non-mandatory initiatives, 285
non-professional investors, 164
Novak, E., 211
novel financing mechanisms, 172
number of backers, 170
numeracy, 280, 287

O

OECD, 275
old, 166
online platforms, 160
outcomes of financial literacy, 278, 290
overconfidence, 281

P

pedagogical benefits, 303
pedagogical value, 304, 322
perceived behavioral control, 305, 308
personal finance, 8, 272, 289
personality traits, 288
photovoltaics, 132
PISA assessment, 280
planning, 282
planning for retirement, 287
platforms, 7
pollution, 130, 136
Pope, A., 154
portfolio companies, 5
portfolio diversification, 287
post-money valuation, 135
potential backers, 158
Principal Component Analysis, 136
private debt funds, 218
productivity, 285
professional advice, 278
professional financial advice, 286
profitability, 282
profitability forecasts, 277
project, 158
project finance, 127
Proof of Stake (PoS), 186
Proof of Work (PoW), 185–186
proper narrative style, 152
providers of capital, 289
public services, 136
Pulitzer, J., 154

Q
quality content, 162
questionnaires, 289

R
rating, 126
recurrent words, 164
redundant, 164
regulation, 7
regulators, 284
regulatory uncertainty, 200
renewable energy, 6, 122
repeated borrowers, 274
repetitive, 165
repetitiveness, 163
repetitiveness of keywords, 153
repetitive words, 150
revenue kicker, 114
reward-based crowdfunding, 156, 163
right message, 173
Ripple, 195
risk, 277
risk premium theories, 95
role of linguistic style for
crowdfunding success, 155
rules of thumbs, 282

S
sales, 286
savings, 287
savvy financial decisions, 289
SBICs, 108
scaling-up, 245
scaling-up mindset, 244, 255, 257,
260, 266
scarce mastery, 167
schooling, 289
sectors, 169
security, 141
seed funding, 322
self-assessment, 280
self-efficacy, 300, 305–306, 311–313,
315, 317–318
self-efficacy development, 7
self-employed, 275, 283
semantic, 165
short-term working capital
management, 290
signaling literature, 159
signaling theory, 155
signal of quality, 159
small businesses, 273
small entrepreneurs, 275
Small Firms Loan Guarantee, 102
smart contract, 188, 191
social capital, 7, 250, 260, 262
social capital dimensions, 254
social entrepreneurship, 8, 299,
301–302
social entrepreneurship competition,
300, 302, 306, 316, 318, 322
social goodwill, 126
socially-isolated, 8
social media, 123
social network, 126
social or environmental impact, 302
social return, 51, 53–54, 69, 71,
74–78, 126
soft information, 211
soft monitoring, 14, 30–31, 34, 36
Spain, 211, 213–214, 218, 236
start-up, 2, 4, 142, 274
start-up experience, 302
start-ups' survival, 288
State Verbs, 168
Statue of Liberty in New York, 154

stock market participation, 287
stocks, 279
story, 164
students, 290
subjective norm, 308
success factors, 162
successful, 161
successful factors, 151
success of crowdfunding campaigns, 150
success rate, 163
success rate ratio, 165
survey, 310, 321
survey instrument, 310
survey tests, 289
survival, 291
sustainability, 273, 289
syndicate, 13–15, 17–18, 24–27, 31, 36–37
syndication, 58–59, 71–73, 77–78, 81, 83

T

tax authorities, 289
taxonomy, 169
technology, 7
technology-based innovations, 6
textual narratives, 161
the crowd, 7
The DAO, 191
tokens, 7
traditional debt financing, 209
transaction costs, 274
trust, 124, 286
trust bonds, 259–261, 263–264, 266
type of project, 151
types of blockchain, 189

U

Udell, G. F., 208
underpricing, 235
unemployed, 283
unique, 166
United Kingdom (UK), 211, 213–214, 222
University of San Diego, 309
unverifiable information, 160
US Financial Capability Study, 281

V

valuation of mini-bonds, 227
value of social entrepreneurship, 318
venture, 8, 273
venture capital (VC), 3–5, 93, 125, 182
venture development, 304
Venture Participation Goals, 312

W

water, 132
weak institutional environment, 245, 248, 262
wealth accumulation, 287
web-based platforms, 154
wind, 132
word Frequency Counter, 165
words, 167
work, 166
working capital, 273
working-capital decisions, 273
workshops, 306, 321–322
would-be investors, 155

Z

Z-spread, 228

www.ingramcontent.com/pod-product-compliance
Ingram Content Group UK Ltd.
Pitfield, Milton Keynes, MK11 3LW, UK
UKHW022105170926
8624IPUK00024B/87

9 789811 202759